'*The Ratcatcher's Grandson* could be considered Puberty Blues' older uncle. Barry, our narrator, gives the reader a remarkable insight into the psyche of two young larrikins embarking on an overseas adventure of a life time. Written in the sixties Aussie vernacular, *The Ratcatcher's Grandson* is real, engaging and eye opening at times. A great walk down memory lane for many fellow travellers who set off from down under to explore the world.' Gareth Wild, Psychologist.

'This story takes place when the author is a young man, and he sets out on an incredible journey backpacking around the world. As a reader you are completely caught up in the gripping, amusing and sometimes racy narrative as he reflects on his experiences and encounters.

'Australian prose and vernacular, the stereotypical representation of the main character, the refreshingly honest insights into his dilemmas, naivety, guilelessness and his innocent determination to succeed, makes this an entertaining, interesting and poignant read.' Lady Joyce Hunt.

The Ratcatcher's Grandson

A Sixties Travel Memoir

Barry White

AIA PUBLISHING

The Ratcatcher's Grandson
Copyright © 2019
Published by AIA Publishing, Australia
ABN: 32736122056
http://www.aiapublishing.com

All rights reserved. No part of this publication may be reproduced, stored in a retrieval system or transmitted in any form or by any means electronic, mechanical, audio, visual or otherwise, without prior permission of the copyright owner. Nor can it be circulated in any form of binding or cover other than that in which it is published and without similar conditions including this condition being imposed on the subsequent purchaser.

Ebook ISBN: 978-0-6485130-5-6
Paperback ISBN: 978-0-6485130-6-3

Cover design by Velvet Wings Media

To those who wonder what's on the other side of the horizon:

It's a cloudless day.
An old man and a boy sit on rocks
that have been there for a million years.
'I'll go there one day,' the boy says.
The old man looks at him, 'Where?'
The boy points at the horizon. 'Over there.'
Both of them look.
The old man thrusts his arm skyward and grabs the air,
a move that startles the boy.
He says to the boy,
'How long can I keep air trapped in my clenched fist?'
The boy stares at the slightly shaking hand.
On the thin sun-damaged skin veins protrude,
blood is forced from the knuckles,
and the fist becomes whiter and whiter.
'For as long as you keep your fist closed,' says the boy.
'How long is that?' asks the old man.
The boy continues to stare at the hand which will soon be ghostly white.
'You can't keep your hand like that for long because it'll die and fall off.
You must open your hand.'
'Ah,' says the old man as he unclenches his fist,
'that's how long things last.
'My boy; live life. Go to the horizon.'

Barry White, January 2002.

Introduction

In the 1830s the family of Emmanuel Rodrigues (later known as Francis Roderick), including three sons, sailed their two whaling boats from the Azores island of Pico to New Zealand. They arrived in Sydney around 1845, and in 1853, Francis Roderick purchased one acre of land at Mullins St, Balmain.

Emmanuel met Scottish boat-builder, William McPherson, and together and separately, they built nearly a hundred boats and ships, mostly at Eagleton on the Williams River north of Newcastle.

In 1876 Richard White immigrated to Australia from Rathmolyon, County Meath, Ireland. He married into the Roderick family, and one of the children from that marriage, John Denis White, worked as a ratcatcher in Sydney's Anthony Hordern Department store.

If those events had not occurred, Barry White, who lives at Jamberoo on the New South Wales South Coast, would not have been a ratcatcher's grandson. Neither would there exist hundreds of Emmanuel and Richard's descendants in Australia.

This memoir is, to the best of my recollection, fact. Writing it would not have been possible had not my mother, Alma, saved all the letters that I had written to her during 1960 – 1963. In 1985, she returned the letters to me packed inside an old chocolate box. These jogged my memory.

Thank you to Graham Tucker and the editor of my book, Tahlia Newland, for their invaluable editorial assistance and encouragement. I would also like to acknowledge all of the inspirational women, including former wives, who have been part of my life. And Australia.

Barry White, 2019.

Glossary of Australian Slang

A blue: a fight.
Basin crop: a cheap haircut.
Bawl: to cry.
Block: (as in 'knock your block off') head.
Bludge: to take it easy, not work hard.
Bobby dazzler: very good.
Bodgie: when used in reference to a male person, it means having long hair. In other usage bodgie means faulty.
Brass razoo: of little value.
Bumper Farrell: a rugby league player who is reputed to have bitten another player's ear off.
Chunder: to vomit.
Clapped out: broken or not running well.
Codger: a man; an old codger is an old man.
Come the raw prawn: to say or do something bad.
Commo: a communist.
Crook as Rookwood: near death or very ill.
Dill: a person who is considered to be dumb.
Dob in: to report someone to someone in authority.
Dodgy: not correct.
Dong: to hit.
Donga: the far countryside.

Donnybrook: a fight.
Dough: money. Big dough: a large amount of money.

Drongo: a foolish person.
Fair dinkum: proper.
Fit as a Mallee Bull: a fit person.
Galoot: a fool.
Get a woolly-bull up you: an insult as in 'go and get stuffed'.
Go the knuckle: to fight.
Gobbledygook: jargon, or difficult to understand.
Gotta: got to do/go.
Knee-trembler: A casual outdoor sexual encounter, usually in an alleyway or against a wall, with the man standing and the woman's knees raised.
Lairing-off: showing off.
Lairy: flashy.
Lurk-man: a man who schemes.
Matelots: sailors.
Middie/Middy: a glass of beer. A lesser amount than a schooner.
Muskeg: Canadian tundra (ice in winter, slush in summer).
Ning-nong: a foolish person.
Not on your sweet Nellie: an emphatic no.
Nuddy: nude.
Once over: looks someone all over.
Orright: all right.
Piddly: small.
Pinch bar: a steel bar used for de-nailing timber.
Piss-pot: one who drinks a lot of alcohol.
Pom: an English person.
Pommies: English people.
Poof: a male homosexual.
Poofy: effeminate in appearance or actions (by a male).

Pox-doctor's clerk: as in 'done up like a pox-doctor's clerk', someone overdressed

Quid: one pound (equal to two dollars).

Ratbag: a fool.

Reffo cut: the haircut of a post WW2 refugee (stylish).

Rookwood: cemetery in Western Sydney.

Rorter: one who cheats.

Schooner: a large glass of beer.

Sheila: a woman.

Shirt-lifter: a homosexual.

Short and curlies: (as in 'got me by the short and curlies') caught me out properly.

Silvertail: someone who is rich.

Skin-full: full of beer.

Snatch it: to resign from a job.

Sook: a soft person.

Squillion dollars: a lot of money.

Stockwhip: braided leather stockman's whip.

Stone the crows: exclamation of wonder/doubt/surprise.

Struth/Strewth: expression of surprise.

Suck hole: one who pretends to like a boss.

Tailor-made cigarettes: manufactured ready-rolled cigarettes.

Ten bob: ten shillings or a half a pound.

Twelve and six: twelve shillings and sixpence (one dollar twenty-five cents).

Two-up game: gambling using a kip (slim piece of wood) to toss two one-penny coins. The game continues to be popular, especially on ANZAC Day.

Tyke: a roman catholic.

Weakie: a weak person.

Wharfie: waterside worker who unloads ships.

Yakka: work.

Zack, Zac, Zak : sixpence (about five cents).

The above definitions are the author's understanding of some of the Australian slang in common usage in the timeframe of this memoir. Nowadays, they are mostly only used by older Australians. The construction industry was a primary source of Australian slang.

Two useful reference books that explain Australian slang are:

The Dinkum Dictionary: a ripper guide to Aussie English: 1994. Lenie (Midge) Johansen. Penguin Books. ISBN 0 670 90728 6

A Dictionary of Australian Colloquialisms: G.A. Wilkes. 1978. Fontana Books 1980.

Chapter One

It's 1958.

I sit in the passenger seat of Ray Bartlett's blue MGA sports car, thinking that his brand new car's a whole lot better than my 1938 Waratah motor bike. Just about anything would be better than my clapped-out motor bike, but replacing it requires a financial commitment, and I'm a terrible money manager.

Mum's always telling me that I ought to knuckle down and save some money.

Ray says to me, 'I know two blokes that are going to Canada.'

I say to him, 'So what?' The state of my finances is such that going to Sydney's satellite cities, Newcastle or Wollongong, would be a stretch.

'They're migrating to Canada,' he says. 'They're going to make big money, then they're going on to Europe.'

I still reckon, so what, but I listen to him.

'Carpenters and plumbers get big dough in Canada, at least twice as much as we make in Australia.'

I shrug. 'So what? They might earn big dough in Canada, but it costs big dough to get there.'

'They told me it's two hundred quid.'

'It may as well be two thousand, because there's no way I can scratch up two hundred.'

'You'd have to save it. You'd have to knuckle down and put some money in the bank instead of spending it on clothes and women and that clapped-out motor bike.'

He sounds just like my mother. I say, 'It's all right for you because you pay less board to your mum than I do to mine … and you get more overtime.'

He stares at my necktie that has my star-sign symbol—a set of scales and the word Libra—printed on it. 'How much did that fucking lairy tie cost? Ten bob?'

I feel the soft silk-like material. 'No … it was twelve and six. It's a bloody good tie. Quality, mate.'

Ray snorts in disgust. 'That thing you're wearing is bloody stupid; it's too thin. They went out of fashion years ago. You look like a pox-doctor's clerk. Plumbers don't wear ties that cost twelve and six. And what about that sports coat, how much did it cost?'

I'm definitely not going to tell him because he'll only take the piss. He'll only say that he could fill the petrol tank of his MGA for a month with the same amount of money. But he's one hundred percent correct; if I stopped buying good clothes I'd be able to save enough to go to Canada.

~

We live in the southern Sydney suburb of Penshurst, five of us: my mother, Alma, my sister, Janice, and my brothers, John and Jeffrey. There used to be six, but in 1954 my father, Stan, died aged forty-two, his lungs riddled by asbestos.

Stan and his mates built our Penshurst house on one of the last vacant blocks of land on the McRae estate. It's a very nice house.

We used to live at Peakhurst in a house Stan and his mates also built. Working-class Australians need good mates if they're going to have their own house.

I liked living at Peakhurst. It had lots of bush and all my mates lived there. Penshurst has no bush, and none of my mates live near here.

Alma, my mother, wanted to move from Peakhurst because she was fed up living next door to the Bennett family. She didn't like hearing their noisy swearing and yelling when they had backyard two-up games; she didn't like the loud cowboy music they played; she didn't like the gunshot-like noises when they practiced cracking their stock-whip; and she didn't like all the rowdy fighting that went on. All the Bennett boys were good fighters.

Bennett's cow finally got Alma to convince Stan to move. The soil outside our front fence was lousy, difficult to grow anything, but Mum had the beginnings of a kikuyu grass lawn. The Bennett boys didn't give a bugger about Alma's struggling grass. They allowed their cow to trample on it and drag its long steel chain over it. Alma sent Stan into the Bennetts' to complain, but how can one man tell a two-up-playing, stock-whip-cracking family of good fighters to keep their cow off our front lawn?

Penshurst has nothing of significance apart from two huge water-storage tanks and Penshurst Park, the park where Stan was wicket keeper for the Peakhurst Waratah Cricket team.

Stan worked for Wunderlich Limited, a company that managed to kill a lot of its employees. At Wunderlich, Stan learnt the trade of metal ceiling fixing, and then transferred to the construction of army camps to house soldiers who would soon fight for the King of England against the Germans. Wunderlich asbestos sheeting covered the camp's walls and roofs, and although Stan smoked cigarettes that might in due course kill him, the asbestos fibres got him first.

In 1951 Stan received a letter saying that his TB chest x-ray showed a shadow on his right lung. A week later he was in Sydney Hospital having that lung removed. My sister and brothers and I weren't told what was happening.

'Your father is very sick,' Alma told us.

We kids weren't told that the clouds of dust that surrounded him when he power-sawed the Wunderlich 'Super Six' asbestos-cement corrugated roofing was killing him.

When Stan came home from hospital, us kids assumed that whatever was wrong with him was now righted.

But mostly all he did was to sit in a 'Morris' chair with his legs resting on a pouf and his body covered by a tartan blanket. When he moved he struggled to breathe, but he forced himself to move; he wasn't going to give in.

A few weeks later he managed to do some walking. He even went the few hundred yards to Penshurst shops to buy the Sydney Sun newspaper.

I worked as a copy boy at *The Sydney Morning Herald* newspaper, and I sometimes saw him when I returned from work. He would stand at the top of Penshurst railway station with the newspaper in front of his face, reading about cricket—the game he loved—maybe about Lindsay Hassett or Arthur Morris, or his hero, the wicket keeper Don Tallon. But most likely he had the newspaper in front of his face while he gasped increasingly shallow breaths.

I found him doing exactly that on a Saturday morning when I returned home after getting a haircut from Johnny Rowles, the best barber south of Sydney Harbour. Some blokes reckoned that Angelo De Marco in Sydney was better, but we thought not. Johnny's haircuts cost five bob, a shilling more than 'traditional' barbers, but 'traditional' barbers were butchers.

We reckoned they did basin crops, but they really did old-codger cuts—short back and sides. Johnny did duck-tail cuts, where at the back of the head the hair met with geometric symmetry slap-bang in the middle. He did American film star cuts—his James Dean cut was very popular—and 'reffo' cuts—the very latest European styles. But his absolute specialty was the crew cut; he probably did the flattest, spikiest crew cut in the world.

I'd had a bobby-dazzler of a haircut from Johnny, and I sat in the train surreptitiously admiring my reflection in the train windows. Jerry Lewis himself would be pleased to have that cut.

Near Penshurst railway station I hung my head out the open doors of the speeding train and hardly a hair moved. I jumped from the train before it stopped, then I ran up the station steps where my father stood, reading his newspaper. I didn't have lung cancer so I didn't gasp for air at the top of the railway steps. I flicked my ticket to the assistant stationmaster, who I knew believed that blokes my age should have more respect for him and should place their ticket in his hand, and went up to my father. He peered over the top of the newspaper, saw my Jerry Lewis crewcut, and rolled his eyes with horror, or disgust—I'm not certain which. But I know he thought it wasn't a good style for a sixteen-year-old who he hoped, in a few years, would be a member of the Masonic Lodge.

Two weeks later I held my mother's hand while we took our last look at my dead father. He lay in a polished-wood coffin dressed in his only suit with one of his three neckties that categorized his status as a middle-class Australian around his neck. I thought it appropriate that he wasn't wearing his wide and lairy 'Taurus the Bull' star-sign tie, and that I was not wearing my 'Libra' tie.

Mum cried. I cried. Dad's mother and father cried. Any one not crying stared at the carpet of Cliff Hardy's Funeral Parlour and wondered why such a young man with a young wife and family had been allowed to die.

I wondered why my mother, a woman who never knew or met her natural mother or father, could be so cruelly treated by asbestos and God?

~

An American, known as 'marrying' Jimmy Mansville, owned the Johns Mansville Corporation— the business his daddy founded— which was the largest asbestos distributor in the world. Jimmy, the little twerp, scuttled the hopes and dreams of a future for our family and lots of other families by knowingly distributing the toxic substance.

The finished products of Australian companies such as James Hardie and Wunderlich Limited, who used Johns-Mansville asbestos, were responsible for worldwide grief and sadness.

All of 'Marrying Jimmy's' long-legged brides quickly divorced him and got away with truckloads of American dollars made from selling the deadly toxin.

~

I was standing on scaffolding at the new Royal Prince Alfred nurses' quarters building caulking hot lead into the joint of a cast-iron sewerage pipe, when I heard a man speak:

'I've got the best life insurance policy available in Australia, and you should come down from up there so I can tell you about it,' he said.

Ah, a life-insurance salesman. Should I tell him to go to buggery?

I thought about my mother and how since Dad died she had to work for measly money in the milk bar next to the Hurstville Savoy picture theatre; and about how she weighs and wraps fruit in the Penshurst Fruit and Vegetable shop for customers who don't give a damn that she's a young widow and don't believe she's as good as them. But they couldn't know that she has to work there because she's struggling to make ends meet.

I thought about that night's meal, which, because it was Tuesday, was certain to be tripe covered by a lumpy white sauce—poor person's food; and about how bad I would feel if I was married with a young family, died of an awful disease at forty-two, and left a struggling wife. I wouldn't want my widow making chocolate-malted milkshakes in the Savoy Theatre milk bar, or coming home from working in a fruit shop with potato dirt under her fingernails.

So I got down from the scaffolding to hear what the man had to say.

I knew nothing about life insurance, so I listened.

He said, 'My company would deduct from your pay one-shilling and nine-pence every week, which means that if you die, your wife will be paid a weekly sum of fifteen pounds.'

'But I'm not married,' I said to the man. 'I haven't got a wife.'

Then I thought about how my father's work mates collected fifty-six pounds at the testimonial cricket match that Mum dragged me and my sister and brothers to. It probably represented ten shillings for every stumping he'd done as a wicket keeper.

I thought about the nothing my mother got from Wunderlich Limited, the asbestos company that killed my father, and I thought about how my father's Masonic Lodge brothers boasted that they'd look after Mum and did near nothing.

So I signed the form and told the man to get one shilling and nine pence deducted each week.

~

It's 1959.

When I tell my mother that Ray and I are going to Canada, she says, '"Oh yes, how?'

'I'm going to save two hundred pounds.'

'Oh yes, how?'

I know why she's sceptical. My weekly wage is twenty-two pounds; ten pounds of which goes to her for my board. As for the rest, I may as well throw it in the air and allow the wind to blow it to kingdom come.

'Just watch me,' I say.

Later, while having our tea, Mum asks, 'Barry, why go to Canada?'

'Ah ... because Ray reckons it would be a terrific adventure. He's very impressed by the Royal Canadian Mounted Police and their red-jacket uniform. Also, Jan's boyfriend Graeme is over there at the moment, and he reckons it's good.'

My mother reminds me of my obligations to her and my siblings.

Her widows' pension isn't all that much, so she needs my financial contribution to the household. My sister Jan and I had spoken about how trapped we felt having to stay at home and keep contributing to the family finances.

I'm focused on my own wants.

So I dump my girlfriend, stop buying clothes or tailor-made cigarettes, make plans to sell my clapped-out Waratah motor bike and look for every bit of overtime: Saturday work.

Car tyres screech. It's Ray Bartlett's MGA broadsiding around the corner near the Catholic Church. I start counting. The car skids to a stop at my mother's house, and I say to Ray, 'Fifty-two seconds.'

He says, 'There was an old Morris in front of me so I couldn't go over the Railway Bridge at top speed.'

I'm sympathetic because old cars often stop me from breaking records when I'm riding my 1938 Waratah motor bike.

'I've got the brochures,' he says. 'They arrived from Orbit Travel today. They look bloody good ... That is, except the fare; it's one-hundred-and-eighty bloody pounds!'

'Shit!'

'Yeah, I know. It's a hell of a lot of money.'

'Does it say anywhere in the brochures that we also have to have two hundred quid in a Canadian bank?' I ask.

'Yeah. It has to be deposited before leaving Australia.'

'Mate, it's going to be bloody difficult for me to make it. I'm going to be short by at least fifty quid.'

There's silence apart from someone else trying to break the record for getting from the Catholic Church corner to somewhere else.

Ray says, 'It's not fair. Pommies that come to Australia for ten quid don't have to have money in an Australian bank. All it costs them is ten lousy quid. Bingo; they're here, then they're off to a hostel and they've got a job next day. I'm buggered if I know why the Canadian government's so tough.'

'Yeah, it's not as though we're going to bludge on them. We'll get a job the day after we arrive. I mean, we're tradesmen; we're qualified. We're not like all those other nationalities from bloody Greece or Poland or Germany. We're part of the British Empire and so are they. They ought to give us some favouritism.'

'Have you sold your motor bike?' Ray asks.

'Yeah.'

'How much did you get?'

'Ah ... fifteen quid.'

'Shit! Is that all?'

'I wanted twenty-five quid, but he knocked me down to fifteen. It was like he knew I was desperate to sell. It was depressing to see the old bike go. Especially since the bloke who bought it went away and got a mate who had an old ambulance stretcher.'

'An ambulance stretcher?'

'Yeah; they piled all the parts on the stretcher and carried it out like it was, well ... something dead.'

'Well ... wasn't it?'

'Dead?'

'Yeah, dead. The fucking thing hadn't run for months, and there's no way you could put all those parts together. It was a deceased bike.'

We hear the sound of two quick changes of gears, then car tyres screeching, and we know that whoever's negotiating the Catholic Church corner has a Lukey muffler. We don't speak because we love to listen to the unique exhaust sound of a Lukey muffler.

'Is there any other way to get fifty quid?' Ray asks.

I remember the life insurance payments of one shilling and ninepence that's been deducted from my pay for five years. 'Yeah; there is. Because I'm now going to be a world traveller, I'll probably never get married and die young and leave a widow, so I could cash in my life insurance.'

But when I telephone the insurance company, they tell me that it's very bad to cancel life insurance. They rip me off and offer a surrender value of twenty quid. Not enough.

But something else comes up.

I work as a maintenance plumber at the Victa Lawnmower factory in Revesby, and on an uncommonly hot March day, someone screams that the factory roof is falling down. All the lawn-mower assemblers rush outside.

Mister Mervin Victor Richardson, the inventor of the Victa lawnmower, orders the plumbers to go inside to save the factory.

We plumbers go in carrying lengths of four-inch galvanized water pipe that we use to prop up the heat-buckled roof struts. Then we work all night welding bits of steel onto other bits of steel. When the saving is done, Mister Mervin Victor Richardson is very grateful, so he gives us plumbers a bonus of an extra week's pay.

It's now certain I'm going to Canada.

~

Ray and I sit opposite a pompous man in the Orbit Travel Company office in Pitt Street. He's acting as if he's the be-all and end-all of travel knowledge. I realise he knows more than we do when he speaks about visas and immigration documents.

I say to him, 'But we don't want to become Canadians; we only want to work there for a while.'

He says, 'If you want to work … you must migrate.'

I think about European migrants with difficult-to-pronounce names that come to Australia on Greek, Italian and German ships that also have difficult-to-pronounce names. There's Sergio Muccuty, a plumber I worked with at Chatterton and Stephens Master Plumbers, the wrestler Emil Korashenko, and the Costantini and Poelakker and Topoljski families whose names I always mumble. They're all migrants.

But I can't reconcile why I should have to be a migrant? My great-grandfather was a migrant; he came to Australia in 1876 from County Meath in Ireland, and when he arrived here, he helped build Australia and the British Commonwealth by working the Redfern area as a tip-carter. And his son, my grandfather, continued to build the strength of the British

Commonwealth by working as a rat-catcher at the huge Anthony Hordens' department store.

And his son, my father, died as a result of building army camps that housed soldiers of the King who went off to save the British Commonwealth from Germans and Japanese soldiers.

Why should I, a fully qualified plumber, be asked to be a migrant? I wonder. My family has done its bit for the British Commonwealth. I mean, I speak English and I don't have an unpronounceable name. My name is White. It's short and sweet and easily spelt, so I'd fit in nicely in Canada. I'd meld very nicely with their Browns and Joneses and Smiths. Canada is part of the British Commonwealth of Nations and so is Australia, and so am I.

The pompous man says, 'Take it or leave it. If you don't migrate, you don't work.'

We sign the migration application documents and leave Orbit Travel so the man can be pompous to his next client; then we go and have a beer in the Wynyard Station Hotel.

Ray says to me, 'Do you reckon our money's safe with that know-it-all bloke? He's got about three hundred and fifty quid of ours.'

'I reckon so. His company makes travel arrangements for *The Sydney Morning Herald*, and I don't think Mister Vincent and Mister Warwick Fairfax would do business with a con-man.'

'But do you know for sure? I mean, the bloke could disappear to Queensland. He could buy a block of land in Queensland with that much money.'

I knew for sure because my first full-time job was as a copy boy at *The Sydney Morning Herald*. It was a terrific job, which I believed gave me status. My mates sometimes tried to cut that status from beneath me by saying that I was really a messenger, thatthe *Herald* wouldn't employ a copy boy who failed his Intermediate Certificate English examination. So I didn't tell them everything.

I didn't mention that I picked up oysters from a King Street fish shop for the executives' lunch, or that I delivered letters to businesses, or that I cleared the *Herald's* post office mail box. And I definitely did not tell them that I sometimes stole a few letters in anticipation of there being a postal-order payment inside for a *Herald* food recipe, or design plans for a Hudson ready-cut house. I told them about the excitement of being in the police-rounds room listening to messages being sent from police headquarters to police cars; of watching a photograph facsimile arriving from London or Washington on a spinning roller—something they never believed. 'That's bullshit,' they'd say.

But the travel excited me most. I saw journalists and photographers leave to cover stories in exotic places: Singapore, Tokyo and Rome.

One of my daily jobs was to deliver the latest edition of the *Herald* and the opposition paper, *The Daily Telegraph*, to the executives' desks. Some mornings I'd be told not to leave Mister Vincent or Mister Warwick Fairfax's papers because they were in London, or New York, or on an overseas holiday. I wondered how they could afford such extensive travel.

And I certainly didn't tell my mates that when I delivered the executive's newspapers, I used to steal a handful of 'tailor-made' cigarettes from the Fairfaxes' nearly-always-full desktop cigarette case. All the travel arranging was done by the Orbit Travel Company, possibly by the pompous man who did our arranging, so I reckoned it was certain our money wouldn't be spent buying land in Queensland.

The Orbit Travel Company also rented premises from the *Herald*, and they wouldn't rent to someone who'd steal money. I trust the judgement of *The Sydney Morning Herald,* so I trust Orbit.

Besides, the pompous man at Orbit Travel was wearing a Libran tie, the same one I have, so he must be all right.

I spend my last few Saturday nights in Australia getting a skin-full of Resch's beer at Shanney's Hotel, then I go dancing at the Hurstville Rivoli, where I avoid any romantic association that would keep me from leaving. I'm still not buying tailor-made cigarettes, and my mother makes sandwiches for my work lunches.

~

June 6th 1960.

The Sydney harbour-side suburb of Pyrmont is busy with taxis and cars and buses carrying hundreds of travellers and their farewellers. Luggage porters balance long-handled wheelbarrows stacked with Globite suitcases that contain the dreams of adventurers. Ray and I, two unworldly twenty-two-year-olds, have our boat tickets sticking out of our jacket top pockets, and we flash our passports about. We feel very important; and we look important too. We wear yachting jackets that, pretentiously, have a map of Australia on the pocket—albeit without Tasmania—and we have smiles a professional boxer couldn't knock off our faces. We don't give a bugger that our mothers and sisters and girlfriends are sad and are crying. We can't wait to get out of here.

The ship's departure is slow, like a dentist pulling a tooth. We hear the announcement: 'All visitors ashore … All ashore who's going ashore.' We share final kisses, hugs, handshakes and tears. In some eyes I detect envy.

My nana panics because she's unconvinced the ship won't sink between Sydney and, and, and … 'that New Zealand place'.

I say to Nana, 'That New Zealand place is called Auckland, and believe me, when this ship sinks, I'll—'

'Barry, don't say things like that,' my mother says. 'Your nana's very worried about you. And so am I.'

People chuck outlandishly priced paper streamers from shore to ship and ship to shore. Few connect. Those that do are tightly held, but a large crane that travels the length of the ship hoisting away gangways soon severs them. Those holding streamers say, 'Oh what a pity.' But the crane driver doesn't care.

The deep sound of the ship's horn repeats many times, bouncing off buildings and echoing in a cacophony of noise.

Uninterested wharfies unhook the ship's hawsers, which then flop into Sydney Harbour. Uninterested English seamen haul the dripping-wet hawsers onto the ship, and the tooth-pulling-like leaving of Sydney continues. I'm wishing that everyone would go home so I can stop waving, but they stay, and we stay, and everyone gets sore arms waving to what are now distant indistinguishable figures.

I should have concerns about my mother's financial welfare. Not getting my contribution for household expenses will make it difficult for her. I should feel guilt, but I don't. Famous explorers wouldn't have thought about their financial obligations. Scott of the Antarctic wouldn't have thought about Mrs Scott when he went off, and neither would have Burke and Wills when they set out to explore Australia's north. I do feel guilty about telling my mother I'll be away for a year. I know it will be years.

Alma's husband is dead, and now she has a might-as-well-be-dead son. She's sentenced to menial, low-paid work to feed her three remaining children and pay her mortgage. She has to continue serving milk shakes, Violet Crumble bars and chocolate-coated ice creams in the Savoy Theatre milk bar, and weighing and wrapping potatoes, onions and carrots in the Penshurst fruit shop.

Ray says, 'Well that's that.'

I say, 'Yeah … that's that.'

We wander off, joining the other passengers on the *Orsova* who are smiling broadly as they explore the ship for the bars, dining room and swimming pool.

I want to get organized, to see who'll be sharing our six-berth cabin.

Ray says, 'That old Canadian bloke we saw downstairs said he—'

'That old Canadian bloke we saw … *below decks*!' I correct him as we head down.

Ray gives me a pissed-off look. 'All right then, *below decks* … if you want to be nautical. He said he didn't know who else will be in the cabin. All I know is that I've got my stuff on a bottom bunk.'

'It might be sheilas,' I say.

'Sheilas? That wouldn't be bad.'

'Imagine it, mate. In the crowded cabin, we'll accidentally, on purpose, rub against their tits and bums.'

'And all their underwear hanging on the cabin clothes line,' Ray says.

'Yeah. But I don't know if that excites me all that much.'

'There'd be no farting in bed, though.'

'Why not? Girls fart!'

Ray's eyebrows rise. 'Oh? Have you ever heard a girl fart?'

'No. But they must. Everyone farts.'

'Have you ever heard your mother or sister fart?'

'No.'

Just after we step inside the cabin, the door opens and three blokes come in. They're foreigners—Victorians.

I say to them, 'Oh, blokes. We were hoping we'd share the cabin with sheilas.'

The old Canadian bloke shakes his head and leaves.

One of the Victorians says, 'Sheilas! You'd be a bit of a ratbag. They don't put sheilas in the same cabin as blokes.'

'Oh well,' I say to Ray, 'that means we can fart.'

We return to the deck and see that Australia is an undulating line on the horizon. There's nothing of size or prominence that impresses us as a final memory. There are lights, but they blend into a glow. No one object is recognizable, but we know that somewhere over there, our families are now cooking an evening meal of meat and three vegetables, and they're, probably, about to settle down on the lounge to watch *Homicide* or *The Bobby Limb Show*.

An experienced adventurer told us that sophisticated travellers eat at the second-dinner sitting, so that's when we eat.

I display my sophistication when I order the apple pie *ah ler mody* from a pompous cockney waiter. He tells me he can't understand what I'm saying, so he asks me to point to what I want on the menu.

'Ah,' he says. 'So you'll be having the apple pie *à la mode* … sir.'

I can't help pronouncing French words incorrectly. We didn't have language subjects at Hurstville Secondary Technical School; we had woodwork and metalwork and technical drawing. I didn't go to a university. My tertiary education was in the building industry where rhyming slang is used and where knowledge of swearing is important.

If a plumbing boss wanted a toilet installed, he'd say, 'Put a bloody shithouse in that fucking room.'

If it was installed out of level, we blamed the 'fish fart', the bubble in the spirit level. We used insults like, 'Go and get a woolly-bull up you,' or, 'Go and bag your head,' or, 'Get rooted.' The receiver of such insults might reply with, 'Keep a cool head there, Curl,' or 'Get rooted yourself.' If I have no money, I'm 'broke', or I haven't got a 'brass razoo', not even a 'zac'. If I'm ill, I'm 'as crook as Rookwood' or 'feeling shithouse'.

So how can I know that *à la mode* means the apple pie is served with ice cream?

Neither can I change the way I speak. All my family and friends speak exactly the same way—except the women, who, as far as I know, hardly ever swear; a damn or a bloody is about all they'll say.

Differences in speech categorize Australians. Those who live on Sydney's middle North Shore or near the Eastern Suburbs are easily distinguished from those who live on the southern side of the harbor. Most of them speak like the announcers on ABC radio. We from the southern side don't listen to ABC—not even the radio serial *Blue Hills* by Gwen Meredith. We listen to stations 2GB and 2UE. We like to hear Jack Davey's quiz programs, and Mo McCackie, Hal Lashwood and Spencer the Garbage Man in *McCackie Mansions*; and John Harper on 2KY ... the people's station.

And we don't much open our mouths when we speak. Words are formed in our throats. We hardly move our tongue or lips, even when we say the word 'elocution'—not that we ever would. If we're surprised, our 'ah' comes out sounding like a crow's squawk. It's reckoned that we don't open our mouths because blowflies might dart in, but there are blowflies on Sydney's North Shore.

I don't deserve the smart-arse comment from the cockney waiter. I've eaten high-quality mixed grills—even gourmet mixed grills that have a fried egg on top of the lamb chop. I've eaten Spaghetti Bolognaise and

Beef Stroganoff and Hungarian Goulash. But it seems those dishes have not prepared me for the S.S. *Orsova's* sophisticated second sitting of dinner.

Ray says to me, 'Remember when we each had a lobster at that restaurant in Brighton?'

I remember, but I don't want him talking about it here.

He tells everyone at our table that I didn't know how to attack the lobster, so I asked Barry, and he took a grip on both ends, bent it and it snapped in half, sending Mornay sauce and bits of lobster flying into the air and onto the floor, tablecloth. and us.

Ha-ha-ha. Now everyone thinks I'm an idiot.

~

I'm very excited about the ship's arrival in Auckland. New Zealand is the first foreign country I've visited, so I go to an 'Introduction to New Zealand' talk that's on in the ship's library. A man gets up and rambles on about cows and sheep and milk production and the kiwi.

He says, 'Do you know that the kiwi can't fly?'

And someone mumbles, 'Of course we bloody well know it can't fly.'

An American woman asks him about buying wool jumpers and the location of 'good' restaurants—stuff that I'm not interested in. I want to know about geysers that spurt hot water into the air and the Maori warriors who defeated the British soldiers—and about the Anzacs.

My sixth-class schoolteacher, Mister Morris, often told us kids that the First World War Gallipoli campaign would forever keep New Zealanders and Australians together. He told us, 'It's a bond formed in blood.' And that might well be true, but I've never met a New Zealander. I've got no idea if they're the same or different from us.

Mister Morris used to point to the Gallipoli-landing picture that hung on the classroom wall above the fireplace that never got lit, and he'd say, 'There we are together, brothers in arms.'

One kid once asked, 'Which are the New Zealand soldiers?'

And Mister Morris couldn't tell him because the Australians and New Zealanders wore similar uniforms and tin hats.

My first view of New Zealanders is the big, tough-looking Maoris on the Auckland wharf. We reckon that most of them must have gone out drinking one night and for a bet they allowed a tattoo artist to go crazy on their skin. Most of them are too big to be good runners, so that's what I'll be doing if any of them pick a fight with me—run.

Ray and I and two of the Victorians have paid four-pounds sixteen-shillings to travel on a bus to Rotorua where we'll see geysers and, hopefully, Maori warriors.

I feel as though I'm akin to Marco Polo or Captain Cook. I'm about to set foot on uncharted shores that I'll explore to find gold, discover mountains and rivers, perhaps even civilize the natives.

We ride away from Auckland in a bus that's better than any other bus in which I'd travelled. I say to Ray, 'What's different?'

'Everything's different. We're in New Zealand,' he says.

'Eucalyptus trees, old cars, people dressed in clothes similar to ours, the roads as bad as Australian roads. Ray, we might well be in Sydney. Nothing's different; it's just a bit greener.'

The grass is so very green and lush. Mobs of sheep graze on small areas of land that in Australia would carry only a handful of stock.

Someone says, 'I've never seen better grass.'

The bus driver replies with, 'We're actually going through a drought.'

I can't tell if he's serious.

The bus driver announces that we will stop for morning tea at Mattamatta and we'll be in Rotorua for lunch. The bus will return to the ship at six p.m. exactly.

I wonder why he speaks the way he does; it sounds strange. At the rear of the bus we all try to speak the same way. The bus driver hears us and tells us we're all smart-Alecs. We all fall about laughing and try to say Alecs the same way he does: elics, arlecs, erlics. We don't get it right, and we can see now that he's really pissed-off, and we know that if we're late at any stop, he'll leave us, and we'll miss the ship's sailing for Fiji.

At the Mattamatta comfort stop, we take comfort in a hotel bar.

Schooners and middies are ordered, but we get a shrug from the barman and he serves each of us a jug of beer. Locals are having quiet cleansing ales, but they don't take well to the crowd of loud-mouthed Australians, and insults are given and received.

Dougie, a Victorian bloke from our cabin, does something really stupid; he says, 'This New Zealand beer's like piss.'

The bar goes quiet.

I say to him, 'Shush.'

We all say, 'Shush,' but he's not going to shush for anyone.

A farmer who has arms as thick as a tree stump says, 'Ind you ussies thunk your baar's batter?'

None of us should answer him with a 'Yes,' but Dougie does.

The farmer says, 'Huw ubout I shuve thut gluss doun yoor throat?'

Dougie wants to fight him, but we drag him back to the bus, and the driver compliments us for not keeping the other passengers waiting. He says, 'It's good that you're back because I'd have left without you.'

I say, 'We know that, that's why we're early. But, mate, can you tell us why those bloody farmers in the pub can't take a joke?'

'What kind of joke?'

'About the local beer.'

'What? You joked about their beer? Now that was pretty stupid. I wouldn't be surprised to see them come after you with some of their Maori mates to—'

'Knock the piss out of us?'

'… yeah.'

So we tell the driver to get out of town fast.

Dougie, the stupid Victorian, moves to the very last seat and stays there. 'Let's get out of here,' he says.

Sometime later, Ray says to me, 'Who farted?'

It's not me, but someone has released an awful-smelling burst of back-end gas. 'Someone's rotten,' I say to him.

The bus driver announces that we'll soon be in Rotorua and does anyone have any questions.

Dougie says, 'Yeah, who farted?'

Older passengers shake their heads because they never say the word fart. Younger passengers snigger.

The driver says, 'That's enough of that foul language. What you can smell is the sulphurous gasses from Rotorua's thermal ponds.'

'I reckon it's the driver that's farted,' Dougie says, 'and he's blaming it on thermal ponds.'

Everyone and everything seems to be farting in Rotorua. Ponds of mud that puff and gurgle and shoot gas into the air are all over the place. We joke about not lighting matches.

A bloke takes off his best thongs and paddles in a pool. 'Christ!' he yells. 'That's hot.'

Someone near him chucks the thongs into the middle of the hot spring, and we all, apart from him, laugh.

A group of Maori women chant and spin balls fixed to the end of lengths of string. The balls whoosh and whoosh around in complicated circular patterns, and we wonder how they can do it without getting tangled. A Maori woman named Rangi then does even more complicated spins.

Ray says, 'How on earth does she do that?'

She gives the balls to him, and he spins them and gets them all tangled. He looks like a goose.

Another Maori takes us to a meeting house that has ornate carved walls and ceiling and he gives us a lecture about the Maori wars, the treaty of Waitangi and the Maoris not being defeated by British soldiers.

I think that what he's saying is wrong, because Mister Morris, my school teacher, told our class that after the Anzacs, British soldiers are the best. He said that the British soldiers beat everyone: the hordes of savage

Indians at the Khyber Pass; the chanting Zulus in South Africa; the French, Germans, Italians, Spanish and Portuguese—they beat them all.

When Mister Morris said all that, one of the kids said, 'But, sir, what about the Americans?'

And he said to the kid, 'Ah … the British were not beaten there; they did a strategic retreat.'

I look at the big, well-muscled Maori men standing nearby, and I don't believe that British soldiers could beat them.

I think about films I'd seen that had the American Indians being easily beaten by gallant British soldiers who were blasting them to kingdom come with their cannons. I remember my schoolteachers speaking about the great exploits of dukes and earls and princes, how they conclusively conquered primitive people in the four corners of the earth so that they might become part of the empire. And now I'm wondering if all that's wrong.

We reckon the bus driver means to leave us in Rotorua, that he'd like to say, 'Oh, they didn't get on the bus, and I couldn't allow my other passengers to miss the ship's sailing, so I left them.' But we're sitting in the bus fifteen minutes before we're supposed to because we're onto him, and we reckon we'd better stop mimicking his New Zealand accent.

At Mattamatta on the return journey to Auckland, we don't want the comfort stop offered by the bus driver; we don't even leave the bus.

Back on the ship, an American man who's leaning on the ship's handrail near me says, 'Well, we've done New Zealand.'

'Done?'

'Yep. We did Australia last week, and we did New Zealand today.'

Ray says to him, 'You've hardly been there enough time to have done a shit. There's two islands, you know.'

The American goes away mumbling something about coarse Australians.

The ship's departure here is similar to its Sydney departure; people are yelling farewells and whistling and throwing streamers. One of the streamers thumps onto the steel stanchion beside me—this is fun. Another hits me on my head, and another rockets onto Ray—this is not fun. We're being targeted.

Ray points at a crowd of louts who don't look like they're saying good-bye to anyone. 'It's those blokes there.'

One of them stretches his arm back, and he flings what must be a tightly rolled streamer our way. Thump; it hits the ships side below us.

Bastards.

I pick up their first missile, take aim, then I toss it. Thump; it hits no one.

Now rolls of streamers are thumping all around us, and other passengers on the ship get involved.

Dougie is frustrated because he's got nothing to throw, so he gets a deckchair cushion and flings it overboard. It wafts for a moment, then does a crazy float to the wharf. Others do the same with more cushions, but the retaliation gets serious when a deckchair crashes onto the wharf.

Some of the ship's crew come looking for culprits. We start waving to the attacking New Zealanders, and they wave to us, and we all yell, 'Good-bye … good-bye.'

My Uncle Harry was an Anzac in the first AIF. He got shot in France. I remember him telling me about the childish games shared by the Australian and New Zealand soldiers. He'd said to me, 'Barry; it was the only bit of fun we got.'

I reckon our streamer throwing is exactly like that.

Childish games continue on the *Orsova* organized by the ship's entertainment Officer, a weed of a man who's always immaculately dressed, except for his very tight short trousers. We reckon he shoves half a toilet roll down his trousers to make it look like he's got a big prick. We tell some of the girls that, and they go around staring at his crotch. None of us know when he gets the time to lie in the sun, but he must do a lot of it because he's as brown as a berry. All the women think he's wonderful. We think he's a ponce.

He swans about trying to persuade passengers to participate in his games, and when that fails, he drags them out of their chairs. 'Sir, you must come to play bingo,' he says.

Ray says, 'Bugger the bingo.'

I also tell him to go away.

The ponce says, 'But you must come; we have wonderful prizes. Most of the passengers will be playing.'

He goes along the deck saying the same thing to others, and almost everyone aged over forty goes to win the wonderful prizes.

I say to Dougie, 'That bloke's a nong.'

He says, 'Yeah, he's a real ning-nong.'

It's difficult to get away from the ning-nong because the ship's bar we mostly frequent is near where the bingo is played. And we reckon he's got the wrong name for the game; we reckon it's housie-housie.

Someone screams out in delight because they've won, and they're awarded a colourfully wrapped prize that turns out to be some of the ship's soap—one of the wonderful prizes.

When the ning-nong finishes that game, he tells us we must come to the horse races. We wonder where the horses are kept and how they're going to gallop along the ship's deck. Dougie learns that there's betting, and he's convinced he'll clean up. He speaks so confidently that we go with him to clean up.

There are no real horses, just wooden cut-outs moved along the deck by bored crewmembers whose only interest is perving on girls sunbaking nearby.

I have a bet on the red horse; it comes near last. Ray goes for the blue one; it also comes near last. Dougie reckons the book is crooked, and he says so. He gets a dirty look from the ning-nong and from his lackey who's setting the odds and handling the betting money.

The ning-nong says, 'Boys, you must come to the quiz because we have great prizes.'

'Grog?' Ray asks.

'No; all the prizes come from the duty-free shop.'

'Any battery shavers as prizes?' Ray asks.

The ning-nong shakes his head and goes looking for easier marks who will certainly be aged over forty.

At the bar that we mostly frequent, we hear quiz questions that only a university professor might answer: mineral symbols, Shakespearean quotes and the names of Greek Gods. Passengers who must be university professors scream out answers and look very pleased. We see the winner presented with a chromed ashtray engraved with P&O lines. I know I can steal the same ashtray from any dining room table. And I do exactly that.

The ning-nong says, 'Boys, you must take part in the talent quest.'

We say, 'No.' We know that none of us have talent.

At our favourite ship's bar, we hear the talent.

A man says, 'I'm going to sing the song Nelson Eddy sang in the film *Indian Love Call*.'

A woman says, 'I'm going to sing Vera Lynn's *White Cliffs of Dover*.' She does and all the old people clap so much that she then does a Gracie Fields' number.

No one does any of Frankie Lane's songs.

The ning-nong says, 'Boys you must come to the deck games.'

'What games?' I say. 'Cricket?'

'No. We play only traditional shipboard games. Today, we're playing deck-quoits and shuttlecock and there are prizes.'

'Grog?'

'No.'

We see good-looking girls wearing bikini swimsuits who jump to hit the shuttlecock, making their breasts wobble about. We reckon there's a good chance that a few breasts will flop out, so we decide to play shuttlecock. But we don't play very well because we can't stop looking at their bikini tops. They easily beat us, and their breasts don't flop out. The girls are excited about winning so they go to deck-quoits, and we go, too, because we reckon that when they bend over, their breasts might flop out. We try to beat them, but they win, and their breasts don't flop out.

Dougie is pissed-off about losing the game, so he accidentally on purpose throws the deck-quoit over the side of the ship, and it plops into the Pacific Ocean. The ning-nong accuses him of destroying P&O property and bans us from further deck games.

He doesn't ask us to participate in the fancy-dress dance, but we do anyhow. We all come draped in bed sheets with eyeholes cut in the sheets, but the ning-nong disqualifies us because we've destroyed more P&O property.

I say to him, 'But we have to see where we're going. Without eyeholes we could walk over the ship's side.'

The ning-nong laughs and says, 'I wish you would.'

It's obvious that most of the passengers want nothing to do with us. Respectable people scoff at us, and the bikini-wearing, good-looking girls travelling with adults ostracize us.

One girl says to us, 'My mother told me not to go anywhere near you hooligans. She said you're drunkards, non-functioning humans, and that your shenanigans will get you thrown off the ship.'

We see the bikini-wearing, good-looking girls who want nothing to do with us sunbaking with blokes who never go to the bar that we mostly frequent. They slide the deckchairs under the girls when they sit, have lots of good white Pelacco shirts that are well ironed—that don't have tram-track ironing marks on the sleeves. We'll never again talk to those girls because they like to read books in the ship's library and sip wine and cocktails at the bar that we never frequent. They listen to classical music concerts and have polite conversations that don't include words we use.

We find other girls who laugh when we do whatever we're not supposed to do. They like to see us do jumping bombs in the swimming pool so everyone gets splashed, and they think we're marvellous when we wrestle with each other. They agree with us when we laugh at those who do circumnavigations of the ship decks wearing nice white shorts and sandshoes that aren't discoloured. Oh, we've got sandshoes, but our sandshoes have aged grass stains and bits scraped off from when we collected cunji bait from the Werri Beach rocks. None of us brought with us our mum's Kiwi-White sandshoe cleaner. We don't scrub our sandshoes with an old toothbrush. We don't give a bugger about that.

Neither do we wear flash-looking airline pilot sunglasses that cost an arm and a leg. We are never seen flushed from exercise and lathered by perspiration or having a white bath towel casually hung from our shoulder to mop up sweat that shouldn't be there in the first place.

We always wear King-Gee Victory Brand khaki shorts and lairy shirts because we're 'two-bob lairs'.

Everyone on the ship is going to get lucky because we lairs are going to leave the ship in Vancouver—but that's weeks away.

Friday 10th June 1960
Dear Mum and kids,
It's a beautiful day; the sea is not too rough and the sun is shining. Last Wednesday we went on a tour to Rotorua, which is located in the thermal region of New Zealand.

New Zealand must be the greenest country in the world; the average rainfall in this area is fifty inches. When we arrived back on board, we stood on deck to watch the ship leave Auckland Harbour. After clearing the Harbour, Ray and I went to the bar and cut a pineapple between us.

On Thursday we just walked around the ship. That night we saw a film with Jack Hawkins in it. After the film we went to the bar and had a brandy lime and soda.

I don't drink too much beer on the ship; I think it makes me seasick. One or two brandies don't have much effect on me next morning.

Today, Friday, we have been up on deck playing deck quoits. We lost.

The bell has just rung for the first sitting of dinner; we're the second sitting. Tonight, the captain is having a cocktail party, and we have been invited. After the cocktail party there is a dance.

The ship reaches Suva on Saturday. I have been told the natives are having a shindig for the Queen's birthday. Ray and I are going on a trip to Deuba to see native dancers and to have lunch at the Beachcomber Hotel. I will tell you all about it in my next letter.

Love, Barry.

Suva is very hot. Primitive Fijian natives wearing red-serge jackets, black skirts and sandals stand on the wharf playing primitive Britannic martial music on primitive tubas, trumpets and trombones.

We expected grass-skirt-wearing, hip-wobbling primitive Fijian women dancing to the beat of drums played by primitive Fijian men. The band plays something familiar, a tune that's not supposed to have words, but we remember some words that we sang to this music when we were Boy Scouts and Sea Cadets.

We sing, 'Oh, the maggots walk down Pitt Street with their boots on'.

No one else on the ship was in the First Beverly Hills Scout Troop or the Kangaroo Point Sea Cadet Unit, so they don't sing. And they probably don't like singing about maggots.

We now realise that New Zealand was not the country in which to be a grand explorer, but Fiji could be. This country is really foreign.

But Suva's shops have Kellogg's Corn Flakes, Arnott's Biscuits, Hallstrom Silent Knight Refrigerators, HMV record players, and on the roads are Holden cars and Mini Minors, so we're thinking that Fiji might not need grand explorers.

Ray asks, 'When's the tour to Deuba?'

'In an hour.' And the sooner the better because I want to see some primitive Fijian warriors.

The tour bus arrives—at least it's primitive. It has no glass windows, but it does have canvas screens that we later find sometimes stay up, but mostly fall down. Its seats are made from wood slats that have splinters sticking out, and there's no spring in the springs, so when the bus goes over the smallest of potholes, the springs bottom-out and splinters lunge into our legs and bottoms. The bus's paint is sun-faded and scratched, and its sides dented in from the lashings of thousands of tree branches. Galloping rust is evident.

Someone says, 'Look out for that tree branch.' But the driver ignores the branch and the warning, and it lashes against the front window then clank-clank-clanks along the bus side.

'Exciting eh?' Ray says.

'Yeah; now we're getting primitive.'

We arrive at the Deuba Hotel where not-so-primitive Fijians welcome us, then they invite us to sit in a grandstand that's not all that grand—a one-horse town grandstand.

Boom, bomb, boom, bomb go the drums, and a mob of grass-skirted Fijian warriors rush from behind a galvanized-iron shed. They yell and yell and yell, and they jump and jump and jump.

Ray says, 'This is good; at last we're seeing some primitive Fijian warriors.'

I say nothing because I'm thinking it's not very primitive.

A warrior who seems to be the mob's leader yells and jumps, then he makes a threatening advance towards the grandstand.

Someone in the grandstand says, 'He's holding a steel axe.'

Someone else says, 'He's wearing a wristwatch.'

Someone else says, 'He's wearing King Gee shorts under his grass skirt.'

A couple of warriors come from behind the shed carrying a cauldron containing a thick, milky, gooey-looking liquid that sluices about. Some of it breaches the side of the cauldron and one of them tries to push it back with a crappy-looking cloth.

The main mob of Fijian warriors stop dancing. They huddle around the cauldron, and we hear angry-sounding words and indistinct chanting.

I say to Ray, 'This looks good. This is primitive stuff.'

He's not so impressed. 'What are they going to do with the dishwater? Wash the breakfast dishes?'

I reckon he's being far too cynical. They'll probably set it alight or it'll change colour.

Nothing like that happens. Instead, a warrior adds something else, another one stirs the liquid, and another soaks a muslin-looking material.

One of the primitive warriors comes near us and says in what I reckon is a New Zealand accent, 'Kava? Will you try our kava?'

No one does anything because no one knows what he's talking about.'

He says, 'Who will be the first to drink?'

Nearly everyone says, 'Drink! You want us to drink that?'

Someone sitting behind us says, 'Careful; it's very alcoholic.'

One of the Victorians says, 'Alcoholic! Oh that's a different kettle of fish; I'll have some.'

We watch while he tentatively sips, then drinks.

Someone says, 'If he's still standing in two minutes, I'm into it.'

Because he is still standing after two minutes, and because his eyes widen with a positive reaction, we reckon it's safe.

Ray takes the coconut shell cup with his two hands—a ceremonious acceptance, almost as if he knows there's a ritualistic way of drinking kava. He sips, then drinks. It must do something to his throat because he croaks, 'Ah, Jesus!'

Most of those over forty creep away in case the kava is forced on them, but we stay and have quite a few.

I say to Ray, 'It's not as bad as that Penfold's Hospital Brandy we drank in Kiama.'

He says, 'Yeah, that was crook; and it's not as bad as that bloody Muscat we had at the Werri Beach camping area.'

Some of the Fijians carefully throw away sheets of hot galvanized iron that cover a smoking hole in the ground, and we eat what comes out of the hole: pork, chicken, seafood and root vegetables.

Someone says, 'Great tucker, eh?'

There's no reply because everyone's gorging food—it's not polite to speak with a full mouth.

The return bus journey to Suva is frightful. The driver must be behind schedule or he's practising to be a stock-car racer, because he ignores reason. No gully or bump in the road is too large to take at speed, and we hope he has x-ray vision because he never slows for any corner. The outside of the bus is being whipped by tree branches and palm tree fronds and vines, but he doesn't slow down.

The kava and the fish, prawns, lobster and other mysterious foods I've eaten are mixing in my stomach. They don't like each other, and I know they're preparing to evacuate.

I'm surprised that everyone else is laughing and joking and yelling encouragement to the driver—goading him on. I move to the rear seat and expel over the bus sides a trail of rejected food. I think it can only help stop the rust spreading.

'Are you all right, mate?' Ray asks.

I give a grunt, which he takes to mean that I'm just fine, or enjoying the view behind or checking the bus rear tyres. I mumble, 'I'm crook.'

And he says, 'I don't know; I reckon he's a good driver.'

Everyone gets off the bus singing, yelling, saying thanks to the driver, and tipping him some Fijian shillings, but I slink away. Everyone goes to buy a miniature carved-wood outrigger canoe. They haggle down the price. I buy without haggling.

The strains of Britannic martial music, then a John Philip Sousa march, followed by the Maori's Farewell, filter through the mass of the ship into the cabin where I lie. I don't give a stuff that I'm not on deck to see the red-serge jacketed Fijian brass band. I hear the ship's horn blasts, and I feel the ship move. If I can feel movement, I can't be dead.

Hours later, Ray convinces me to join the group while they drink the ritualistic few beers before dinner. I drink lemonade, and everyone laughs at me. I don't give a stuff.

There's loud discussion about the prices paid for miniature carved-wood outrigger canoes, but I don't take part.

Ray says, 'I beat the price down to a quid.'

Dougie says, 'I got mine for nineteen shillings.'

I paid only fifteen bob—by far the lowest price. But I don't boast, because I reckon the Fijian I bought it from thought he'd catch the dreaded disease I had if he stayed near me too long, so he sold it at a loss.

Circular Quay, Sydney, 1960.

Right:
June, 1960: Entrance of Rotorua Maori Village.

May 1960: Ray and Barry at the farewell party, Laycock Road, Penshurst.

Chapter Two

I'm very excited about arriving in Hawaii. Others must be excited, but they're not saying anything, and I reckon they're trying to look cool, calm and collected when they're not. I reckon they can't wait to drive one of those big yank cars, strut about on the famous Waikiki Beach, and have a beer in the famous Don the Beachcomber's bar.

One of the bikini-wearing girls is parading on deck, so I ask, 'Are you excited?'

She says, 'No. Why? It's just Hawaii.'

It's all right for her to say *just* Hawaii. It's all right because she's done a lot of travelling. She's been to New Zealand twice, and she's had a holiday on Lord Howe Island.

I've been hardly anywhere, so I hope to see this girl in a few years' time, then I'll be off-handed and say, 'I've been almost everywhere.'

Ray asks me what we spoke about, and I tell him. 'She's very excited about arriving in Hawaii, and she can't understand why we're not.'

He says, 'Why did you say we're not excited? I'm bloody-well excited and you told me last night you are.'

It's dumb that I told him about something that didn't happen. It's dumb because he's a good mate and mates should be truthful and shouldn't be offhanded about their emotions. I'm now stuck with what I said. I say to him, 'I'm … a little bit excited … just a bit.'

Many passengers skip breakfast because they'd rather watch the ship being manoeuvered by huffing, puffing little tugs to the Aloa Tower wharf. I'm on deck before dawn when the Hawaiian coastline is a long series of bumps on the horizon, and I stay there to watch the bumps become mountains. The pilot comes aboard the ship, and I guess he goes to shake the hand of the captain and that the captain says to him, 'Good morning pilot; the ship's all yours.'

The little tugs' engines labour to push the ship sideways, then they wait until they have to nudge it back a bit. The final sound of their labouring has the ship softly touching the wharf. Hawsers are thrown and tied, then the tugs rest. The ship signifies its gratitude by sounding long blasts of its horn, the deep sounds hit buildings and concrete to reverberate as one long noise that's surely going to startle Hawaiians having a sleep in.

I notice the bikini-wearing girl, and I say to her, 'Exciting, isn't it?'

And she says, 'Yes, it's very exciting.'

Ray doesn't come on deck to see the ship's docking because he wants a bellyful of breakfast before we go ashore, so he doesn't see all the hard work done by the tugs.

When he does get on deck, the bikini-wearing girl says to him, 'Isn't it exciting?'

He says, 'No.'

We stand at the ship's handrail looking at the United States of America, and it looks nothing like what I expected. There's no one on the wharf who looks like the Americans I've seen on television: no hip, blond-haired blokes like Kookie from the *Seventy-Seven Sunset Strip* television show, and no one's roaring up and down the street in brightly-painted hot-rod cars that have no muffler. There's no tight-sweater-wearing, big-breasted American girls waving and yelling, 'Hi there, you big-bronze Australians'.

All I can see are large proportioned Hawaiian women standing around having a natter. I wonder why they're there, but once the gangway's positioned, they dawdle onto the ship and flop floral leis over people's heads. That's not so bad, but I see them rubbing their noses against anyone who has the misfortune to be within grabbing distance. I decide to keep out of grabbing distance, but I don't succeed, and I get a sweaty nose-rub. Ray's saved only because he's far too tall: only a Hawaiian of Amazonian height could rub her nose against his.

While lined up in a queue that's waiting for American immigration officers to ask the questions they're supposed to ask, I see the bikini-wearing girls showing off and giggling and forcing their shoulders back so their breasts look bigger.

I say to Ray, 'I reckon those girls are trying to impress the American immigration officers.'

'Yeah?'

'Oh yes. And, from the look on the American's faces, I bet they'd like to take them to Don the Beachcombers to get them drunk.'

'Yeah.'

'Then they'll take them to their flat for a bit of nookie.'

'Yeah. I reckon … lucky bastards.'

'The girls?'

'No, the fucking blokes … the yanks.'

I notice one of the girls rubbing her crotch on the edge of the table, and I wish it was me she was rubbing against.

Ray says, 'American's don't have flats; they'd take them back to their apartment.'

He's right. Americans have different words for lots of things, so I'm going to try to remember their words. I should say auto instead of car, gas instead of petrol, dollar instead of pound, and pounds instead of stones. I'm going to have trouble converting my twelve-stone-five weight into pounds, so while I'm waiting to be processed, I do the calculation on paper. I say to Ray, 'One-hundred and seventy-three.'

He stares at me. 'What?'

'That's what I am; one-hundred and seventy-three pounds.'

'That's how much you've got in the Canadian bank?'

'No, that's what I weigh.'

He's got no idea what I'm talking about. He says, 'Who cares?'

'I care. I want to be ready in case they ask my weight.'

'Why the fuck would they ask your weight? They're not going to ask that. They're more likely to ask …'

'What?'

'I'm fucked if I know, but they won't want to know your weight because that's in your passport.'

'Exactly! But it's in stones. They don't have them; they have pounds.'

We get to the table, and Ray and I go to it.

The pimply-faced immigration officer says, 'One at a time.' He points at Ray. 'Sir, get back in line.'

I give him my passport. He opens it, looks at the photograph, then looks at me, then at the photograph.

I say to him, 'I'm one-hundred and seventy-three pounds.'

He says, 'Excuse me?'

That's my weight, one hund—'

'Sir, the American Government doesn't care.'

I see him glance towards the girls who want nothing to do with us, and I know all he cares about is getting them drunk, then up to his apartment.'

'Over there, that's where we've got to go,' Dougie says when we've cleared customs. He's really excited, and so am I and everyone else.

'Over there for what?' I say.

'That's where we hire a car.'

'Hire an auto,' I say. 'You should say auto instead of car. That's the way Americans say it.'

But he's not interested.

'They've got 'em; they've got convertibles.'

Convertibles!

For days we'd discussed what car we should rent, and in the end no one was thinking about anything other than a convertible—preferably a Chevie.

Dougie's mate asks the man at the desk, 'How much?'

'Ah, about thirty dollars.'

'Shit ... thirty dollars!'

We decide not to hire the car at the wharf because we figure the car hire companies are fleecing the tourists, and we're too smart for them. We're not like the other stupid Australian boat people who are happy to pay an outlandishly high price. They may be fools but we're not.

Ray says, 'Let's go into Honolulu. We'd have to get a lower price there. I mean, for that kind of dough, I could buy two new tyres for the MGA.'

He's saying that because it's his way of boasting about having owned a great car.

Dougie and the other Victorian bloke are impressed. 'You had an MGA?'

I believe getting the car in Honolulu's a good idea because I want to be cautious about how I spend money. I can't help thinking about my motor bike and I say, 'Christ all bloody mighty; I got less than twenty dollars for my motor bike!'

'Twenty dollars? That's all? It must have been a heap of junk.'

'It was a heap of junk, but it's not right that you should say it.'

The other Victorian bloke says, 'I bet I know who got all the best sheilas ... and it wasn't the bloke on the motor bike. What engine did it have? It did have an engine, didn't it?'

Ray laughs. 'Yeah, but it was detached from the bike's frame. When he sold the—'

I push Ray, and he pushes me, and we all push each other, and an American policeman gives us a dirty look.

Honolulu looks exciting. I see some Americans with blond hair who do look a little bit like Kookie from *Seventy-Seven Sunset Strip*, and I see a few brightly painted hot-rod cars, but they do have mufflers. I look for tight-sweater-wearing big-breasted American girls, but I see none.

Dougie says, 'There's a car hire place.'

So we go there.

The plan is to drive around the island, see some huge surf, have a swim without getting drowned in the huge surf, then to round-off the day, have a few drinks at Don the Beachcomber's.

I reckon it's exciting.

Ray says to the man behind the counter, 'G'day mate. We want to hire a car for a day, a Chevie convertible. What'll that cost us?'

The man has a blank stare—either he's not listening or he's off with the fairies.

Ray says, 'Well?'

The man's mouth is slightly open, and he rubs his tongue along his bottom lip. 'Eh?' he says.

I've been practising my American words so I say, 'Buddy, we need an auto for a day.'

The man stares at me, then he blinks his eyes.

At least I've got communication going.

He says, 'What kind of car?'

I'm wondering why he doesn't say, 'What kind of auto?' I say, 'We want a—'

Ray butts in: 'We want a Chevie convertible.'

The man goes to brochures stacked in neat rows on the wall. He selects one titled 'Our Extensive Hire Fleet' and lays it on the counter. 'Sir,' he says, 'point to the car you want.'

Ray says, 'I don't have to point. We know what we want; it's a Chevie convertible.'

There's no way this American's going to understand an Australian accent, so it's up to me. I say, 'A Chevrolet! The car in the advertisement that goes …' And I sing, 'Tour the USA … in a Chevrolet.'

The man smiles. He understands. 'We ain't got any.'

The man's speech needs correcting so I say, 'You haven't got any.'

All he does is nod his head and say, 'That's correct.'

Now we're all confused.

'We only got Vauxhalls … it's because of a convention. There's a lot of tourists from the mainland, and there's two ships in port, and … and we're fresh out of cars.'

Ray says, 'You've gotta be kidding. Vauxhalls are a heap of shit. They've got no guts.'

I'm hoping that Ray and the other blokes will shut-up and leave the speaking to me, but I'm not going to tell them to, because we'll all start pushing each other, and we'll never get a car, not even a Vauxhall.

Even though I'm the most practised at using American words, I can't fathom what he means by 'convention'. 'Mate, this is supposed to be a car hire business, right?'

He nods.

'Well, I reckon it's not all that smart for a business to have a convention of only having Vauxhalls?'

I'm not getting far because he again looks confused. 'It's … it's a railroad convention!'

Ray says, 'Do what you like, but I'm not driving a bloody Vauxhall.'

The man says, 'Vauxhalls are very good cars.'

'Oh yeah,' says Ray. 'So why is it the only car left? Why isn't your Vauxhall running around Honolulu with tourists in it? I'll tell you why; it's because no one wants to be seen in one. That's why.'

This is not a good turn of events because Ray's supposed to be our driver. It had to be him. I can't be let loose on American roads. I'm a motor bike rider. I got my license to drive a car only two months ago, and I'm still having trouble getting used to not having a front-wheel brake lever. He's the obvious driver because his cars have been a sporty four-seater 1938 Morris convertible, then he had an MG TC, then after that an MGA. I know it's going to be a huge blow to his ego to have to drive a Vauxhall, but no one's going to see him, no one important, and I won't tell anyone.

Dougie shouldn't drive the bloody thing because when I spoke to him about driving he said, 'A number-two wood.' He's got no idea. And his mate hasn't even got a licence.

Ray says, 'Dougie will have to drive.'

No one's saying anything. We all remember the stupid things Dougie did on the boat: the throwing overboard of the deckchairs and the deck quoits; the stealing of useless souvenirs, and the many other exploits he'd told us about, all equally stupid and all believable.

We're afraid that he'll drive off the end of a cliff and kill us all.

But about Ray's abilities, we're confident. I'd told them about his driving record and his world-record time of seven minutes to get from the Werri beach camping area to Kiama Post office. I'd mentioned his responsible attitude in keeping below thirty-miles per hour between Sydney and Surfer's Paradise, because the brand new MG A's engine had to be run-in, and him driving his MGA in a parade at Mount Druitt race track carrying the famous singer Frank Ifield. And I'd told them about his world-record time to get from the Penshurst Catholic Church corner to my mum's house. After that, the driving job was his. And now he won't drive!

We're looking at the Vauxhall. It's painted bright blue and the upholstery is blue. It's almost enough to make Ray puke. I hear him mumble something that includes 'hopeless' and 'heap of shit'.

The car hire man says, 'There it is; take it or leave it. It's the only car we have left.'

We take it.

As soon as Dougie turns the car onto the road, we know we're in for a hair-raising experience. He goes left towards oncoming traffic, and innocent Americans going about their business have a traumatic event in their day.

Dougie's looking at the gear stick saying, 'Where's second; where's second gear?' He looks up and sees wide American yank-tanks fitted with huge chromed bumper bars all speeding towards us, and he says, 'Fuck!'

The yank-tanks brake; their wide tyres screech, and a lot of blue smoke surrounds them. The Vauxhall brakes, but its puny tyres give off a little squeal. The yank-tanks turn away and we turn away. It's chaotic.

Ray says, 'You stupid bastard; go to the other side of the road.'

But Dougie's still saying, 'Where's second fucking gear?'

At the same moment he finds second gear, Ray grabs the steering wheel and twists it to the right, which sends the Vauxhall into sharp rear-end skids, but we do get a much more impressive tyre squeal. The Vauxhall does a spectacular jump over the road divider, rips through a garden bed and somehow ends up facing the correct way.

I say, 'Shit, that was close.'

Ray says, 'Turn right here.'

Dougie pokes his arm into Ray's face.

'Aah! You're using the wrong arm,' Ray yells. 'You've got to put your arm outside the car.'

I yell, 'Use the fucking indicator on the steering column.'

The engine's roaring because now Dougie doesn't know where third gear is.

'Change gears,' I yell. 'The fucking engine's going to blow up.'

Understandably, Dougie's now quite pissed-off, and I'm relieved that he steers to the roadside. The car skids to a stop on loose gravel, and a cloud of dust rises around and above. None of us say thank Christ, but it's certain we're thinking it. Dougie pulls the bonnet catch and gets out. I'm not surprised; there has to be big damage to the engine.

Ray lights a cigarette and draws deeply. He says nothing, just twists his head from side to side.

Dougie does something under the bonnet, then slams it shut. 'I fixed it,' he says.

I've got no idea what he's fixed. 'You fixed what?'

He gets back into the car. 'I've fixed the speedo cable.'

'Speedo cable! What was wrong with it?'

'It needed disconnecting.'

'Why?'

'So we can travel as far as we want for free. I can't believe that an American car hire company doesn't have seals on the speedo cable.'

'I can't believe it either,' I say, 'but I suppose they're used to having their cars rented by honest people, not crooks like you.'

~

On the other side of the island, we see huge waves—and swim without drowning—spectacular scenery and some tight-sweater-wearing, big-breasted American women, but we only have one very expensive beer at Don the Beachcombers. We go to buy petrol at a service station but instead, we buy gas at a gas station. Dougie reconnects the speedo cable, then we return the pretty-well-exhausted Vauxhall.

Dougie gently, nervously even, stops the car outside.

The car hire man comes out smiling and says, 'Hi, did you have a great day?'

Dougie gets out of the Vauxhall shaking his head and saying, 'Great day? No, it was bloody awful.'

The smile disappears. 'Awful?'

'Yeah, awful. You Americans drive on the wrong side of the road.'

A confused frown. 'We drive on the right side.'

'It might be the right side, but it's the wrong side. We reckon the left side's the right side.'

The man takes a clipboard and goes to get the details. 'This can't be correct,' he says, 'You've only travelled six miles!'

'It's correct all right. It was so nerve-racking driving on your roads that we only went to Waikiki Beach and stayed there all day.'

The car-hire man's no fool; he knows something's wrong, but he's not a mug, because he accepts the explanation. There are four of us: Dougie, who's obviously quite mad; Ray, who's six-feet-two tall, broad shouldered and a Robert Mitcham look-alike; Dougie's Victorian mate who never says much but looks like the type who can go the knuckle, and me, a mild mannered bloke who no one should be afraid of, but who just might have a superman suit that he could change into.

The man says, 'That'll be twelve dollars.'

We pay, then walk to Waikiki Beach where we surf small waves and take a ride in an outrigger canoe. Because the bloke who's paddling the canoe is twice the size of any of us, we pay the full asking price.

~

There's undisclosed apprehension about how life will be after we leave the ship in Vancouver. When it comes to displaying or discussing emotion, Australian males are unskilled, unpractised and unprepared. Young Australian males have never been encouraged—which means they're not allowed—to show hurt at school, at home, on the football field, at work, in wars or with friends or lovers. Being told not to be a baby starts when they are babies and continues through life. If there's an injury that's bad enough to 'bawl your head off', convention won't allow that reaction. An 'Oh that hurt,' will get the response, 'You've only broken your arm so there's no need to bawl your bloody head off like a big sook."

For a male child, being called a sook is as bad as being called a girl, but a male adult being called a sook is tantamount to being a poofter.

None of us are sooks.

I already know Dougie has no special work skills when, while lounging around on the deck one day, I ask, 'What kind of job are you going to look for in Vancouver?'

'Oh, any job.'

'Labouring?'

'Yeah, if there's nothing else.'

'What else can you do ... I mean, most jobs require training, and you haven't got any training.'

'I wouldn't mind being a park ranger—you know, in a National Park or something like that.'

'Do you know anything about being a ranger? Do you know anything about animals or trees or birds or …'

'Yeah.'

'Yeah what? Tell me what you know.'

'I know how to skin a fox; I know how to chop down a tree; I know how to blow bird eggs, and that's just for starters. I know loads of stuff.'

'That's great. So you're going to offer yourself to the Canadian National Parks with those qualifications?'

'Yeah. No worries. They'll want me as soon as they see me.'

I ask Dougie's mate, 'Do you reckon there'll be jobs for milkmen in Vancouver?'

'There ought to be. Everyone drinks milk. I'm pretty good at my job so I should be a shoo-in to get work straight away.'

Ray asks me, 'What if there's no work for plumbers, what will you do then?'

I wouldn't mind working in an office. The fact is, I'm sick and tired of working in dirt and mud and wearing old work clothes. 'I might get a job in an architectural office,' I reply. 'You know, designing buildings, stuff like that.'

'Do you reckon the classes at Hurstville Technical High School, the drawing classes where you couldn't even use a scale rule, is enough training to get you a job with an architect?'

'Why not?' A moment later, I ask Ray, 'If carpenters aren't needed, what else will you do?'

'Ah … there'll be something. I wouldn't mind being a racing car driver. I've had experience driving sports cars. Or even a stock car driver wouldn't be too bad.'

'How will you get that kind of work?'

'I don't know.'

We don't show worries, concerns, or fears. Those emotions are for our inner being, they're kept inside us only be thought about before going to sleep and immediately after waking. Those thoughts are had while sitting alone at the bar, or while under the shower, or while writing a letter home.

'Everything all right mate?' Ray asks.

'Yeah, great. I can't wait to get ashore.'

'Missing home?'

'Nah.'

Canadians on the ship are surprised that we chose to arrive in the autumn, when work can be difficult to get, only a few months from winter when work's impossible to get. But are we worried? Nah.

We're now not jumping bombs in the swimming pool, so we pack away our swimming trunks, and the bikinis belonging to the girls who want nothing to do with us also get packed away. Outside the ship, temperatures go lower and lower. The cooling tropical breeze becomes a chilling autumn wind, and it's cold enough to freeze the balls off a brass monkey. We hear blokes boasting about scoring, about them winning the lottery of life, about them meeting girls who were prepared to have uncompromising sex on deck. But we know it's bullshit, because when we ask probing questions, the uncompromising sex becomes a nearly successful knee-trembler, or a simple kiss.

We try to get some of the uncompromising sex and, unless Ray's telling me lies, we end up failing.

Few of us openly display our emotions; hardly anyone, apart from girls, say anything about missing home and families. I think about my mother and hope she's not struggling, although even if she is, what can I do? Go home? The grass will need cutting about now, and I wonder if my brother John can do the job without running over the mower's electric lead. The steep backyard is like a jungle. Will John do what I never would do? Will he dig and scrape and shovel dirt to terrace the slope into formal gardens? Jesus, I hope so, because I don't want to have to do it when I return to Australia.

I think about Rosemary, the girlfriend I dumped, and I question what I should do about getting my dirty clothes clean. Should I try to wash them even though I don't know how to iron? I think about dividing my money into weekly amounts to force me to be frugal. I think about how long I can last without income.

Everyone's having similar thoughts, but no one's saying anything. It's not discussed because 'it's not the thing to do'. Only a weakie will admit they have apprehension about the future.

It's always windy now and often raining, so we mostly stay within the ship, and that means drinking. Because our stomachs and heads need recovery, we nearly always miss breakfast. We don't indulge in much loud behaviour or lairing-off, and show some interest in what's offered by the entertainment officer, especially talks about Canada.

I'm drinking tea and eating cream-filled cakes when a bloke sitting nearby says, 'Yesterday I had tea and cake with a Canadian who works for the government, and he was telling me how high unemployment is.'

'Unemployment?'

'Yeah, it's supposed to be about ten percent.'

'That can't be right. The Canadian Embassy said nothing to my mate and me about high unemployment.'

'I'm simply telling you what he told me. He said that during winter, loads of construction workers get laid-off because the weather's too cold to work outside.'

I think about the holidays Ray and I had in the Snowy Mountains at Kiandra where we'd mucked about throwing snow and trying to ski. I remember the army boots we used as ski boots—we'd heated a steel rod to burn a groove into the leather heel to locate the ski-bindings. I think about how we'd helped to construct a ski lodge for the Bush-walking Association and the fun we'd had. It was great, but never so cold that we couldn't work outside. Then I remember how my toes got frost-bitten and I spent three nights in the Snowy Mountains Authority hospital at Cabramurra.

I should realise that Canadian winters are significantly colder than any could be in Australia, and that working outside will be difficult, impossible even. But I don't.

We both take another cream-filled cake. I gorge mine.

His hovers outside his mouth. He says, 'The Canadian told me about the cost of living. Food's dear, rent's dear, and ...'

I swallow the cake and wipe cream from my lips with my arm. 'What about grog and fags?'

'Oh, they're cheap.'

'And cars?'

'They're cheap, too.'

'But unemployment's high?'

'He said that in Vancouver it's about ten percent, but in Calgary and Edmonton and Winnipeg it's even higher ... fifteen percent.'

'Shit!'

During pre-dinner drinks, I tell the others about the conversation I had with the Canadian who works for the government.

Dougie says, 'Well, I should be all right because my job's inside.'

'What do you mean your job's inside? You told me you're thinking about being a park ranger. Park rangers work outside ... they range in the mountains and hills, spend their time in the donga, and they bloody-well hardly ever go inside.'

Ray says, 'Dougie, in the two weeks we've known you, you've never mentioned what you do, so ... what do you do?'

'Well, now I know there's high unemployment for outside jobs,' he replies, 'I'm going to be an inside man.'

'Yeah, but doing what?'

Dougie gets up and says, 'I'm going for a beer.'

We watch him go.

Ray says, 'The bastard didn't answer. I reckon he's a bullshit artist.'

'I reckon you're right. But I tell you what, he'll do better than any of us because, as you've said, he's a bullshit artist and bullshit artist's do well anywhere.'

We all say, 'Yeah.'

~

Everyone, apart from me, is on deck as the ship sails past Vancouver Island. I'm probably the last to contact the virus that ravaged the ship, and it couldn't have come at a worse time.

Someone says, 'You ought to come look at the scenery. There's pine trees everywhere. Bloody pines … there's not a eucalyptus tree in sight.'

Someone else says, 'You won't believe it, but there's snow on the mountains. It's only June, winter's a while away and they've got snow!'

I struggle to the deck to see all of this, but I vomit over the side, and everyone looks at me and I feel stupid.

Back below deck, newspapers are spread on the cabin bunks, and all I hear from the readers are gasps and swearing.

'There's nothing,' someone says.

'Are you certain these are the papers that advertise jobs?'

Someone else says, 'There's some jobs in this paper. One for car salesmen … and here's another for cladding salesmen.'

'What's cladding?'

'Buggered if I know, but it says no experience necessary.'

'There's one in this paper,' Ray says.

We listen.

'Reliable people required to canvass in exclusive territories promoting our prestige magazines. The successful—'

'That's not a fair-dinkum job. That's another salesman's job.'

I raise my head to say, 'Listen you blokes, I'm so fucking crook I couldn't give a bugger about jobs … in fact, I want to go home.'

We pack our suitcases and place them outside the cabin for porters to carry ashore. Often-worn, unwashed clothing takes up more than half the space in my suitcase, but I don't give a bugger.

Someone says, 'We ought to give the cabin steward a tip.'

'Why?'

'Because that's what we're supposed to do. Everyone does it.'

'Why?'

'Because if we don't tip the steward, our bags will, accidentally, be left on the ship and end up in England.'

'Ah …How much do you reckon? Ten bob each?
'You heard what I said—accidentally left on the ship.'
'All right, how much?'
'Five quid each; that ought to be about right.'
We each give the steward three quid and take a chance.

Three quid is enough because our bags arrive on the wharf where they're opened by customs. The man who opens mine looks inside and quickly closes it. He shakes his head and tut-tuts.

There's no welcoming committee. No signs saying, 'Welcome to Canada'. No brass band playing. No politicians to shake our hand to thank us for coming. And there's no one from the Canadian Government for us to ask about the rumour of high unemployment. Uniformed immigration officers look at us as though we're bludgers. They search our passport for a visa, then they thump a stamp beside it. We go from the wharf feeling unwanted, lost even, and probably for the first time, empathise with the experience of millions of refugees and immigrants who'd arrived in Australia.

We rent a flat to use as a base, a secure place to gather thoughts and to re-enthuse; this is where all the invitations for job interviews will be sent.

I have to do something about getting clean clothes, so I have my first experience in a laundromat. I don't separate whites from coloured clothes, and all my white Chesty Bond's underwear is now pink. We buy groceries and wonder at how little we get for ten dollars. The flat immediately becomes a pigsty because we now have more than the one bag that was allowed in the ship's cabin, and there's no cabin steward to clean up.

The bathroom and toilet that's shared with the occupants of two other flats is soon a haven for disease. We reckon we shouldn't have to buy a toilet brush; we reckon one should be supplied or that those in the other two flats should get one.

The other blokes wash their clothing in the bathroom, then they hang them to dry in the flat, so there's always dripping water and the hazard of faces being lashed by someone's underwear.

Ray has a friend of a friend, who has a friend who lives at Ladner. He makes contact because it's certain we'll be given a free meal, and we need advice from them about getting work. We get invited for supper and that confuses us. Is it cakes and biscuits, or is it meat with three vegetables?

We're both mystified.

I say to him, 'Americans call supper what we call tea, so did you ask them if it's tea we're going for?'

'Of course I did. I said, "We'll see you for tea," and they said, "Whatever … tea or coffee."'

'Does that mean we eat there?'

He doesn't know.

On the bus to Ladner, I think about my stomach. I say to Ray, 'Mate, this is a long bus trip so they better bloody well feed us.'

At the house there's a small committee, and they fall about welcoming and saying nice things and asking how George is.

I have no idea who George is, but Ray remembers that his mother had mentioned that name. He says, 'George is good.'

'What's he doing these days?'

'Oh, not much.'

'And, Barry, do you know George?'

'Not well.'

They're disappointed because they learn nothing from us about George. We're ushered to the sitting room, which is actually the lounge room, and I whisper to Ray, 'You bloody idiot, who is this fucking George they expect us to know. We've got to tell them something … anything.

Ray says to them, 'George has a job in a factory.'

They give us blank stares. 'Why? Can't he get work as an architect?'

'Oh, yes; he's, ah, he's designing factories.'

They say that's strange because he went to Australia to build Pizza Hut restaurants.

'Oh he is … but he's also designing factories …'

I interrupt: 'He's designing and building factories for Pizza Hut … factories to store pizzas.'

They still have blank stares. One says, 'But pizzas are made when they're ordered, they make them …'

We need to get the conversation away from George. I say, 'Are there any buffalo around here?'

'Buffalo? There's never been buffalo here.'

'Oh, well, what about bears or reindeer; any of those?'

'We don't have reindeer. Reindeer are in Norway. We have elk and moose.'

At last we have a topic away from George. 'Wow, that's interesting. How big do they grow?'

They tell us about their neighbour who has a stuffed moose head that we simply must see, and they tell us that a rogue elk destroyed someone's back fence. Thirty minutes later they're still talking and hope is fading about getting meat with three vegetables. They say, perhaps we can continue this while we have supper, and we follow them into a room that has a table set with what our mums would call 'best'.

We eat meat and Ray foolishly asks if it's moose or elk.

'It's Alberta beef,' the man whose house it is says with an indignant look.

We ask questions about getting work, and they tell us they have a friend who's looking for labourers to dismantle a garage. They give us his phone number.

We too often say, 'That doesn't happen in Australia,' or, 'We do it differently,' and, 'Unlike here, there's plenty of work in Sydney.' We can tell they're pissed off, so we make excuses, and we're out of the door to return to Vancouver, back to the safety of our flat.

In what we hope is the correct bus, Ray says, 'Why did they give us ice cream with coffee?'

'Dunno, I'd have thought that Adora Cream Wafers or Iced Vovos would've been the go.'

'What about the phone number? Should we ring the bloke about the job?'

'I suppose so, but it is demolition work.'

The irony doesn't escape us that our first job in a new country is pulling down a building.

~

'Guys,' the man dressed in funny-looking overalls says, 'you start on the back and …'

I don't want to offend the man, but I'm not comfortable being a guy. I mumble, 'I'm not a guy; I'm a bloke.' But he doesn't hear me.

'… take the cladding from the outside wall while I get the inside boards off.'

We look for tools. Ray says, 'Have you got a pinch bar?'

'A … what?'

'A pinch bar, so we can lever the weather-boards away from the studs.'

'What?'

'The Canadian's got no idea. He says, 'Take this crowbar to ease the cladding from the two-by-four uprights.'

Ray takes the bar. 'Ah, good, a pinch bar.'

This Canadian can't tell us anything about demolishing buildings because we're just about experts.

Back in 1957 the Sea Cadet group NLTD Sirius which we were part of was given a dump of a building attached to Sydney Technical College. The college had to get rid of the fibro-and-weather-board clad building to build something else on the site. A pretend-to-be-sailor, a Lieutenant Commander O'Connell, was in charge of the Sea Cadets. His real job was with the NSW Lands Department, but at weekends he did a Clark-Kent-like transformation when he exchanged his suit and tie of little authority for a navy uniform with loads of authority. His second in command, Chief Petty Officer Switzer, was by day a panel beater, and at weekends he screamed Navy-language orders at us.

This unlikely duo commanded about twenty pretend-to-be-sailors who, apart from Ray and I, had no knowledge of construction or deconstruction.

The motley crew arrived at the demolition site with all manner of unsuitable tools, ready to help the 'experts': Ray and me. They went berserk using their borrowed hammers and axes, striking and smashing at everything, and pretty soon we had a building with only timber uprights and a roof. The two officers did their best to minimize damage. They ran about ordering the crew to be careful, to stop breaking glass windows, to not break into the timber and plaster sheets inside, but it was no use because the kids were in a frenzy of destruction. I was a fourth-year plumbing apprentice, and Ray was a fifth-year carpenter apprentice, so we had the knowledge. The other kids were counter-jumpers at S.R. Buttle, the grocers, or fitting-and-turning apprentices at Garden Island, or pen-pushers in the Rural Bank, or station attendants with the NSW Government Railways. So they knew nothing about the subtleties of construction. Ray and I yelled orders, but the little bastards ignored us and continued destroying everything that might have been useful.

When it was time to go onto the roof, everyone wanted to climb the ladders, so Ray and I went up, then pulled the ladder onto the roof. This didn't stop them; they climbed walls to get to the roof. The Lieutenant Commander blew his whistle, but they took that as encouragement. We, the experts, couldn't get the roof screws loosened, so we told the crew to use their American screwdriver, and they bashed every screw top in sight to smithereens with hammers and axes.

Ray, the expert, put his foot through the Caneite ceiling and tumbled to the floor below, and I broke a water pipe. We were physically unhurt, but our pride was damaged beyond repair. We threw our professional tools into the back of his MG and left the crew and officers to self-destruct.

Remarkably, the job got done, and the building was reconstructed. It now stands at the entrance of the Cook's River at Tempe, and is, I believe, still a Sea Cadet unit.

Back on the garage demolition, Ray tells me to de-nail the weather boards and then to stack them. I do as I'm told because he's the carpenter. My turn will come when the pipes get taken apart.

'Where's the boss?' I ask.

'I saw him take a few sneaky looks from around the corner,' Ray says, 'and then he went back, shaking his head.'

'In admiration?'

'No, he didn't look all that happy.'

'Why? He'd have to be happy. The back wall's coming down quickly.'

'I reckon he's not happy about how many weather boards I'm splitting.'

'You haven't split that many … have you?'

'About half.'

'Oh. What's he expect? He's only paying us a dollar an hour. Look, I'll pretend to get a drink of water, and I'll see how he's doing.' I trample through long grass to get to the tap where I take a sneaky look and see that he's done hardly anything.

I say to Ray, 'The bastard's done hardly anything. He's got a stack of timber a third the height of ours.'

'Many split ones?'

'No.'

Something rustles in the nearby grass. I look and yell, 'Christ Almighty it's a snake.'

Ray stops hammering and runs backwards. 'Shit! It's a snake.'

~

Australians know a lot about snakes. They know that the only good snake is a dead one. They know that snakes are all right as long as they're in the middle of bush hunting for things that twitter or croak. They know that snakes sunbake on hot rocks and live in holes in the ground and are kept in the zoos and that's all right: that's acceptable. But away from those places they're the enemy.

Young Cubs and older Boy Scouts are taught that hot days and long grass means snakes. Boy Scouts in the First Beverly Hills troop use to tramp through bush singing: 'Hot days, long grass … snakes. Hot days, long grass … snakes.' We chanted to let the snakes know that the tough Boy Scouts were coming, so that the nasty snakes should wriggle away to their holes in the ground. When Boy Scouts had to climb over a fallen tree or a rotting log, they'd cautiously look over it, and then they'd bash the living Christ out of the log or tree with a stick because snakes hid in those places and they loved to sink their fangs into Boy Scout's legs.

We didn't see all that many snakes, but we knew they lurked. As a five-year-old, returning home from Peakhurst School, I used one of the secret short-cut tracks. I generally used the track that started at the back of the incinerator and finished at Greenland's Avenue—not a good track because it went through long grass near puddles of stagnant water and right beside where fathers dumped lawn clippings and the contents of the garbage bin they forgot to put out.

Despite knowing this, I used it because I was afraid that Frankie Bennett would be hiding on the other one, waiting to spring out and punch the shit out of me.

I sometimes armed myself with a tree branch to dong any snake, but more often I'd run like a greyhound, jumping over logs and tall grass in a single bound, and arrive home breathless. Then I'd change from my good school shorts and shoes into old mucking-around-in-the-paddock clothes. The gang would be waiting in the cubby house, a secret place where girls aren't allowed and where, we hope, snakes can't find us. I tried to leave the house without making a noise, but the fly-screen-door hinges squeaked and the door closer—the strong steel spring from a 1928 Essex Super Six car—thumped the door shut.

Mum always called from the kitchen, 'Watch out for snakes!'

And I would.

I saw my first really big black snake when my father and I were returning from a cricket match at Penshurst Park. He was the first-grade wicket-keeper for Peakhurst Waratahs. We were happy because the Waratahs had a big win, and dad had taken three catches and done a stumping. He was always happy after a stumping.

He says, 'Anyone can catch a ball, but a stumping's what good keeping's all about.'

It's all downhill from the bus stop to home, and we jog. He holds his sweat-soaked leather inner gloves, and I've got his outer gloves that are stained red from the new ball used in the last four overs. He's in front of me, then he feigns a limp so I catch up to him, and run ahead. The matches in his pocket rattle and coins jingle.

I yell, 'You can't beat me.'

He does for a while, then I get in front.

Near the Van Gelder's house, a thick, long snake wriggles onto the road and Dad yells, 'Stop!'

I stop dead and he puts his arm around my shoulders. He says, 'You wait here while I go to Van Gelder's to get a mattock.'

I watch the snake, and the snake's watching me, and I reckon it's thinking it's the boss, that it's going to bite me if I come any closer.

Dad returns with the mattock. He gently pushes me back, then he goes for it. He swings the mattock high above him, then brings it down with a resounding thump. But he missed. Now the snake's aware that it's being attacked, so it curls around to face the enemy. Dad raises the mattock again and it strikes the snake a glancing blow. The snake's now very pissed-off, and it strikes. Dad's not won the trophy for being best wicket-keeper on Penshurst Park for no reason; he's won it because he's very quick on his feet, so he dances backwards.

Again, he raises the mattock, strikes and connects, divorcing the snake's head from its body. Both ends wriggle about in a frenzy. Dad struggles to free the mattock head from the bitumen road, but it's like Excalibur—King Arthur's sword—it's stuck in. He screams words I'd never heard before, which I guess to be magic words, because the mattock comes free. He dances backwards, and then darts forward to push the snake's head away with the mattock. He then kicks the still-wriggling body, and dark-red blood splashes join cricket-ball red on his white cricket boots. The body rolls to the roadside, and he sighs and smiles.

Itinerant snakes going about their own business on Baumann's Road had no hope of survival when my father got his hands on a mattock.

~

Ray stumbles back from the snake, pointing the crowbar at it and yelling, 'Get away from here, you bastard.' He throws the bar, but it misses the snake by a large margin.

'You missed!' I yell.

Ray gives me a dirty look.

We both retreat while keeping our eyes on the monster. Monster? Not really; it's only a little bugger, but it *is a snake*.

I see leaning against the wall what I know to be a mattock, but what Canadians must know as something else. I yell, 'It's all right, mate; I've got a mattock.'

'You've got a mattock?'

'Yeah. Stand back.'

Ray looks relieved. He knows a mattock is a snake equalizer. He knows that with a mattock the most ferocious snake can be defeated; he knows that a mattock is the atomic bomb of snake killing. 'Well, get the bastard,' he yells.

I creep towards it and raise the mattock over my shoulders. I mean to aim for its head, but it's wiggling around, so I'll have to strike it anywhere. While the mattock's hanging in mid-air, I think back to my father's killing of the black snake and his failed first strikes.

As the mattock comes down, I see I have the wrong end—the pointed axe-head end, not the wide end—in position to hit the snake. I attempt a correction, but I bugger it up, and the mattock hits the ground awkwardly.

'You missed it,' Ray yells.

I give him a dirty look.

He takes the mattock from me. 'I'll get the bugger.' He goes toward the snake.

I notice that he turns the mattock so that he'll strike with the right end—the hoe end. His father must have trained him.

He swings the mattock above his head. The snake's now seeing a six-foot-two man holding a long mattock handle with the hoe-head end in the correct position. The snake's looking up at the sky thinking that an atomic bomb is about to hit, and it's shitting itself.

The mattock hits it with a loud wallop and divorces the snake's head from its body. Deep-red coloured blood squirts from the snake, some of it landing on my trousers.

'I got him,' Ray says.

It's an act of bravery deserving the Victoria Cross.

'Bloody good work mate. An excellent shot.'

The boss comes to see what the ruckus is about. 'What's going on?'

We're smiling because we reckon we've not only saved our lives, we've probably saved his. Ray says, 'It's all right; I got the bastard.'

'You got what?'

'The fucking snake.'

'What snake?'

'This one.' He pushes the snake's body with the mattock. 'Its head's here … somewhere. I got it with the mattock.'

'You got a what? With a what?'

'Snake with a mattock.'

'Mattock?'

The man's not reacting the way he should; he should be rejoicing and congratulating us.

'Yeah,' I say, 'Ray got the bastard with the mattock.'

He says, 'What the fuck's a mattock?' Then he sees the snake and says, 'Why did you kill a Garter snake? They're harmless.'

Now we're confused. 'Garter Snake! Harmless?'

'Of course it's goddamned harmless. All they do is eat mice.' He goes to the snake, lifts it by the tail and says, 'The poor little thing.'

We work for two days demolishing the garage. The boss pays us twenty Canadian dollars each, equal to ten Australian pounds, about half the average weekly Australian wage for five days work. The money's important, but not as much as the snake, or as useful. In our story telling it becomes a huge rattlesnake that was going to kill the Canadian and us.

I counter accusations of, 'Ah that's all bullshit' by my showing the snake's blood on my trousers.

There's one aspect we agree on: Canadians should be trained by Australians about how dangerous snakes are, and all Canadian households should be issued with a mattock.

C/- Y.M.C.A Vancouver.
25 June 1960
Dear Mum.
Everything the Canadian Government told us is not true.
We had tea with Ray's contacts that live seventeen miles out of Vancouver at Ladner. We have also been looking for work, and we have registered at the unemployment office. I went to the Plumbers Union office and amazingly, they wouldn't let me join until I take some kind of trade test.
We are renting a flat in Vancouver that costs nineteen dollars a week, and we can live on twelve dollars each week for food. People here are confident we will soon get work, so don't worry about me.
If we don't get work here, we'll travel inland—perhaps to Calgary.
Quite a few of the boys from the ship have bought cars and driven to Toronto. Most of them have less money than us.
Love to you all.
Barry.

Chapter Three

Ray and I look a bit stupid rugged-up and sitting on the park bench, but someone told us we must visit Vancouver's Stanley Park.

Nearby stands an intricately carved Indian totem pole. It looks like all the rest. We're not too interested in totem poles.

We have to make a decision. Do we stay in Vancouver where there's no work or do we try elsewhere? Dougie's gone; his wild imagination has him easily getting a job in the Banff National Park or at the Banff Springs Hotel. He is, at this very time, sitting in a bus going to success; we think he's heading for failure, but he's comfortable living in his fool's paradise.

I say to Ray, 'We could go and get drunk.'

He says, 'Yeah, that'd be really sensible.'

I'm joking and I hope he is.

I look up at the totem and try to imagine what advice it would give, but it's there already, the carved face on the totem is looking east.

I say to Ray, 'We should leave Vancouver and go east.'

'East?'

'Yeah. We should go to Calgary or Edmonton or Winnipeg.'

'Why not North, or South, or West?'

'Well, South's America, and we're not allowed to work there; West's the Pacific Ocean—we just came from there—and North, well, North's too bloody cold.'

'But those cities are nowhere near the ocean. I'd rather be near water. I've always lived near the water, that's where—'

'So have I. But we can't get work near the water. Let's go inland … you choose the place.'

Ray's a very responsible person; I've never known him to make a rash decision, so I understand that he needs to consider.

He says, 'We'll go to Calgary.'

Oh, that's a bit quick. 'Why Calgary?'

'Because I read in the Vancouver paper that there's something called the Calgary Exhibition and Stampede there; it's on next month.'

'What's an Exhibition and Stampede? It sounds corny.'

'Dunno, but it's supposed to be the largest outdoor exhibition in the world.'

'Bullshit! The Sydney Royal Show is.'

He gives me a look of disgust. 'I'm simply telling you what it said in the newspaper. It's the largest, the fucking biggest.'

I know what he says is wrong, but when a mate's so certain, especially when he says fucking, it's smart not to argue. I say, 'All right. Let's go to Calgary.'

~

The Greyhound bus's second stop during our journey through the Rocky Mountains is in Revelstoke.

The driver says, 'We'll stop here for thirty minutes, and then we'll attack the Big Bend.'

I reckon the driver's being a bit melodramatic when he says, 'attack'. I say to him, 'Are you trying to scare us?'

He laughs. 'No, but there's roads to drive on, and there's roads to … well, the Big Bend's a road that can break hearts, cars and buses. We're going through in good weather, but in winter no one goes through, they close it.'

'Oh.'

'It's steep and winding and narrow and treacherous—a real sonofabitch. Buses only get through the Big Bend if the Big Bend wants it. You got to treat the Big Bend like a woman: don't take risks; don't go too far; don't think you got it beat, and hug the curves.

I say to Ray, 'This bloke's an actor. He's got no idea that we've been on dodgy roads. Remember the road through the Brindabellas? Remember when the Kombi van floated in that river?'

'Yeah, this Big Bend thing can't be as bad as that.'

We look at the length and width of the Greyhound bus, and it's lots bigger than a Kombi van. 'Do you reckon this bus could do the Brindabella Road?'

'Shit, no. It couldn't get more than a few miles. It couldn't turn the corners.'

We reckon the bus driver's lost because he's got the bus pointing at sheer cliffs.

Ray says, 'He's going to have trouble turning around; there's no way there'll be enough room.'

The bus is now on a narrow gravel road that has a mountain on one side and a two hundred-foot drop to a river on the other. Either the driver can't turn or he doesn't intend to.

I say, 'He can't go up here … Christ, he is. He'd better get away from the side of the road; he'd better get into the middle.'

We see cars coming toward us in the distance. 'Shit! It's a two-way road. This can't possibly be two ways; it's too narrow.'

A man's sleeping on a seat on the other side of the aisle. He twists his body into a more comfortable position.

I tap him on the shoulder. 'Hey, mate; is this road both ways?'

'Eh?'

'Does this road have traffic going up, and down?'

He nods, turns his back to us, then closes his eyes.

Ray says, 'I'd rather be going down than going up. At least we'd have the cliff beside us instead of that bloody big drop.'

'Yeah.'

On the right side of the bus, a fast-flowing river with rapids rushes by. I can't help but be mesmerized.

Occasionally, Ray mumbles words—different words and different emphasis. There's 'shit' and there's 'shiiit'; and there's 'fuck' and there's 'fuuuck', and there's 'bloody hell' and there's 'blooody heeell'. I don't look because I know I'll say exactly the same as him.

The driver announces that he's going to stop at Boat Encampment. We have no idea what it is, but it's certain the bus needs a rest, and if everyone's got brains, they should say to the driver, 'Well done.'

A sign tells us that the elevation is seven-thousand feet. That's the highest I've ever been

After that, we drive south, travelling more downhill than uphill, and the cliff face is on the other side of the bus. Now I see what Ray was seeing, and I often say, 'Sh…it.' The bus back-fires. Low gears slow it, stopping it from rocketing downhill. I remember the bus driver saying that the Big Bend breaks hearts, cars and buses—now I believe him.

The bus arrives at the town of Lake Louise, and we're astonished at the beauty. The surrounding mountains reflect on the water, and I say to Ray, 'That's a memory I'll never forget.'

He's a bit more blasé. 'Do you ever remember saying that about Sydney Harbour?'

'Yeah.'

I think I know what he means: that we see things that impress, and then when we see something more impressive, we forget the first impression. Deep and meaningful thoughts from Ray are few, so I wonder what's happened to him. 'Are you taking the piss?'

'No … it's just what I reckon … like, I know when I see a Maserati or a Ferrari, I forget about my MGA.'

'Oh. I see.' He's probably right, but I can't tell him because mates don't go on with bullshit like this.

We pass the Banff Springs Hotel and wonder if Dougie's got a job there or if he's already patrolling the National Park or if he's drunk in a pub. The bus passes the Bow River rapids, which to me are insignificant compared to those I saw on the Big Bend highway river.

The driver says, 'Those are the rapids in the movie *River of No Return*. That's where the famous scene was filmed, the one that has Marilyn Monroe rafting the rapids.'

I'm impressed because I saw the film at the Hurstville Savoy theatre, and I remember being very excited about Marilyn's nipples stretching the tight, white, wet blouse. I also remember that image being the cause of a wet dream, and I'm hoping that when I go to Hollywood I'll get the chance to see Marilyn, and I'll say to her, 'Thanks for the memory.'

Ray says, 'That driver's got to be wrong. Marilyn Monroe was in the middle of the bush in that rafting scene; remember?'

He's right. I easily visualize it. There's this immense rush of water that's tossing the raft about; Marilyn's hanging on to a big oar like grim death, and she's twisting it to stop the raft from hitting huge boulders. Behind her is a forest.

I say to the bus driver, 'But in the film—'

'I know, I know, I know. Everyone says, "But in the film there's no big hotel behind her and it's all bushy." The guys around here saw the filming and they say there were hundreds of people gawking, but in the actual film you see none of them.'

I'm not going to forget what the bus driver said. I say to Ray, 'I'll ask Marilyn when I see her in Hollywood.'

He says, 'Oh gord.'

It grows dark and, eventually, we see lights in farmhouse windows, then fifteen minutes later, we see lights in houses and small buildings positioned on the roadside, then come a few streetlights, and soon we're in the suburbs of Calgary.

We're very interested. Most of what we see flashes past as a blend of hundreds of different lights, advertising signs for car yards and shops and houses. Occasionally, something deserves a longer look, and our heads twist as if we're watching Ken Rosewall and Lew Hoad playing tennis.

I'm not yet an experienced world traveller, but I'm thinking that darkness is not the time to enter a new city. The bus goes on dimly lit narrow streets that have shabby-looking buildings. Tonight must be garbage night because all the bins are out. We see people having a good time, many walking like they've already had too much to drink, some of them yelling obscenities at the Greyhound bus. It's easy to tell that they'll soon be fighting, or stealing, or locked-up by the police. I'd heard the term 'wrong side of the tracks', and I know what it means. In Sydney it's the South side of the Harbour: it's Surry Hills, Redfern, Liverpool and Riverwood, not Lindfield, Gordon, St Ives and Lane Cove. The right side of the tracks is anywhere that's located next to a place of the same name, but has 'heights' after it. All the carpenters, plumbers, labourers, and process workers are on the wrong side of the tracks. All the doctors, lawyers, solicitors and managing directors are on the right side.

Ray and I come from the wrong side of the tracks, and that's where bus stations are always located.

I see a building lit up like a Christmas tree, and I say to Ray, 'What's that?'

'Dunno.'

'It must be important. Perhaps it's the Town Hall.'

The man on the other side of the aisle who's been asleep in his seat since leaving Vancouver says, 'It's the Calgary Brewery.'

'Brewery?'

The man nods. That's all we're going to get out of him.

Ray says, 'If that's a brewery, we ought to pay it a visit.'

Outside the bus terminal stands a friendly man from the wrong side of the tracks. He's got loads of personal things crammed into two cardboard boxes wrapped up with fraying rope. I should say to him that his rope would be better if it was back-spliced, that I used to be a Sea Cadet and I know how to do that, but he'd probably think I was being too pushy. He'd probably say that he likes his ropes with frayed ends.

The man says, 'You guys new in town?'

'Yeah.'

He looks at our suitcases. 'Where you from?'

'Vancouver.'

'No, I mean where you from, them bags say you ain't from Canada. Them bags got labels on them … it looks like ship's labels.'

'Oh, yes; they are ship's labels. We're from Australia.'

He rubs his hand over his chin and scratches more than two days of whiskers; droplets of what looks to be dandruff fall. He says, 'I knew you weren't from here. I can tell by your jackets. Are you in some kind of team?'

'Team?'

'That thing on your pockets, that map thing. That's Australia, ain't it?'

He's right; it is Australia.

It seemed like a good thing to do to have the pockets of our yachting jackets embroidered with a map of Australia, but the novelty's wearing off because whenever we wear them, we're different, and I'm fast learning that it's not all that good to be different.

I should've known because an old journalist at *The Sydney Morning Herald* told me about a man who was taken by a shark. The shark selected the man because he wore a bum-crack-hugging French swimming costume. Had the man worn Australian Speedo swimming trunks, he'd still have two legs instead of one. The shark wouldn't have selected him for dinner; it would've taken a piece of someone else. He said, 'Son, that's what happens to people who are different.'

The friendly man from the wrong side of the tracks says, 'Where you boys staying?'

It's a good question. We have no idea. If this man were wearing nice clothes and his lovely wife and children were with him, and if he were from the right side of the tracks, we'd ask him if he had a spare room at his house.

Instead I say to the man, 'We thought there'd be a travellers' aid office in the bus terminal; we were going to ask them.'

He says, 'They'd tell you to go to the YMCA.'

We get directions from him and we walk off struggling with our suitcases.

Ray says, 'Have you ever been to a YMCA?'

'Only one; I went the Sydney YMCA for a photo-club meeting.'

'Photo club? Nudes?'

'Yeah, as if.' Despite the instruction I got that day, my photographs were lousy so I'd decided to finish my plumbing apprenticeship.

The Calgary YMCA looks welcoming, and I'm hoping that when we book in, they won't ask my religion, because I'll say none, and they'll probably tell me to go to away.

I'm writing my details on what the woman behind the reception desk said was a registration form, and I realise I've never before registered to stay anywhere.

The caretaker at the Werri Beach camping area, or the man at Surfers Paradise camping ground doesn't want such details. All they want is five bob a night and to know when the campsite's going to be vacated.

The woman gives us a key for room A8 and points in the room's direction. We struggle upstairs carrying suitcases that now seem twice as heavy than when we left the bus station. It's a stiflingly hot room because they have heavy cast-iron radiators similar to those in the Crown Street and the Royal Prince Alfred hospitals, so we turn the heat off and open the windows. During the night, we close the windows and turn on the heat.

~

I've only ever sat in a restaurant booth at Repin's Coffee Inn in King Street, and I liked it. It was just like in American movies—James Dean sits in booths, so do Marlon Brando and Marilyn. My father built one in our house, but we call it a nook. Sitting in a booth's fun, but a nook's awful. Mum and I usually sit at the open end of the nook; my brothers and sister are in the trapped end because they're small enough to slide onto the floor to crawl under our legs to get out. Mum's always saying, 'I don't know why your father built this.' But I reckon she's to blame because it's her kitchen and she planned the room

Now I'm sitting in a booth in the YMCA coffee shop and Ray's mumbling about tea bags. He's saying over and over, 'They don't have leaf tea, only those stupid bags, only bags.' He stops mumbling to ask, 'Have you found it yet?'

I'm flipping through the pages of the Calgary newspaper, looking at advertisements for the movies *Exodus* and *Fanny*—they're both classified 'Adult', and I wonder if we'd see Leslie Caron or Eva Marie Saint's nipples stretching their tight white blouses.

I say, 'I've got what's on at the pictures but there are no positions vacant pages.'

'Oh.'

'There's a story here about unemployment rising to ten percent.'

'Ten percent! Shit.'

'What's unemployment in Australia?'

'Dunno, I don't think we have any.'

Behind us a voice says, 'Are you blokes Australian?'

'Yeah; you too?'

'Yeah. We arrived yesterday from Toronto.'

'We got here yesterday from Vancouver.'

Everyone says something very ocker: Well, blow me down; I'll be buggered; stone the crows; blimey Teddy Charlie. We're Australians and we're going to sound like Australians—at least our kind, the wrong side of the tracks Australians.

'Any of you blokes got a job?' one of them asks.

'No; you?'

'No. That's why we're here, there's nothing in Toronto.'

'Do any of you have a trade?' I ask.

'It wouldn't be any different. There's no bloody jobs.'

An Englishman and an Irishman are listening and they join us.

I ask, 'Are you blokes working?'

'No.'

'What's the matter in this country? I've not met anyone who's got a job,' Ray says.

The Englishman says, 'I'm a clerk.'

Then we hear what the other two Australians do, and we all look at the Irishman.

He says, 'I'm a poet.'

For a while nothing's said, but eventually one of the Australians says, 'A poet … I can understand why you've not got a job. What did you have to do to be a poet?'

'Five years at Trinity College.'

None of us know what or where Trinity College is, but I guess it's some kind of high-fee private school like Sydney's Barker College and the 'tyke' Saint Ignatius College. I say to the Irishman, 'So you're a silvertail, eh?'

He doesn't know what I mean, but I know because I went to the head of the river rowing regatta with my lost mate. He's lost because his parents, who own a grocery shop at Peakhurst, send him to Sydney Grammar School, and he wears a stupid-looking straw hat and a poncy-looking suit, and we lost him from that day.

I'd told my Uncle Harry where I'd been, and he said, 'Out with the silvertails eh? Barry, they'll get their just desert when the revolution comes.'

And my Uncle Harry knows about such things because he was a digger in the First World War and was shot twice. Uncle Harry once showed me a thick wallet stuffed with photos. He had that wallet in his top pocket of his uniform when he was shot, and it had a bullet hole through all the photos. 'It saved me, Bro.'

I ask him, 'What revolution?'

But all he does is ramble on about workers' rights and distribution of income and silvertails controlling capital. I know nothing about all of that so I just say, 'Oh.' But he continues on about how the NSW Premier Jack Lang should nationalize all the banks.

Again, all I say is, 'Oh.'

~

The next day and the next, we meet at the YMCA, but now we're a gang because two New Zealanders, a Rhodesian and a Scot join us.

The routine of meeting for breakfast to exchange information about possible jobs expands to end-of-the-day meetings at a pub, where we should get our heads punched in because all we do is criticize.

During consumption of the first few beers, our voices are moderate and we make reasoned comments, but too much alcohol transforms us to loudmouths, and we're fucking the country, the people, the system, the beer and the Canadian mindset of being too bloody serious.

Ray says, 'I was interviewed for a job as maintenance man for a school board.'

The Englishman says, 'Board? Ah, yes, very appropriate for a carpenter.'

I say, 'I inquired about joining the Mounted Police, but they only take Canadian citizens.'

The Irish poet goes off into doggerel: 'There was a young man from Australia / who went with his Masonic regalia / to the police office in town …'

We don't allow him to finish because it's pathetic and nothing rhymes.

The two New Zealanders talk about making money by playing American football, and we all laugh and say how stupid the game is.

We give the Rhodesian the nick-name 'Ridgeback', and he fools about like a dog. A group of Canadian drinkers near us, who are all too serious, scoff and send some serious Canadian abuse our way.

Nothing happens because we know we can't fight everyone in the pub, and they seem content to verbally abuse us. I'm not that happy being called a cocksucker so I tell them they're drongos and if they continue coming the raw prawn there's going to be a blue. They don't know what I mean, and the English and Rhodesian don't either, so we all laugh, and I'm pleased that there's no donnybrook.

One of the Australians says, 'I telephoned the unemployment department office, and I told them their country's fucking hopeless, and they hung up on me. They wouldn't even listen to what I had to say.'

None of us consider compromising. We all think it's the Canadian Government's fault that we have to live at the YMCA, that we can't get work, that we spend too much money on alcohol, and that we can't afford to buy a car, and for everything else we can't have or get.

~

Ray and I go to the Greyhound Bus Station to get our tools of trade that have arrived from Vancouver, and we lug them to the YMCA. Ray carries his well-crafted wooden carpenter case that has dovetail corners. Inside the case are dovetailed sliding drawers for nail punches, and attached to the lid are neatly fixed leather straps for storage of sharp wood chisels. I carry my battered steel Australian Army ammunition box that's a disgrace.

Canadians who must've been in the war give me funny looks, and I guess they wonder if I've got .303 rifle bullets inside.

At the YMCA, a different woman manages the desk. I ask for the key for room A8, and she gives me a blank stare and does nothing.

I repeat the room number, and still she does nothing. I'm thinking that she's scared because I'm carrying an ammunition box, so I say, 'It's my tools. I'm a plumber. We've just got them from the bus station.'

She looks puzzled, and I wonder if the YMCA employs people who are deaf and dumb—and I reckon that's good. I write the room number on her desk pad, and she says the room number using North American pronunciation.

I repeat the number, 'Yeah, A ate,' and she smiles and gives me the key.

I feel embarrassed about her difficulty understanding my Australian accent. Although she's a very good-looking woman, I could never ask her out because we'd not be able to talk about anything.

I have no more anxiety about how I secure my valuables—passports, travellers' cheques, bank books, personal references, trade certificates and cameras—because out go some of my plumbing tools, and in they go. Then, to make certain they're unstealable, I snap shut a stolen New South Wales Government Railway padlock.

Ray says, 'You're a fuck-wit; a robber will take the whole box.'

But I reckon robbers are smart enough to know that lugging a heavy steel ammunition box along Calgary's footpaths is inviting the police's curiosity.

'What about when our room's cleaned? It can be broken into then.'

'Oh yeah, as if the maids will have a pinch bar with them. Anyhow, we're in the YMCA; they don't let robbers in here. They only let honest people in.'

'But they let us in.'

~

We think we're spending too much money at the pub so we all decide to drink less and, to get fit.

The YMCA has an indoor swimming pool, sauna and gymnasium, but we reckon that parallel bars, wrestling mats and the boxing ring are too serious for us. We meet in the sauna, and the attendant criticizes us for not showering first. After lots of sweating, we jump into the swimming pool, and the attendant criticizes us again. He says, 'You must shower before going into the pool, and as this is men's only night, you must not wear swimming clothes.'

We're all prepared to shower, but none of us are very happy about swimming in the nuddy. We do what we're told because we're not allowed in the pool without our dicks and balls swinging in the air. I make the mistake of diving in; my balls smash against the water and it bloody-well hurts.

I start screaming underwater and continue until my head gets to the surface where my scream echoes in the building. I reckon it's the first time 'fu...ck' has been heard in the YMCA.

We huddle in a not-too-close group at the shallow end of the pool where we Australians admit that we've never before swum in an indoor pool. The Englishman says he's never swum in an outdoor pool. I'm thinking about Sydney's Ramsgate Baths and the North Sydney Olympic pool and the shark-proof, wire-enclosed pools at Parsley Bay and Sans Souci, and I'm wondering what swimmers there would make of seven blokes standing around in the nuddy talking.

The Englishman tells us he's going to the USA where he's going to make a squillion dollars. We ask him about his Social Security card, which he says he hasn't got, so we tell him he's a nong and that he'll be deported and never allowed back in to the USA.

Our healthy lifestyle lasts a few days, and then we're back to needing recovery sessions each morning. We try Prairie Oysters—a dry biscuit with a dab of butter scraped on filled with HP sauce—and 'V8' vegetable juice. The HP sauce burns our tongues, and the 'V8' ingredients—carrots, tomato, celery, beetroot, lettuce and, worst of all, spinach—does nothing except make us thirsty, for a beer.

The waitress in the YMCA coffee shop says, 'You ought to be ashamed of yourselves. What would your mothers think?'

The Rhodesian bloke says, 'I heard the Calgary Brewery has tours, and after the tour, they give out free beer.'

Free beer!

I reckon the Calgary Brewing Company is pretty good because they have structures outside festooned in coloured lights that all the Calgary kids love to see. They also have an aquarium, a fish hatchery and a museum. Loads of things to introduce kiddies to the normality of alcohol and the smell—because all breweries stink. The breweries know they'll get complaints from people living near, so they do things to make them appear good. The Calgary Brewery is a good-but-cunning corporate citizen.

I've been in a lot of breweries. I've even worked in some. Resch's Brewery has the custom, and so do most other Breweries, of dispensing a couple of freebies to their workers from an on-site bar.

The bar's only open for a short time, so as soon as the knock-off whistle goes the workers all rush to get in the free-beer queue. It's never a social occasion because we have to catch buses, trains and trams to our local watering hole. Even there, it's difficult to get a skin-full because at six o'clock the publican says, 'Time gentlemen please.' Then, because everyone pretends not to hear him and because everyone's got a few schooners yet to be scoffed, he screams 'TIME GENTLEMEN … PLEASE.'

Toohey's, Tooth's, Foster's, Cascade, Swan, Four X, and all the rest has the same custom.

'Are you certain they give free beer?' I ask the Rhodesian bloke.

He's certain. He says, 'They take reservations for the inspection tour.'

'Reservations? Like when you go to a play?'

Ray laughs. 'Go to a play? You?'

'I did once; I took my mum to the Theatre Royal to see something called *The Mikado*. I made reservations, and the tickets were mailed out. To tell you the truth, it was bloody awful, but she enjoyed it.'

'What was the play about?'

'Dunno; lots of blokes in Japanese dresses and sheilas with funny hair, and they all sang lots of songs.'

Ray says, 'You didn't tell me you'd gone.'

'Of course, I didn't. You don't go around telling mates that you've been to a fucking play. They'll think you're a poofter.'

The Rhodesian says, 'Well, it's nothing like that. The brewery doesn't give out tickets.'

'Well why do they take reservations?'

'Fucked if I know.'

I get the job of phoning the brewery. 'G'day, we're a group of Australian tourists that are interested in beer, ah, interested in seeing how beer's made, and we're told that you have a tour.'

A woman says she needs names and I give her Jones, Smith, Black, another Smith because it's a common name, and Bartlett.

Ray says, 'Why'd you give my correct name? Why didn't you give me a bodgie name like the others?'

'Because … because …' I've got no idea why his name just slipped out, but I'd better come up with something. 'Because one of us will have to wear a tie.'

'Why?'

'Because we have to look the part; we can't all look like piss-pots.'

When we turn up for the tour, about fifteen people mingle in the Calgary Brewery foyer; most are Canadian, there's one American and us. Ray has convinced me that we should both wear a necktie and our yachting jackets with the map of Australia and the word 'Australia' on the pocket. We could be part of a National team, Olympians even.

The man in charge says, 'Good morning. My name's Greg, and I'm your tour guide. I have here a name badge for everyone. They must be worn.'

Greg's too bossy so I don't like him much.

He calls out names and all the other tourists get theirs but we get it mucked up because we don't know who of us are Smith, Jones or Black. Ray goes to get his name badge, and we stand there like gooses.

Greg says, 'Which of you is Mister Jones?'

The Rhodesian and I say, 'Me.'

We take the rest of the name badges from Greg, and I become a Black.

We're all chattering when Greg asks for our attention and we're still chattering when he yells for our attention. He says, 'You guys wearing the fancy coats. Will you stop talking?' He pauses to look around the tour group, and we all hang on his words. 'Now … we will commence the tour. At the completion of the tour we will return to that room.'

He points to an adjoining room where the beer-manufacturing process is posted on a huge board with lots of coloured light bulbs.

'There,' he continues, 'you will have the opportunity of participating in a quiz about the beer-manufacturing process. It's all multiple choice; simply select the answer you want, press the button beside it and that light will illuminate.' Greg goes to a control panel and pushes a few buttons. Lots of coloured lights flash on and off.

Ray says, 'It's like Bob and Dolly Dyer's *Pick a Box*.'

Greg seems not to know that Bob and Dolly are Australia's quiz show kings. He says, 'If, and I mean if, you get fifteen of the twenty-two answers, you will be awarded the …'—he swells out his chest and his voice grows louder—'The Calgary Brewery Amateur Brewmaster's Certificate.'

Obviously, from the way Greg announces it, this certificate is up there with the Nobel Prize.

Greg wears a look of expectancy, as if he's wanting ohs and ahs, but they don't come.

It's a good opportunity to get some respect, so I say, 'That's terrific.' And he smiles.

We follow Greg into the factory where they store barley.

'Ladies and Gentlemen, ten million pounds of malt is used annually and that is ground at the rate of six-thousand pounds each hour …'

One of the Englishmen says, 'Forget about the barley; let's get to the finished product.'

'… As it makes its way from the lauter tun, the brewing liquid, which is now called sweetw, passes through the grant where the first of many laboratory tests are done.'

Ray says, 'Who the hell cares?'

The Rhodesian says, 'Shut up or we'll be thrown out without getting any free beer.'

One hour later Greg tells us it's the end of the tour, that we will return to the examination room and we all think, 'Thank Christ.'

Greg says, 'Are there any questions before we finish?'

We all think, 'Finish? We can't be finished. We haven't been given our free beers. Quick, someone ask him a question.

One of the Englishmen says, 'Can you explain the importance of good water in the manufacturing process.'

Greg has a big smile. 'Yes, sir. That's a very good question. The sixty-four-year-old well, together with four others provide …'

He goes on and on about the water's importance, its chemicals, the temperature and flow rates, and we think he'll never shut up. Then he invites us to the board with coloured lights for the test of our beer knowledge.

We go to the board and press anything. Few lights illuminate which means we're mostly wrong.

Greg says, 'When you've finished the test, come to the bar where we'll try some of our wonderful product.'

The fair dinkum tourists ponder over the questions and answers, but we rush to see the unlocking of the refrigerator.

'Let's get stuck into it,' someone says.

Greg panics a bit and says. 'Gentlemen, gentlemen, don't crush. There's a beer here for everyone.'

There probably is, but no one wants to chance missing out.

The Rhodesian says, 'A beer? There'd better be more than *a* beer. We've been here half the day for *a* beer?'

We each get a beer. Gulp, and it's gone.

Greg looks anxious.

Ray whispers to me, 'We've got to use our nous here.'

He's quite right.

Explaining nous is difficult. Firstly, it's not just Australians who use nous, but Australians have taken its use to a high level.

The concept was defined for me once in a building-site lunch shed. Imagine the Titanic sinking. Is a nousy bloke the one who sits in a deck chair near a lifeboat holding women's clothing so he's ready when they announce, 'Women and children first'?

No, that's not it.

83

Is a nousy bloke the one who checks if icebergs are about and then cancels his ticket so he won't be on board?

Not that's not right either.

A very nousy bloke won't have left Australia in the first place.

The boss said, 'If you blokes are nousy, you'll all get back to work.'

And we all went, because we're nousy.

The only one who didn't understand was Sergio Ponti. He'd only been in Australia for a year, but he soon learned the meaning.

In a fine example of the idea, Ray places his empty glass on the bartop. 'That was terrific. What beer would you blokes compare it to?'

Nous comes into play.

One says, 'When I was at the Carlsberg brewery in Denmark …'

Another says, 'There's a New Zealand beer that's …'

Another says, 'The Czech beer I like is …'

Another says, 'The Germans have a brew that's …'

I say, 'The chief brewer at Resch's used to tell me …'

Greg's impressed. He goes to the refrigerator, gets out five of that and five of this, and we're drinking again. He says, 'Try our heavier lager.'

Which we do, then we try another kind.

It's nousy to do what Greg expects. Some of us hold the beer to the light; some smell it; some roll it in their glass, and I say, 'This one hangs well on the side of the glass.'

All the other tourists leave, and we know it's no fun drinking alone so we stay to keep Greg company.

The next day, we continue with the YMCA coffee shop ritual, and we continue to be criticized by the waitress. Some in the group go off on adventure, and others who are passing through Calgary join us. We exaggerate about what we've been up to and so do the newcomers. Someone reckons they're going to hitchhike to Texas where they'll buy a cheap car then drive it to Panama. Someone else reckons that can't be done, then someone else says it can because he's driven to Columbia. Nearly everyone would work in the USA but without a social security card it's risky. There's stories about deportation from there, and stories about great jobs paying huge money. One bloke made a fortune working on the 'DEW' line, but he can't explain why he's staying in the low-cost YMCA. Australians and New Zealanders who arrive from Europe tell us about awfully low wages. Some boast about how many countries they'd 'done', and those of us who hadn't yet 'done' Canada get pissed off because we can't yet boast about anything. Mountains are climbed in Europe and adventure had in Morocco, but all we can boast about is ripping-off a Fijian native when buying a miniature outrigger canoe.

We all go to the pub and it's on again. Everyone tries to better everyone else. A Welsh bloke goes to take a photo in the hotel and there's trouble.

The barman says, 'You ain't allowed to take photos.'

'Why?' the Welshman asks.

'It's the law. There's no taking photographs in hotels.'

'But that's fucking stupid.'

'Do you want me to get the police?'

We settle down, then we decide to move to another table.

The barman says, 'You ain't allowed to carry beer from one table to another.'

'Why?'

'It's the law. Walking around holding beer's against the law.'

The shouts get mixed up, and we have more than two beers each.

The barman says, 'It's against the law to have in the possession of one person more than one beer.'

'But that's fucking stupid.'

We need to buy beer to take to a party, but we can't get it at the hotel; we must go to a liquor store, and we must have a license.

It's difficult being a serious drinker in Alberta. But it's not only Alberta.

An Englishman says, 'I was going to see your Rolf Harris in Vancouver, but I wasn't allowed entry into the mixed bar without a woman accompanying me.'

'Why?'

'Because, that's the law.'

I should say to him, 'It's not 'my' Rolf Harris. I hate his music.' But I don't say it because at parties I'll be singing, 'Tie me kangaroo down, sport' along with the rest of the Australians. And when I'm singing the line, 'Keep your cockatoo cool, Curl', I don't want him asking why I'm singing music I hate.

We criticize Canadian liquor laws, but we don't say anything about the stupid Australian six o'clock closing, and we agree that it'll be great in England where we'll be able to drink what we like, when we like.

The Englishman says, 'Except for the few hours after lunch when the pubs are closed.'

~

Ray gets a job with a local school board, and I get a job with Canadian Comstock working as a plumber on the Calgary University extension. Money's coming in, so we decide to rent, but instead of getting a swishy apartment, we take a converted garage that's in the back yard of a house. The single room is almost a hovel, but it's cheap.

One day I'm bronze-welding copper pipes and bashing holes in walls, when I see a bloke wearing King Gee Victory brand overalls. He's got to be Australian. He's actually looking for me.

He says, 'G'day, I'm Noel the Australian carpenter; are you the Australian plumber?'

'Yeah.'

'Do you play rugby?'

'Yeah.'

'Good. I'm in the Calgary Hornets team and we're looking for players. What about coming to our training tonight?'

'Okay.'

That evening I stand on grass covered in a crunchy layer of frost looking at blokes of six nationalities throwing and kicking and screaming, 'Pass it to me.' I'm a bit confused because they're not stopping to play the ball, and I realise its rugby union they're playing. I've never played union; I've only played rugby league with the Sea Cadets.

Noel says, 'Got your boots?'

'No, only sandshoes.'

'That's all right; come on for a run.'

I go on for a run; someone passes me the ball. Lots of blokes push me to the ground, and soon I've got football boots scraping my head and body. I'm hanging onto the ball like grim death, and they're all yelling, 'Release, release.' I don't know what they mean. I wish they'd let me get up to play the ball, but all they do is yell, 'Release.' I'm tired of football boot sprigs scratching my face so I let go of the ball, they all yell and wrestle after it and leave me lying on the frost.

For an hour I chase after them and the ball, and I realise I know nothing about rugby.

Fitzpatrick, an Irish bloke, tells me he's the captain, then he says, 'You've never played rugby, have you?'

'No. I played rugby league.'

'That's obvious. Do you want to play rugby?'

I don't immediately answer because they're all madmen; they all have bruises and cuts and scars and bandaged knees. I say, 'But I've not …'

He says, 'That doesn't matter. We need players. What position did you play in rugby league?'

I'd only played in the front row of the Sea Cadet team because that's where I was put, but I was always far too light to play that position. I say to Fitzpatrick, 'Front row. I used to be the right-side prop.'

He says, 'Good you're our new right prop.'

Training's over. We're all in a pub doing serious drinking, and I enjoy the companionship. Noel introduces me to Stuart. I like him straight away.

'G'day, I'm Stuart Acason from Boulia in Queensland. Where're you from?'

Stuart does the I've-been-here-and-there spiel, and I do the I-haven't-been-anywhere-yet response. He mentions farmers, and I say that Australian farmers are on a good wicket, that they're doing great, but he says they're not. I ask how he'd know, and he says because he's been a share farmer and a contractor cleaning out irrigation ditches and that he's always worked on the land.

Because I don't know what I'm talking about, I decide to shut my mouth.

I discover that Rugby and alcohol go together like bookends. Soon I'm at a party every weekend and I love it.

The team discovers that I'm not a very good front-row forward or a good rugby player, but they've got no one to replace me so I stay in the team. After every weekend I'm bruised and sore and sorry, but I love being part of the group—a team that doesn't win one match but has more parties than anyone else.

Noel tells me the party's at the New Zealanders' flat this week, and I'm there.

Next week it's at a Canadian girl's apartment, and I'm there also.

We, the blokes, the heroes, the players, never bring anything but grog to parties. But we do bring a lot. The pommies are as tight as fishes' arseholes, and they always turn up short. We watch the poms when they come in the door, and we notice few of them go to the laundry to put their grog with ours.

A South African says, 'Thet mon was a bit leight-on when he arreved.'

'What man?'

'Thet mon thet's pooring a stuff scotch.'

South Africans are always difficult to understand, but they're never light-on bringing grog to parties.

'The bastard. I reckon I'll try to get onto his sheila.'

'You'd better not. I saw him king-hit one of the Canadians on the Saracens team. He packs a mean wallop.'

'Oh.'

We never think that alcohol's harming us, that it's destroying brain cells and that we spend too much of our incomes buying it. A Monday morning conversation might go something like this:

'How are you blokes feeling?'

'Shithouse. How else would I feel after the party last night?'

'What party last night? The party was on Saturday.'

'Shit. *What day* is it?'

'Monday. The Rhodesian blokes brought you home, yesterday, Sunday. You were still as pissed as a fart.'

'Oh. I must have had a good time then.'

The Calgary Brewery's Amateur Brewmaster's Certificate is a trophy I want, but the only way to get it is to do Greg's boring tour again, then attempt his coloured lights test.

I've always wanted a worthwhile certificate to hang on my bedroom wall.

I didn't get the High School Intermediate Certificate; I was beaten in the first round of a certificate fight at the Mortdale Police Boys club; I can't run for nuts; I got no badges or certificates in the Boy Scouts. I've got nothing.

Oh, I do have a cricket pennant, but that's because during the finals a higher graded team than mine was short one player. I had my leg in a plaster cast and went to watch the team play. The captain told me that if I went onto the boundary and stopped any ball that came my way I'll get a pennant if they won. I didn't stop any balls, but they did win and I got a pennant: *1950/51 Peakhurst Waratah Boys' under Sixteen Competition, Runners up.*

I'd love to have the Brewmaster's certificate to put with my cricket pennant.

We go back to the Calgary Brewery in a 1951 Ford that one of the blokes bought for two-hundred-and-fifty dollars, and we're confident.

'No mucking about this time,' Ray says, 'The brewery guide's going to chuck us out if we muck about.'

'Yeah,' I say, 'It's our last chance for glory.'

'Glory?'

'Yeah, glory. There's not many of these certificates; I reckon I'll be the only one in the St George area to have one.'

It's difficult keeping the two English blokes focused. They don't have the right attitude. One of them says, 'All I want are a few free drinks,' and the other one says, 'I'm only drinking their beer because it's free. I mean, really, their beer is …'

'Piss?'

'Perhaps that's the appropriate word. I don't understand why you Australians enjoy drinking beer that's so light. There's little taste and it's served so cold.'

We're always hearing from the English about their beer; they go on and on about their ales and bitters and something called scrumpy, but when it comes to being at a party, they'll bring nothing but drink anything. They've got deep pockets.

Greg's getting his tourists organized when he sees us. 'You guys back again?'

'Yeah,' I say, 'Last time we weren't serious; this time we are.'

He looks at his papers. 'There's no reservation on my list in your names. There's no Jones, Smith or Blacks, and there's certainly no Bartlett. You know that reservations have to be made. You're definitely not on this tour.'

The other tourists stare at us, sniggering and whispering.

One of the Englishmen says, 'What about the group from London University? Are they registered?'

We booked as a group of five from London University.

'Oh,' Greg says, 'you're the London group.'

'Yes,' I say. 'We're really are keen to get the Brewmaster's certificate.'

'Well, London group, if you're that keen, come over here and I'll give you each a certificate.'

The other tourists mutter that it's not fair.

We know it's not fair; we also know that Greg doesn't want us to muck up his tour or give us any free beer.

The Rhodesian whispers, 'He's playing games with us; if there's no tour, there's no beer.'

I say, 'It's not fair if we get the certificate and all of you'—I turn to point at the tour group—'all of you have to do the tour to get a certificate.'

A Canadian bloke says, 'Yes, we're locals; overseas people shouldn't get preference over locals.'

Greg knows he's beaten. He gives us nametags and off we go again.

Greg says, 'Ten million pounds of malt is used annually, and it's ground at the rate of seven-thousand pounds each day …'

Ray says, 'What?'

'What do you mean by, "What"?'

'I'm saying "what" because it doesn't calculate; it doesn't pass the eyeball test, and they're different figures from the last tour.'

Greg says, 'Excuse me?'

'I said it doesn't pass the eyeball test.'

'Eyeball test?'

'Yair. If you multiply the—'

I tell Ray to shut-up. We don't want his math spoiling our chances for the certificate or free beer.

He says, 'But I'm right; do the calculation.'

We say, 'Mate, SHUT-UP.'

We'll have to work hard to get Greg on side now.

I say, 'What's that big machine over there?'

Greg looks relieved. 'Oh, yes, that's the lauter tun, the liquid goes from there to the …'

Ray's pissed-off about being told to shut-up. He says, 'This is boring.'

One hour later we return to the reception room. We anticipate spending ten minutes doing the test then get into the free beer. We go straight to the test board. What was that called? How much did they use there? Where did it go after that? What's the name of that lauter thing? We press buttons, get seventeen lights and yell, 'Hey, we did it!'

Greg's already got the certificates ready. He seems keen for us to leave, but we're not going without having our free beer.

He says, 'Congratulations.'

We say, 'Thank you,' and wait, but nothing happens. He just stands with a sick smile on his face.

'Well, Greg, where's the beer?'

'There's no beer today.'

'What?'

'You heard me.'

'But there's always free beer after a tour.'

'Not after this tour. You "blow-into-town" guys that come here to take jobs from local people piss me off. Why don't you stay in your own goddamned country? Even if there were beer in the refrigerator, I wouldn't give you any.' He unlocks the refrigerator and opens the door. There's no beer inside.

All the other tourists have gone so we must decide what to do—punch his head in, or leave?

Greg says, 'When you arrived, I offered to give you certificates, but you said "No." You insisted on doing the tour.'

'But what about the other tourists?' I asked. 'Did they know there'd be no beer?'

'Of course.'

The Rhodesian bloke looks pissed-off; he's rolling on the balls of his feet like a prize fighter, and I'm thinking the P's: punches, police, patrol wagon, pyrrhic victory.

The Englishman takes his certificate. We take ours, then we all leave.

We go to a pub and decide on revenge.

Ray says, 'We shouldn't ever drink Calgary beer again, but that's no good because it's the local brew and it's the cheapest.'

One Englishman says, 'We can write to the brewery manager, but that's no good because he'd only commend Greg's actions.'

The other Englishman says, 'We can stop drinking beer and drink rye whiskey instead, but that's no good because we don't much like rye.'

I say, 'We can stop drinking all alcohol, but that's no good because we know we can't stop.'

The Rhodesian bloke says, 'I don't give a fuck about what you lot won't do because I'm going to blow up the brewery.'

Christ; he might just do it.

One week later, Ray and I and many thousands of Calgary's citizens watch the Calgary Exhibition and Stampede street parade. We see the Canadian prime minister, John Diefenbaker—but we're not too excited about him—and the famous cowboy actor, The Cisco Kid—we're a bit excited about him. Then we see some of the chuck-wagons that are going to race around the Calgary exhibition ground—we're very excited about them. The real excitement comes for Ray when a group of Canadian Mounted Police wearing their distinctive red-jacket uniforms march past.

'Bloody hell,' he says, 'this is what I came to Canada to see. Mounties!'

1960, Calgary.

Barry and Ray rent a garage to live in. It isn't nice, but its cheap and warm.

Barry and Ray looking for work.

After the NW Territory camp.

Chapter Four

My job as a plumber at the Calgary University construction site abruptly came to an end, eliminating my only source of income. I should have been managing my money, purchasing only essentials, but I spent most of it on partying and beer, and sometimes food and rent. I'd saved no money, and the likelihood of work was slim due to outside construction work slowing for the winter months. Unemployment in Alberta remained at over ten percent.

Then the Scottish bloke who supports the Hornets Rugby Union team told me that the Alberta Trailer Company, a provider of construction and mining camps, was looking for a bull-cook.

I had no idea what a bull-cook did.

He explained that it was nothing to do with cooking bulls, that it was a Canadian term for a person who does camp maintenance, etcetera.

I had no inkling about what the etcetera involved; neither did I care. I was near enough to being broke, and no other work was on offer.

'The camp is one hundred miles north of Fort Nelson … on the Simpson Trail,' the Scottish bloke said.

'I don't give a bugger where it is; I'll take it.'

I'd only met the Scottish bloke a few times, but he helped me, as he'd help any fellow traveller. Had I not got this job, I'd be broke and living on the charity of friends, which is not unusual. Many travellers sleep on floors of apartments, bludge meals and hope something will happen to change their circumstances. I was lucky.

My Queenslander mate and landlord, Stuart Acason, drove me to a place on the outskirts of Calgary where I would meet the rest of the crew.

I'd been instructed to carry, in one bag, warm working clothes and nothing unimportant, for my survival in the isolated North West Territory. I did, however, pack my trusty Yashica 35mm camera.

Seven large flat-top trucks are parked there. They have twenty-five- to-thirty-foot-long shiny aluminium caravans with no wheels—trailers the Canadians call them—loaded on their back tray. A crowd of handy-looking, winter-clothed men stand nearby.

I have not the slightest idea what's going to happen.

A bossy man, who I later learn is the camp boss, gives instructions, and soon we're off, heading north. I sit beside a driver in one of the trucks who tells me we are in for a two-day road journey. Should we all make it, we're to meet outside the Fort Nelson Hotel.

We pass through Edmonton, then Dawson Creek in Northern British Columbia to join the Alaskan Highway at Fort St John. I am astonished at the physical beauty.

On a few occasions, when the driver sees others in our convoy of trucks parked at a truck-stop, we stop. Nothing much is said. These blokes have done it all before.

Without any communication between trucks, we arrive outside the Fort Nelson Hotel.

~

Treading lightly is the best thing to do at the Fort Nelson Hotel. Don't stare at anyone. Don't be different. Don't speak loudly, and don't get involved in buying rounds of drinks. Not staring is going to be difficult because an unusual collection of men inhabit the bar of the Fort Nelson Hotel, and I reckon they're all tough. I hear an English accent and wonder why that man's living so dangerously. He's either a fool or very confident that he can handle himself. If he were big and tough-looking it'd be all right, but he's not.

He's shorter than I am, and he's got a stupid haircut that has long strands of hair going from one side of his head to the other in a hopeless attempt to hide baldness. I'm pleased he's amongst the cluster of men next to the cluster I'm in, because I'd be uncomfortable if he were closer. I hear him say that he lives in Mexico, that he used to be in the Royal Navy, that it's his third winter in the Northwest Territory and that he's a good mechanic.

One man in my cluster says to me, 'You and that guy speak the same.'

I say, 'No, we don't.'

And he says, 'Yes, you do.'

I try to not speak loudly but it's difficult. I say to him, 'That man's a pommy and I'm Aussie.'

The Englishman hears me and says, 'Are you Aussie?'

'Yair, I am.'

'Well, I'll be a son of a moose, an Aussie up here. I'm Mike Schonberg; what's your name?'

'Barry … I'm Barry White.' This is exactly what I didn't want. I'm now with someone who's identified himself as different.

'So … you're with Frontier Geophysical?'

'No, The Alberta Trailer Company.'

'What are you? The cook?'

'I'm the bull-cook. And you?'

'I'm the most important person in the crew; I'm the mechanic,' he says in a loud voice.

All the others hear him and they roll up their eyes. One of them says, 'Bullshit.'

Mike hardly takes a breath while he tells me that he joined the Royal Navy as a boy seaman, that he served in submarines, that his submarine was stationed for a year in Sydney and that he now lives in Mexico City.

The smart thing to do is listen without saying anything so he runs out of things to talk about or runs out of breath.

He says, 'There's no work in Mexico that pays decent money so I come up North every year. I hate leaving the wife and kids, but it's her father's fault; he should get me a good job with one of his rich friends. He could do that easily. Then I wouldn't have to come up here and winter with these cowboys.'

'Cowboys?'

'The Canadians. Cowboy is what I call them. They're all quite stupid.'

This man's going to get his face punched in, and so might I if I stay here. I can pretend I'm not listening; I can argue with him or I can leave. I say to him, 'Excuse me, mate, I need to go to the toilet.'

I have a pee, wash my hands and face, and comb my hair. It's better to stay away for as long as I can. Two men come in; we nod, and I know I have to go—lingering in a toilet's asking for trouble.

All conversations in the bar include lots of swearing: fuck, cocksucker, goddamned, bastard, motherfucker and more; sometimes all the words are used in the same sentence. I see an opening to the serving area, so I ease myself between men who want to thump everyone they don't like. Mike's on the other side of the room; I ignore him, but he sees me and yells, 'Hey, Aussie, I'm over here.'

I pretend not to hear, but he comes to me. 'Oh, you've got another beer. You didn't get me one.'

'When I left you hadn't finished.'

'I am now.'

'Yeah, so you have. You'd better get another.' This Englishman's both a loudmouth and a bludger. I rejoin my cluster.

Mike gets a beer and looks for me. He says, 'Hey, you've left me again.'

The Canadian I'm talking with says, 'Oh, here comes the limey.'

The moment Mike arrives, he talks, 'As I was saying, nothing happens in the camp without me. I've got six four-wheel-drive Dodge Power Wagons, a Caterpillar bulldozer, a diesel power generator and …'

The Canadian turns his back on us. I know why.

'… if I don't keep them going, the whole camp stops.'

More men enter the hotel. The clusters are now one big mob. A strong smell of body odour permeates the air, and I reckon it's because the room's heated and hardly anyone removes padded winter clothing. It's really strange to have snow and ice and cold wind outside but sweating bodies inside.

Mike says, 'So you're from Sydney. It's a great city, especially the harbour. The beer's not all that good but the women are. I used to drink at pubs in the Rocks and near Garden Island and …'

This Englishman can talk underwater. It's clear why he was in submarines.

I cringe when he says, 'Canadian's are a bit strange, aren't they?'

'Strange?'

'Different to us, you know. They're like Americans, and us, we're British.'

'I'm not British.'

But you're like the British … reasonable people. We drink tea and drive on the same side of the road and sing *God Save the Queen* and have pounds, shillings and pence. Canada may as well be an American state.'

I may agree with some of the points he's making, but I don't want to hear or discuss it here. I say to him, 'My beer's finished,' and I go to the bar, but he calls out, 'Get me one.'

Before leaving Calgary I had ten dollars, now I've only got a five-dollar bill and loose change, probably seven dollars in total. Plans for my money don't include buying loudmouth Pommies beer. I'm going to spend my five dollars protecting my feet. I need to buy socks.

I say to Mike, 'Better get your own beer because I've got to have a crap.'

He says, 'Son of a moose, you spend a lot of time in the can.'

Instead of going to the toilet, I go outside where the exploration crew stand around, and a collection of idling vehicles trail exhaust gases into the air. They're lined up like a western wagon train, with the camp boss's utility in front, then the power wagons, the shooters truck and the seven trucks with their caravans on the back.

I walk along the street to the small Hudson's Bay shop where I buy five pairs of thick wool socks. When I return to the pub, Mike is outside. He lifts the hinged side of the diesel power generator and takes a look at it.

'God it's one of them,' he says. 'This must be the worst generator they could get.' He closes the lid and says to me, 'Where did you go? I was going to buy you a beer.'

'That'd be unlikely. But if you must know, I went to buy socks.'

'Socks? That'd be unlikely.'

The camp boss counts heads—twice. 'Goddamn, we're one short.'

'Yeah, it's the cook,' someone says.

'Goddamn. I told that guy to not go away. I told him. I told that goddamned cocksucker.'

One of the crew that's sitting on the running board of a power wagon says, 'He went to buy saucepans.'

'Saucepans! Oh hell.'

Off goes the camp boss, and off we go back inside the pub.

Mike gets the owner of the pub in a conversation. He holds his arms out to simulate a submarine diving and says, 'Then we blow just enough ballast to plane beneath the surface and …' He sees me. 'Hey, Aussie come and meet the publican.'

'G'day.'

'Hi, your friend here's showing me how he manoeuvred his submarine.'

'His submarine?'

'Yes, the one he commanded.'

Commandeered is more like it.

I say to the publican, 'Mate, that pom's a bit of a lurk man. You'd be a nong to believe what he tells you.'

The publican doesn't know what I mean.

I wish I had time to explain to him that I've known loads of lurk men, that the building industry is where the world's top lurk men are trained. I was trained there. I'd tell him about the lurk man who stole a builders' square from the ICI Chemicals site in Botany, that he shoved one end of it down his trousers and the other along his arm under his shirt. The lurk man knew he was going to look strange, that the security man would challenge him, so he carried a raincoat over his arm. Everyone was going home, and half way to the security gate, it started to rain.

Someone said, 'Hey, mate, put your coat on.'

The lurk man gave a sick grin and said, 'A bit of rain won't hurt me.' Everyone else ran because we didn't want to get wet, but he walked with a funny walk, as if he were sleepwalking, his arm stretched out in front and his leg stiff.

The security man in his hut looked out at everyone. He knew stuff was being pinched, and he wasn't going to let it happen on his shift, but the lurk man said to him, 'They're afraid of a little rain, but I'm not,' and he walked past the security man with the builders square undetected.

I wish I could tell the publican about truck drivers, and wharfies, and clerks, and police, and all the others who practise lurks in their jobs. That lurk men know how to 'acquire' the things they and their friends want, that nothing is beyond being acquired. That lurk men always have a plausible excuse—they tell very good stories that, according to the lurk-man code, can involve all manner of lies.

Lurk men love nongs, because nongs know nothing and they're easily conned. Anything and everything can be acquired from a nong.

I wish I had time to explain all of this to the publican.

Mike continues. Using a matchstick as his submarine, he says, 'Perhaps if I had some liquid, perhaps a beer, I could show you the emergency dive, the one when I give the order, dive dive *dive*.'

The publican agrees, and Mike says, 'Better get two; one for the Aussie.'

The publican may not be a nong because he tells us about barring two Caterpillar drivers from his pub.

Mike says, 'Cat drivers can be awkward; I remember one who—'

The publican cuts him off—he must reckon it's his turn to hold forth. He says, 'I warned the two Cat drivers about kicking chairs that guys are sitting on but they keep doing it, so I toss them out.'

'Fair enough.'

'About ten minutes later,' he continues, 'I hear engine noises outside, so I go to see what's going on. Those arseholes had started their D8 Cat, had the winch unwound and the steel-wire rope wrapped around the hotel veranda support poles. I'm about to tell them to piss off, but they take up the slack on the rope, and one of them says, "Do we do it?"'

'Jesus, what happened then?' I ask. 'Did you call the Mounties?'

'No. I lifted the ban and invited them inside for free drinks.'

'Very wise; very nousy.' I reckon it's my turn to bullshit. I say, 'In Australia the—'

But the publican interrupts me. He says, 'Then there's the time when Darcy the "shooter" got a bit out of control.'

'He had a gun?'

'No, he's the shooter, the explosives guy in a seismic crew. Darcy sat in that seat over there, and I see him and he sees me, and I get really pissed off because he knows he shouldn't be there; he knows he's been barred from coming in here. I tell him to get out, and all he does is show me the two sticks of jelly he's holding, then he gets a cap from his pocket and he says something.'

'What?'

'There's too much noise for me to hear but I read his lips. He's saying, *"boom."*'

'Boom?'

'Yes, boom. That's what he's going to do, *blow up* my hotel'.

'Jesus. What'd you do? Call the Mounties?'

'No. I poured a very stiff rye whiskey, put it on the bar, beckoned him over, gave it to him and told him he can have as many as he wants.'

I'm still keen to tell some lies about rogue koalas, killer wombats and fighting kangaroos, but the camp boss puts his head in the door and yells, 'You goddamned guys get out.'

Mike says, 'There, I told you I'd get you a beer.'

~

The wagon train of trucks drives down a narrow, smooth, icy road that's like an Olympic bobsled run. Deep banks of snow, pushed there by a road-clearing plough, flank both sides of the trail. Falling powder snow will soon cover the tyre tracks. I'm squashed in the cabin of a truck with the driver, the cook and a bloke who says he's the flunky.

The riding of my clapped-out motor bike on Sydney roads has me unprepared for this adventure. I say to the driver, 'Not much of a road.'

He says, 'This early part's good; wait until we get on the Simpson Trail and the tracks cut last week by the Cats.'

'Rough?'

'The Simpson's rough enough, but as for the tracks? Who knows?'

The sound of a truck horn blowing three times has our driver peering ahead. He says, 'That's the boss telling us there's something on the trail.'

We see a sled towed by four dogs that's pulled off the trail. The Indian on it looks annoyed. He waves his arm, but the truck engines drown out whatever he says.

'The driver says, 'Goddamned Indians; they think they own the trails.'

The flunky says, 'They do, don't they?'

'They used to, now the Government does. This is now *our* road.'

'The Government bought it from the Indians?' I ask.

'No, they took it. We can't have Indians owning land that's got oil. They'd do nothing with it; they'd be content to not touch it; they'd leave it in the ground.'

I feel like saying something, but I might get thrown out of the truck.

We arrive at a junction that has many signs, some hanging from trees, some nailed to trees, some lying against the snow, all of which have roughly written messages. Others, those professionally painted, are on wooden stakes driven into the ground.

I say to the driver, 'How long have they been there?'

'Not long, the boss would've put ours there a few days ago when he went in to see if the campsite's ready. Every seismic crew that's in here this winter puts up signs. It's a bit of a game, though, because crews don't want other crews to know much about where they are. It's to do with the bidding. All the oil companies try to keep their competitors guessing. The less they know the better. Some of those signs are there to confuse; companies want other companies to believe they're somewhere, when they're not.'

I say, 'To confuse? I reckon I am. Why have a sign that's wrong? Wouldn't people get lost; they'd go one way when they should go the other?'

'Yep, that's the way it works. That's what supposed to happen.'

Ahead I see the boss quickly paint over a direction arrow and do another pointing to another trail.

The Frontier Geophysical trail is rough and narrow. We brush against trees and snowdrifts and slide about even though the tyres are fitted with chains. The truck driver takes quick, anxious glances at his rear-view side mirrors, does frequent gear changes to slow and quicken speed, and hardly ever brakes. The truck ahead thumps against snow banks and does fishtail swerves. Our truck does the same, and from comments made by our driver, I realise that all the trucks are having difficulties.

I glance at the cook; he's fingering through food invoices and shaking his head. Occasionally, he says something about prices charged or substitutions made by suppliers for something he ordered. He's completely unconcerned about what seems to me to be our impending death.

The truck driver curses everyone and everything, and says that most of the other drivers can't drive for shit. The wagon train slows. The camp boss stands beside the trail waving his hand, and the truck driver reaches to put on a restraining harness.

I say to him, 'Trouble?'

'No, there's no trouble if the riverbank's not too icy.'

'River bank?'

'Yeah, a branch of the Petitot.'

'There's a bridge?'

'Shit no; there's no bridges up here. The river's frozen over; we cross the ice.'

I look for my restraining harness, but there isn't one.

The truck goes down a steep embankment in low gear. It slides about, but the driver controls it. The one ahead of us doesn't do as well; it slides one way, then the trailer it's towing jack-knifes over the edge. The camp boss swears his head off, and the truck's driver gets out of his truck looking, and no doubt feeling, like a dill. Moments later all the drivers are yelling and pointing and swearing. They quickly set winch ropes around trees, and soon get the impossibly positioned trailer back on the trail. Then we're on the flat river ice, tons of weight on ice of an unknown thickness that will surely break, and we'll all be drowned in freezing water.

Five hours later, we arrive. Our destination turns out to be an area of muskeg flattened by the blade of a D9 Caterpillar.

The camp boss yells orders, and trucks go in all directions, backing into each other and into fallen trees and snow-banks. He tells arseholes to reverse trailers to there, and cocksuckers to reverse to the other side, then he does a count which reveals that the truck towing the ablution trailer is missing.

All the cook cares about is his cookhouse. He knows that if he's not got a hot meal for the crew, he'll be in big trouble, but when he opens the trailer door, he sees pots and pans and everything else on the floor. He blames the flunky for not stowing them properly.

I see Mike rushing about, and I ask him, 'What's the panic?'

'In an hour it'll be dark,' he says. 'The fucking generator has to be running; power leads need to be laid; the cook's got to have light; the trucks have to have their oil sump elements plugged in; two power wagon engines need looking at; it's twenty below zero, and *you* ask what the panic is?'

'Oh. Am I supposed to do anything?'

'If you don't get every oil heater filled and lit, and the cook's trailer connected to bottled gas, and all the beds made, and water connected to the ablution trailer, I reckon the camp boss will kill you.'

'*Make the beds?*'

'Yes, that's one of your jobs.'

'Make the fucking beds? *Not bloody likely*. I don't even make my own bed.'

'Please yourself. But if you don't, you'll be hitchhiking back to Fort Nelson in twenty below and not a thing on the trail but you and wolves.'

Now I'm panicking.

The trailers are positioned in a circle, and I think about movies I'd seen of the American West where Indians attack settlers' wagon trains that are laid out in a circle, so I wonder if there's something I don't know.

I get oil in some of the heaters, but the cook says to me, 'If you don't get the gas bottles connected, and I don't get hot coffee and food for the crew, there'll be trouble.'

I ask him, 'Who makes the beds?'

'What?'

'The beds. Mike tells me I have to make all the beds.'

'You can do that when the gas's connected.'

'The gas can wait. It's the beds *I'm concerned* about. They didn't tell me in Calgary that I have to make beds.'

'Of course you have to make beds. That's the bull-cook's job. But forget about that, get the gas on.'

'Okay, okay, but I'm *not making* fucking beds.'

'If you tell the camp boss that, he'll—'

'He'll what? There's nothing he can do.'

'Isn't there? Being here's like being on a ship. He can do anything he likes. Tell him your gripe, but I know what'll happen, and it won't be pretty.'

A while later, the gas is connected, the lines bled of air, pilot lights lit, the cook has coffee brewing, and I'm still stewing about making the beds.

The ablution trailer arrives with the whole of one side smashed in, and the camp boss goes off his brain. He pushes the truck driver, and the driver pushes him, and the boss king hits him.

I'm still stewing about the beds so I say to the boss, 'About the beds—'

'If you don't get those goddamned beds made,' he says, 'I'm going to kick your arse in.' Then he goes away and gives the truck driver another couple of king hits.

I feel demeaned making others' beds. The camp's hierarchy is structured around authority, physical size and what job is done. I have no authority. I'm average size and build, and my job is second from the bottom; only the flunkey rates below me.

I've been in the Boy Scouts, Police Boys Club, Sea Cadets, Peakhurst Boys Club, rugby league and cricket clubs and I'm a plumber—all masculine activities. I've not had any preparation for what I consider to be non-masculine bottom-of-the-pile status. Nearly everyone in camp will be battling the elements, slaving their guts out doing physically demanding work, and I'm to make beds? I'm supposed to do the soft jobs that a woman might do? If I'm not careful, the men will label me as a weakie; they'll call me names; I'll be the fairy Australian; they might even reckon I'm a poofter. I have to show the crew that I'm their equal, that I'm capable of looking after myself, but how do I do it? I can't do what's done in the movies. I can't pick a fight and knock the toughest man in camp off his perch. I could try, but I'd probably get myself killed. The only way to handle the situation is to swear, so I say shit, fuck, bastard and prick, which are all understood, but other Australian words like galoot, drongo, mongrel, bludger and ratbag are not, so I use Canadian swear words. I quickly get the reputation of being foul-mouthed, but that's better than being a fairy or a poofter.

No one can challenge the camp boss's position as cock-of-the-walk—everyone reckons he's a bastard—but positions below him are competed for. The cook gains high status because he provides for our stomachs; then come the geologists—no one knows what they do, but whatever it is it must be important. Mike comes in next because he's in control of the power generator and without electricity we're buggered. After him is the surveyor—he's the only one who knows where we are, where we are supposed to go and in which direction. The crew rate in the middle with the driller, the shooter, the bulldozer driver and the roughnecks. I should be at the bottom, but I'm an unknown quantity, and I do have responsibility for the gas connection to the kitchen, so the flunky comes in last.

Mike knows his position, but he's accustomed to manipulating British navy officers, so there's a continual struggle between him and the cook for higher status. He tells me how much money he's paid, which is twice as much as me, which, he says, makes him twice as important as me.

It takes one day to establish routines. The exploration crew leaves camp at seven in the morning when it's still dark, then they travel on mostly unused tracks to the prospect where they work in twenty-below-zero temperatures for the next ten hours. They return in darkness at six in the afternoon, completely pissed-off and ready to vent their frustrations on anyone who gets in their way or looks sideways at them. Everything has to be prepared for their soft arrival: hot coffee, hot water, hot trailers, and a crash hot mechanic. Now is when all mechanical problems have to be fixed. The cabin heaters and truck engines which have run continuously for ten hours always have something busted or something that's making a noise. As soon as the trucks arrive, Mike connects power leads to the heaters in the oil sumps, and he's ready to prioritize mechanical repairs. He only ever does what he wants to do.

Now, after the first day working at the prospect, the crew tests everyone who supports them. The cook knows they'll complain about their lunch so he has a special meal prepared. The mechanic knows they'll complain about the smallest problem so he's ready to nod and sympathize. The crew knows they'll complain to each other about each other—they'll bitch about snow being tramped into bunkhouse trailers or about outside gear being thrown on 'their' bunk. I'm prepared for complaints about trailer heaters not being warm enough and beds being badly made. But I'm not prepared for the toilet rush.

How can I know that many of the crew won't shit in the freezing cold? That they wait for a warm toilet, that there'll be a rush to get one of the four, and that those who don't get a seat will bash on cubicle walls, then do their business in a wash basin. I'd have thought that four shower cubicles wasn't enough, that the crew would be anxious to get their sweaty bodies clean, but hardly anyone does.

After the meal few linger near the kitchen; sleep is all they want. Mike has told me about his love of gambling, so he organizes a game of cards, a friendly game not involving money, playing for matches. Mike's a good lurk man; he's got it all worked out how and when he's going to suggest a nickel and dime game, small stuff, as he puts it, just to make it interesting. He knows when he's going to upgrade to a serious game, a game using money that, as he puts it, doesn't make a noise when it hits the table. At first there's few who have the energy to play so he plays two-handed cribbage, then when more show interest, I hear him say, 'Gentlemen, the game's dealer's choice and tens are wild.'

There's mumbling and positioning of the dealt cards, small-value coins bet, then a joyful yell by the winner. Mike says, 'All the winners laugh and tell jokes, and the losers say, "Shut up and deal those bloody cards,"'

Everyone says, 'Yes, that's what happens.'

I'm surprised when Mike takes losing so well, and I think I've misjudged him.

Next morning the crew leaves for another ten-hour day, and Mike and I sit in the warm mess trailer drinking coffee and hearing the cook yell at the flunky.

He says, 'Cobber, we've got to stick together. It's *them* and *us* in this camp.'

'Them and us?'

'Them, the Americans, and us, the British.'

'I'm not British, I'm Australian. And the Canadians aren't Americans.'

'They may as well be; everything they do mirrors America.'

'I wouldn't know; I've not yet been to America, but I reckon the Canadians won't be happy about you saying they're Americans, just as I'm not happy about being lumped in with you pommies.'

'But you have British heritage.'

'*No, I don't*. My great grandfather came from Ireland. We hate the British.'

'But you sing *God Save the Queen*. I've been in picture theatres in Sydney when everyone gets up and sings. Son of a moose, we don't even do that in England, but you Australians do.'

I think about what he says, and he's right. I don't know how I can argue. How can I say Australians are not British when at all public and most private events we all get up and sing about God saving our gracious queen and long may she reign over us?

I say to him, 'Mike, your last name's Schonberg, that means you're not British, you're German—certainly European.'

He says, 'Did you know that the Royal family has German ancestry?'

That can't be correct, so I say to him, 'Bullshit!'

'It's not bullshit. The Queen's German and the Duke of Edinburgh's a Greek.'

'*Oh*.'

Mike gives me titbits of information about himself, almost as if he's testing me, seeing how I react, seeing if I'm surprised or suspicious.

He tells me that during three winters in the Canadian north he doubled his wages by gambling, that he always returns to Mexico on a train because that's where big money gambling's done. I ask him if he cheats, and instead of reacting angrily, he laughs.

He says, 'Bazza, if you're caught cheating up here, you don't go home with all your limbs intact, and if you cheat on a train, you get pushed off between stations, at fifty miles per hour. Of course I can cheat, but I don't; I don't have to, I *always* win.'

I let him teach me to play cribbage using nickels and dimes and after the lesson he writes in his small black notebook that I owe him twenty dollars.

Card games happen nightly after that, and Mike wins large amounts of money from some of the crew. I watch while he roars, 'Son of a moose, I won again,' then he writes their names and how much they owe him in his small black notebook.

Night after night sensible men go on a fruitless chase to win back money they've lost and, nearly always, they end up owing him more.

Most of Mike's mechanical work is done after the crew comes back from the field, but that's when the card games are so he has to devise quick ways of doing the repairs or delaying them. If he's on a losing streak, the repair gets done immediately, but if he's on a winning streak, trucks remain untouched.

He's on a lucky streak when a truck needs a major repair. He says to the camp boss, 'I'll have to take the engine out.'

The boss says, 'Then do it.'

'But the block and tackle needs setting up.'

'Then do it.'

'But I need to rig an 'A' frame.'

'Then do it.'

But he doesn't do it. He hides the 'A' frame pipes under snow then he tells the boss the pipes are missing, and next day they're miraculously found. It's always a battle of wits, but Mike wins most encounters.

There's no undercover, heated area for him to work in. If the job's under the vehicle, he lies on a tarpaulin. If it's an engine problem and it's snowing, he rigs the tarpaulin over the bonnet where he'll do fiddly work using small nuts, bolts and screws. He can't wear gloves, so his hands are bare in thirty below zero temperatures.

He spends a whole night replacing springs on one power wagon, and he says to me over breakfast, 'If that cowboy breaks the rear springs again he can fix it himself.'

I have some sympathy. But how much sympathy do I give a man who has in his little black book my name saying I owe him twenty dollars. I say to Mike, 'Oh yeah. So you're going to tell that big bloke he can fix his own power wagon?'

'Yes.'

'You're full of bullshit. The boss will sack you.'

'Oh, then who'll fix the trucks? Him? You? *The cook?*'

'They'll get someone in Fort Nelson to replace you.'

'How? You saw all the crews ride off into the bush. There's no one left. All the mechanics have gone.'

'They'll get one from Edmonton or Calgary.'

Mike smiles. 'Why do you think they employ me? Eh? Why employ someone who comes from Mexico? I'll tell you why; it's because there's a shortage of mechanics with camp experience. There's plenty that can fix a noisy tappet or clean a carburettor in a nice warm workshop in town. But there's not so many who'll do it out here. Besides they'd need to have diesel experience and know about D9 Cats and diesel-power generators. There's not too many of them. That's where my submarine experience gives me an advantage, power if you like. They'll not get anyone quickly.'

I'm uncertain what to say, so I say, 'Bullshit.'

He's not impressed by my lack of empathy. He says, 'It's all right for you and the rest of the crew. You're all inside in the warmth while I'm in sub-zero temperatures. I have to lay on my back on the ice fixing things that shouldn't get broken in the first place. If those cowboys took some care ...'

I laugh. 'Sub-zero temperatures! That sounds appropriate for a sub-mariner.'

He says, 'Really, it's not a joke. Ah, sod it.' He goes away mumbling to himself.

I have more sympathy for the seismic crew who stay ten hours every day in below-freezing temperatures, where they roll and unroll thick electrical cables from coils strapped to their chests and backs. And for the drilling crew lugging drill-stem pipe and sloshing about in drilling mud and quickly freezing water. I should tell Mike their jobs are worse, but I don't.

He's on the other side of the camp when he yells, 'Son of a moose, tonight I'm going to tell those cowboys I'm not doing repairs that are caused by carelessness. I'm going to tell them I'm not going to lay for hours on the ice under their truck. That's what I'm going to do. I'll tell them to go and get ... what's that Aussie saying about bulls?'

'Go and get a woolly-bull up you.'

'Yep, that's what I'm going to tell them, I'm going to tell them to ... what's that other Aussie saying about birds?'

'Birds?'

'The black birds; you know.'

'Oh, *crows*. It's stone-the-bloody-crows.'

'Yes, that's it; I'll say to them, stone-the-bloody-crows and get a woolly-bull up you.'

'Great; they'll understand that.'

I see him an hour later, and he's muttering, 'Stone the woolly crows and get a bull up you.'

I laugh.

He says, 'You can fucking laugh, but I'm taking them on tonight. I know I can't refuse to fix the trucks but I can make a point.'

I say, 'Good luck. The camp boss will be no pushover.'

'He won't be, but I've got a plan that'll show those cowboys for what they are.'

'Drongos?'

'Ah, that's a good one. I'll use that too. They're drongo kick bulls that want stoning like woolly crows. How's that sound?'

'Great!'

Mike tells the crew what he'd rehearsed, and he gets no reaction. I hear one of them say to Mike, 'Listen, you limey cocksucker, that goddamned truck's heater had better work tomorrow or I'm not going to work. You hear me? I'm not going to be all day without heat.'

Mike tries the mixed-up woolly-bull thing again, and the Canadians have no idea what it means.

Every day now trucks return with more things broken, squeaking, rubbing, or busted, and it's inevitable that the camp boss confronts Mike. Strangely, Mike calmly listens to all his criticisms. He nods, shakes his head and smiles, so I know something's up.

I go close to them and I hear Mike say, 'I agree … I understand … I see … of course.' Then he says to the boss, 'I've got a suggestion. I want to do a study into which trucks get the most repairs, and the causes.'

The boss looks confused and bemused. 'A study? Why, I err … all right; if you think it'll help.'

That evening Mike carries an official-looking clipboard holding sheets of paper on which he's drawn lines, graphs and columns. He struts about the trucks looking at springs and bodywork, then he opens the engine bonnet, sticks his head under and takes notes and ticks items on a check list.

The cowboys have no idea what's happening, but they react predictably, and they don't cooperate. Mike sucks as much as he can from the moment. He nods, says technical mechanical words, and taps engine parts, all the time making notes on his papers. His actions are that of a person responsible for a huge fleet, a fleet as large as New York's taxis.

In the mess trailer, the crew does some of their own scheming. There's no card playing tonight.

The study has consistency for two days, then nothing's the same.

Mike says to me, 'Those cowboys are trying to get at me.'

'How? What are they doing?'

'Something's happening with the distances travelled. Some trucks are doing fifty miles a day. Others are doing only five. There's something rotten in the state of Denmark.'

I've got no idea what Denmark has to do with trucks in the Canadian North West Territory. 'Oh. Shouldn't all the trucks travel about the same distance?'

'Exactly. The sons of moose are disconnecting their speedo cables.' He goes away muttering about a new plan, and I go to make all the bloody beds.

I'm getting on well with the crew. I'm doing what they're doing—goddamning and son-of-a-bitching everything, and when they criticize the goddamned, limey, cock-sucking, son-of-a-bitch of a mechanic, I keep my mouth shut. It's not in my interests to defend him and be alienated by the crew. Besides, there's a developing situation in the cookhouse that gives me cause for concern: the cook and the flunkey are not getting on.

There'd been squabbles from the beginning about unimportant issues like where pots and pans are stored, how long vegetables are prepared before being cooked and the frequency of cleaning floors, but now they're arguing about everything. The camp boss has told the flunkey that in the scheme of things, he's rated at one, whereas the cook's nearly at the top at ninety, and the boss reckons he's a hundred. The outraged flunkey tells the boss that the cook has a secret stash of alcohol, but the boss says, 'I'm the one who gets the supplies from Fort Nelson and I know I've only brought into camp one bottle of cooking sherry.'

The flunky gets no sympathy. No one's got any respect for him because all he does is peel vegetables, wash pots and pans, clean the kitchen, and give the crew dirty looks when they want more hotcakes or eggs, or less mashed potato, turnip and parsnip—jail food's what they call those vegetables.

So the camp boss tells the flunkey he's a liar and he's got to get on with 'his' cook, and that he doesn't give a fuck if he's got to bow and scrape and lick the cook's shoes.

The flunkey has a moan to me, and I say to him, 'Mate, they'll piss you off. You'll have to do some serious crawling, and you have to suckhole to the cook.'

The camp boss asks me, 'Do you like working here?'

I say to him, 'Yeah, I love it.' He's not going to get the truth from me. He's not going to hear me say that I detest making beds, that some of the men are idiots, that the cook's a self-centred, pompous prima donna, that he's a fucking dictator. He's not going to hear that from me, at least not until three months pass when I get my last pay cheque.

He says, 'If something happens to the flunkey, you'll have to help the cook.'

'Something happens? What *could* happen?'

'If there's an accident, or something.'

'Accident?'

'Like, if he was to go.'

'Go where? There's nowhere to go. There's only Fort Nelson and that's a hundred miles away. You're the only one who goes there.'

He's annoyed by my feigned naiveté, and his face goes red. He points his finger into my chest and says, 'Listen to what I'm saying, you fucking arsehole. What I'm trying to tell you is that you might have to do the flunky's job, just for a while, if he goes, just until I get another guy.'

I know that the camp boss can do whatever he wants. I know that my job as bull-cook rates only slightly above the flunkey; that he and I are the dirt and dust in the camp dustpan, the ones and twos in a deck of cards. I have no money and no prospects. My financial worth is zero. The camp boss is the captain of the ship, and he can, if he wants to, maroon me in Fort Nelson. So I'm going to tell him what he wants to hear. I say to him, 'Yeah, I'll do the job … until you get another flunkey.'

Saying that to the camp boss means significant erosion of my leisure time. Time that I need to practise playing my harmonica, which I have to do during the day because the bulldozer driver's tired of hearing squawky notes, and he's threatened to shove the goddamned thing down my goddamned throat. Also, I'm getting used to having a bit of a sleep after lunch, so that'll have to stop. Then there's the cook to contend with, so I say to the camp boss, 'But there's one thing you've got to know; if the cook abuses me like he does the flunkey, I'll kick the son of a bitch in the balls.'

The cook and the flunkey's angry voices can be heard throughout the camp. I hear the cook say, 'You have to stir the goddamned custard. It's always going to have lumps if it's not stirred.'

I hear bashing of saucepans, more yelling, then the kitchen-trailer door bursts open, and the flunkey runs out saying, 'Shove the custard up your arse.'

The cook yells obscenities as runs after the flunkey. I notice custard on his white chef's jacket that's dripping onto the snow. It doesn't look all that lumpy to me.

The flunkey zigzags between trailers, then runs along the trail and takes cover in the trees.

I say to the cook, 'What happened?'

He says, 'That's the last time that son of a bitch's going to be in my kitchen.'

Two hours later the crew return from the prospect. Thirty minutes after that the flunkey's being driven by the boss to Fort Nelson away from the revenge-seeking cook.

That night I wash all the pots and pans and dishes. The custard-encrusted pan is the most difficult to clean.

It's to my great relief that the camp boss returns next morning with a replacement flunkey, a man who was fired by a cook in another camp and who the boss found sitting on the front step of the pub.

The new flunkey's an Italian, he tells me, 'Thata lasta cook isa madaman.'

I ask him why he's a madman.

He says, 'Ia tella him the hama shouldnota cook for a threea hoursa. And he goa crazy.'

I wonder if there's an itinerate band of sacked flunkies who don't get on with cooks wandering the Canadian North.

Peace reigns in the kitchen, but war goes on between Mike and the exploration crew. I reckon he's put himself out on a limb because now no one wants anything to do with him, except to play cards. They all want to win back their money and get their name out of his little black book. The whole lot play as a team who're all out to get him. Away from the card games it's 'them' and 'us'. I want to be in the 'them' group with the exploration crew, but I get lumped into the 'us' group with Mike, the cook and the flunkey. Mike appoints himself as our leader, and he's focusing on achieving his selfish aims.

He says to 'us', 'We have to come up with a plan to expose to the camp boss those cowboys who're stuffing-up my study.'

The cook's not interested in doing that. He says, 'What about doing the important things first? Like exposing the phony complaints being made about my food. We should do something about that. It's more urgent than your stupid vehicle study.'

Mike argues with the cook, and on his say so, the cook gets dumped from the 'us' group. The new Italian flunkey doesn't understand what we're doing, so he's also dropped. Now, instead of being a group, we're a couple, and that might not be for long because I'm not fully convinced that Mike's aims are important.

I say to him, 'You're being a bit melodramatic. After all, it's only some bloody statistics. It's not as though it's important.'

He says to me, 'Aussie, you're either in this with me or you're out with the cowboys. Take your pick.'

I say, 'I reckon I'm mad to be on either side. I don't want to get offside with the crew. They don't think *I'm* the bastard. They reckon *you're* the bastard.'

'Bastard?'

'Yeah, bastard. You're the poncy pom. You're the one who's treating them like drongos. And I tell you what's probably going to happen. First chance they get, they'll beat the shit out of you. In my Irish grandmother's words, they'll give you two black eyes and a pumpkin face, and they'll tear your trousers in a terrible place.'

Mike grins then he laughs. 'Well, son of a moose, that's a mouthful of Aussie slang. Had you said that to anyone else but me, they'd give you a blank stare. They'd not have a clue. Now as I understand it, you're saying they're going to bung on a blue with me, eh?'

'Yair. And how do you know what a blue is?'

'You forget that my submarine was stationed in Australia. I used to hang out in the pubs near Garden Island where there were blues every day. That's where I learnt to use the word 'cobber'. I used to tell the Aussie matelots that their language is not as colourful as our cockney, and that most of their slang came from my lot, the poms.'

'Oh.'

'So don't think for one moment those cowboys will get the better of me. I'm too smart for them. Besides, this is all a game; it's something to make life interesting, a bit of fun … but they don't know that.'

He's fooled me. I took his antics seriously. I suppose I might act in the same way if I had a wife and family thousands of miles away and I missed being with them. I can nearly understand why he does what he does, that it might be a bit of fun. I miss my mother and brothers and sister, but it's not the same as having a wife and kids. Perhaps I shouldn't be too critical of him. Perhaps I need a diversion, something to get my mind away from making beds. Perhaps the crew, the 'thems', also need it.

That night there's yet another confrontation between Mike and the 'thems' that should develop into a fight, and it surprises me that they get satisfaction by using abuse, but it's surely got to go further.

~

It's seven in the morning. The crew, as per normal, are bad tempered and uncommunicative while they prepare for a day's work at the prospect. The activity is not unlike preparation for a grand prix race. The shooter's truck waits at the explosives' safe where it's carelessly loaded with enough jelly to blast us all to kingdom come, and in the recording truck, the scientific boffins check their dials and gauges and instruments. The crew loads sensitive geophones that have been repaired, and they untangle and rewind long lengths of thick electrical cables. Oil-sump heating elements are disconnected; fuel tanks are filled; tyres are checked, then the trucks are lined up with engines idling while the crew eat their breakfast. The crew build their own lunch, so the cook has laid out on a table plates of meats, thawed seafood, salads, freshly baked bread and cakes, and anything else he reckons they'd like or he wants to get rid of. When he first did this, everyone took too much food and the camp boss chipped him. But the cook knows men; he knows they'll settle, that after a few days they take only what they'll eat. And he's correct.

During breakfast there's not much eye contact, and except for an occasional grunt there's hardly any conversation. That's the way everyone wants it. Mike's busy outside tuning rough-idling engines and checking rear springs. I keep out of the way because it's nousy not to be anywhere near the grumpy bulldozer driver or anyone who wants to thump someone they'll not see for the rest of the day.

Those who are smart have a major toilet stop before they leave, and few, if any, bother to clean their teeth. There's not going to be any kissing where they'll be.

The camp boss sets a good example by uttering ape-like grunts, then he pushes used plates onto the floor and orders the Italian flunkey to clean them up. He gorges a huge stack of hotcakes with three soft-fried eggs on top and a veil of maple syrup over it all and dripping into a lake of the same syrup. It's a sickening sight.

He drinks his coffee in gulps then he stands and roars. 'Okay, *you guys*, let's do a day's work.'

This is when I venture outside, especially today, because Mike's got his new plan going. I see him with his head under the engine bonnet of a power wagon that's causing him the most trouble.

The Canadian cowboy driver says to him, 'Limey, I hope you've got that goddamned spring fixed, this time.'

Mike says nothing. He gives the springs a cursory glance, then he goes to each tyre, gives it a kick and listens. Whatever he's doing looks very professional.

The trucks do a kind of Le-Mans-style, standing-start leaving of camp, and I hear Mike call out, 'Take your usual care.' Then he says to me, 'We'll be seeing them soon.'

Because the cook and flunkey are often the only ones in camp, the two-way radio is located in the mess trailer. Sometimes I muck around with frequencies and change channels trying to find something interesting, but all I hear are guarded, coded even, conversations. Frontier Geophysical and all the other exploration crews' geological results will be used by oil companies to decide if they bid for a prospect, and how much they'll bid. Some crews have their prospects marked in a grid pattern that only they know and competing camp bosses spend many hours trying to fathom.

Sometimes I hear conversations about accidents; other times there's banter about ice hockey teams and sex.

It's certain our radio's in the best location, because if there's an accident, the cook can rush to it with hamburgers or cake and hot coffee.

Mike, the cook and I are having third and fourth cups of coffee when a voice on the radio says, 'Mobile to Frontier base ... mobile to Frontier. Over.'

It's the boss's voice.

Most often, anyone near the radio ignores it, because the caller will know that whoever answers is having coffee when they should be working. Surprisingly, Mike takes the call. 'Frontier base to mobile; we read you. Over.'

'Mobile to base; there's some trouble with the Cat's hydraulics. Get out here in the spare truck and get it fixed. Now. Over.'

Mike's got a big grin. 'Base to mobile; advise your location. Over.'

The boss sounds pissed off. 'Mobile to base; Mike you fucking well know where we are. I told you an hour ago; we're at the start of grid six. Over and out.'

Mike rubs his hands. 'Son of a moose; the plan's working.'

'What plan?'

He glances at the cook, and the cook knows he's not wanted.

'I'll tell you on the way. Come on let's get the gear. Let's go.'

I say to him, 'I'm going nowhere. I've got my jobs, and the beds have to be made.'

Nothing I've ever done has depressed me more than the feeling I have when making the beds. The exploration crew's work is difficult and tough but it's satisfying; they're doing a *man's* job.

When I enter the crew's bunkhouse trailers, I'm questioning why I'm doing work a woman would normally do. Obviously, they can't have women in an all-male camp; they'd be too much of a distraction. The cook tells me that I'm the youngest bull-cook he's seen in a camp, that generally old men do the job. That most of them are no-hopers who don't care what work they do. But I reckon they'd react the same way as me about this crew's disgusting habits. They throw their stinking work clothes on the floor; their bed sheets reek of perspiration; mud off their work boots soils their blankets. and worst of all, there's girlie magazines that they've used for sexual excitement. I'm now not making a bed without wearing leather gloves, and even then, the beds get roughly made.

I have no option. It's work here or nowhere.

Mike says, 'But you've got to come with me. I need you. You're part of the plan.'

'I don't care. What if the Cat repairs take all day? What happens then? We'd get back to camp late and there won't be time to get all my jobs done.'

'But mate, you must come. *Please.*'

He's pleading so there's much I don't know. There's more in this than meets the eye. I say to him, 'I'll come with you on one condition: you make some of the beds.'

'What! Me make the cowboys' beds? Not blooming likely.'

'Okay, then, off you get. Go to find the bulldozer alone. I really don't care.'

I can almost hear his mind ticking. His face shows the angst of wondering 'will I, or won't I?' He says, 'All fucking right; I'll help make the beds, but only because I want to. You hear, only because I want to, not because of any pressure from you.'

'Right; It'll take half an hour. You make the beds in the six-bunk trailer. That's the easiest.'

Of course it's not the easiest; it's the hardest. It's the one that stinks, the wanker trailer. Pigs live in there.

I'm surprised that Mike loads few tools. I know nothing about bulldozer hydraulics, but I do know everything's big, so he should need hammers and large spanners and tubing and oil.

I wonder how he has the knowledge and confidence to speed along the trail because he told me it's one he'd not previously used. He approaches blind corners at high speed when he should slow, and he slows long before there's a gully or tree stump. We pass trails branching off to the left and right that are covered in deep snow, so it's certain they haven't been used this winter. But other trails have prints—a wolf or larger animal? Could they be human prints? Where do they lead? Do they lead to sites like ours but from winters past, or might there be an Indian camp?

We turn onto a newly cut trail that has trees torn from the muskeg and pushed to each side. Is this the trail we should be on? There are tyre tracks, but are they from our crew, or were they made by others months earlier? I think about stories of people lost in the Australian outback, and I can't help making comparisons. There, like here, is no place to be uncertain. There, like here, tyre tracks made by others should not be followed unless there's good reason. We might easily go in the wrong direction, travel ten miles, be caught in a big snow storm and get lost in a white out.

A story told in camp is about two seismic workers taking a wrong track, having engine trouble then spending a night outside. They start a fire, feed it with every part of their vehicle that's burnable, thaw frozen trees then burn them. Next day they follow their tyre marks, but they get them mixed up with other tyre marks and they get lost, and one of them dies.

Mike says to me, 'What are you doing?'

'It's a map. I'm drawing lines for the different tracks we travel, in case we get lost.'

'Lost? *Me*? I've sailed submarines around the world. We sailors have a built-in compass. I know exactly where I am and where I'm going.'

'Oh yeah? I suppose the captain of the submarine regularly asked you for advice, you, a diesel mechanic that has no fucking idea about navigation. If you know about navigation and you've got an in-built compass, what direction are we going now?'

He looks out the window. 'North, we're definitely going north.

'Great; so there's only a thousand miles between us and the North Pole. Mate, I'm doing my map.'

We come to a junction that has many tyre marks which confirms it's the wrong trail, and a bit further on we find the right one.

I say to Mike, 'In what direction are we going now?'

'South.'

'Thank, Christ. If that's so, we're heading for America and warm weather.'

I'm relieved when I see the mobile drilling rig in the distance.

Norman the driller says, 'What are you guys doing away from the comfort of your warm trailers?'

Mike says, 'A spot of bother with the Cat, old chap. We're here to save the day. Any idea where it is?'

I hate the patronizing language he's used, and I say to him, 'Why the overkill on your accent? Do you enjoy having these blokes hate you?

The poor buggers are slaving in the snow and ice handling heavy drill pipe and you ...'

I don't finish because Norman talks over me saying, 'Hey, you limey bastard, piss off.'

My sentiments exactly.

Fresh Caterpillar tracks on the trail lead west, so we follow them. I say to Mike, 'What's this new plan you spoke about?'

He doesn't answer. I don't push him because we're on a very dodgy trail, and I don't want to crash and die.

Bulldozers cut trails through the muskeg at exact locations decided upon and marked by the surveyor. He and the chainman have the loneliest of jobs. Every day they go into virgin bush with their theodolite, tape measures, wooden pegs, heavy hammer and rolls of coloured ribbon. They bush-bash through deep tracts of snow, marking where the bulldozer driver must cut new trails, and they mark points where the driller bores shot holes. Only once did I have to assist the surveyor, and that was enough for me: I couldn't wait to return to my 'women's-work'. It took only one day to be convinced that surveying was not for me.

The chainman told me his greatest fear is wolves. This part of Canada has few animals apart from wolves and rabbits. During summer when the ice and snow melt, thousands of square miles become a stinking quagmire that's called muskeg, and any larger and less mobile animal than a wolf dies in the thick, slimy, bug-infested ooze. Rabbits, being small and light, manage to exist and eat little, which is just as well, because there's little to eat in winter, but the wolves eat the rabbits. It's not difficult for a wolf to find where the rabbits run, because rabbits mostly use the same track and the snow gets compacted. A wise wolf—and most are wise—simply hang about the track and wait for dinner to amble past.

The surveyor and chainman often see wolves, but the wolves show little interest; they'd rather have an easily caught rabbit. But they're there, and just like sharks in Australian waters, they're feared. Wolf tracks are easy to see in winter. There's four vertical leg holes forced into the snow followed by the mark of their underbelly dragging over the snow. Wolf howls have great psychological effect, and few humans alone in the bush don't have fears.

The chainman told me that his greatest fear is when he has to shit in the open. He said, 'Somehow a goddamned wolf knows that when a human's squatting they have no defence.'

I said to the chainman, 'If that happened to me, I'd be the only Australian with the epitaph, 'Killed by a wolf while shitting'.

He said, 'You'd be famous.

Mike's twisting the steering wheel, and the power wagon's weaving around large clumps of tree and snow. I say to him, 'Is this supposed to be a freshly cleared trail?'

He says, 'It will be when the Cat driver does his back run. At the end of the day, he'll turn around and do a clearing cut.'

Minutes later we hear, then see the bulldozer gouging away at the bush.

'I'm stopping here,' Mike says. 'We'll wait until he sees us.'

'But he's a quarter of a mile away.'

'Yes. But if he decides to reverse, he's not going to look behind; he's just going to back up and anything there gets squashed.'

Yeah, it's a good idea to stop here. I don't know what'd be the most unlikely epitaph: killed by a wolf while shitting or killed by a reversing bulldozer.

Mike gives a long blast on the power wagon horn, but there's no reaction from the bulldozer driver. He says, 'Most of them are deaf.'

I say, 'And they're big blokes. I see him in camp but he never says anything.'

'They're big because they sit all day, and they look bigger because they have to wear a lot of clothes. Can you imagine what it's like jockeying that big D9 around at thirty below zero?'

'No. He can have it all to himself.'

'I can't even get him to play cards. All he wants to do is lie on his bunk.'

'Yeah, I know. And he doesn't take his dirty boots off, either, there's always mud on his blankets.'

'Well, here's your chance to tell him, because he's seen us. Why don't you tell him right now to take his boots off before he gets onto his bunk?'

'Yair, *as if.*'

Mike drives the power wagon to where the bulldozer waits, and I hope that he doesn't use any of the 'old chap' English talk. He says, 'How's the hydraulics?'

The bulldozer driver says, 'What? Can't hear you.'

'How's the hydraulics?' Mike yells in his ear.

'How's what?'

I now understand why few want to drive the big D9 and why they're paid big money.

Mike yells into his ear, 'Thanks for asking the boss to call me out. I owe you one.'

The man frowns, one big roll of skin above his eyebrows comes down to cover the top of his eye sockets, skin on his cheek bones goes up, and his eyes become small evil-looking slits on his face. He says to Mike, 'Piss-off limey.'

The man's exactly the same here as he is in camp: gruff-mannered and angry. I reckon his order to piss off should be obeyed, immediately.'

I say to Mike, 'Come on, let's go.'

We watch the bulldozer driver slowly climb up to the driver's seat of his big yellow beast. I now partly understand the man's attitude. Anyone who sits alone for ten hours with that huge engine roaring in their ears doesn't want small talk at the end of the day.

I say to Mike, 'Is he a wrestler?'

'No, why?'

'That wide leather belt around his waist. It looks like a world championship-wrestling belt, it's like the one Chief Little Wolf wore at the Sydney Stadium.'

'Little Wolf? Never heard of him. That belt's a kidney protector. Those blokes have a lot of trouble because they're bouncing around a lot, so they wear a belt.'

'Oh, well, he's big enough to be a wrestler.'

Puffs of smoke come from the engine's exhaust chimney, and the bulldozer reverses at us. Mike's earlier warning is correct: they don't look behind. The huge thing slews left, the front blade drops and it easily pushes down trees. Then it reverses, and I'm ready to abandon ship. It stops barely three feet from us, then it goes forwards. Mike drives the power wagon into the gap in the trees, quickly reverses, then drives away.

He says, 'Nice bloke that. He knew we'd have trouble turning, so he made it easy for us.'

I ask, 'Why are we here? There's no trouble with the bulldozer's hydraulics.'

'Of course there's not. I asked the dozer driver to get the boss to call me out. It's part of my plan. We need to have a reason to be out here. Now we can check the speedometers on all the power wagons. Get it?'

'No.'

'Look; I've taken a record of our mileage, so tonight I compare it with the cowboys, and if it's different, that proves to the boss that they're deliberately—'

'Jesus Christ, are you telling me that you've brought me all the way out here to do that, to play childish games?'

'Yes, good isn't it?'

'Bad, isn't it? We're here just for you to prove a point, so that's why you brought so few tools.'

'Yes. This is my day … er, our day, cobber.'

'You're a vindictive bastard. I want no more part in this, and don't call me cobber; it's an Australian word and shouldn't be used by pommies. Right? Use it once more and I'll hit you.'

During the drive back to camp, he and I say nothing, which is just as well because there's a fierce blizzard and near whiteout conditions.

Thirty minutes later the crew, who've been forced to stop work, arrive back in camp.

There's little for me to do. I fill the trailer heaters with fuel oil and top up the fuel tank on the power generator.

Some of the crew—it should be all—take showers. Some of the crew—it should be all—remove dirty work clothing, and some of the crew lie on their bunks.

I hear angry voices and wonder if I should investigate. It'll be none of my business. Someone's said something that someone's taken exception to, or someone used the wrong soap, or someone's girlie magazine has been taken, or someone's farted in a trailer. I hear my name mentioned, so it *is* my business. I open the trailer door and I see two of the crew wrestling on the snow; one of them has a bowie knife. There's lots of cursing and swearing. Whoever they're talking about is a bastard, a cocksucker, a son of a bitch, a cunt and a prick.

Provided neither of them get stabbed, its good end-of-the-day entertainment.

Then, amongst the cursing and swearing, I hear my name, but why? It's got nothing to do with me. I take a step backwards. The fighters see me, and they stop wrestling. They're very angry men. One of them says, 'There's the bastard,' and he points his bowie knife at me.

I'm reasonably certain they're not angry with me, but I don't take a chance. I retreat—quickly.

They are angry with me, but why? I start running, and they're up and after me. They slip and I slip, but I stay in front. We're now in darkness, and I reckon I've got a comfortable lead on them, so I hide behind a large bank of snow.

I'm trying to fathom why I'm their target. There's no reason I can think of, but even so, discretion seems to be the better part of valour.

I'm winded, each outgoing breath is a short-lived vapour mist. I hear my heart pounding and realise I'm wearing indoor clothing. My body shivers. I don't yet feel cold, but I soon will. I say to myself, 'This is ridiculous.' I consider yelling to them that I did nothing, but it'd be stupid to disclose my hiding spot.

Again I'm thinking about epitaphs: killed with a bowie knife by two crazy Canadians. It's not good.

'Are you there, cobber … Cobber, are you there?'

It's Mike calling me, but is it a trap?

Snow's now pelting down. I feel it building up on my head, collecting on my eyebrows, and hitting my cheeks. I can't stay here. I must tell him where I am, so I poke my head over the snow bank and say, 'G'day, have those crazy Canadians gone?'

Mike throws me a parka and says, 'They've gone. They're back in camp.'

'Have you got any idea what that was about? I've done nothing to them. There's got to be some kind of mix-up. There's no reason they'd want to put a knife in me … is there?

In the darkness I can just see Mike's face and he has a guilty look. He says, 'Cobber …'

I must be recovering my confidence because I say to him, 'Don't fucking-well call me cobber.'

'Cobb … oh, all right then, mate; there's something I should tell you.'

'What? Tell me before I freeze to death.'

'Ah, this afternoon when I helped make the beds, I realised one of the beds was the cowboy's, the one giving me all the trouble, so I … ah, I decided to make his life uncomfortable.'

'Yeah?'

'Well, I ah, I went to the rubbish bins and I got some—you know, that's where the rabbits go to eat the food scraps'.

'Yeah.'

'So I got a good load of their shit and I—'

'You *didn't;* don't tell me you—'

'Yes, I did. I put the whole load in the cowboy's bed.'

'Christ. You dumb bastard.' I walk back to camp, and he follows me like a naughty puppy.

He says, 'Not only his bed; I threw some in his clothes drawers as well. I was on a roll. I mean, they were frozen; they were just like little marbles. I guess that after a while the heat in the trailer made them very sloppy.'

He's now smiling, and I'm fuming. I aim a punch at his nose but connect with his cheekbone and feel pain in my wrist.

He says, 'Son of a moose, cobber; that hurt.'

3 April 1961
Calgary.
Dear Mum
Last Tuesday night the party chief told us we are breaking camp and going out of the bush next morning. We all got up at 1.30 a.m., had breakfast and were underway at 3.00 a.m. I had to stay until the last truck hooked up to the last trailer, so I didn't get to Fort Nelson until 10.30 a.m.

The whole crew stayed in Fort Nelson overnight where we did some partying. Next morning we set out for Fort St John, arriving at 9.00 p.m. What a day that was. Everyone's happy to see the last of the bush, Fort Nelson and Dawson Creek.

It's great to be back in Calgary, to be clean again and to wear normal clothing.

As I write the winds are blowing at forty miles an hour, and a big snowstorm is expected ... in April?

Love Barry.

1960, North West Territory: The Simpson Trail Junction.

Twenty miles from camp and not quite making it across a frozen lake.

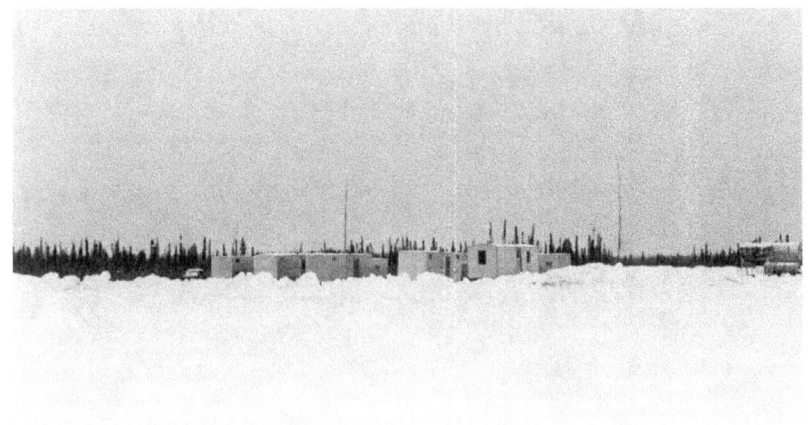

Seismic Camp.

Mike, 'Son of a Moose', Schonberg on the NW Territory border.

Barry and Mike at the NW Territory border.

Barry and Dodge Power Wagon.

Chapter Five

The seismic camp boss struts about because he thinks he's the King of the Castle and that no one will challenge his authority, which is mostly correct, but the boffins know they have power.

They prove this when the most boffin of the boffins, the man who's the interpreter—the one who can tell what's underground—orders the surveyor to map and mark new trails in virgin territory on the other side of the prospect. When that's done, he's going to order the Caterpillar bulldozer driver to go cut new trails.

The camp boss objects. He says, 'That means that when the new trails are cut, the whole camp will have to move. That area's six miles from here at the other end of the prospect. If we don't move camp my guys will need to travel an hour before they can start work.'

All the interpreter says is, 'Richfield Oil wants it done.'

And straight away we're getting ready to move camp.

The title 'interpreter' is very impressive, but I don't rightly know what it means. After the crew return to camp each afternoon, the interpreter goes to the laundry trailer where he uses photographic processing equipment to develop long strips that have lots of fluctuating lines that are supposed to represent what's under the ground. When I ask how the lines get there, he rambles on about shot shock waves racing underground, hitting rocks of different densities and then bouncing back to ground level. He says to me, 'See that there?' and he points to what could be marks a blowfly has made, 'Well, that tells me the rock is pre-Cambrian.'

I don't know how he knows that, or even what he means. What I do know is that he's a bloody nuisance, because I've now got a profitable sideline of washing clothing for some of the seismic crew, and I need to hang it to dry where he hangs his long strips of what's supposed to be underground. One day he's got his strips hanging, and I want to hang clothes, so I bundle his strips up. When he sees what I did, he goes off his brain and says I spoilt a whole day's exploration and I'll be sacked, but that doesn't happen because all the strips are dry, and I knew that.

I begin to understand the importance of the strips when I see them being placed in a locked cabinet and then taken by the camp boss to Fort Nelson in security packs addressed to Richfield Oil.

Moving camp must be complicated because nearly everyone's in a panic. They're all talking about what needs to be prepared and how quickly it has to be done, and in what order. Someone says that the Alberta Trailer office in Calgary needs to get four prime-mover trucks here to tow trailers to the new site, and someone else says that's wrong, they'll need eight.

There's also a rumour that a light plane carrying Richfield Oil 'big bosses' will arrive tomorrow, and the camp boss confirms this by panicking. He says in a voice that must be heard a hundred miles away, 'What! *Tomorrow*! Goddamn! How can I get the goddamned Cat here to make an airstrip, *by tomorrow*!'

Then the Cat driver explodes. It's the first time I hear him put more than a few words together. He says to the camp boss, 'What! You want me to ride the goddamned Cat from six goddamned miles away to here, then flatten goddamned snow on the goddamned lake so a goddamned plane can land?'

'Yes. It'll be here tomorrow,' the boss says.

'Goddamn. You want me to do all that, and you want it done overnight?'

'Yes.'

'Then, when I've done it, you want me to ride the goddamned Cat another goddamned six miles to the new goddamned area to flatten a new goddamned campsite?'

'Yes. It has to be ready in two days.'

'Well, fuck you,' the bulldozer driver says, and it looks like that's the end of story.

The camp boss explodes. He calls the bulldozer driver a goddamned useless arsehole and if he doesn't get the goddamned son of a bitch Cat here, he'll get the fucking thing himself.

~

I'm looking forward to the landing of the plane that's just buzzed the airstrip, because I reckon it'll crash or break the ice and sink in nearly freezing water. It drops height suddenly, then it rises, and then, slowly and carefully, its skis touch the lake ice and plumes of snow shoot away from the skis. When it stops, the interpreter assists grim-faced men out of the cabin, and because I'm standing near and because they don't know I'm just the lowly bull-cook, they give me an American, 'Hi'.

Two hours later they get back on the plane, and I watch while it sits there having the guts revved out of its engine, the propeller drawing snow up and forcing it behind in fluffy sheets. Then it's as if hundreds of elastic bands restraining it are released; the plane springs forward with its engine roaring and drawing even more snow from the lake top, then it's in the air, and it's goodbye Richfield big bosses.

~

A truck ahead of the one I'm in that's towing a bunkhouse trailer speeds at an incline, but it's too steep and it slows, then stops, and then it begins to slide back.

The man beside me says, 'Shit! It's going to hit us.'

Our driver brakes. His truck skids to a stop. He attempts a controlled roll backward, but the trailer jack-knifes and crashes into a snow bank. He says, 'God-dammit.'

I watch the trailer sliding at us. 'Fucking hell, it's going to ...' It just misses us, and stops to teeter over a deep gully.

The camp boss runs from his truck, god-damning and cock-suckering everyone. I'm laughing, but he doesn't see me.

Some broken wheel chains are removed from the trailer, then everyone's around talking about blue ice and black ice and saying, 'We ought to ... We got to ... You've got to ...' The camp boss tells them they're mad, and he orders slings to be attached and winch ropes looped around the biggest trees.

Eventually we get back underway and the track becomes flat. I say to our driver, 'It's a smooth trail.'

'We're on the lake.'

'I hope it holds us.'

He says, 'If it held the Cat it'll hold us.'

I hope he knows what he's talking about.

The new campsite looks the same as the old one, and just like at the old camp, trailers are positioned in a wild-west wagon-train circle of defence. After the experience of the first camp, I know what I must do. Immediately, I connect gas to the cookhouse and fill the trailer heaters with oil, then light them. Mike gets the power generator running, so now we have power, warmth and hot food—the three ingredients that make the crew happy.

With the new campsite comes a remarkable uplift of spirits. Everyone's civil, even the camp boss is smiling, and the bulldozer driver says, 'Hi, Aussie'—the first words he's spoken to me.

I reckon this new spirit is because we acted as a team, and we all depended on each other, but one of the seismic crew says it's because we crossed a sacred Indian lake and we're now on Indian lands which have good energies. Whatever the reason, the Czechoslovakian bloke's getting on with everyone; the American's not boasting as much; Mike is not going on about pommy superiority; and the cook's not fighting with his flunky. Yet.

After-supper gatherings in the dining trailer are jovial. Mike's not always winning card games; jokes are told—even the punch lines are listened for—and best of all, yarn spinning is done. One bloke says he drove from Calgary to Edmonton during a snowstorm and made it in two hours—that's got to be bullshit. Then another bloke says he did it in one-and-a-half hours—that's definitely bullshit. Huge elk and deer are hunted and trout too large for a frying pan are caught. Those boasts are passé when bigger and angrier elk are hunted and trout are caught that don't fit in the back of a pick-up truck.

Men tell of feats of strength, of eating, of money made and lost, and of sexual conquests, and then others better them. Canadians are disadvantaged because other Canadians know when something's an outrageous lie, but for Mike and me, it's open slather—carte blanche.

One man tells an outrageous story about a giant grizzly bear that does everything an army can do, and when all the Canadians nod to support him, I know I'm being had, but I don't tell them I know.

So then I'm off. I've got mobs of kangaroos terrorizing farmers; swarms of taipan snakes invading a town; and a huge school of tiger sharks destroying a fishing fleet. Mike supports my lies, and then he's off.

He says, 'In the Royal Navy, we trained whales to escort submarines through mine fields.'

And I say, 'Yeah, I heard about that.'

Then he says, 'When our submarine was in Cape Town, a huge school of piranha fish attacked it.

And I say, 'I also heard about that.' Canadians seem not to know that piranha fish live in South America.

Soon no one believes anything that's said. This frustrates the American because he's telling us about using a bow and arrows to hunt, which I know is true because he's shown me photographs of him holding a shiny trophy that he'd won.

Because the Canadians know little about Australia, I attempt a final yarn. I say, 'Hunting is taught to all young Australians. In fact, my father used to carry me in his backpack when he hunted.'

Mike asks, 'What age were you?"

'Less than two. It was before I could walk. Dad used to reckon that kids needed to learn early.'

Mike says, 'That's true; I was told that when I was in Australia.'

The American believes me, but the Canadians will take more convincing, so every opportunity I get I reinforce my yarn.

A Canadian asks, 'Aussie, how would you catch a moose?'

'That'd be easy, I say. I'd use good bait. I'd use … I'd use sponge cake.'

'Sponge cake!'

'Yeah, sponge cake. Research by, ah, the University of Sydney veterinarians has found that animals have a sweet tooth, and sponge cake is what most animals like best.'

A Canadian says, 'You're full of shit.'

Which I am, but Mike bursts in with, 'What he's saying is true. I know because I read a story in an Australian newspaper about that.' He then goes on and on, establishing credibility for my yarn, and I wish he'd shut up. But he doesn't shut up, he says, 'I tell you what, let him prove it. Challenge him to catch a moose.'

He's definitely gone too far; there's no way I can catch a moose. They're bloody big things with big horns coming from their heads and they're dangerous, but I'm prettysafe because no one has seen a moose around here. The great American hunter, Davy Crockett, couldn't even catch a moose here. He'd have to be content catching wolves or rabbits.

The cook says, 'I'll make him a sponge cake.'

And everyone says, 'Yeah.'

I say, 'It'd need to be an Australian-style sponge having cream between layers and loads of passion fruit icing on top,' which I'm thinking the cook can't possibly do.

He says, 'I'll look for the recipe in my international recipe book.'

I'm stuck with Mike's stupid challenge.

~

In the new prospect area, the seismic crew work their guts out for ten, sometimes twelve, hours every day. I've worked out a system that has me completing my jobs in three hours so there's plenty of time for me to read borrowed magazines. I practice playing my harmonica, or drink coffee while discussing with the cook, or with his flunky, and with Mike about our solutions to world affairs. The flunky's a difficult person to discuss serious issues with because he's for dropping nuclear bombs on any country that doesn't do what 'we' tell them to do. So he's got India and Pakistan and most of South America and all the Arabs and definitely Russia destroyed. Mike's all for sending in the British Navy, especially the submarines, and the cook doesn't care what happens. All of them say that it doesn't matter much what Australia does because we haven't got all that *much* to do *much* with. I reckon that's not true, and when I tell them that, proportionally, more Australians were killed in World War One than were killed from any other country, they say we must have been careless, and I get pissed off because my uncle Harry was wounded in France.

There's much better things to do than argue about world affairs, so when I see a pair of snowshoes in the camp boss's trailer, I ask him if I can use them.

Everyone laughs at my first attempts because I try to work out right from left snowshoe, and there isn't any right or left. Then I put one snowshoe over the other one and I fall over; then I don't lift my legs high enough and I trip; then I turn around using jumping moves, and they reckon I look stupid, that I look like a kangaroo hopping. But I don't care because these snowshoes are my excuse to get away from the complications of discussing world affairs.

Along the trail a few hundred yards, there's a different world; the noise of the power generator doesn't dominate, and there's no one to laugh at my snowshoe stumbling. I venture off the trail into deep snow, and I do very well until the snowshoes get caught on bits of fallen trees, making me fall over. Snowshoe imprints in the snow are easy to follow back to the trail, but to make certain I don't get lost, I steal some surveyor's ribbon and tie it to trees as markers so I can go further into the bush.

Small tracks on the snow show animal activity. Some may be from field mice, many are from rabbits, but there's a bigger track that must be from wolves.

I've got city knowledge of Australian wild animals. I once saw a kangaroo grazing in a paddock; I've seen dead wombats squashed onto the Pacific Highway, and at an animal farm west of Sydney an emu pecked at my arm. I know a bit about animals from other countries because I've often visited Sydney's Taronga Park Zoo where a llama spat at me, and where, after riding the cradle on an elephant's back, I stood in its huge shit.

What I know most about are snakes and lizards and spiders and frogs and rabbits; all of those are seen in the suburbs. But I've never seen a wild pig or buffalo or dingo, nothing that has four legs that can hurt humans. Wolves can hurt humans.

I hear from the seismic crew comments such as, 'How did you go today Aussie? Did you get a moose?' And, 'How's the big white hunter from down under?' But I'm not concerned about the sarcasm because I'm having fun. I'm playing a game.

I say, 'Today I was close to a bloody big moose but I was upwind, and it got my scent and it ran away. Or, 'I heard stampeding hooves, so I reckon I was close to the herd.' I tell them all manner of rubbish.

Something that's not rubbish that I tell them is, 'There are more rabbits in one Australian state than all of Canada or America.'

The American says, 'More than we've got in Texas?'

'Jesus, we've got *more* rabbits in a big paddock than what's in bloody Texas.'

The American says, 'That's a load of crap,' and I know I can't let him get away with saying I'm talking crap.

Mike can sniff moneymaking opportunities, so he says, 'If you blokes want to put your money where your mouth is, I'll take the bets, I'll back the Aussie.'

A Canadian says, 'How can we prove who is right? We ain't got no books up here; we can't telephone anyone to check his story.'

As evidence of rabbit knowledge, I tell them about the pommies bringing rabbits to Australia so they had something to hunt, and Mike says, 'Oh yeah, blame us English.'

Then I tell them about the myxomatosis disease that was introduced to kill billions of the little bastards. And I tell them about the longest fence in the world, the dingo fence, which I say is the rabbit fence. And I tell them that farmers and their dogs herd thousands of rabbits into wire enclosures and then club them to death, and I tell them about large tracts of land so riddled by rabbit burrows that the land collapses.

They don't believe any of this. I tell them that I and most Australian kids kept pet rabbits. They say, 'If everyone hates rabbits so much, why keep them as pets?'

Mike says, 'The kids ride the big ones to school. The small ones are eaten. Australians love stewed rabbit.'

The American shuts up, and the Canadians are very sceptical. One of them says, 'If you know so much about rabbits, catch some and let the cook make you a stew. Go on.'

Everyone's saying, 'Yeah.'

So I have to do it.

In the Sydney suburb of Peakhurst all the kids tried to catch rabbits, but unlike our fathers and older brothers who used a twenty-two rifle or a strong-spring rabbit trap, we had to use wire snares. Occasionally our fathers invited us kids to go with them on the train to Penrith or Gerringong to see them knock off a few bunnies, but more often than not we'd be left at home.

Few of us succeeded in snaring a rabbit, but that didn't stop us from trying. We dreamed of walking down Baumans Road holding a rabbit by the ears and saying to Mum or Dad, 'I've caught a pair.' And that's the confusing thing about rabbits: one is called a pair when we all know that two's a pair. The rabbito man who comes in his horse and cart has many skinned rabbits in an ice chest strapped to the back of his cart.

He yelled out, 'Rabbito, rabbito; Any fresh rabbits today?'

Sometimes my mum gave me the money to buy one for our dinner, and I had to say to the rabbito, 'One pair please,' and I'd watch him go to his ice chest that dripped enticing melted ice water on hot days. Occasionally, I'd put my finger in the water, but even though I was tempted, I never licked my finger, because the water had been around dead rabbits. And I never looked inside the ice chest because I knew it held the bodies of lots of rabbits, and I reckoned it'd be a gruesome sight. The other horse-and-cart traders that came—the clothes prop man who most of us kids were scared of, and the fruit and veggie man that no one was afraid of—had horses that looked half-dead. But not the rabbito; he had a frisky horse that had the devil in its eyes, and I reckoned that was because it knew it had a load of dead things behind it.

Now, back in Canada, Mike gives me a roll of insulated copper wire that I strip by melting the plastic over flames on the cook's stove. The cook gets pissed off because the place now stinks, and he tells me to get out of his fucking kitchen. I shape the wire easily into a noose, and it works well because when I push my hand through the noose, it tightens. I reckon it'd even hold a wolf if one was silly enough to investigate and push its paw through.

I search for narrow tracts of well-trampled snow, because that means rabbits use it as a road. I tie the loose end of the wire to overhanging branches, and then I tease out the noose. I've got many nooses set so that makes me a trapper, and like all trappers I have to regularly go to check them and get my kill.

But I'm not having a lot of success, and every night I'm quizzed by the seismic crew, so I have to come up with excuses.

I tell them that I forget where I put half the snares, and they say I should mark the branches with surveyor's ribbon. When I say, 'Something big must have been snared because it pulled the wire from the branch,' they tell me to knot the wire like a fishing line tied to a hook. When I say, 'There were no fresh paw prints on newly fallen snow,' they tell me to move the snares, which I do, but I'm still unsuccessful.

I feign disappointment about my failures, but in fact, I really don't care. I'm enjoying being in the open. My lungs seem to object to breathing the overheated air in the trailers. They want me taking gulps of icy oxygen that no one's ever before had inside them. The only occasions when I question the sense of being alone is when I hear wolf howls, but I'm not too afraid of them. When I say this to the Canadians they reckon I should be afraid. They tell me stories about wolves attacking grazing sheep, but I accept that this is life—like dingoes attacking sheep; it happens. But when they tell me about attacks on cows, moose and deer, and on isolated humans, I have new respect.

A Canadian says, 'What if one of those bastards cornered you? What would you do?'

I tell him, 'I'd dong it with a lump of tree.'

Others nearby say, 'You're full of shit.'

And they're right.

I drive the spare Dodge Power Wagon to check my snares, and I do what I'm told to do—take blankets, matches and food with me, and the sponge-cake moose bait.

I tasted the first sponge cake the cook made, and it was terrible, nothing like the sponge mum makes. Mum's sponges are really Mrs Jenkins' sponges because that's what's written on top of the receipt she uses. Just as she has Mrs Baxter's biscuits and Mrs Van Gelder's fruit cake. But I can't expect to get in the North West Territory of Canada cake of the quality of Mrs Jenkins's sponge, because she doesn't give her recipe to everyone; it only goes to close friends.

A suggestion that I should go further away from camp to set snares is good, because where I am now has loads of well-trampled rabbit roads. I've set most of the snares when there's a noise of a snapped tree branch falling—probably that's what it was. But when I look up its not. It's a bloody wolf.

'Fuck!'

Obviously I've got to get away. *Fast.*

But one of my snowshoes gets caught amongst an under-snow tree branch, and I fall. I get up quickly and try to run, but snowshoes aren't designed for running, so I fall again.

Fuck!

I visualize the classic defensive pose: arms protecting head. But that's not going to be much good because the wolf's will rip my arms to shreds, so I've got to bash it with a snowshoe, but they're attached to my boots with a long rawhide strap.

Fuck!

I look at the wolf to see how much time I've got to get a defence going. I've got loads of time—it hasn't moved—but I still say, '*Fuck!*'

It's got to be planning its moves. It's got to be getting its mind into stalking mode, or perhaps it's waiting for the rest of its pack. I get untangled, and I run quite well on the snowshoes. I make the trail and the safety of the power wagon, but the bloody snowshoes are too big to fit in the wagon's cabin, so I jump onto the back tray.

I stare at the wolf and it stares at me, and I grab a roll of rope and throw it, saying, 'Get out of here you, bastard.' The rope lands near enough to scare it off, but it doesn't move. This is a very inactive wolf. I'm staring at it and it's staring at me, and I realise I'm staring at a wolf that doesn't have ears, or a tail. This is either a very disadvantaged wolf, or it's dead.

Then I remember hearing about the Canadian Government having a bounty on wolves, something like the bounty offered by the Australian government on dingoes, and I now know this wolf has earned a hunter a few dollars.

I get off the truck, take off the snowshoes and hold one of them in front of me as if it's a sword. I close in on the wolf and see that it hasn't been shot. It's been snared. Fencing wire wraps tightly around its throat, and more wire winds around one of its legs.

I say, 'You poor bastard,' but I reckon I wouldn't say that about a snared rabbit.

Possibilities flood my brain: if this frozen wolf fooled me, it will fool others, particularly those Canadians who have been treating me as a joke. Yeah.

I say to the wolf, 'Mate, a taxidermist couldn't tell if you're alive or dead; you've got a great future.'

In another three months when the snow melts and the muskeg thaws, this wolf will sink into the ooze and probably only be discovered in a million years when an archaeologist's trowel scrapes its bones or scull, which is less than a wolf such as this deserves.

I gently push the wolf. It falls over, and I try to drag it to the trail. It's heavy going because it's completely inflexible. Its legs dig into the snow and get caught on tree branches. I fall over and find my head near its head, and I imagine feeling and smelling its breath.

I say, 'Mate, you can have better than this. '

When I get back, Mike's mucking about with the power generator engine, the cook's preparing apple pie and the flunky's bitching about everything in general.

I say to Mike, 'You're not going to believe what happened to me.'

He says, 'I don't give a fiddler's fart what happened to you because if I don't get this generator going there isn't going to be any power.'

'Believe me. You are going to give a fiddler's fart, because I've got a wolf!'

He stops mucking about and says, 'You've got a *what?*'

'A bloody full-grown Canadian wolf.'

'Bullshit.'

'Fair dinkum.'

He wipes what must be near-frozen hands on an oil-soiled cloth and says, 'Let's have a cup of tea and discuss this.'

When the crew returns later, I think the surveyor has made a mistake when he announces that the temperature is fifty degrees below zero. He says to me, 'It's the coldest I've ever been,' and I say to him, 'Me too,' and he laughs.

He says, 'It'd be strange if I can't say I've been in lower temperatures than an Australian. You don't even have snow there, do you?'

'Oh, we have snow all right, but nothing like here.'

'Look up there,' he says.

I look upwards at something amazing. Veils of floating angels fill the sky. Well, that's what I reckon they look like.

'It's the Aurora Borealis—the northern lights.' Then he shushes me.

I do what I'm told and I shush. I hear crackling sounds that the surveyor says are gasses and electricity and magnetic forces.

He says, 'You won't see that anywhere else.'

I don't have the heart to tell him that when I was a child, my parents sat me on the front fence at Peakhurst where we watched the Aurora Australis. I would tell him about our aurora if the Australian veils of floating angels were more spectacular than the Canadian veils of floating angels, but theirs is much better.

The surveyor opens his tripod, connects something scientific-looking and peers through it, then he writes figures in a notepad. Under torchlight he points to the figures and says, 'That's where we are.'

I believe him because he's a lot smarter than I am.

The fifty-degrees-below-zero night gives birth to a bitch of a morning. Perhaps it's now colder, but I can't ask the surveyor or any of the weather-experienced Canadians because they're all panicking, and so is Mike. Most of the power wagon engines start because they've had heating elements in their sumps, but the differentials and wheel bearings are frozen. Mike's going around with a gas flame trying to unfreeze them. The wagons that do get going tow others that don't, and lots of yelling and screaming goes on.

I'm not concerned about power wagons because I've got my wolf to think of, but when I speak to Mike about it he says to me, 'Son of a moose; I've not got time to talk about a fucking wolf. I've got my hands full with these fucking trucks.'

I reckon he's got his priorities wrong, and I reckon he shouldn't be speaking loudly because the wolf's a secret. I tell him to keep his voice down.

He tells me to go and get lost.

The camp boss screams orders at everyone, particularly Mike. Norman the driller needs unfrozen water to flush his equipment; thermos flasks that contained hot soup or coffee that were unintentionally left in wagon cabins are now frozen and split open, and clothing that was adequate yesterday is now inadequate. Everyone's very pissed off. There's going to be trouble, so I go into the warm dining trailer to drink hot coffee, and I realise that I've got the best job—even if it is the lowest paid.

The cook yells at the flunky and the flunky yells back as good as he gets. Outside, engines rev and blokes yell. Then I hear the wagons leave and relative peace descends. Mike comes into the dining trailer, forgetting to stomp his boots on the grate to remove snow, and the flunky yells, 'Clean your boots.'

Mike wants breakfast and the cook yells at him, 'Breakfast is over.'

Mike says, 'This is fucking ridiculous. Why am I here when I could be lying in the Mexican sun?'

I could answer him. I could say he's here for the money, but that's bleeding obvious. That's why we're all here.

I say to Mike, 'Do you want to get my wolf?'

Mike and I drive off in the power wagon, following yesterday's tyre marks on the trail. I'm grateful he's with me; it's too easy to take a wrong turn that will peter-out miles from anywhere or anyone. And if there's a mechanical problem, the only thing I can fix is a flat tyre. If we do get stranded, I'm well clothed. I'm the only one in camp who wears Australian white King Gee Victory brand combination overalls. The Canadians reckon I look stupid, but they don't know that these King Gees were worn at the 1957 Bathurst car races when I was a flag marshal. If they knew that, they'd be envious. Underwear, then long johns, then a flannel shirt and trousers, then a football jumper, then the King gees, then a parka cover my body, so if we're stranded I'll live.

Tradition and inhibition prevent the Canadians or Mike from wearing King Gees; they've got to wear a shirt and long trousers, and when they bend over their backs are exposed. I wear heavy leather work boots and old-fashioned rubber overshoes. The Canadians reckon the overshoes look stupid, but they don't think them so stupid when I simply unlatch two catches and slide them off when I go into the dining trailer The flunky never has to yell at me to stomp my boots on the grate to remove snow.

Mike says, 'Are we still on the right trail?'

I'm not certain. We seem to be following yesterday's tracks so give him a confident, 'Of course we are.'

He says, 'Any ideas about what we can do with the wolf?'

'There'll be loads of things.'

'Such as?'

'We could train it then sell it to a circus.'

'Be serious.'

'I am being serious.'

He doesn't know what to make of my circus idea. He says, 'The thing is dead; isn't it?'

'Yeah, but it doesn't look dead. I reckon at a glance, and if there's not too much light, you'd take it to be alive.'

'So ... its condition's good?'

'Its condition is that it's dead, but it's in a good dead condition.'

Mike thinks. He tosses around ideas, but before any get developed, I say to him, 'There's only one problem; it hasn't got ears or a tail.'

'Jesus, what happened to it?'

'I reckon bounty hunters have ... whoa, stop; there it is.'

We stop, and I lead him to the frozen beast.

Mike's very impressed with the wolf's condition, and he reckons he's got a plan, but we first need to get the wolf to the power wagon. I suggest carrying it, but he's used to thinking like a mechanic so we unhitch the wire-rope winch line and wind it around the wolf's body.

I yell, 'Take up the slack. Careful; a bit more; a bit more. Stop, stop, stop.'

The wolf's uncooperative. If it doesn't change its attitude, there's a danger that the winch rope will decapitate it. I wiggle its body from under a tree branch and tell Mike to take up the slack again. He guns the engine, the tree branch breaks, the wolf goes flying through the air and lands with a thud on the trail.

Mike jumps out of the truck. 'Son of a moose!'

We throw the now slightly damaged wolf into the truck and cover it with a tarpaulin in case any of the seismic crew sees our cargo. On the return journey Mike tells me his plan. It's a good plan.

~

The bitch of a morning has been for the seismic crew a bitch of a day. Because the interpreter had trouble reading yesterday's recordings, he'd ordered everything they'd done to be redone. So they worked for ten hours in thirty below zero. Rightfully, the interpreter's being called a son of a bitch. I reckon the crew have good reason to be tired and bad tempered.

Swearing is a release, so everything they say is prefixed or suffixed with words such as cocksucker, or fucking, or goddamned, or asshole which is really arsehole, or other very descriptive cussing words which are really cursing words.

All of my jobs are done, but I still cop some of the prefixes and suffixes. Mike gets them all. Someone has to.

The resting wolf stands at the back of the kitchen trailer where frozen foods are stored. It's got to be happy amongst roasts and tee-bones steaks and seafood, although I don't think it would like vegetables all that much. We've got it well hidden, but I still glance nervously in its direction; we must keep it a secret.

It's been dark for two hours when the six o'clock dinner gong is sounded and everyone rushes into the dining trailer to avoid the wrath of the cook, and to get the best seats—those furthest away from the door.

I don't rush because I'm not supposed to get a best seat. According to Mike's plan I have to get the worst seat, the seat that's copping cold air when the door's opened.

Now everyone's inside, Mike and I go to get the wolf from its lair. We drag it to a mark I'd made on the snow. The wolf has to go on this spot because that's where light from the dining trailer falls when the door's opened.

We stand the wolf on its legs, but it keeps falling over.

I say to Mike, 'Dig four holes in the ice with your screwdriver.'

He says, 'I haven't got a screwdriver.'

'All mechanics have a screwdriver.'

'Mine are in my bloody tool box.'

I try to bend its legs, but they're frozen solid, and I'm afraid they'll snap off.

Mike says, 'What about some of those jam tins on the rubbish heap?'

He gets four jam tins and into each one goes a leg, then we put snow around each leg and stomp it down. The wolf now stands proud.

'It looks real,' Mike says.

'It is *real*. It's just that it's real ... ah, dead.'

I go and sit in the worst seat, and the cook gives me a dirty look. He says, 'Where's the limey?'

I say, 'He's dead,' and everyone cheers.

Mike pushes open the trailer door and it bashes back against the wall. He points at the man who's always bitching, the man who hates Mike, and says, 'Your power wagon hasn't got its heating element plugged in.'

Everyone looks up, wondering who's guilty because they know it's not them.

The man says, 'Limey, you're full of shit. I plugged the goddamned thing in myself.'

Mike says, 'You're the one who's full of shit; your wagon's not connected.'

And that's enough to start it all.

Mike says to the man, 'You ... dingo!'

I say to Mike, 'He doesn't know what a dingo is; use pommie language.'

So Mike says, 'You've got the guts of a chicken!'

I don't know where he gets that from, but it's definitely an insult; it's punch up stuff.

The guts of a chicken man jumps up, but he's blocked by two tables, so he gets on the first table and hops to the second. Sauces and vinegar and pepper and salt and plates go flying, and everyone gets out of his way.

I open the door and rush outside. Mike follows me, and so does everyone else because they all want to see the limey bashed up.

The wolf's placed exactly right. In the part light it looks like a major threat. It looks like it's raring to attack.

Mike stops running, points and says, 'Look, it's a WOLF!'

Everyone stops.

I say in an even louder voice, 'Stand back. I'll get the bastard.' I run straight at it and, as planned, do a pretty good rugby tackle.

There's a lot of confusion. Some of the men retreat to the dining trailer; some run away and some stand transfixed. I lie on the ice completely winded because the bloody wolf is frozen solid. I've just tackled what felt like a brick wall.

They must hear my gasps for air, but between gasps I get out, 'I ... I ... got the bastard.'

The wolf's not moving and I'm not moving except to give it a few half-hearted kicks so it might appear to be a little bit alive.

Some brave souls come closer, and I hear, 'Shit. Fuck. Goddamn,' and, 'I'll be a son of a bitch,' then, 'What's those jam tins doing here?' Less brave souls arrive, and I hear, 'That goddamned wolf *ain't got no ears,*' then another says, *'It ain't got a tail either.'*

Someone shines a torch on the wolf and there's mumbling and accusing looks.

I say, 'I bit its ears off. I did a Bumper Farrell on it.' But no one apart from me knows what that means.

Mike says, 'Wolves don't have ears or tails, do they?'

I start to laugh, and Mike laughs, and the man who has the guts of a chicken laughs, and then everybody laughs. The cranky cook comes and he laughs, as well as the flunky and the camp boss.

I get no sympathy for my bruised shoulder.

~

The crew continues to hound me about catching a moose, which I don't do. But I do snare a rabbit, and the cook offers to make it into a gourmet dish—if I skin it.

I admit to not ever skinning a rabbit, but a Canadian does it, and I'm later forced to sit as a film star might with twenty men watching every mouthful of a bloody woeful rabbit stew.

I wonder if when the wolf was alive it did anything that it was proud of? It may have fathered packs and packs of pups; it may have hunted and killed a huge bear or moose; its howl may have put fear into millions of rabbits, but was it ever proud? Well, now it can be, because it gets propped at the entrance to our camp. And what a fearsome sight it is with its mouth gaped open and teeth bared. Its last dying gasp for oxygen, its howl for help, its howl of pain becomes in my photograph of it, a mouth ready to tear its victim apart. This wolf has what none of us are likely to have: fame in death.

For the next two months the Canadians say to me, 'You be careful, Aussie; there's wild animals out there.'

3 April 1961

Calgary
Dear Mum,

The trip back to Calgary took four days of hard driving in the 'power wagons'. We didn't mind though as we were on our way home.

Last Tuesday night the party chief told us we were going out tomorrow. We all got up at 1.30 a.m. and had breakfast, then we were underway at 3.00 a.m. I had to stay until the last truck hooked-up to the last trailer, so I didn't get to Fort Nelson until 10.30 a.m.

We stayed in Fort Nelson that night and headed to Fort St John next day. It was a long day. We didn't reach there until 9.00 p.m.

In any case, we were heading out of the bush and were pleased to see the back of Dawson Creek and Edmonton. Four of the blokes and I stayed with Garry the driller at his parents farm outside Calgary. Stuart was in Banff skiing.

It's good to be clean again and wearing normal clothes. Tomorrow I will call at the Alberta Trailer Company office to pick up the rest of my money. I have decided to phone you tomorrow, so when you get this letter I will have spoken to you. The wind is blowing at 40 mph and a big snowstorm is expected.

Love Barry.

PS. I shaved the North West Territory beard off yesterday, and I'm glad it's gone. I weigh 174 pounds, or 12 stone 6 pounds. Wow.

1960, North West Territory Camp:
Barry and Carl McQuade smoke cigars.

Richfield oil bosses come to see what their money is being spent on. Yes, I did get to fly in this plane.

The 'Wolf' chases Norman the driller.

1961, NW Territory: Dodge Power Wagon recording truck.

The seismic crew have their monthly beer in the dining trailer.

Back view of the kitchen and dining trailers at camp one.

Chapter Six

I'm very confident that the Alberta Trailer Company will give me the job as maintenance man for the five-hundred-and-sixty-bed trailer camp.

The man doing the interview says to me, 'Mister White tell me about …'

'Please call me Barry.'

He frowns. 'Mister Barry?'

'Barry's my first name.' I've made a mistake interrupting the man. I should've let him continue using the Mister title.

'All right … Barry. Tell me the experience you've had that qualifies you for this job?'

I tell him that I've got loads of experience, that I was employed by Alberta Trailers to work in a seismic camp in the North West Territory.

The man looks at my written application form that probably has two mistakes. There's certainly one because I've always had trouble spelling 'originally', and I know I wrote it as 'originly'. The other might be that I've exaggerated my qualifications.

The man says, 'So you were the bull-cook in the Fort Nelson camp?'

'Yes.'

'But *this* job's for a maintenance man.'

I wonder why he's going into so much detail. I've got runs on the board with this company; I've endured the rigours of a winter in the bush. I'm proven. I say to him, 'I'm a qualified plumber.'

'A plumber? Then why were you working as a bull-cook? Surely you could've done better than be a bull-cook?'

'Necessity. There were no jobs for plumbers. I was broke.'

'Broke?'

'Short of money.'

The man scrutinizes my application, and I hope he doesn't know how to spell originally. He says, 'You don't say anything about your experience with refrigeration.'

I've not got the slightest idea how refrigeration works but I say, 'I've had experience with that.'

'What about ice-making machines?'

I'm thinking it must be a trick question because ice making isn't complicated—ice is made by filling a tray that has compartments with water, then it's frozen in the top part of a refrigerator. I say to him, 'No worries.'

He says, 'There may be some basic electrical work; can you do that?'

I say yes to everything because in my short experience job hunting in Canada I've learnt that everyone lies. I worked as a plumber for three months during construction of the nuclear reactor in Sydney's Lucas Heights, so I'll even tell him I'm a scientist, but he doesn't ask about that and I get the job.

~

It astonishes me how different it is approaching the Canadian Rocky Mountains compared to what we think are mountains in Australia. The Great Dividing Range west of Sydney is seen from ten miles distant as a long green-grey line on the horizon and is approached by travelling a gradual incline. Rock-hugging Angophora grow where eucalyptus won't, and from a distance the Dividing Range peaks seem soft. The Rocky Mountains from fifty miles distant are seen on the horizon as an undulating line of peaks and troughs that look like a graph-line plot, and are approached by travelling on a vast flat prairie. Pine trees skirt only the lower parts and above that is high, steep rock face with no softness. Both have physical features that are impressive; both claimed the lives of long-time-ago explorers and both are icons.

I'm staring at the Rockies, but Clive, the driver of the car, is chattering away.

He says, 'I could be setting up another camp in Texas, but I chose to do the Pincher Creek one.'

'Because it's a bigger camp?' I ask.

'Yes, that's one reason, but the other is that I'm away from home too much and my wife's fed up being alone. At least from here, I'll be able to go home on weekends.'

I find Clive interesting because he's the only embalmer I've met. I say to him, 'How does being an embalmer qualify you to be in charge of constructing a trailer camp?'

'Because I've got contacts. I know a guy who's a vice president on the Alberta Trailer board.'

His answer confirms my recently learnt practice of lying during job interviews. 'Why did you choose embalming? It's a bit gruesome, isn't it?'

'No, you get used to it. That wasn't my first choice of job. My parent's chose that line of work for me.'

'Yeah, that happens.'

I remember my first job—a messenger and copy boy at *The Sydney Morning Herald* newspaper. My parents were mystified how a boy who was in classes 1E, 2G, and 3F, all the lowest and least academic, a boy who can hardly write sensible sentences and who doesn't know a verb from an adjective, can have a future with a newspaper, especially *The Sydney Morning Herald*. But in Australia in 1953, there's no such thing as unemployment and there's not enough kids to fill all the available jobs.

At least my parents didn't tell me what job I should do.

Clive says to me, 'I realise it's a strange occupation. When I was dating, girls' parents asked me what work I did, so I'd tell them I'm training to be an embalmer, but I get horrified looks. So after that I lie, I told them I worked in a food market. It's easier. I kept more girlfriends that way.'

'I reckon I'd react the same. I've only seen one dead person. That was my father.'

'Oh, sorry.'

'Thanks. It was five years ago.'

'We don't get over bereavements like that quickly.'

I reckon that's what he's supposed to say, that it's all part of his funeral and embalming training, that he's really not so sorry.

Then he says, 'The country's looking beautiful.'

I reckon changing the subject's also been part of his training.

'Yeah, it's so green—nothing like Australia.'

Clive's driving is unnerving; he gets behind other cars and tailgates, and I reckon it's because he's used to being in funeral processions. Drivers ahead of us show their annoyance by speeding then slowing, but he does the same, and they get really pissed off.

He says to me, 'They told me at the office that you're a plumber.'

'Yeah.'

'So why aren't you plumbing? You'd make lots more money.'

I don't want to explain to him that the same day I sat the Alberta Plumbing Board exams, I also had to play rugby. That I was writing answers to questions I found easy, but I couldn't stay to finish because I had to pack down in a scrum and get physically abused in rucks and mauls. I'm not going to tell him that the Plumbing Board sent me a letter stating that I failed, that I can't work as a plumber until I answer all their questions. So I lie; I say, 'I want to do something more interesting.'

'Like being a bull-cook in a seismic camp in the Northwest Territory?'

The subject needs changing. I say, 'How long does it take to be an embalmer?'

'Four years. How long for a plumber?'

'Five years … it's beautiful country.'

We stop outside a bar in Fort Macleod. There may be a fort somewhere but I don't see it.

Clive says, 'You get something to eat while I go inside to call the office.'

It's an order and he's the boss, so I should do as I'm told, but I've seen antics like his played by better performers. I say to him, 'But there's a phone box over near the food shop.'

He says, 'I'll go in here … it's quieter.'

He's going for a liquid lunch, and that explains the smell of alcohol he's tried to cover up by sucking small white lozenges and keeping the car's side window open.

'You should try Ombo Junior,' I say to him, but he doesn't understand because Canadians mustn't have the little green bottle of breath freshener that most Australian alcoholics use.

We arrive at the location of the sulphur plant. Apart from the loads of pipes and steel, and bulldozed earth and poured concrete, it's a magnificent site, and I wonder why anyone would want to stuff up such a place.

Clive slows the car and says, 'You're going to hear people calling me 'Fearless'.'

'Fearless? Why? Are you a judo expert, or something?'

'No. It's a nickname that I didn't choose. It goes back to when I was learning embalming, in fact, to the first day at the mortuary. I was sent to the refrigerated storage room to get something—I don't remember what—and when I opened the door to go inside the dark room I felt for the light switch and, and felt a hand.'

'Fuck! Don't tell me it was—'

'No, not a corpse's hand; it was the hand of one of the embalmers. They were doing a first day on the job thing. You know, a kind of induction.'

'Oh, and the joke backfired on them. You weren't scared; you were fearless?'

'Something like that. It's a great location here, isn't it?'

'Yeah, why would they construct a monstrous processing plant here? This is a superb area; they're going to stuff up all this beauty.'

Clive grunts. I reckon it's not much good talking beauty to him.

A man dressed in bib-and-brace carpenter's overalls walks out of a trailer with the sign 'office' painted on its front. He says, 'Hi, Fearless.'

Clive says, 'What's the status?'

The carpenter says, 'There's twenty trailers parked on the grass and another twenty on their way.'

'Twenty! Goddamn, there's nowhere to put them.'

The carpenter's not very concerned—in fact there's a hint of a smile on his face. He says, 'We're following your plan; nothing's been changed.'

I see the reason for the carpenter's concern. Each trailer is fifty-feet long and ten-feet wide and sits on two four-wheel bogies. Prime mover trucks that towed the trailers have unhitched them and parked them all over the place, so if there's a plan being followed and it's Clive's plan. It's a bad plan.

The carpenter says to me, 'Hey, you.'

I wonder how I should react. 'Yeah?'

Clive says we should go to hustle up the site prep guy.

'Let's go, then.'

And we go to hustle.

It's a busy area. Caterpillar bulldozers are gouging two blade-width flat areas across the hillside. I remember that Cat drivers don't always look behind when they reverse. The carpenter lives dangerously and goes directly behind the Cat. I give it a wide berth. I see him scoff at my caution, and he says something I don't hear.

I tell him to get fucked, which he doesn't hear.

When we get within hearing, he says, 'That goddamned Fearless hasn't got any idea, but he's the boss.'

'Why do you call him Fearless?'

'Everyone calls him Fearless. That's been his name for years.'

We hear the sounds of a revving car engine that's becoming frantic, and we see that Fearless has tried to do what only a four-wheel drive should do. His car looks ridiculous bottomed out on a pile of dirt, its back and front wheels off the ground.

The carpenter says, 'Stupid arsehole.'

'Should we go and help him?'

'Hell no. Leave him.'

It's obvious that Clive's disliked by his workers, so since I'm one of the workers, I have to show my dislike, but carefully.

The carpenter asks, 'Coming from Calgary, did you stop to do any drinking?'

'Drinking? Do you mean alcohol?'

'Of course, I mean fucking alcohol. What else would you drink?'

'There's water.'

'Oh, a smartarse limey, eh?'

I think, *oh not another Canadian who thinks I'm English*. It seems that anyone who speaks English without a North American accent has to be English. I ought to suggest to him that it'd be safe to label the Welsh, Irish and Scots as English, that they wouldn't mind, that they'd accept it as a compliment.

I reckon it's time for me to be assertive—to straighten the bloke out before he thinks he's on top of me. I say, 'Listen to me you fucking dim-wit, call me a limey once more and I'll push your teeth down your throat.' I wait for his reaction. Had someone said to me what I said to him, I'd expect a response, so I'm ready for fight or flight.

He doesn't disappoint. He says, 'Buddy, I don't give a damn. Do what you have to do, all right?'

I've been on the site for only an hour, and now I'm about to get my head punched in. I consider, fight or flight? I must fight. The repercussions of fighting will be I'm hurt or he's hurt, I'm sacked or he's sacked, I'm dead or he's dead. I have a last try for peace. 'Mate, in Australia we'd—'

'Oh, you're *Australian;* you're not a limey?'

'Yeah.'

'Ah well, that's different. I thought you were English.'

'What's wrong with being English?'

'Everything. Polish guys like me take lots of crap from limeys.'

'You're Polish? You don't sound Polish.'

'I came to Canada after the war when I was a kid.'

'But I've heard Canadians tell Polack jokes. I've heard Polacks refer to themselves as Polacks.'

'That's allowed, but limeys can't call us Polacks. I just love fighting limeys.'

I'm thinking that if this bloke likes fighting, I should be his friend. I say to him, 'Mate, I'm an Irish Australian. The Irish don't like the English, but they don't go around thumping them.'

The carpenter says, 'But the Irish—'

We hear, 'Hey, you guys! Come back and give me a push.'

Clive needs our help, and I'm pleased to end the conversation about race hate.

~

There's supposed to be one-hundred-and-twenty trailers coming to the campsite, each of them towed by a prime mover owned by a driver who wants a quick turn-around. When the prime movers and trailers arrive, they need to be parked, unhitched, and later relocated to position end to end. When they're located, the trailers are jacked up, the bogies removed, railway sleeper supports placed under them, a covered hallway constructed, and more trailers located on the other side of the hallway. It's a complicated procedure that requires a good plan. Fearless is the planner.

Ten trailers arrive and ten more and ten more, and we've got a huge trailer jam.

A prime mover driver asks me, 'Where will I put this baby?'

I'm buggered if I know because there's no more room so I tell him, 'Mate, ask the boss. That's him over there.'

He says, 'Who's the boss?'

'It's Clive.'

'Oh shit. They put that dumb cocksucker in charge of this camp?'

Behind this prime mover are another ten towing trailers, and it's easy to tell the owner drivers from those that are company owned. Company men pour coffee from thermos flasks and laugh and tell jokes, but the owner-drivers are angry.

Clive runs about, pointing and waving and yelling. He often goes to the boot of his car to, so he says, refer to the master plan. I reckon I can help sort out the mess. I need to see the master plan, but he doesn't allow anyone near it.

I say to Clive, 'I reckon this is enough to make a man turn to alcohol.'

He gives me a quick guilty glance and says, 'It's not my fault; it's the goddamned plant. They've screwed up with the delivery schedule. Everything's arriving two days early.'

A man in a pick-up truck skids to a stop beside us. He's wearing a tie, which means he's got authority. He says, 'Who's in charge of this fucking mess?'

I look at Clive and walk away.

Clive points at the parked trailers, at those not parked, at those lined up to be parked, in the direction of Calgary, and at the sky. God is being blamed?

The authority's face goes from an annoyed flush to a deep red, and we hear loud angry voices. The authority points in all directions, including God's, and I reckon the authority's asking God to strike Clive with lightning.

He says, 'Do *you idiots* know what you're doing?'

Clive says, 'Of course.'

'Well, if you know what you're doing, you'd better do it quickly because there ain't no way anymore goddamned trailers are going to fit in the space I was asked to prepare.'

The authority drives off spinning the pick-up wheels and leaving us in a cloud of dust.

I look at Clive and I don't feel any sympathy, but I do have admiration because I would've told the authority to go to blazes.

Clive says to me, 'I'll phone the office.' He beckons me to follow.

I want to be with him when he speaks to the office because I reckon he's looking for a scapegoat, and I'm a likely candidate.

At his car I go to the passenger side, and he goes to the boot. He says, 'I'll just check the master plan.'

A moment or two later, he joins me in the car. I smell something, but I'm not certain what. He's irrational, saying, 'What can we do? What can we do? Goddamn it, what can we do?'

I feel like correcting him, to suggest he's saying too many *we's,* that he should be saying, what can *I do?* I think about his boasts of establishing camps all over North America, about how he made it clear that he's the boss, but I realise how easily I could be blamed for the fiasco.

He says, 'Those sons of bitches in Calgary have done this to me on purpose!' Then he says a lot of words that could be Spanish, and even without knowing the language, I know he's swearing.

Self-preservation is my main concern; if Clive's secure, I'm secure, so I tell him I've got a suggestion. 'Mate, there's a way out of this.'

'How?'

'I reckon we should employ some construction workers that are about to quit for the day; we offer them cash for the hours they work for us—everyone likes a bit of tax-free cash.'

He's listening.

'We can borrow a power generator from the construction camp, which together with lights from the trucks should let us see well enough to get, say, ten trailers located. Then we can send ten trucks back to Calgary. What do you think?'

'But there's twenty trucks!'

'Yeah. But if we get the construction boss to lend us one of his Cats, we can flatten another area to park ten more trailers.'

He nods. 'We'd have to work most of the night.'

'Yeah.'

Clive's telephone conversation with Calgary is a wonderfully measured piece of one-upmanship. He's clear about it not being his fault but theirs, and out of the goodness of his heart he's going to get them out of trouble, but he needs a thousand dollars cash to pay the men. He gets what he wants and then is so grateful to me it's sickening. I wish I knew some way of exploiting his gratitude.

We use the construction workers for only one night because the Fort Macleod unemployment office sends us six carpenters and four labourers, so we're now a total of thirteen. That's got to be unlucky for someone but not me, because Clive promotes me. I become his construction manager, and I get more money.

Trucks arrive with roofing sections to cover the walkway between trailers, and I direct operations like a general. Everything's going fine.

Clive tells me, 'Aussie, you and I are a good team.'

I tell him, 'You stay in your shed pondering over the master plan and leave me alone, and the job will be completed on time.'

Over the next two weeks, we locate one-hundred-and-twenty trailers including installing electricity, water and sewage.

Clive takes the Calgary bosses and the 'authority' on a pre-occupancy inspection. They all smile and congratulate Clive, and when they're finished, they drive away in their cars without saying anything to us workers.

Clive struts about like a rooster in a chook pen, and we all wonder how he managed to get the credit for all the work we've done. I label Clive as a bludger, con-man, lurk-man and a rorter. The Canadians soon incorporate those terms into their descriptions of him. I say to a carpenter that the reason I'm not snatching it is because the hard yakka is over, and I don't want to walk out on a soft cop. When I explain what all those words mean, he starts to talk about snatching it, then all the crew are saying snatch it and a bit more Australian slang gets into Canadian usage.

Clive detects the disharmony so he decides to take the crew to Pincher Creek for end-of-job celebratory drinks.

I say to him, 'Who's paying?'

'Me.'

'You?'

'I'm going to use cash that's over from what Alberta Trailers gave me to pay the construction guys.'

And I reckon he's a bastard because its money he should've used to employ them for another night.

~

Len, the newly arrived camp boss, says to Clive, 'I knew you'd get all the trailers located on time. There was talk in Calgary that you'd not do it.'

Clive says, 'The Aussie and I have a good team. I took all of them to Pincher last night to celebrate.'

Len says, 'That was generous. You paid for that?'

'Yes.'

Because Clive said we're a good team, I don't tell the camp boss that he spent company money on alcohol, or that I had to drive a very drunk Clive back to camp.

'It's just as well that you're a good team,' says Len, 'because in three days, the cooks, flunkies, cleaners, bed makers, a clerk and a commissary manager are arriving. We'll need to test all the cookers, refrigeration, lighting, heaters and air conditioning, so I'll need you guys.'

I absorb what we have to do, but I repeat one word aloud, my nemesis, the thing about which I know nothing; *'Refrigeration.'*

Len says, 'Calgary told me you're okay with refrigeration. That's right, isn't it?'

'Yeah, that's right. But from my experience in the Fort Nelson camp, the heaters take a lot of setting up. Then there's the gas cookers; they take a lot of adjusting, and you'd know how important it is to keep cooks happy, and there's—'

Len interrupts, 'You're right; you've got enough to do. I'll get refrigeration guys from Pincher.'

I immediately like the man; he's saved me from refrigeration-induced self-destruction.

After we're all set up and everyone has arrived, Len has the cooks prepare food, and he gets some alcohol from somewhere for a camp-opening celebration at which he plans to announce pecking order and responsibilities. The crew that located the trailers are now out of work so they're cussing, and the cooks, flunkies, cleaners and bed makers are now in work, so they're laughing. Kurt, the executive chef, who's German, says he's worked in the world's best restaurants, and the commissary manager, Donavan Archie McConnachie doesn't say anything because he's a nousy Irishman, and he wants to get the lie of the land. There's an announcement from Len that he acknowledges Clive's outstanding effort in locating the trailers, and Clive acknowledges his outstanding effort as being outstanding.

I ask Len, 'Where's Clive going next?'

'Fearless? He's probably going to a new camp in Pakistan.'

'Pakistan! Does he know that?'

'Not yet; I'm about to tell him.'

I'm drinking Calgary Bitter beer, Len's drinking rye whiskey and Clive looks like he's drinking water.

I say to Len, 'Fearless must be off the grog.'

He says, 'Fearless not drinking! He's on vodka. He always drinks vodka because it can't be smelt on his breath.'

'Oh.'

'Did he drink much when you were locating the trailers?'

'Not that I could tell; I never smelt it. I … ah, so he's been on the vodka.'

Len nods.

'But I never saw him drink.'

'Did he have any reasons to go to his car?'

'All the time. That's where he kept the master plan.'

'That's where he keeps his vodka. It's in the trunk. He's got a first-aid box there that's not got bandages in it. The guy's an alcoholic, and it's going to kill him. We're all concerned about him, and we're going to do something about it.'

'Ah, such as sending him to Pakistan. He's not going to get any vodka there.'

Whenever I look at Clive, he's got a glass full of his water, so I guess he's carrying vodka in a hip flask. I say to Len, 'Clive told me why he's known as Fearless.'

'Oh,' Len says, 'why?'

It's from his mortuary days. Apparently he was not scared by—'

'Not scared!' Len laughed. 'He was scared all right. The story is that when he felt the other guy's hand, he ran up the stairs with a load of shit in his pants. That's why he's called Fearless. It's not because of having *no fear*; it's because he *was fearful* … so afraid.'

'Oh.'

A new crew member I've not met, and who's supposed to be the clerk, goes past us and says, 'Hello, Mister Enz.' I reckon he's a crawler and a homosexual.

Kurt, the executive chef, snaps orders at his cooks, and I reckon he's been trained in the Hitler youth.

Donavan Archie McConnachie, the commissary manager, drinks something called Guinness, and he's talking to Clive, and I reckon they're both nearly pissed.

Next day Fearless leaves the camp to go to Pakistan. One of the cleaners finds stored under his office trailer many empty vodka bottles. We're surprised that one's still full, and I reckon he'd pay a fortune to get that bottle in Pakistan.

There's anticipation in the mess trailers about the first serving of breakfast. Len wears an Alberta Trailer uniform. Kurt wears a starched 'whiter than white' chef's outfit and an even-whiter chef's high-hat that must be impregnated with starch. The catering crew stand to attention behind steaming food warmers, and Kurt says to his cooks, 'Gentlemens, ve are professionals, zo be professional at all times.' Then he says to Len, 'Open zee doors.'

In wander hard-nosed, cynical construction workers who are about to criticize everything: eggs too soft or hard, bacon too crispy or floppy, hotcakes too small, toast too thin, wrong cereal, plates too small, coffee too weak. It's a hostile jury.

Afterwards Len speaks with Kurt, and they look pleased. Len tells Kurt that it was a satisfactory launch because no food was thrown back to the cooks. It's just as well because Kurt, who stood defiantly at the exit of the serving area unsmiling and with his arms on his hips in a 'complain if you dare' pose, would have defended his cooks' food.

Everyone not working in the kitchen starts to hate Kurt's overprotective attitude to all in his domain. He prefixed everything with *my*: *my* stoves, *my* floors, *my* refrigerators and *my* menus. I give him the nickname 'Reply', which soon becomes popular.

When he knows this, he asks me, 'Vhy is my name 'Reply'?'

I explain that to get a nickname is honourable. That Australians give and get names other than their own when they're popular.

'But vhy 'Reply'. Vhat's it mean?'

Then I have to explain about Cockney rhyming slang: frog and toad for road; tit for tat for hat; steak and kidney for Sydney, but he still doesn't get it.

He says, 'My name's Kurt zo zhouldn't zee name rhyme. Zhouldn't it be somezing different zan Reply?'

I'm trying to explain what a curt reply is. How similar 'Kurt' is to 'curt', but we don't use 'curt' because it sounds like 'Kurt', so we use 'Reply'. But I get nowhere. Later when I see him he's got the look of a worried man, and when I tell him he looks as though he has the weight of the world on his shoulders, he doesn't get that either. I reckon Kurt's brain has a humour vacuum.

Len's a good manager. He's got a sense of humour, and he's fair, but even he can't relate to the cooks. Compliments are welcome, but criticism is not. They're bastards. They're only happy when they get everything they want, and when there's no interference—that applies to everyone except Kurt.

On paper Len's at the top of the pecking order although Kurt fights him on many issues. There's some professional agitators amongst the construction crew who are unhappy about the first breakfast. They complain to Len, but Kurt won't have a bar of it unless the complaints are made to him face to face. Len tells them that, and they send the union delegate who's skilled in industrial-relation negotiating, but he's no match for an arrogant German executive chef. Kurt does give his chefs a pep talk, and at the evening meal, they serve smaller portions to those construction workers they suspect of complaining.

Canadian Bechtel, the builder of the sulphur plant, told their construction workers they'll get the best food and plenty of it, but Calgary's told Kurt that he's on a tight budget so he's using strict portion control.

Every day more construction workers arrive in camp. Three hundred are accommodated and fed, and food costs escalate. Kurt tells us at a camp management meeting that steak was to be served three times a week, but he's going to reduce that to two. We all know that means trouble. We know that hard-working construction workers want their steaks because on the steak days everyone ignores the low-cost spaghetti bolognaise, Hungarian goulash, pizza and chili. Even the European construction workers ignore those traditional meals, and they tuck into barely cooked, juicy steaks. Kurt's convinced that the men will accept the elimination of a steak meal, but most of us know different.

Len says to Kurt, 'Something's brewing.' And Kurt thinks he's talking about the coffee.

I agree that something's brewing because I overhear groups of construction workers talking about mutiny, but I say nothing.

Len says, 'I heard there's going to be a union-led demonstration, that the agitators are telling the men they don't have to accept less steak, that in fact, there should be more.'

The construction workers see me using plumbing tools so I'm doing what they consider a 'real' job, and they're friendly. I can't dob them in. I can't tell the caterers, the non-construction guys, those who wouldn't know how to do a hard day's work, about the intended mutiny.

After the camp meeting, I'm surprised to be summoned to join Len in Kurt's office for a crisis meeting. I know some skulduggery is happening when I see a huge Bavarian cake on the table. I like cake.

Kurt cuts large slices, and he and Len tuck into it, but I don't because I'm suspicious.

Kurt says, 'Eat your Bavarian cake.'

'No thanks; it's a bit too rich for me.' My mouth salivates.

Len tucks into his, and just as Kurt takes a large bite of Bavarian, Len says, 'Tell Barry your idea.'

Kurt goes to speak and bits of cream shoot from his mouth. I expect him to apologise, but he doesn't. He's not the least bit embarrassed. He clears his throat with a gruesome screech and says, 'Ve're' here to dezide ow to handle zee unreasonable demands of zee construction crew.'

'Very unreasonable,' Len says.

'I vill not accept hostility to my chefs. Ve are creating outstanding meals for zhose men, and vhat do my chefs get in return? Hostility. If zee men vill take only one steak zhere vood be plenty, but zhey take much more.'

Len holds up his hands to calm Kurt. 'Your idea of vouchers is good. We give every man three steak vouchers a week, and then they can eat them all at once if they want, but they only get three. When the vouchers are used there's no more steaks.'

'It iz goot,' says Kurt.

I say nothing because I'm not affected. I get as many steaks as I want. In fact, I am tired of having steak.

Kurt says, 'It'z agreed zhen. Barry vill stand near zee entry to zee serving area and collect zee vouchers from zee men.'

'What! Me collect *what*?'

'You collect zee vouchers from zee men.'

'Not fucking likely. They'll *kill* me!'

Len's looks uncomfortable, and I wonder if it's because he's not convinced the voucher idea is good, or that he knows the collector will be in danger. He says, 'You'll have help. We'll have the commissary man help you. That way it'll look more …'

'Stupid.'

'What do you mean by stupid?' Len asks.

'The commissary man! Donavan Archie McConnachie! He's over sixty. How in hell is a sixty-year-old man going to stop a six-feet-four bulldozer driver from having a steak? Have you told Donavan about this?'

~

Donavan comes down the steps from the commissary holding a small metal box secured by a large padlock. The box used to have a piano lock, but everyone told Donavan it was inadequate, and one of the crew proved it by opening it with a bent nail. Donavan had a highly qualified pressure welder fix a steel hasp and staple to the box, then he made a special trip to Pincher Creek to buy a padlock, and when the commissary's open, the box sits on a shelf like a house ornament. The construction crew muck about by asking for shaving cream or tobacco, and when Donavan's got his back turned, they lift the box and shake it. Donavan gives them satisfaction by feigning panic, then he says 'Put that back or I'll thump the bejesus out of you.' The box can easily be stolen but then all the fun would go out of commissary visits.

It's certain that Donavan's capable of greater things than selling the few personal-care products, magazines, tobacco and candy because he was, until forced into retirement, a conductor on Trans Canadian Railways. He likes to boast about his starting as a brakeman and finishing his twenty-five-year career as the railway's top conductor. It's ironic that the rows of shiny aluminium trailers are very like a Trans-Canadian train. Donavan has a strong affinity for 'his' commissary trailer, just as he had for 'his' railway caboose carriage.

He says to me, 'My caboose was the best decorated on the line. I had my family photos on the wall, and when I retired it was like losing my home.'

I'm hanging about the commissary because I'm hoping to get Donavan's opinion about us collecting steak vouchers from the construction crew. When I tell him what's proposed he says, '*What?*'

I'm uncertain if the '*what*' is because of his railway-caused deafness or if he's surprised. 'It's true; we have to collect steak vouchers.'

He says, 'What's a voucher?'

'It's something like a ticket. Yeah, like a railway ticket.'

'Tickets for steak?'

I tell him about the crisis meeting with Len and Kurt and their voucher idea.

He says, 'I won't be doing any of that. I won't be refusing a working-man his meat. I'll tell them what I think.'

He goes off to do just that, and I reckon it'd be nousy for me to become scarce.

With so many trailers and so much equipment there's bound to be many problems, and it's my job to fix the problems, but hardly anything's breaking down so I'm having to use my nous to make it appear that I'm busy.

Old codgers are the best teachers of the Australian skill known as nous. I had the good fortune to have been a pupil of a master practitioner, tradesman plumber Tom McGlinn, who I reckon, could've been world champion. Old Tom reckoned that a boss is only happy when his employees are working flat as a tack.

I said to Tom once, 'But we can't work all the time. We have to have a rest.'

He said in a dramatic voice worthy of a commandment-issuing God, 'Use your nous when resting.'

Tom taught me to always carry something, preferably eighteen-inch pipe Stillsons; to never stroll in the open but to go quickly; to never disclose your inability to do any job, rather if you can't do the job, tell the boss you ran out of time. Old Tom taught me loads of nousy things.

And that's why Len the camp boss congratulates me for always being busy, when I'm not. Preventative maintenance is the cover for my inactivity, and because nothing's breaking down, my preventative maintenance gets the credit. That's what I say, and it's believed.

I manage to avoid Len and Donavan for hours, but Donavan finds me. I slip the Zane Grey cowboy book I'm reading into my jacket and say to him, 'I'm under the trailer, checking the water pipes.' And I give the pipes a couple of solid whacks.

He says, 'They've told me about the, ah, the steak tickets.'

'The vouchers?'

'Yes, them things. And I can't believe that you and me have to be steak policemen. The men will hate us. They'll *hate* us.'

'Can you think of any way of getting out of it?' I ask.

'No.'

One hour before supper, we report to Kurt for steak duty, but half an hour before then, I cut a fuse to an ice-making machine. It's nearly suppertime, and already some of the construction crew are lined up at the dining trailer doors hungering for their steaks. I wonder why the cooks haven't discovered that the ice making machine's not working, and I'm losing hope, but then Kurt comes to me asking if I've got my tools?

I say, 'Of course I have. I've got my pipe Stillsons.'

'Goot because zee ice machines is broke.'

'I'll go straight to it.'

Donavan says to me, 'You bastard.'

I say to Donavan, 'My great-grandfather was Irish. I got my bastardry from him.'

I manage to extend the ice-machine repairs until meals are finished, then I join Kurt and his chefs for a post-supper discussion about steaks. I explain to a chef why the ice machine broke down. 'The cable to the refrigerant gas was crossed with the condenser, and that sent the billingsgate rupture valve into delay.'

He's impressed by my gobbledygook, and I hope I don't have to repeat it.

Donavan sits beside me. 'You left me on a limb.'

I say, 'You'd have done the same to me, but I got in first.'

'You left me—'

'An old man.'

'An old man, all by myself to face the wrath of men deprived of their steak. You ought to be ashamed of yourself, you, spalpeen.'

Attempting an Irish accent, I say, 'Jaysus Donavan, I'm honoured, I haven't heard anyone being called a spalpeen since my Irish grandfather died, and he said that to people he liked.'

Donavan must know something about nous because he smiles.

I say, 'Mate you've got to consider what my options were. I'm not a Canadian and I'm young so there's a fair chance I'd get a knuckle sandwich—'

'A what?'

'Knuckle sandwich; a mouthful of knuckles; a fist in my mouth. Those riggers and carpenters and welders wouldn't think twice about hitting me. But you, why you're an older Canadian—'

'Irish Canadian.'

'All right, Irish Canadian. It's an unwritten construction law that you never beat up an old man.'

A chef standing nearby says, 'That's correct; you're a *very* old man.'

Even old men get tired of being told they're old, but to be told you're very old is too much. Donavan says, 'I ain't that old.'

'Oh yes you are,' says the chef.

'No, I'm not. I ain't that old that I can't make you eat those words.'

I think about what my mother says is my Irish temper. It's three generations removed from being in Ireland, but Donavan's is not. He was born an Irishman. I watch his face as it reddens, and I know his anger is percolating and there's no consideration of flight. He looks about, grabs a sugar bowl, looks for a better option but sees none, and then he throws the bowl at the chef. It's a good shot. The chef ducks, but it smacks him on the side of his head and sugar goes everywhere. The chef looks for a weapon, but there's only a bread and butter knife a few tables away, and he must believe that to get that he'll lose the momentum of retaliation, so he runs head down at Donavan. He misses. His momentum takes him to where the bread and butter knife is, and he grabs it.

I feel guilty about causing the problem so I stand between them with my pipe Stillsons raised ready to strike. I say to the chef, 'Mate, cool down.'

But it's no use. He lunges at me with the knife. I feel my chest for blood or guts but there's nothing. I'm hardly sore.

We face each other. I've got pipe Stillsons raised, and he's got his blunt bread and butter knife.

I say, 'Back away or I'll dong you with these Stillsons.'

He says, 'Oh yeah, I'll cut you open with this knife.'

Another chef says, 'There'll be no cutting with that blunt knife.'

I reckon I've got the best weapon. A wallop with Stillsons will break teeth, possibly it'll break bones, certainly it'll bruise.

I hear laughter and see Donavan falling about and pointing at us. 'No one's killing anyone with those.'

We both know he's right. The chef laughs and does a mock lunge at me, and I laugh and swish the air with the Stillsons.

Next weekend I go to Calgary, and Stuart Acason, a mate from the rugby club, tells me he's quitting his job. He's driving his VW Beetle to Montreal to collect his brother who's arriving from England. After Montreal they're going to New York, Key West, Texas then to Mexico City. He asks if I want to go.

I return to Pincher Creek to give Len my notice, and I ask for a reference. He says it's company policy not to give references, so Donavan helps me break into the clerk's office where we steal company letterheads, and Donavan writes me a very glowing reference.

1 September 1961.
Calgary.
Dear Mum,

Just a short note. I'm helping Stuart clean his flat ready for the next tenants. Last night the Rugby Club presented Stuart and I with a pewter mug that's engraved, 'Hornets Rugby Union Football Club 1961'. It's something I'm proud to have, especially as I didn't play that many games.

On Saturday we'll be in the USA and I'll write as often as I can, but mostly it'll be on postcards.

Please continue writing to me at the Pincher Creek camp address, they'll send the mail on to me.

Love, Barry.

Chapter Seven

Stuart Acason's a very experienced traveller, and he's smart. I know that because he's lived in London; 'done' the continent; lived in Calgary for a year and he works in an office. He even knows how to use a typewriter—not many blokes can do that. I know little, so I suppose I should take notice of what he's saying; but I don't.

He says to me, 'Why hitchhike? '

'Because it's cheap, mate.' I've got loads of time on my hands, and now that winter's here, there's not much chance of getting any work in Calgary. Instead of sitting on my bum I may as well be travelling. That's why.'

'You'll be murdered. South of the Canadian border, Americans wait to prey on hitchhikers. I've read about it in the Calgary Herald. There was a story about one a few weeks ago.'

'Don't be stupid. Who'd want to murder me? Apart from my camera, I'll have nothing worth murdering me for.'

'That's *it* then?'

'Yeah, that's it.'

Because he's a mate, I know his concern for me is genuine. That's what mates do; they look after each other. We both play football with the Calgary Hornets Rugby club, and it's the same when there's a game on—we look after each other. If a bloke knees him or me in the back or throws a punch in a maul, we wait until the referee isn't looking then we do the same thing to the bloke.

There wouldn't be a need for me to go hitchhiking alone if my mate Ray hadn't dumped me for a woman. He's returning to Australia to get married—his priorities all wrong. I told him he should stay here and sow some wild oats. But, no, he got on a train to Riverside in California to see Stirling Moss race in the American Grand Prix, then got on the Orient liner *Orcades* to return to Australia.

I have to hitchhike because I've only got the money I earned in the North West Territory, which, if I stay in Calgary, is enough to get me through the winter. Then in spring I might get a job, but that leaves me in the same city for a year, and that's not what travellers do. That's not adventure. I have to leave.

Stuart asks me, 'Where will you go in America? Do you have an itinerary?'

'No. The Scottish bloke who follows the rugby team reckons he can get me a truck ride to Great Falls in Montana.'

'Then what?'

'I'd head south.'

'You're *crazy*, you stupid bugger. You can't just head south; you've got to be going to somewhere.'

I don't tell him that he's quite right, that a sensible person would have a destination, so I make one up. 'I'll head for Hollywood. It's near Los Angeles, isn't it?'

He says, 'Jesus you're bloody hopeless; *of course* it's near Los Angeles. Look, mate, do me a favour. Buy a map, and I'll put a cross on it, and I'll also put a cross on Calgary so you can find your way back.'

'I won't be back. Eventually I'll get to New York; I'll get a job on a ship, go to Europe, then I'll send you a letter telling you where to send my stuff.'

Stuart's always got loads of other people's stuff in his front room that he later sends off to Peru or Mexico or London or Africa.

~

The description given to me of the truck driver I'm to meet isn't all that good, so I'm a bit of a nuisance to tired and hungry diners in the Calgary truck stop. Some of them appear suspicious, as if I'm a bum trying to cadge a free meal or coffee. Others seem amused that a bloke who's got a scruffy haversack on his back and an Australian Army slouch hat on his head is in their diner searching for a man he doesn't know. Whenever anyone comes in, I look at them expectantly, hoping they're my truck driver, but they ignore me. A short man wearing a bright Hawaiian shirt under his parka comes in, and I reckon he's not a truck driver. He orders coffee then says to me, 'I guess you're looking for me.'

I say, 'G'day. You're the Alberta Trailers driver?'

'Yes. You're the Australian?'

'Yeah; how'd you guess?'

He laughs. 'There are always guys in here trying to get rides, but there's not too many that wear bush hats.'

'Oh, so it's a bit obvious.'

'A bit.'

'Thank Christ you're here. Everyone's been giving me strange looks.'

'I can't say I blame them. We don't get too many in here wearing hats like that.'

'It's an army hat. I thought it'd help me when I'm hitchhiking. Americans will know that I'm Australian and not a murderer.'

'Murderer?'

'Yeah, there's lots of stories about killings in America, especially hitchhikers on the open road.'

'Is there?'

'Yes. Well, not lot's, some.'

'I've not heard any. Anyhow, let's drink our coffee then we'll get going.'

He tells me his name is Peter, that he takes camp-site trailers all over North America, that he wishes he wasn't married with three kids, a mortgage and a clapped-out family car, and that he would like to visit

Australia one day. I don't tell him that he's got a fat chance, that he's living the adventurer's nightmare.

While I was waiting for Peter to arrive at the truck stop, I drank four cups of coffee to legitimize my presence there. I prefer to drink tea, but everyone in the diner is a tired, tough-looking truck driver who's gulping cup after cup of jet-black coffee. I imagined the biggest of them saying something like, 'Look at the funny little man drinking his English tea,' then I'd have to defend myself and I'd certainly get beaten to a pulp.

I say to Peter, 'Can I get you another coffee?'

He accepts, so I have to have my fifth cup.

'Where are you going after Great Falls?' he asks.

It's a sensible question that deserves a sensible answer, but by not having a firm destination, I'm able to go where rides take me. It'll be a fine way to see America. Fine, but unusual, but to be unusual in America is courting trouble. I say, 'Disneyland. I'm going to Disneyland.'

'That's great. One day I'll take the wife and kids there. All I need is the money.'

It seems my hitchhiking destination is very credible—it's where North American fathers want to take their wife and kids—so that's where I'll go.

I don't get to see the great falls in Great Falls. Peter offers to let me off in the conservative-looking town centre, but I know I'll be an oddity and likely questioned by conservative police.

Instead, he leaves me on the town outskirts, telling me that it's doubtful anyone will give me a ride while I'm on this road. But I don't care. It's the start of my adventure.

One hour later, I look back at the steep hill I've walked up, and I'm thinking he's right. The few cars have whizzed by, the drivers not even waving or giving encouraging blows on their horn. Already I'm a failed hitchhiker.

I wonder about my technique, but it's exactly the same as I used in Australia, where I was very successful; I got many rides. I'd had girlfriends who were 'geographically impossible' and where, after fleeting kisses at their front gate, I'd successfully hitched a ride home.

I consider my appearance and presentation, and I reckon I look the part. My battered haversack has an Australian flag sewn to the back; I'm wearing denim jeans; my shirt's not yet crushed, and most car drivers should recognize my hat as Australian. I'm certain that I'd be a good and interesting travelling companion to an American who's driving south to Disneyland. All I need is the chance.

A long flash-looking car with loads of chromium on front comes along. I hold out my thumb in the internationally recognized 'please give me a ride' position. But the car whizzes past with a toot of the horn and the driver holding up his thumb in the internationally recognized 'up you' position.

I yell at him, 'You *bastard*.'

I'm hot and wish I had some water. Should I eat the fruit I've got, or should I ration myself because I may be here for days and days. I sit on a tree stump. There's no sounds: no bird whistles; no rustling grass that's hiding scurrying about little lizards, and no engine noise from approaching cars or trucks. It's too hot to be wearing denim jeans so I change into my khaki 'King Gee Victory Brand' shorts.

Why hasn't anyone given me a ride? Is it because I'm going up a hill and American drivers don't stop because they're reluctant to do hill starts. Perhaps it'll be better after I get to the top and I'm going downhill?

A man who looks nothing like me comes down the hill. He wears army fatigues, proper hiking boots, a peaked baseball cap, and a proper backpack with steel supports. I remain seated. I glance down at my well-worn tennis sandshoes and then at his boots that are laced to well above his ankles. They're nice boots.

He glances at me, and our eyes momentarily meet. I say, 'G'day,' but he ignores me.

I remember Stuart's warning about hitchhikers being murdered, so I look around for a stick or rock. I see a pretty good throwing rock I can use if I'm attacked, but first I try to be friendly.

I say, 'Howya goin, mate, orright?' But he continues to avoid eye contact. I size him up and reckon that if he attacks and he's not got a knife, gun or length of motor-bike chain, I can beat him. I still try to be friendly. He might be coming back from Disneyland and could give me some tips about hitchhiking in America. I say, 'Mate, you're not very friendly. Aren't you going to say g'day?'

He starts running.

I yell, 'What's *wrong* with you, you bastard,' but he breaks into a sprint. I watch in amazement. His backpack wobbles about and bashes against his body and he stumbles on the rough roadside. 'You ignorant cunt,' I yell, 'I hope you never get a ride.' He's soon out of sight.

Minutes later I hear an engine. I prepare myself in the internationally recognized hitchhiking position, but just as I'm about to put on my big please-give-me-a-ride smile, I see that that the car has lights and a siren mounted on its roof.

The car slowly passes me, then it stops, and a man dressed in an official-looking uniform gets out. He says, 'Hi, I'm the border patrol officer.'

There's little need for him to tell me that he represents authority, because he's got all manner of badges and stripes sewn to his shirt, and a gun and handcuffs strapped to his belt.

I stand very still.

He says, 'Are you from hereabouts?'

'No, mate; I'm from Australia.'

'Alrighty. Sir, have you got ID? A passport?'

'Yeah.'

'Can I see it?'

'Yeah, it's in my haversack; I'll get it.' I reach around to put my hand into the side pocket.

The man says, 'Sir, do it slowly.'

I think that's a strange thing to say. He's got to be a busy man and the quicker he gets what he wants, the quicker he can get after illegal immigrants, perhaps go after that man who ran away from me. He's obviously a suspicious character. I'm certainly not.

I slowly get my passport and go to give it to him, but he takes a step backwards and his hand drops to near his gun. 'Sir, stay where you are. I'll come to you, and then you give me the passport in an outstretched arm. Understand?'

'I'm beginning to. You think I'm here illegally. Here look in my passport. It was stamped last night at Sweetgrass.'

He cautiously takes my passport, and without looking away from me, he opens it at the photograph, glances down, glances up and down again. Then he flicks over the pages, locates the visa, rubs his finger over the immigration stamp and says, 'It looks okay; you've got a visa until January ten.'

'Yeah.'

He gives me the passport and says, 'Sir, what are you doing way out here? You're not hitchhiking, are you?'

I'd seen many signs stating that hitchhiking is illegal in Montana, so there's no way I can plead ignorance. I say, 'Hitchhiking? Isn't that illegal? I'm not hitchhiking.'

'Well, what are you doing way out here, sir?'

'I'm walking.'

'Walking to where, sir?'

I wish he'd stop calling me sir, but I'm not about to tell him that. I say, 'South. I'm walking south. I'm going to Disneyland.'

'Disneyland! Why, that's a thousand miles from here. You can't walk all that distance.'

'Probably not. I'll probably get tired of walking, then I'll get a bus, but I assure you, I'm not hitchhiking.'

This man's no dill; he knows I'm hitchhiking, but he also knows I'm not worth the aggravation of arrest and the accompanying bookwork. Arresting a seemingly stupid Australian who reckons he's walking to Disneyland isn't going to further his career in the immigration service.

He says, 'Sir, good luck. Just remember that hitchhiking in Montana, Idaho and Nevada is illegal. Just don't get caught by the Highway Patrol guys. Try getting rides in truck stops, no one will bother you there.'

The immigration officer gets in his car. He calls out to me, 'Did you see that guy running down the road. He could be Army, doing a training exercise.'

'Yeah, I thought he was an illegal. I reckon you should check him out. He looked suspicious.'

And he goes to do exactly that.

Big rigs with all manner of advertising painted on their trailer sides sit outside the Big Belt Mountains truck stop. The smell of long-time-brewed coffee, hot cakes and sweet-smelling maple syrup, important staples of American truckies, waft in the air. I'm a naive tenderfoot going into a saloon packed with gunslingers so I enter gingerly.

Another country-and-western song sung by another nasal-sounding cowboy that's lost another woman blares from a juke box. Most customers sit on barstools and swivel to see who's come in the front door. I sense hostility. The gunslingers wear a uniform: grey or dark blue trousers and jackets that probably cover tattooed bodies; boots that lace-up high above their ankles; more than two days of beard growth, and baseball hats. A cloud of tobacco smoke mixed with grilled food fumes hangs in the air.

I shouldn't simply slink in. I must be assertively friendly. I say to the staring faces, 'G'day; I'm an Australian who's trying to get to Los Angeles; can anyone give me a ride?'

One man says, 'Australia?'

'Yeah; I've just come from Alberta. I'm on my way to Disneyland.'

Another man says, 'Disneyland; yep, I'd love to go there myself.'

Conversation flows—they know I'm not a threat.

A man says, 'Goddamn, what's an Australian doing here in the Big Belt?'

'Accident. I've been hitchhiking. My last ride left me a mile down the road. The bloke told me I should come here, that it's a friendly place.'

I sit with three burly men who have big stomachs caused by beer or from sitting too long on truck seats.

A waitress wearing a tatty apron and holding a tatty order pad stands impatiently waiting for a food order, and I expect her to lick the end of her poised pencil. One man scrutinizes a much-handled menu.

The waitress says, 'You guys want to order?'

I glance at the menu and see some of the reasons for the men's big stomachs: pies, and fried everything else.

The waitress does lick the end of her pencil, then she parrot-fashion calls the day's specials—all fried something.

The three men order fried somethings, and the waitress turns to me saying, 'You want to eat?'

'No thanks; I'm all right.'

One of the men says, 'You got to eat; we's all eating. This meal's on us.'

I'm certainly hungry, but I'm thinking about the custom of hospitality. One of these men is going to give me a ride to Los Angeles, and when that happens, I should pay for all their meals. I can't afford to do that—my daily food budget's only three dollars. If I don't eat, though, the men will be offended, so I say, 'I'll have what they're having.'

This is a mistake because fried eggs and fried bacon come, then hotcakes, then pecan pie and coffee. During the meal I exaggerate my answers to their questions: kangaroos become household pets; snakes hide behind every bush, and when that goes unchallenged, I raise the stakes to include huge man-hunting spiders.

One of the men says, 'Well, we'd better get going.'

I've been entertaining them for an hour so I say to them, 'What about a ride to Los Angeles?'

'Los Angeles? We're going to Calgary, Canada. You're welcome to come there with us.'

'But I've just come from *there*. I don't want to go back.'

I've got coffee running out of my ears. When I finish drinking one cup, the waitress comes to re-fill it, and she points to whoever paid for it. I give what I hope are friendly waves of my hand and say, 'Thanks.'

Slices of pie arrive: first blueberry, then apple, then cranberry, then more of them all. I'm stuffed. I could live in this truck stop for months without ever paying anything.

A voice from behind me says, 'You want to go to LA?'

I say, *'Do I what?'*

The man that asked the question says, 'Eh. Do you what?'

Clearly this Chuck or Frank Junior or Billy-Joe doesn't understand the Queen's English as spoken by an Australian, so I shift into American speak and say, 'Goddamn, I sure do.'

He says, 'Me and my buddy are back-hauling a load of wheat from Winnipeg Manitoba to LA. You're welcome to ride with us.'

'Great!'

The man's buddy says, 'Our eighteen-wheeler's heading for home. We'll be there in two days.'

Sitting on the engine casing between John and Jack in the cabin of their eighteen-wheeler isn't all that comfortable, except when one of them goes to rest in the sleeper bunk behind. I continually answer their questions about Australia: politics, lifestyle, why the Queen of England is also the Queen of Australia, and how much money truck drivers make in Australia. They're especially interested in Australian English, and before long I'm sprouting all the slang I know. I talk, and they laugh, so I keep talking.

Whenever they stop the truck for food, they insist on paying, and I continue to amuse. I say, 'I should shout you for something.' And they fall about laughing and yelling-out, 'Shout, shout, shout.'

After driving all night, Jack says, 'We'll soon be at Millie's.'

I don't know what that means, but I'll do anything or go anywhere to get my bum off the hot engine casing.

John says, 'We're going to have a free Thanksgiving lunch in Eureka.

I say, 'Free lunch: eureka!'

He says, 'So you've heard of our Eureka.'

I realise he doesn't connect the word to its Greek meaning.

'We're going to make you an honorary truck driver.'

Something is definitely happening at the Eureka truck stop because trucks and trailers of all sizes and makes are parked there. It surprises me that they're positioned so exactly: all the truck fronts in a perfect line with the spaces between of equal distance. It's just like a used-truck sale yard—at least the way it should be.

I say to Jack and John, 'I've never seen as many trucks in one place. There's got to be at least fifty! Where'd they all come from?'

'Everywhere; guys come from out of state to be at Millie's Thanksgiving. She's been doing it for fifteen years. She's probably been preparing it for weeks. You'll be amazed at how good it'll be.'

But I'm still looking at the trucks.

They know them all. John says, 'There's that rig we saw on that long climb out of Memphis, and there's the rig those two Polacks drive.'

Jack says, 'There's the rig Rick sold last year.'

And they both say, 'Little Joe's here and there's Jones's rig.'

By American standards mid-twentieth century Australian road transporters use inferior equipment. In the nineteen-fifties, rail carries most inter and intra-state freight, and British-made trucks carry any that isn't—Bedfords, Ford, Foden, perhaps a Thornycroft, a few Autocars, and ageing ex-army blitz wagons. Few sophisticated prime movers or huge aluminium-covered trailers can be seen on Australian roads, just the occasional American International or Mack towing a shiny aluminium trailer, and they get a lot of attention. There's no huge interstate transport companies. Brambles, a Newcastle-based business, is yet to expand Australia wide, and Ken Thomas' TNT and Peter Abeles' Alltrans are struggling small businesses.

Jack and John's truck is an impressive Peterbilt, a sixteen-forward-gear monster that attacks steep hills with the tenacity of a bull. But anxieties such as truck payments to the finance company, whether they'll get late payment for the next haul, and will mechanical repairs be necessary are the same as for all owner drivers, American or Australian.

As we walk towards Millie's, I notice they occasionally take admiring glances at their Peterbilt. The front of the truck appears as if its thinking, 'There go my owners who wash, nurture and load my belly with freight.' Pride in ownership is certain.

There's no need to open the front door of the Eureka truck-stop to know that a party's on. From outside I hear yells and laughs and screams.

Jack goes in first, to immediate recognition: 'Hey, you old road buck, have you got your ...'

'Hey, there you are, John'.

I linger outside. I'm a stranger in this family, and space is needed for brother to greet brother.

'Jack, you son of a gun.'

'Goddamn, it's you guys!'

'Who said they'd never make it?'

There are few women in the room. One, a particularly big woman wearing an apron embroidered with sampler patterns, comes to Jack and gathers him in a tight bear hug. She says, 'Honey, I knew you wouldn't let Millie down.'

John says, 'To get here we had to drive all the way from Alaska without stopping.'

Everyone looks at me. I feel like a rabbit amongst a pack of dingoes. I can stay where I am, or go inside, or do the unpredictable. I go straight to Millie and hug her. She doesn't know what to do.

Jack says, 'This guy's our new off-sider. Meet Barry.'

She says, 'Hi Barry. Welcome to Thanksgiving at Millie's.'

I should try for an American accent, perhaps a southern drawl, a long-voweled hiiiii. But I say, 'G'day, howya goin?'

Millie looks confused. 'Eh. What'd you say?'

Jack laughs. 'He's from the wilds of Australia; he's talking Australian.'

John says, 'But we've learnt his language. Go on, Barry, say something else.'

They hadn't told me I was to be the entertainment, but I can't let them down. I say, 'Blimey-Teddy-Charlie, you blokes are gunna make me look like a drongo, youse are comin the raw prawn.'

Jack looks serious when he says, 'You're as mad as a cut snake.'

I'm surprised he remembers something I'd said earlier, but it's nothing like my accent, it's more a cockney one. I burst out laughing. I laugh at him, while John laughs at Jack, and Millie laughs at them, then everyone laughs at everyone, and no longer feel like a rabbit amongst a pack of dingoes.

Between Millie's haw-hawing and spluttering she says, 'Give these three guys a beer.'

I sit in a booth with them and think I should shoot for more credibility, so I decide to become an Australian rough-riding champion. Around my waist I wear an impressive cowboy belt with a longhorn steer on its buckle. I wore it during Calgary's Stampede week, when all us city dwellers paraded about in mostly borrowed western clothes pretending to be Tom Mix or Gene Autry or Hopalong Cassidy.

Stampede week's when accountants and bus drivers and dressmakers become wild west cowboys and cowgirls, and everyone struts around walking bandy-legged like they've spent years in the saddle.

Stuart Acason, the bloke I flatted with in Calgary, was born in Western Queensland, and his background includes clearing irrigation ditches, share farming, riding horses and branding cattle. He used to talk about wild-west stuff, about rodeos and roughriding, and how the Warwick rodeo was the best in Queensland, and then he'd correct himself and say best in Australia, probably the world. He'd spoken about Wally Woods, Australia's all-around champion cowboy, and how he reckoned Wally could beat these North Americans any day of the week—blindfolded. He told me that during the Second World War American troops had competed in friendly—if that can ever be so—Australian rodeos.

I remember some of the special rodeo words he used, so I reckon I can easily pretend to be a champion. That is, provided no one produces a horse.

I get up as if I'm going to the toilet and say loudly, 'Are any of you blokes on the rodeo circuit?' I place my thumbs into my belt so the buckle's seen and hope like hell no one says yes.

Everyone looks at the buckle, and before they see too much, before someone says they bought a buckle like that, I take my thumbs away and say, 'I ride bulls on the Australian circuit, and I'm over here to see your best riders ride the best bulls in the world.'

Someone says, 'Yep, that's correct; us yanks are the best.'

Everyone nods approval. They're happy, and I'm happy to have them believe I might be a champion.

I come back from the toilet and see John and Jack's puzzled looks. Jack says, 'So you're a rodeo rider?'

'Fuck, *no*. I can hardly sit on a horse let alone one that's moving up and down. I told the blokes that because, because … it's a bit of fun. We'd call it, ah, character reinforcement.'

John says, 'We'd call it bullshit.'

'And you'd be one-hundred percent right, but don't dob me in, because all your mates now think I'm pretty tough.'

'So we shouldn't tell them you're on your way to Disneyland to say hi to Mickey and Donald Duck?'

'Fuck no, they'll think I'm a shirtlifter, or something.'

'Shirtlifter?'

I ride in John and Jack's Peterbilt across Nevada into California then to Los Angeles. I consider leaving them to explore sites and when I tell them this, they say, 'Why? There ain't nothing to see.'

We get to the outskirts of Los Angeles, and I'm excited about seeing Hollywood and its film stars, especially Marilyn Monroe. Four-lane highways are now ten-lane freeways, with overpasses and underpasses that'll take a mistaken navigator many miles away from their correct destination. I can't help comparisons:

The widest road in Australia is on the Sydney Harbour Bridge, and I've always been impressed, but it only goes a couple of miles. Los Angeles freeway constructors have taken their concrete art to ridiculous heights—roads rule. Cars are mostly big and bulky with loads of chromium and glass, and all drivers seem intent on crisscrossing over every lane.

John and Jack are excellent drivers on open highways, but now they show signs of wanting to own the freeways. Jack's arms spread over the steering wheel in the ten-to-three position of a racing-car driver as if he thinks he's king of the road. My head does a tennis-match twist: a huge building on the right; a huge movie theatre on the left; a car-sales yard as big as a football field on the right; a gigantic shopping centre on the left. I can't see what's behind the Peterbilt, but I hear evidence of near misses.

Jack relays a strange commentary about some of his moves. He says, 'All right you guys; this is now my lane.' And his arms twist the steering wheel to twenty-five to one, then back to ten-to-three. I feel the load of Manitoba wheat in the trailer move about.

John's supposed to be navigating, but he looks at his road map infrequently. He says, 'We exit in another mile, I guess.'

'Exit right or left?'

He doesn't know so he studies the map. 'Goddamned if I know, but to be on the safe side, go to the middle lane.'

Jack doesn't look at his side mirrors before his arms twist to five-to-five, and the big rig jerks into the middle lane. Behind us car tyres squeal and horns honk.

John says, 'I figure we have to exit now.'

'Right or goddamned left?'

'Ah ... right ... I guess.'

The truck goes right, then he says, 'No, it's a left.'

I look to the left and see a red-roofed car that's going to be in our way. I say, 'Jack there's—'

'Get out of my way you bastard,' he says.

Inside the truck cabin, we hear very little of the sound of one of the nine wheels on that side of the Peterbilt abrading the paintwork on the red-roofed car.

Jack glances at his side mirror. 'There seems to be a bit of trouble behind.'

John says, 'What happened?'

'Some guy's hit another guy and … oh shit; he's now hit someone else.'

Jack asks, 'This exit?'

John says, 'Yes, but keep your eyes on the exit road; we don't want to cause accidents.'

~

Disneyland's Anaheim car park is nearly full of empty big cars with shiny chromium fronts, their passengers probably now speeding in a bobsled down the Matterhorn or riding on Dumbo the flying elephant. Everyone's excited, and I am too. I was planning to get post cards of Mickey and Donald Duck to send to John and Jack. But at the Los Angeles street corner where they stopped the Peterbilt for me to get out, a policeman riding a strange three-wheeled motor bike told them to get the hell away from the corner. So we never exchanged addresses.

I queue at the entrance gate eager to go inside, and I'm not the least unhappy to pay the entrance fee. Nearby, cars drop off excited passengers, and I see a red-roofed one that has a huge tyre abrasion on its side. I hope they enjoy Disneyland.

28 November 1960
Los Angeles. California
Dear Mum,
I have just had the most fantastic day. I went to the beautiful, marvellous, huge Disneyland Park.

I met an Aussie named Bert at the YMCA, and we went to Disneyland together. At first sight, I felt like running as fast as I could to see the place, but I controlled myself and kept with the mob. It cost $4.75 for fifteen rides and was good value. I almost couldn't believe it—me, Barry White, at Disneyland.

I saw Roy, the big bloke from the Mickey Mouse Club, and I got him to do a drawing for John and Jeffrey, which he signed. Tomorrow I'm going to Hollywood.

The trip from Calgary to Los Angeles only cost me $5.00, but since being here I have spent $30.00; too much.

Love Barry.

At Las Vegas I played the five-cent machine but moved to the dollar machine to have a 'free' photograph taken. Two weeks of hitchhiking had taken its toll; since leaving Calgary I had lost ten pounds in weight.

Chapter Eight

The man's got an air of superiority, and I feel like telling him to get the smirk off his face. I should say to him that if he thinks his smart, starched-white shirt with epaulettes and his job as Albuquerque Bus Station manager makes him better than me, he's wrong. I should do that. I should say to him, all he's got is a smart starched-white shirt with epaulettes and nothing else, but I don't. I don't say it because he's the only one who can help me. I tell him that his bus company has lost my haversack.

He says, 'Your *what?*'

So I tell him again.

But he still answers with, *'What?'*

I wonder how he got his job when he can't answer a simple question.

'Your men put the haversack on the bus in Flagstaff, and now it's not on the bus. Somehow your bus company has lost it.'

He says, 'We don't lose things. We're the largest transporters of people in the United States of America. If we lost people's things, they wouldn't travel with us.'

I think about saying that he should roll up the sleeves of his smart starched-white shirt with epaulettes and go to the baggage area to look for my haversack, but I realise it's no use saying that to a man that doesn't even know what a haversack is.

I describe it to him in detail. 'It's made of canvas and has pockets on the side and shoulder straps at the back, and an Australian flag sewn to the top flap. It's the haversack I used when I was a scout in the first Beverly Hills troupe.' But all he does is laugh. Laughing at a visitor to the United States of America when that person is in dire straits is wrong. I reckon he shouldn't have the job as bus station manager.

He says that he checked the manifest.

I have no idea what he means by manifest. I laugh and say, 'What's that got to do with my missing haversack?'

He says, 'Sir, you changed buses at Winslow and at Gallup, and our manifests show that your hav … what did you call it?'

'Haversack. It's a haversack. You have them in America; I've seen people carrying them.'

He smiles. 'Our manifests show that your hav-er-sack was not on our bus at those changes. My guess is that Continental Trailways screwed up.'

I smile, wondering if a bus-station manager is allowed say screwed up. I say, 'Well someone fucked it up,' and he tells me not to use obscene language in his bus station. I say that he can't tell me not to use obscene language when he's using it. He starts to explain but I interrupt him:

'I'm not leaving your bus station until I get my haversack. I'm going to Calgary in Canada, and if I don't get my haversack now, I'll never get it. It'll never catch up with me. Everything I own is in it.'

He says, 'Sir, you do what you have to. We're doing all we can to resolve the problem. I suggest you come back tomorrow.'

Then he leaves me standing there like a goose. He goes towards a door that has 'Manager' written on it, thinking he's dealt with his problem passenger. I reckon he thinks I'll go away. But he's wrong.

I call out to him, 'I'll still be here. I'll be sitting on your polished timber seats. I'll stay here all night if I have to.'

He opens the door, goes inside and closes it behind him. But I follow him and stand close to it. 'Whenever you come out of your office, I'll ask you about my haversack.'

If my hitchhiking had been successful, I wouldn't be here arguing with the man. If everything had gone as well as it had with John and Jack's Peterbilt truck, I would know exactly where my haversack was. Getting rides between Los Angeles and San Francisco was easy. I'd even been selective about who I'd ride with and only put my thumb out for newer cars. But between San Francisco and Bakersfield it all fell apart.

Something went wrong. It couldn't have been my technique because I know it's good. Jack and John had told me so. I thought about how I looked to American motorists bored by their own company or tired of listening on their car radio to Little Richard or Bing Crosby. They wouldn't be able to see that I hadn't shaved for days, but they'd notice my clothing. A problem for hitchhikers is getting clothes washed and dried and ironed. There are places called Laundromats in America, but how do hitchhikers get a load to wash? Hitchhikers only have one or two of everything. Oh, they might have more than two sets of underwear. I've got four, but a bloke looks bloody stupid washing his Bond's underwear in a bloody big washing machine. I wash mine in garage toilet washbasins or under taps in parks, but drying them is a problem. I used a method of tying them to the back of my haversack so they'd flap about, but I realised drivers who are tired of listening to Little Richard or Bing Crosby and who might be thinking about giving me a ride would think it strange. I wouldn't give a bloke a ride who had Bond's underwear tied to his haversack. Then there's my two shirts. They never get ironed, and I reckon car drivers notice. They probably say to themselves, look at that rough-looking bloke wearing a crumpled shirt. How does he expect to be given a ride? He hasn't even taken the trouble to iron his shirt.

So I get less selective. I try to hitch rides in any old car, and I try in truck stops—without success.

I should ask someone what I'm doing wrong. When I get my next ride, I'll ask if there's anything American hitchhikers do that I'm not. I'm prepared to change my style. Perhaps I should get a small American flag and sew it to the back of my haversack and whistle the Star Spangled Banner? Perhaps I should speak with an American accent and tell everyone my name's Chuck or Bill Junior or Mike? There's plenty of Chucks and Bill Juniors and Mikes in America—I bet they'd get a ride—but there's not too many Barrys.

It took me two days to get from San Francisco to Bakersfield. It shouldn't take two days to travel a hundred and fifty miles. I should've taken a side trip to Sequoia National Park to see the biggest and oldest trees in the world, but I was riding in a Mexican bloke's old car, and I didn't want to take the chance of having to sleep rough. North American National Parks have lots of wild bears. I was told in Canada about a brown bear biting off a bloke's head. The bear pulled apart his tent, threw him in the air a few times, then it took his head off in one almighty bite.

But it's not just the bears. There's rattlesnakes and wolves, and maybe even be a deranged murderer hiding in a National Park. America has a lot of deranged murderers, and I reckon an Australian sleeping under a tree would be an easy target. Can you imagine how my mother would feel receiving a telegram saying your son's been murdered or has had his head bitten off by a bear?

Hitchhiking in America is stupid enough, but there's no need to be absolutely stupid and sleep rough in a park full of bears and murderers.

I decide to hitchhike during the day so I get to a bus station by nightfall, then I buy a ticket on a bus going west. By doing that I get some sleep on the bus and there's little chance of being murdered.

At daybreak one morning, the bus arrives at a small town at a drug store that doubles as the bus terminal. I get off the bus and walk away from the town.

I know I'm going in an easterly direction because I'm facing a hot early morning sun, but soon the sun is on my right, so I'm going south. I look at my completely unsuitable map that has only major roads, large towns and cities marked. I walk for an hour, but I'm uncertain where I am or where I'm going. Apart from the Greyhound bus, no vehicle passes me, and I feel frustrated. I'm wearing heavy denim trousers that are great for travelling because they never look dirty, but they're too hot, so I stop walking to change into crushed and wrinkled khaki shorts. It's an opportunity for a car to come, for its driver to see a man standing in Australian Bond's underwear and for the driver to laugh his head off. But none comes. Even fate's against me.

By noon a few cars pass, but the drivers must have been happy listening to Little Richard or Bing Crosby so they don't stop. I'm feeling hungry because I haven't eaten since last night, and even then it was only a hamburger without beetroot. I did ask for beetroot but the man in the greasy-spoon café said, 'What's beetroot?'

It gets boring hearing the stomp of your own feet hitting the ground, so I hum and sing. I sing; *tramp-tramp-tramp along the highway*, but I only know the first line of that song, which I repeat and repeat. I look for birds resting in trees, listen to bees flying past my ear and I sing more songs: *row-row-row your boat gently down the stream, merrily-merrily-merrily-merrily, life is but a dream*. I kick pebbles along the road trying to break my own record for the number of times kicking the same pebble. I get to fifty-two kicks which is, I think, a world record. My throat's dry and my lips are cracked. But there are no front yards to sneak into to get a drink. It's a miserable situation.

Then I smell food. Something familiar, but I'm not certain what. A truck carrying vegetables goes past without the driver even blowing the horn or giving me a friendly wave. I yell out, 'You lousy bastard.'

The straps on my haversack are blistering my shoulders, and I think about other intrepid explorers. I remember reading that Scott of the Antarctic, Sir Edmund Hillary, and Burke and Wills had to ditch some of the gear they carried, so I'm thinking I should do the same. I compare their predicaments to mine and I decide to wait a few more hours before ditching postcards I'd been collecting, or my shaving gear, or my writing pad.

The food smell gets stronger, and I'm certain it's coming from a large building about a mile distant. Smoke pours from chimneys, and the truck that passed me drives inside. Cars are parked out front, and as I get closer, I can read a sign which says it's the something-or-other Onion Processing Company. Bloody onions! I hate onions.

An old man sits in a small hutch behind a gate, so I ask in my best American accent, 'Is there a town near?'

He gives me a hostile wave, and I hear the word 'hobo' said.

I call out, 'You old bastard,' and continue walking.

Now I'm even more miserable. There and then I decide that if I don't die of starvation or thirst and if I ever get to a town, I'll buy a bus ticket to Calgary.

As result of buying that bus ticket, I'm now scrutinizing the baggage load of every bus that arrives or departs from the Albuquerque Bus Station, a building that could easily win last prize for architecture in Afghanistan. I watch as drivers carelessly load and unload everything from bundles tied with rope to Samsonite suitcases. There are no haversacks.

I see a driver who was driving a bus many hours earlier and he says to me, 'You still here?'

I say, 'Yeah, my haversack's not going in or out of here without me knowing.'

He shrugs and gets into the driver's seat of an aging Greyhound bus. It must be a local bus because the Greyhound Bus Company seems not to give a bugger about the comfort of short-trip travellers. The shiny new ones are all on interstate routes where they have to compete with the Continental Trailways Bus Company. No bus driver gives a bugger about my problem. The bus-station manager comes to dispatch the aging Greyhound, and when he sees me, he goes in the other direction.

When there's no bus baggage to search, I sit on the polished-wood seats designed for discomfort and, like everyone else, watch everyone watching everyone else. Faces show excitement, anticipation and tiredness. Kit-bag-carrying American servicemen wear bored expressions because they're being transferred to Fort something or Camp something. Mothers fuss over children who don't sit still because they're excited about going on an adventure in the big shiny bus that has a skinny greyhound dog painted on its side. A down-and-out man surreptitiously swigs from a bottle that's hopelessly camouflaged in a brown paper bag. But it's the mystery people I mostly watch. They take some guessing. They're sitting one moment, standing the next; they go in and out of the toilet or go outside and don't return for hours. They seem not to have any baggage, and when buses arrive or depart, they do nothing, not even pretending they're meeting anyone. The smart mystery people know how to be no one in a country where everyone's supposed to be someone. America is an identity crazy country because everywhere they ask you for an ID thing. I reckon the mystery people are nobodies—they don't have any identity. I bet they don't have any possessions or even a family photo album.

Moments after I got to the bus station, a bloke asked me to give him a dollar for a beer. I said, 'No, mate I'm a tourist, and I'm not giving you one of my hard-earned dollars so you can buy a bloody beer.'

He stared at me and said, 'Uh, a tourist in *Albuquerque?*'

I understood his surprise.

He said, 'Man, where you from?'

I said, 'Australia.'

And he said, 'So you speak Spanish.'

'No. I speak English.'

He went away shaking his head.

I wonder why the Albuquerque bus station is even worse than Sydney's Central Railway Refreshment Rooms. Why do they have hard wooden seats that are so bum unfriendly? Why are the toilets so dirty? Why does the restaurant only serve fried foods, coffee and apple and blueberry pies? Why does the front door give off blood-curdling squeaks every time it's used? And why is the wall and ceiling paint peeling, and the cactus in the only two planter boxes dead? I mean, how can they kill cactus? They hardly need any water. This place is so unfriendly.

An unseen person with a speech impediment announces the bus from OklahomaAmarilloandallpointseastisarrivingatbaysix. Who gets pleasure out of dragging-out the name of every town and city at which buses from New York, New Orleans, New Hampshire or Newfoundland stop? How do Albuquerque's down-and-outers and deros get any peace and quiet when there's an idiot hiding in a back room blasting their eardrums with towns and cities from here to Canada?

Sydney's down-and-outers and deros are luckier. There's no idiot hiding in a back room at Central Railway Station's country platform blasting them with the names of all the stations from Sydney to Melbourne. It's sobering being at Central Station in the early hours of the morning when the paper trains are loaded with *The Sydney Morning Herald* and *The Daily Telegraph*, and on Sundays, the scandal paper *The Truth*. This is the time when down-and-outers and deros use lurking and nous skills. The coppers park their Black-Maria or Birdcage with its wire prison attached to the back in no-standing areas, then slowly strut along the rows of seats to decide who they'll arrest. On cold windy winter nights, those who don't care about arrest records welcome a warm cell. The crafty ones with nous know the rules of the game. They know that a respectable-looking bag, or moving about the station, or going to the toilet, or meeting arriving trains, or looking often at the big clock, or scrutinizing the arrival and departure board is a good ploy. If a bloke wants to have a sleep, he finds a used ticket and dangles it from his pocket so the coppers can see it. They can sleep because they don't have ear-splitting calls of the next train from CootamundraWaggaWaggaandWangaratta

The Albuquerque area is the traditional home of many Native Americans who do the same as many Native Australians; they often visit their extended families. When white settlers decided to steal Native Indian lands, the Indians didn't pack up and leave, they stayed to scratch out a living, and that's what they still do. Most are positioned at the bottom of the economic ladder, where work opportunities are few, liquor stores get a lot of their money and where most travel is by public transport.

I see a particularly big Indian and a particularly small white American doing some smart lurking. They do all the right things to make them appear legitimate: they meet buses; they use the toilet and drink the dishwater coffee served from the restaurant. They're professionals. Before the city police arrive to do a patrol, they go—disappear. When the police leave, they're back. They're skilful lurkers. They're not going to be arrested for loitering. There is, in any case, a cockatoo system that has the first person seeing the cops tapping his heel on the floor three times. I only twig to this after hearing a three-tapping sound coming from near the door, then the bloke sitting near me immediately stomps the heel of his boot three times.

The coppers come to me and ask if I sleep on the seat? I say 'No. I'm waiting for my haversack.'

I reckon they think I'm a bit mad because they go to the bus station manager's office and he comes out and points at me. The coppers nod and transfer their attention to someone who is not waiting for a haversack. But the mystery people don't accept me, because they know I'm different. Someone leaves a book on a seat, so I take it and begin reading. It's about a cowboy called Tex who rides a horse named Piebald and who is trying to find and shoot a man named Gonzales. This book's nowhere near as good as the one I found in the San Diego Armed Services YMCA that was written by a Mister Steinbeck. This book has no bartenders or cowpunchers or dogs with the name Doubletree Mutt, so I only pretend to read it. I keep my face down and avoid any eye contact with the mystery people. Sometimes I nod off and drop the book, but I quickly get it again, open it at any old page and don't even look up. I get very good at rolling up my eyes so I can look at what's going on, but no one knows I'm looking.

I hear that the bus from Denver-Colorado-Springs-Pueblo-and-LasVegas is arriving at bay four, and I roll up my eyes to see families with children, American servicemen, men wearing wide-brim Texan hats, Native Americans, African Americans, and nervous-looking Mexicans who, probably, don't have visas. A man wearing a flash-looking shirt that looks as though it's made of silk dawdles toward the toilet door. His shoulders are dropped, and his face has a hangdog look so I guess he's come from the Las Vegas gambling tables. He stops outside the door, looks down at the suitcase he carries, decides to leave it outside, then he goes inside—probably for a quick pee. Immediately after the door closes, the particularly big Indian and the small white American strike. They go towards the suitcase, and without breaking his stride, the particularly big Indian grabs the suitcase handle and off they go, out through the squeaky-hinged front door.

I think, *'Oh.'*

The man who has peed comes from the toilet, goes to get his bag, stops, looks around, panics and races to the baggage-storage area. I know that area very well because every hour or so I have a good look for my lost haversack. I know his bag's not there. It's gone out the front door carried by a particularly big Indian.

I keep my head down, pretending to read the cowboy book, but I can see the man rushing about holding his arms out. I hear him say, 'My goddamned bag was just *there*. Now it's *not.*'

I know that the man in charge of the baggage storage area is absolutely bloody hopeless. I know from my experience that he doesn't give a fuck about people's bags, but he plays the part, and they both stand where the bag had been. I see the lips of the man in charge of the baggage-storage area move, but I can't hear what he says.

I hear the man who lost his bag say, 'But it *was* here. *Right here.* Some goddamned motherfucker has taken it.'

I think he shouldn't be saying mother-fucker when there are mothers and their children about, but he keeps saying it, and I keep my head down, pretending to read the cowboy book.

The man stands near me and asks, 'Did anyone see me put my bag over there? Goddamn, I just arrived from Las Vegas.'

I mumble, 'I guessed you'd been there. I reckon you've lost all your money on the crap tables or in one of the thousands of slot machines.'

He says, 'I only left it for a minute. I only went to the john for piss. When I came out it was gone. One of you must have seen who took it.' He goes along the row of seats asking, 'Did *you* see who took it? Did *you*? Did *you*?'

It's becoming difficult not to look up. Everyone shakes their head and says, 'No.'

I have some sympathy for the man, but I don't want to get involved. All I want is to get my lost haversack and get on a bus going to

Calgary. I reckon it's not up to me to help him. There's plenty of Americans here who haven't lost their haversack and who must have seen the particularly big Indian pinch the bag. They should say, 'I saw the goddamned bastards that stole your bag.' An Australian tourist shouldn't have to be the one.

The ruckus moves away from me, and I think about my own problem. What if a particularly big Indian has already stolen my haversack? If that's happened, the theft should be investigated, and here I am wasting time seeing another particularly big Indian stealing someone else's bag. I notice the door to the bus station manager's office is slightly open, so I decide to confront him. I don't knock.

I say, 'Have you found out where my haversack is?'

He looks up and smiles.

I say, 'This is no laughing matter.'

He says, 'We've located your, ah, bag. It's in Flagstaff, Arizona and should be here tomorrow.'

I say, 'That's good. Do you know at exactly what time tomorrow?'

'No. Just keep in contact'.

I go away smiling. Immediately I have greater empathy for the man wearing the flash-looking shirt that looks as though it's made of silk. I see the poor bastard sitting with his hands cradling his head, and he's sobbing. I think, *fuck, I suppose I should help him.*

'G'day, mate. I'm an Australian tourist and I saw the bloke who pinched your bag.'

He looks up at me and says, 'Excuse me? Did you say *you saw* who took my bag?'

'Yeah. I saw two blokes knock it off. They took it right after you went into the toilet ... it was a bloody stupid place to leave it.'

He says, 'You saw two *what?*'

I realise that I should be speaking in my best American accent so I do. 'Blokes—guys. A bloody big Indian bloke and a short-arse white American. When you asked if anyone saw who stole it, I said nothing. I didn't want to get involved because this stupid bus company's lost my haversack. But now it's been found and should be here tomorrow.'

'*Your bag* was lost and now it's found?'

'Yeah, that's right. Are you having trouble understanding my best American accent?'

He nods. 'You are speaking very quickly.'

'Australians do that. Speak quickly. I've had a lot of trouble being understood. When I was …'

He nods again and says, 'Uh, uh.' He's not interested in my social observation of when I was …

He asks, 'Which way did the guys go?'

I point to the front door. 'They didn't muck about. As soon as you went inside they picked your bag up and buggered-off quick smart.'

He gets up saying, 'Goddamn, let's go outside to see if they're there.' He grabs my arm and pulls me.

'Mate, you've got Buckley's. They'll be well away by now.'

The man pulls me towards the door, and everyone in the bus station looks. I reckon they think I'm one of the suitcase bandits. He's naïve to believe that the particularly big Indian and the particularly short European American would hang around the scene of the crime, but he keeps pulling me, and I stumble over his legs.

I say, 'Hey, keep a cool head, mate!' But he's not going to be able to keep a cool head because he's lost his suitcase, and he's lost the plot.

Some passengers come through the doorway, and he pushes them aside. They probably think he's a plain-clothed policeman who's making an arrest, and that I'm a murderer or an alien without a visa. I don't want them thinking that, so I say, 'He's had his bag stolen and we're after the crooks.'

He stops outside and asks if I can see them.

A station wagon stops. I notice it has phony wood panels along its side, and I reckon they're big-time cattle ranchers. I remember seeing cars like this in cowboy films. I also reckon they shouldn't be at a bus station but at an airport getting aboard their private airplane. They look at us with puzzled expressions.

I say, 'He's had his bag stolen and we're after the crooks.'

They show no sympathy and hurry inside.

He asks, *'Can you see the guys?'*

'Don't be ridiculous; you can kiss that bag goodbye.'

'Goddamn it really pisses me off.' And then he asks, 'If you saw the guys take my bag, why didn't *you* stop them?'

He makes a fair point. I wondered if he'd get around to asking that. When the thieves knocked-off his bag, my immediate reaction was to call out, but I quickly considered the repercussions. I'm a badly dressed foreigner who has not shaved or properly slept for a week, and I'm wearing crumpled clothing that needs a wash. I look terrible. If I saw someone like me hanging around a bus station, and I'd had my bag stolen, I'd accuse me of being the robber. I know that it's best not to stick out like a sore boil, but to be part of the crowd. Not be obvious. Then there's the size of the particularly big Indian. He looked as though he can handle himself and might even have a tomahawk or bowie knife or be a champion shot with a bow and arrow. I'd seen films at the Beverly Hills picture theatre in Sydney where American Indians throw tomahawks great distances, and their skill with a bow and arrow is legendary. The man was a mug to leave his bag outside the toilet, and I wasn't going to get myself killed helping a mug.

I say to him, 'I didn't realise they were stealing your bag. I thought they were your friends who were taking your bag outside to their American station wagon that has phony wood panels along its side. Mate, you're stupid for leaving your bag. Only a mug would leave his bag in a bus station.'

He stares at me and grunts.

We go inside the bus station, and that's the end of that. I head straight for my uncomfortable polished-wood seat where I plan to have a sleep. He goes to the bus station manager's office.

A bloke sitting beside me says, 'There must be some trouble because here come the cops.'

I open my eyes to look. Fuck, they're coming towards me.

They ask, 'Are you the guy who saw this man's bag stolen?'

I sit upright and say, 'Yeah that's right.'

The policeman squints and I wonder why. 'This guy says you'd recognize them. Is *that* correct?'

Another policeman with two stripes on his shoulder stands in front of me and gives me the once over. A grunt comes from his throat; he nods and says, 'Err another bum.'

I'm certain he's referring to me and consider saying to him that I'm no bum. I'm a fully qualified plumber. I used to be in the Sea Cadets and the Scouts and I don't normally go around without shaving and wearing crumpled clothing. But I say nothing.

The policeman says, 'Well, what's your answer? Would you recognize them?'

I say, 'Yes.' But I realise I've made a mistake; I should've said no. But it's too late. I try to back-pedal. 'It, it all happened so quickly. I only *think* I'd recognize them … I'm not really certain.'

The two-striped policeman says, 'Sir, *come with us.*'

I sheepishly follow them to the bus-station manager's office.

Inside the office, the two-striped policeman asks what language is spoken in Australia.

'English, the same language as you.'

'So you're speaking English now?'

'Bloody oath.'

For thirty minutes they quiz me. They ask why I'm at the bus station? How I got there? How long I'm staying? Where I'm going? Do I have a hotel where they can contact me? And finally, do I have a passport? The policeman without stripes takes notes. He says, 'A.U.S.T.R.A.L.I.A.' as he writes in his notepad.

'Yeah, A.U.S.T.R.A.L.I.A.'

The two-striped policeman says, 'That's all the questions I have.'

211

'Good, can I go now?'

'No. We want you to come downtown.'

'Downtown?'

'Yes. There's a fair chance that those guys are still on the streets. We'll cruise around for a while.'

I shake my head. 'Mate, it's got nothing to do with me. I've done my bit. You cruise the streets.'

The two-striped policeman stands up. I reckon he's doing that to appear dominant, but he fails because he's shorter than I am.

The no-striped policeman takes a firm grip on my arm and tows me behind him, saying, *'He's coming.'*

I protest, 'But … but, I've got to wait for my haversack. The stupid bus company's lost my—'

'Greyhound's not a stupid bus company,' the bus-station manager says, 'Continental Trailways lost your … your thing. Greyhounds found your … thing.'

I'm the only non-American and the worst dressed in the room, which places me low in hierarchy, so I go where I'm towed.

They put me in the rear of a Dodge police car with a big sheriff's star painted on its doors. A siren and blue lights sit on its roof. If the policemen decide to turn it on—and I hope they do—it'll flash on and off. I think about what else I'd be doing if I wasn't riding in the car, and the answer is nothing. I'm much better off sitting tall in the back of the car with people on the street looking at me and wondering if I'm a disguised detective investigating some horrible crime. The man who lost his bag sits beside me, but he looks nothing like a disguised detective. I'd bet people on the street think he's a criminal. I'm trying to come to grips with the police's theory that the robbers might still be on the streets when I know they'd be holed-up in their hideout.

I'm enjoying seeing the sights but hope that the streets we're cruising are not typical of Albuquerque. If they are, Albuquerque's a dump.

The two-striped policeman says to me, 'You said you vaguely remember how they were dressed, but do you remember anything else? Did they have scars, a limp or any visible tattoos? Did they have hair or were they bald?'

I have no idea but I reply, 'I'm thinking.'

I have a good time glaring at people carrying their groceries, or taking home their dry cleaning, or walking their dog, or standing on a street corner chewing the fat with a neighbour. I glare because I want them to think I'm a dinky-di detective. I want people to panic and run away so I can say to the two policemen, 'Hey! They look suspicious,' so they'll turn on their siren and flashing light to chase them and the car will screech its tyres when it broadsides around corners. While I'm in the police car there's no danger for me making eye contact because everyone I glare at looks away. I think it's likely there are a lot of guilty consciences walking the streets of Albuquerque.

The two-striped policeman repeats his question, 'Well, is there anything else you remember?'

I say, 'I've got a mental picture, but I'm not certain. One of them was an Indian, but there's lots of Indians on the streets.'

I'm happy for the policemen to continue driving me around. I even think about giving people on the street a wave—a King-like casual wobble of my hand—but I know that no one waves to anyone sitting in a police car.

People on the street look life-toughened. The policeman driving the car tells me this is Albuquerque's skid row and the man whose suitcase was stolen says, 'Yep, I used to live here.'

The no-striped policeman says, 'Why don't we try a few bars?'

I say, 'I thought police aren't supposed to drink on duty.'

Neither of them is amused.

'That's not a bad idea,' says the two-striped policeman, 'We're not getting anywhere here. Why not try those two bars on Sixteenth Street?'

Now I'm really confused. Of course they wouldn't be going for a drink? The car stops in a no-standing area outside a bar, and I say, 'When you go inside, how will you recognize them?'

They say, 'We can't, but *you* can.'

I think that if they think I'm going into a bar in a down-and-out part of town to identify the particularly big Indian, they've got rocks in their head. I tell them exactly that.

The two-striped policeman says, 'Sir, that's exactly what you're going to do.'

I still don't like being addressed as a sir, but the policemen and most other Americans don't care because they like saying sir.

'Sir, if they have this man's possessions to fence it's a good chance they'll be in one of two bars. They'll try here or another bar we know.'

The man who had his bag stolen says, 'That's correct.'

I suspect the man's no angel, that he's also a bit of a crook.

I say, 'Look you blokes, let me get this straight. Do you expect me to go inside to see if that bloody big Indian's there?'

The policemen and the man whose bag was stolen say, 'Correct!'

I'm pissed-off with this idea. 'If he's inside and I see him, what the hell am I going to do? The Indian bloke's bloody huge. He could eat me for breakfast.'

The policeman says, 'Don't worry. We'll be close enough to handle any trouble.'

They may be confident, but I'm not. It's all right for them because they each have a long black nightstick they can dong him with, and if he got completely out of control, they have pistols dangling from their belt.

I say, 'You'll need to be close to where I am because I know how tough American Indians are.'

'Oh, and how the fuck would you know?'

'The Beverly Hills Picture Theatre in Sydney. That's how I know. Almost every Saturday afternoon I saw films where Indians attacked settlers' wagon trains, and US Army Forts, and cowboys drove mobs of cattle. I know from those films that Indians fight very well, that they sit on horses out of sight over the tops of hills, then they race down to attack when no one's looking. I know that once I'm inside they could hack me to bits with their tomahawk and take my scalp. … Are you blokes sure this is a good idea?'

They nod. They think it's a great idea. 'Here's what we'll do,' says the two-striped policeman, and he tells us.

The man whose bag was stolen nods in agreement at every part of the plan.

I say to him, 'It's all right for you because you don't have to go into that bloody bar to confront the big bastard.'

He says, 'It's a good plan.'

I reckon he'd reckon that any plan to recover his bag is good. I say, 'It's a lousy plan.'

The no-striped policeman says, 'Let's go over it again.'

'Don't bother. I understand.'

'We want to make sure you've got all the details.'

'Christ! I'm not stupid.'

I'm not completely convinced they're convinced that I can even speak English, but that's my fault. I'd purposefully used many Australian colloquialisms in my speech, and I have many more ready to use.

The no-striped policeman does go through it again. 'You go in the front door and walk slowly to the end of the bar. On the way in, look at those on your right, on the way back look at those on your left. That's where the booths are, on the left. If you see either of the men, you come back out the front door, then we'll go inside to do the arrest.'

'Look, you blokes, I'm not a drongo. I understand. But tell me this; how are the Indians in there going to react to me, a white Australian, strutting through their bar?'

The two-striped policeman says, 'Ah fuck, kick him out of the car and push the arsehole inside.'

I say, 'Listen there's no need to …'

The man whose suitcase was stolen asks, 'Will I push him out?'

I don't give him the satisfaction. I get out and settle myself. I know I have to appear confident, but not cocky. There's little that can happen to me if I go straight in and out. I'm an Australian and we are the ANZAC's, the most feared soldiers on Earth, and an Anzac would beat an American Indian every time—probably.

The one-striped policeman says, 'Get the fuck into—'

'I'm going. I'm *going*. Keep your shirt on.'

I push open the bar's door and go inside. It's just as the police explained, a long bar on the left and booths on the right. Most of the people in there are American Indian men. An unshaved face and crumpled clothes is de rigueur, hardly anyone looks at me. I could be taken as a local coming in for a quiet drink or to be looking for a friend. I slowly walk to the end of the bar making sure my glances are casual and not maintaining eye contact. I considered putting on a limp but decided it was over acting. I slowly return to the front door, managing only once to not avoid eye contact. It was only for a couple of seconds with an inquisitive Indian barman. I think about doing something stupid like holding up my arm in a traditional Indian greeting and saying, 'How!' But I don't. I go out of the bar and into the arms of the no-striped policeman.

'Did you see them?'

'No, mate; they're not in there.'

The two-striped policeman asks, 'Are you sure? Did you look at everyone?'

'Of course I did. I'm bloody certain the Indian bloke's not there. I'd recognize him by his size.'

'What about we go in to take a look,' says the other policeman.

The two-striped policeman shakes his head. 'No. They'll realise we're after someone so they'll only phone the other bars to tell them we're around. Come on; let's go to Johnson's bar to check it out.'

The man who lost his bag nods to another man who wears crumpled clothing and hasn't shaved. The policemen stare at him as he goes into the bar.

I have a smug look as we go back into the police car. I say to them, 'I reckon I did that very well.'

They grunt.

On the way to Johnson's bar, I wish they'd turn on the flashing light and the siren, but they don't. I remember when I was aged sixteen and I tried to join the New South Wales police cadets. I stuffed bananas into my mouth and stretched my body upward before standing on the weight-and-height-measuring machine. I remember the police cadet sergeant saying, 'Sorry, son, too short and not heavy enough. Try again in six months.'

I did try again, but the result was the same. I say to the Albuquerque policemen, 'I tried to join the police force in Australia, but I wasn't big enough.'

They say, 'Not big enough? Hey, you're bigger than both of us are.'

'Australian coppers are big buggers. I'm five-foot ten so I'm a short arse.'

The two-striped policeman says, 'You'd be big enough now because you're full of shit. Here's Johnson's bar so cut the crap.'

The no-striped policeman says, 'We'd better change our plan here. This bar's only got one door. You'll go in and come out the same way. You'll do exactly the same as before. Only here check out both side of the bar on the way in. We'll wait a minute then we'll come in.'

'What if I see him, and he sees me before you come in, and he *goes for* me?'

'If that happens, you go straight to the wall-phone at the end of the bar and dial the emergency number.'

'What's the number? Here, write it on my arm.'

'It's written on the phone booth. Oh, and you don't need coins.'

'But what if—'

'Don't make a federal case out of this piss-arse little thing,' the two-striped policeman says. 'Just do what he tells you. I'm goddamned tired of your maladramatics —'

I interrupt him: 'It's melo, melodramatics.'

'Uh!'

'You just said maladram—'

'Listen her you smart-arse mother-fucker …' He turns to the man who had his bag stolen and says, 'Push the mother-fucker out of the car.'

And he does exactly that.

The no-striped policeman gets out and says in my ear, 'It's an emergency number, so when the officer answers tell him to send backup to Johnson's bar. Tell him that officer Baxter's making an arrest, *Got it?*' I feel the spittle from his mouth hit my ear.

'I got it. But remember, I'll probably be cornered at the back of the bar with the whole Indian tribe trying to get at me, so you bastards come in quickly.'

The policeman pushes me towards the door. A man comes out, looks at me, looks at the policemen and scurries away. My confidence is gone, my Anzac courage lost. I'm nervous and certain to be a liability if things go wrong.

The light inside is dim, so I blink, trying to get my eyes accustomed to it. The bar doors slam shut behind me and curious drinkers turn to look. Nearly everyone's an American Indian. *Shit.*

I try to do a slow amble towards the end of the bar, but my legs go off in a panicky quick walk. I see the particularly big Indian sitting in a booth with three other particularly big Indians. I gasp and go to the wall phone. Had I been in Australia it would be odds-on for the phone not to work, for some stupid bastard to have wrenched the hand-piece off and scratched on the wall 'Norm loves Gloria' or 'South Sydney forever'. I hear a dial tone, look at the emergency number and dial it.

Someone says, 'Police emergency; can I help you?' I think about saying send a thousand cars to Johnson's bar. But I don't, I whisper in my best American accent: 'Officer Baxter's making an arrest at Johnson's bar and he wants backup.'

I'm certain everyone in the bar hears what I say. I nervously glance at the particularly big Indian. He's looking at me. I still have the phone in my hand so I say into it, *'And make it quick.'*

The two policemen come into the bar. The door slams shut behind them and everyone looks. The policemen see me at the phone, so they know I've made the call and that the Indian's in the bar. We walk towards each other and meet beside the particularly big Indian's booth.

The two-striped policeman says, 'Which one is he?'

I say a squeaky-voice, 'He's right bloody *here!*'

'What?'

'Right beside us!'

Four particularly big Indians stare at us with guilty looks. The policeman stares at them.

I take a step away from the booth and point at the Indian. 'It's him!'

The two-striped policeman says in a very officious voice, 'Is it this man who stole a bag from the Albuquerque bus station?'

I know I'm supposed to answer, but I'm still staring at the Indian, who I realise, even though he's sitting and I'm standing, has his head above mine. I point at him and say, 'Yeah, that's the bloke.'

It's just like in a television detective show, like in *Peter Gunn*, or *Seventy-Seven Sunset Strip*. I feel like a bit of a hero.

The no-striped policeman walks over and stands at the door, presumably in case someone does a runner.

The other policeman asks me, 'Is his partner here?'

I look around the room and everyone has a guilty look. I remember seeing *Ali Baba and the Forty Thieves* at the Beverly Hills Picture theatre and I think that being here is like being in Ali's cave: they all look like thieves. Apart from two men, they're all American Indians.

'No, the other man was a paleface.' I hardly believe what I say and from the look on the policeman's face, he hardly believes it either.

He says, '*What?*'

'Ah, shit. No, he's not here; he was a European American.' I feel I should say that I know the Europeans stole all your land. That was why you had to sit on horses hiding over the tops of hills, and why you had to attack wagon trains and cowboys who drove cattle over your hunting grounds and killed all the buffalo. But I reckon that'd be useless because I can read hate for me in the Indians' eyes.

The distant sound of a police siren means that the cavalry is close, and I wish I were riding in the car that has its siren sounding and its light flashing.

The no-striped policeman says in a loud voice, 'Everyone remain seated and there'll be no trouble.'

I hear the police car skid to a stop outside, and I reckon they're in a no standing area. Two policemen holding long nightsticks push open the doors. The doors bash against the wall then spring back to hit the policemen. Everyone, including the police in the bar, sniggers.

The newcomers flush with embarrassment. One says, 'You got the guy?'

The two-striped policeman says, 'You're goddamned right we got him. It's a positive ID.' He looks satisfied, and I wonder about the validity of that. It's obvious the particularly big Indian is not a master criminal and all the police are doing is taking a father away from his family. I regret my part and feel like shit. I should thank my lucky stars I was too short and not heavy enough join the New South Wales Police Cadets: I'd be a lousy copper.

The two-striped policeman handcuffs the particularly big Indian and says, 'Let's go.'

I follow sheepishly. I don't chance a look at anyone in the bar because I know they're all thinking that I'm a goddamned, cock-sucking, son-of-a-bitch, and I reckon they're right.

I ride in the police car with two gloating policemen and a now very talkative man who seems to think that his lost bag will shortly not be lost. He asks, 'Did the guy say what he'd done with my stuff?'

The policemen don't hear him because they're talking about going back to the bar to fit other lost-stuff crimes onto other particularly big Indians.

I say to the man, 'The Indian bloke reckoned you had nothing of value so he threw your bag into the Rio Grande River.'

His expression takes on an agonized look. 'Ah fuck.'

The particularly big Indian said no such thing, but that's what I would have done.

All I hear from the policemen is more gloating: 'We got the goddamned bastard;' and, 'We got him good;' and, 'Yep, we got the arsehole.'

The man who had his bag stolen is nearly bawling, muttering between near sobs saying, 'He *threw* it in the god damned river. He threw all my stuff in the Rio Grande. Shit.'

The police car screeches to a stop beside other police cars on land adjoining a building that looks totally depressing. The sound of screeching tyres behind means that the other police car is following too close, or that Albuquerque police car drivers like to perform dramatic stops.

I look around to see loads of battered eight-cylinder yank-tanks parked nearby which all have stickers saying, *Impounded,* and I'm certain these heaps of mechanical junk don't belong to any of Albuquerque's elite. It's odds-on they're family cars of native Indians.

The particularly big Indian is roughly assisted from the other police car, and I wonder how he was able to fit his bulk in the narrow back-seat space. He has some blood on his forehead so I assume he had an accident with a policeman's nightstick. The Indian glares, and I read hate for me in his dark eyes. I understand.

A policeman says, 'Let's get him inside.'

We go through a security door to an elevator, where we stand close to each other and smell each other's body odour. Stale perspiration dominates, but there's another smell that's strange, and I wonder if it's something that's permeated into the wooden walls: it might be the smell of fear.

We front up to a charge desk where the particularly big Indian is ordered to empty his pockets—poor-person possessions: loose coins, dirty handkerchief, a crumpled pack of Lucky Strike cigarettes and a book of matches with Pat's Bar printed on its cover. I ask myself, is *he* a criminal?

A fat-faced detective who I reckon should be sucking the soggy end of a cheroot takes me to an interview room. He says, 'We know the guy you did the positive ID on. He's been here before.'

I say to him, 'Was it for murder or bank robbery?'

He stares at me with his lips tightly closed, his cheeks puffed with air and breathing heavily through his nose. He looks like he's going to blow out birthday candles. A pah sound comes from his mouth which turns out to be the beginning of the word, past. He says, 'Past history on the man is that he's a petty criminal …'

I think, *I could have told you that.* Big-time criminals, no matter from what country, don't pinch suitcases containing cheap, used, crumpled clothing.

'… who's spent periods of up to six months in the slammer.'

'Slammer?'

'Yep, the slammer. Our local jail.'

I say, 'You call your local jail the slammer? I thought only Humphrey Bogart used *slammer* to describe a prison. And he only uses it when he's talking about places like Sing-Sing or Alcatraz.'

He briefly considers my comment, but the sarcasm goes over his head.

The telephone rings. He answers and says 'Yep, yep …' and another, 'Yep.' Then he tells me that the call was to say that they'd recovered the stolen bag.

I say, 'That's very impressive.'

Again he tightly closes his lips and puffs his cheeks. I wait for him to utter another word beginning with a pah sound and out it comes. 'People like this Indian guy should be behind bars. What'll happen now is that you'll be notified when the court case comes up and—'

'Court case? I won't be here for *a court case*!'

'Oh yes, you will; you're the star witness.'

'Star witness I might be, but in Albuquerque I won't.' I tell him about the trials and tribulations of my lost haversack, which he writes in a notepad.

He says, 'This, um, haver-thing you lost. What exactly is it?'

I explain and he says, 'Oh, you mean a backpack!'

I think about backpack and decide that word is eminently sensible. I wonder why Australians use the word haversack. I now know why no one understood me.

I say, 'Mate, I would really love to spend time in your beautiful city, but the truth of the matter is that I'm nearly broke, so if I'm forced to wait until the trial, you'll have to support me. Perhaps I could live at your house.'

He again tightly closes his lips and puffs his cheeks, but this time no pah sound follows. He shakes his head vigorously and air comes from his mouth like a deflating balloon. 'I'll, I'll, I'll see what I can do.' He leaves the room and returns moments later, smiling broadly. 'You can make a written statement; the chief says that's okay.'

I wonder what an Indian Chief has to do with the court case, but I say nothing.

The detective uses one finger to type my statement and asks me how to spell Australia, which I spell, A.U.S.T.R.I.A. And he types exactly that.

When we're done, Albuquerque's finest won't drive me back to the bus station, so I get on a local bus and pay my own fare.

The bus station manager greets me with a broad smile and fumbles in his pocket. 'Hi, here's your claim ticket for your—'

'Backpack,' I say, cutting him short.

'It's a haversack,' he says. 'I looked it up in the dictionary. The dictionary says that a haversack is made of canvas, and yours is.'

If that's true, I've learnt an American word for nothing. 'Mate, I've only just learnt to use the word backpack. It's a backpack for as long as I'm in America. I'm fed-up with you yanks not understanding me.'

I look at his starched-white shirt, and say, 'I notice you don't have epaulettes today.' Without epaulettes, much of his pompous authority is gone.

He stares at me. 'What's epaulettes?'

I decide not to tell him; he can look it up in his dictionary.

I get my backpack and open the top flap. Everything seems to be there. If anyone has opened it they've not ventured below the dirty underwear stored on top of everything else. I sit on a corner seat with my back protected by two walls and place my backpack on the ground, then I put my leg through the shoulder strap—no one's going to steal my bag. I want to sleep, but self-preservation instincts win over tiredness. I remember from the Beverly Hills Picture Theatre Saturday afternoon screenings that American Indians are very vengeful. Indian family ties are very strong. I watch the many Indians in the bus station and know they're watching me. If I close my eyes, they'll take revenge for what I did to their blood-brother. They'll kill me and hang my scalp outside their teepee.

23 December 1960.
Dear Mum and kids,
I suppose you'll get a surprise to get this letter from Calgary. I arrived here yesterday by Greyhound bus from Winnipeg, Manitoba. I stopped in Chicago to think the whole travel thing out and decided it would be nice to spend Christmas day with people I know. I realise it will be disappointing for you to read that I've returned to Canada rather than travel to England and then home to Australia.
I need to think things out to decide what I should do, but it does mean getting a job and saving more money.
I've enclosed a map to show you where I've been.
Santa will bring me nothing, not a cracker.
Love Barry

Chapter Nine

In the Mexico City traffic our VW beetle is too small for safety. Mexican drivers seem to be off with the fairies, and we reckon it's because they've drunk too much tequila or that they hate VW beetles. No one here has any respect for three lost Australian travellers. At any moment we expect to be squashed by a truck driven by another crazy Mexican.

We might be safe if we can find where 'son of a moose' Mike Schonberg lives, then park the VW and only drive it again to get out of the city.

I'm in the cramped space of the back seat with my imitation crocodile-skin overnight bag and blankets and sleeping bags and everything else that doesn't fit in the boot of the VW, which is not really the boot because it's in the front of the car. Stuart is driving and his brother David is navigating. I don't interrupt their debates about going the wrong way, turns, speed and nearly having trucks hit us. I don't say anything because I couldn't do any better.

Mexico City is lousy: it stinks; it's polluted; everyone's mad, and there must be lots of crooks because most houses have high security fences and all windows have steel security bars. We take many wrong turns onto back streets that shouldn't be streets, because they're just two-wheel tracks of dust-filled potholes. Stinking garbage and litter are everywhere. We see jerry-built shanties roofed with rusting materials that should be sent to the rubbish dump, and it's certain that Mexico City's elite do not live here.

We're prepared for contrasts in living standards because all the Mexican towns and cities we've come through have been the same: so many with little, so few with lots.

Roadside camping is not recommended, but we're three tough and fit Anzacs who aren't scared of anyone, so we camp anywhere. The night before arriving in Mexico City, we camp in hills to the north, and we take turns watching a bloke, who probably is a bandit and related to Pancho Villa, stare at us while we cook our ritual meal of stewed vegetables. That's all we ever have. At night it's freshly cooked in a big saucepan, then it's reheated for breakfast, then it is spread cold on bread for lunch.

The three of us reckon the bloke watching us is an advance bandit; he's got us spotted and he's waiting for his *bandito* gang to arrive. Stuart tries to trade a plate of stew in exchange for our safety, but he gets nowhere. All the bandit does is stare. We sit away from the fire on a canvas groundsheet, eating our gourmet dish, and the bandit cautiously comes to the fire where he cooks a cob of corn that has very little corn on it. This *bandito* is not a threat, but sleep that night is had with one of us on guard.

~

Mike 'son of a moose' Schonberg's house has, like all others near it, a decent front security fence. We park our VW behind it.

I've told Mike that none of us has much money so he's not to suggest a card game, and he assures me that the thought never entered his mind. I don't believe that and remind him how he fleeced the Canadian cowboys in the North West Territory camp, and that thoughts of playing cards and fleecing people are always in his mind.

He says, 'Son of a moose, I'd never take money from friends.'

I remind him that he won twenty dollars from me.

He takes us to the floating gardens of Xochimilco, the University, and a one-sided bullfight. Then he says, 'That's it; there's nothing more to see,' so we leave a day earlier than planned. We don't go to the Palace of Arts or the National Museum or anything else Mexico City is proud to have tourists see. Mike goes to find a card game.

We plan to make Acapulco in one day, but the silver city of Taxco and 'Montezuma's revenge' stop us. Montezuma has already taken loads of revenge on me. I became acquainted with his malady shortly after crossing the American and Mexican border, but Stuart and David were untouched, until they ate the meal Mike's wife cooked.

My bout of Montezuma made me into a joke. I frequently yelled, 'Stop the car; stop the car!'

All I get from Stuart was, 'If we have to keep stopping, it's going to bugger-up our mileage goal for today.'

Every night he and David slept well in our small tent while I was outside in the darkness squatting on the desert sand while shining a torch in circles hoping I don't see snakes. When I do sleep, I have nightmares about rattlesnakes biting me on the bum, and I know if that happens I'm going to die because I've been told no one's going to suck poisonous venom from my bum.

Now they've got Montezuma's revenge and I'm not sympathetic. I reckon it's a sin to throw away sandwiches that Mike's wife made for us.

David says, 'Well you eat them.'

Stuart goads me, 'Yeah, go on; you eat the bloody things.'

I smell the fillings, then chuck them out the car window. I hope they're found by one of Pancho Villa's men with only a mere corn cob to eat.

From a distance Acapulco looks far too rich for broke Australians, but when we get to the outskirts of the city, we see loads of broke Mexicans, so we reckon we can exist here. Then we see the beachside boulevard with its tall palms, luxurious hotels and villas, and we reckon that's out of our league and it's going to be difficult. Our Canadian license plate invites touts to swamp us with offers for girls and rooms and anything else money can buy. When we speed away, the persistent ones stand on the VW's back bumper bar and our calls of, 'Piss-off' and 'Vamoose, you bastards' gets two of them off, but one hangs on for grim death. Stuart brakes suddenly, loosening his grim-death grip and he's now being dragged behind, but we don't care because he could let go.

When we stop, we're again besieged, and my two Spanish phrases—'Where is the post office,' and, 'I have a trunk and two suitcases'—are not understood or appropriate.

We find the morning beach and it's for us because there are loads of fabulous-looking women. But we can't leave the VW without security so we roster guard duties: I'm first.

I try sitting in the car, but it's too hot and touts swamp me with offers, so I lock the doors and sit in the shade of a tree. The car's a magnet for thieves. After they try the doors to see if they're locked, if they produce a screwdriver, I yell at them to vamoose. They then give me a dirty look and go to another car.

It's Stuart's turn to guard and my turn to look at the fabulous-looking women. I go to join David, but he's yelling vamoose at two Mexicans so I yell vamoose with him.

Our vamooses must have Australian accents because one of three males that are also watching the fabulous-looking women says to us, 'Which part of Aussie are you from?'

I say, 'Sydney.'

David says, 'Stuart and I are from Boulia.'

'Where the hell's that?'

David says, 'Back of beyond.'

'Oh.'

'And you blokes?' I ask.

One says, 'Rockhampton.'

Another says, 'Melbourne.'

And the other one says, 'Gosford. We arrived here yesterday. Last night we slept on the afternoon beach, but the coppers moved us on early this morning.'

The Rockhampton bloke says, 'I'm going for a swim.'

His two mates say they are too, and David says he is, and they all say to me, 'Mind our gear will you, mate.'

So I'm on guard duty again.

When they return from swimming, the Gosford bloke says, 'Let's go and have a beer,' and I know I'm not going to cool off in Mexican seawater today.

In the glossary of drinking terms, having a beer means having a shout each, and there's now six of us in the shout, so we'll be having a few beers. If we go to have a few beers and we have a couple of shouts each, it extends to getting pissed, and if we go that far, we're going to get a skin full and most of us are going to write ourselves off. And that's all right because Mexican Cerveza is cheap.

During the first shout, we form our first impressions of everyone else. Malcolm from Rockhampton is as thin as a steel star post and hardly stops talking. I reckon he won't make the end of the second shout. Robert from Gosford is a short-arse bullshit artist whose done everything and been everywhere, and although he talks tough, I reckon he can't fight his way out of a paper bag. Bill from Melbourne is a dark horse; he says little, but I reckon he can do much, and I'm certain he'll be as steady as a rock at the end of the second shout. I'm certain Stuart will be standing at the end because I've seen him handle long rugby parties in Calgary. And I reckon I'll be alright, but David's not well trained for a twelve or more shout of Mexican Cerveza.

We select a cantina where we have a good view of our parked VW and of the other blokes' Ford, then we go to the bar's swinging entry doors like a gang of gringos. Short-arse Robert goes in first and he gets hostile looks, but the bar doors keep swinging as our gang goes in, and few eyes continue looking at us once they see we're six gringos.

'G'day, mate, give us six cold ones,' Malcolm says as if he were in his Rockhampton local hotel.

The barman doesn't know what he means. '¿*Excusa, senor?*'

Malcolm doesn't know what that means so he says in a louder voice, 'Six beers. Six beers.' He points at each of us. 'One, two, three, four, five, six. *Six beers.*'

David's practised his Spanish so he says, '¿*Habla inglés?, senor?*'

We all laugh because we know what that means, and we know that if the barman spoke English, he'd have known what Malcolm said.

The barman says, '*No entiendo suyo inglés.*'

We all laugh again because the barman's said the bleeding obvious.

I point at a beer bottle, then point at all of us, and we get six beers. There's no further need to attempt conversation.

At the beginning of each round of drinks, we do a 'here's mud in your eye', or 'down the spout', or 'here's to ya'. No one but other Australian yobbos will understand our slang or our dirty jokes and other buffoonery.

The barman gets very comfortable with us because we're paying for our drinks, and we're laughing, and we're not a threat.

He says, 'You are not American gringos.'

We tell him we're Australians, and to prove it, Robert does a fine rendition of *The Bastard from the Bush*. When he gets to, 'Will you have a cigarette mate?' We all say, 'I'll have the flaming packet says the bastard from the bush,' and we fall about laughing.

The Mexican drinkers think we're mad.

Talk gets to where we'll sleep. Because of the other blokes' experience with the police, the beach is not an option.

Stuart suggests pitching our tent at the end of the beach amongst trees, but Bill's heard from two Americans that the police patrol that area, and we all reckon that Mexico is uncivilized because it doesn't have camp sites.

Only brave Mexican touts linger outside to sell their wares to six drunk Australians, but one of them could get lucky because none of us are in a fit state to have anything but a soft bed and a clean toilet. One of the touts is sitting on the front of the VW, he speaks English and tells us he's guarded our cars from the other thieving bastards, and he's got a very clean, very cheap, very good, very close place we can rent—which must be bullshit.

David's gone philosophical. He says, 'If you were floating down a crocodile-infested river on a raft constructed of logs tied with rotting vines and you see a huge waterfall ahead, and on the riverbank is a man, a Mexican man, who says "Take this rope because I can save you." What do you do? You grab the fucking rope. And that's what we should do. We should grab this bloody Mexican's rope and take his very good place to rent.'

None of us knows what he's talking about.

Stuart says, 'David's been in England for two years.'

We nod our heads. Poor bugger.

Our trusted tout stands on the back bumper bar of the VW pointing left and right. We go where he points and hope he's got a firm grip because if he falls off, the Ford close behind carrying the other three blokes will run over him.

He directs us to a narrow driveway on a hill. At the driveway's end, we know he shouldn't have been pointing here because we're outside a mansion that overlooks the morning beach. Stuart slows our VW. Before it's stopped, the tout's running beside us smiling.

Stuart says, 'We can't afford this. He's dreaming.'

The tout acts as if he's been trained in an Egyptian bazaar. He walks backwards with his arms apart, saying, 'Come in; you must see it first, come in, sirs.'

All the sirs say, 'He's dreaming,' but, entranced by the view, we follow him along a wide balcony. We look down over the tops of palms to the morning beach and the ocean and see the view that only millionaires get.

The tout seems to know what we're thinking. He says, 'You will wait here. I will get a special price from … the owner. You will see; you will see.'

There's a cluster of us, and a cluster of the other three Australians, but each cluster is saying, 'We can't afford this place.'

Our tout returns with a little old man who's yelling and pointing and probably swearing in Spanish. All the while our tout's saying, 'Everything's all right; I'm getting a good price from him.'

The little old man says lots of stuff to us in Spanish. We all nod and smile. We reckon he likes us.

'I've arranged a special deal for you,' our tout says. 'For five-hundred pesos you have the house for five days.'

We don't believe it. David says, 'That's only twenty-five quid. That's just over four quid each, we'd be mugs not to take it.'

Malcolm decides to haggle. He says, 'Too much money; you must make it less.'

We all tell him to shut up, but he doesn't.

The tout talks to the old man who's looking angry. They yell a lot, and the old man leaves. The tout, says, 'Gentlemen, the villa is yours.'

We strut about as though we're millionaires. We look down on everyone on the morning beach, and they look up at us. I reckon we'll now have no trouble getting the fabulous-looking women to notice us.

Stuart gives some fabulous-looking women a wave of his hand, and they wave back, so we all wave at them and already Robert's talking about having a party.

The villa has four bedrooms, each with a double bed, and because no one will share a bed with a bloke, two of us will sleep on the floor.

Malcolm says, 'Stuart and David can share a bed because they're brothers.'

But they refuse, both saying, 'I'm not sleeping with him.'

The only ones sharing our beds will be the fabulous-looking women, and that's how the beds will be allocated, the first four of us to get a fabulous-looking woman to the villa, get the beds.

Stuart looks in the kitchen and tells us there's no food. Some of us will have to go grocery shopping. He reckons we should all put in fifty pesos, that he'll be the treasurer and he and I should buy the food. I know why he does that. He'll get to eat what he likes.

It's not so difficult shopping for Mexican groceries because I only select cans that have pictures of the contents on the labels. Stuart doesn't select any cans because he likes only fresh fruit and vegetables. Almost everything I select, he criticizes.

It was exactly the same when we flatted in Calgary. There, Barry Ambrose and Stuart and I would combine our ten dollars each and we'd do our shopping weekly. I'd take canned frankfurters and something called Spam from the market shelves. Barry Ambrose would take a sticky cake and something called jelly sauce from the shelves. Stuart would reject the lot and take cabbage, spinach, celery, beans, potatoes, carrots, and a leg of lamb. Good tucker he called it, all the makings of a good healthy stew.

Stuart always cooked the stew because he'd seen us throw out carrot and celery tops and the very outside cabbage leaves. He reckons that's where the nourishment is. We never argue because Stuart is as fit as a Mallee bull and he never gets colds. And he can run like the clappers, so if we eat what he eats, we'll be just like him. That's the theory.

Even while we travelled, from the first meal after leaving Calgary and for every nightly meal through twenty-three American states, Stuart cooked his stew. Excepting when he chucks in curry powder or when he finds something that's supposed to have a million vitamins in it, the ingredients are always the same. The quantity's also the same because he always fills the big boiler to the top and squashes down the lid. There's always enough stew to feed a battalion, and that's just as well because there's now six Australian mouths to feed and that equates to a battalion.

Bill looks at our provisions. He's not happy. 'No biscuits and no cake, and who's all that vegetables and fruit for?'

'*You*. I'm cooking,' Stuart says. 'If *you* don't like what I cook, you do it.'

'But that's all bloody rubbish; there's nothing there I like.'

'That's what you're going to get.'

Bill says, 'Well you can stick it up your arse. I'm not eating any of that.'

There's momentary silence—the silence that might precede the outbreak of hostilities; the silence before the first shot of war is fired.

Robert picks over the provisions, sees some meat and holds it up saying, 'Calm down, mate; there's meat here.'

'Meat?'

'Yair, meat. Stuart's going to include meat with all that … other stuff, aren't you?'

'If I must.'

David says to his brother, *You must.*

And that's about the end of that.

It's decided that we'll buy lots of Mexican cerveza, that we'll drown Stuart's stew in beer. When the money's collected, Bill says, 'I'll go get the beer'—he looks at Stuart—'then I'll get what I want.'

And that's the very end of that.

Sunbaking in the afternoon sun on the morning beach is impossible, because our villa and all the others are in front of the sun and we're in shadows. All the fabulous-looking women and the sellers of shade hats have followed the sun to the afternoon beach, and we now know why there's a morning and afternoon beach.

Bill isn't convinced it's because of the sun. He reckons that during mornings it's high tide on the morning beach and low tide at the afternoon beach, then in the afternoons, it's the reverse. We all hope Stuart doesn't tell him the facts of life. That it's the Pacific Ocean we're looking at, the same ocean at both beaches, but he does.

He says, 'You stupid bugger, it's the Pacific.'

And Bill says, 'I *know* that.'

Stuart can't help himself. 'If *you* know *that*, how can the tide be different at beaches a mile apart?'

'Because I say it is, and I don't give a fuck what you say.'

'Christ! Have a look at that,' David says. We all look at nothing. 'You just missed her, it was Elizabeth Taylor *in a bikini.*'

We all say, 'Bullshit.'

He says, 'It was her—fair dinkum!'

Everyone's pleased that a fight's been avoided.

We don't get any fabulous-looking women to join us for Stuart's stew or to drink Bill's cerveza. All night the blokes are at each other's throats.

Breakfast is fried stew on toast that only Bill won't eat.

We all look when a long, shiny, fancy American car parks beside our VW and the Ford. We hope it's the fabulous-looking women. That they'd heard about us and are visiting. But it's not. Four Mexicans wearing white-cotton shirts that I reckon are elitist—a kind of made-the-grade, I'm-better-than-you statement shirt worn outside trousers like a safari jacket—get out of the car and walk confidently towards us.

We're not impressed by their confidence or their fancy shirts. We remain seated. They jabber away in Spanish.

David knows the most Spanish words. He says to us, 'They're saying something that sounds like *es lavable*. I think that means it is washable. But I don't reckon they're here to talk about washing clothes.'

One of the men says, 'Who are you?'

I say, *'We'll ask* the questions; who are you?'

'We are Senor Garcia's guests.'

'Who the fuck is Senor Garcia?'

'Senor Garcia is the *owner* of this villa.'

'Oh.'

They are four and we are four. That's an equal confrontation, but Stuart calls to the other two who are inside to come out—*quickly*.

'What's going on?'

'These blokes reckon that they're here to stay in Senor Garcia's villa.'

'Tell them to go to buggery. Tell them we got here first.'

One of the Mexicans says, 'We will go and return with the *Policia*.' And they go.

The Mexican's firmness mystifies us. If Senor Garcia does own the villa, who is the man we rented from? Surely he's the owner; he must be Senor Garcia. We go to ask Senor Garcia, who is living in the small flat under the villa, what's going on.

Senor Garcia says he *no hablar english*, and that's not good enough so we shout at him, but he still doesn't understand.

Robert calls to us from the balcony, 'Ah … a cop car's just arrived.'

We reckon that's good because they'll sort things out.

One of the police says, '*Buenos dias senors, hablar Espanol?*'

We say, '*No.*'

Stuart points to David. 'He can speak a little Spanish.'

David says, 'Don't be stupid; I can't speak enough Spanish to handle this.'

The policeman now speaks nearly perfect English. 'Who are you? What are you doing here?'

All of us answer at once: 'We're Australians.'

'We rented this.'

'This place is ours.'

The rush of words confuses the policemen. One of them says, 'Australiano? Not Americano's?'

Malcolm says, 'American? No bloody fear. We're Australians, and we rented this villa fair and square.'

The policeman doesn't understand. His response is one word, 'Passports?'

We hear the sound of a siren. Another police car speeds into the driveway and we're well outnumbered and outgunned, because all the police have pistols.

We go to get our passports, but a policeman says, 'One at a time, the rest of you stay here.'

We do as we're ordered. When one of us goes inside for our passport, a policeman who acts like he's about to arrest a mass murderer or a bank robber accompanies us.

I'm regaining my confidence, so I say to a policeman, 'What's this all about?'

'Senor, I will ask the questions. You will be silent.

Bill's really pissed off and says in his finest Australian quickly-spoken accent, 'Listen to me, you, we rented this place from a bloke, and we've paid up front. So don't you start pushing your weight around with us.'

The policeman says, '*Excusa*, speak English, *please.*'

'I fucking-well am speaking English. I, I.' He splutters and a dollop of something from his mouth jets forward and lands on the policeman's uniform.

The policeman says, 'Is this person crazy?'

David says, 'That *might well* be true.'

They take oodles of time inspecting our passports, and one of them says, 'Australiano turistas. Not Americano? Australiano. *Ah.*'

Bill says, 'Yeah, we're Australians, you bloody ratbags.'

The policeman looks puzzled. 'Rat. Rat and a bag?'

It's all developed into a farce. Clearly we've been conned by Senor Garcia's caretaker, we don't have any law on our side, and we should do everything we're told to do by the police. We tell the police how we rented the villa, and they laugh. We say that we should get our money back from the caretaker. They laugh again.

'You have five minutes *to vamoose.*'

We've got right on our side. But we've got no might. We're helpless.

~

We reconnoitre a possible squat at the other end of the afternoon beach that's amongst the trees, and we're all in a mess. The policeman's order to vamoose was reinforced by him saying, *'Rapido*, rapido, *rapido.'* So everything got stuffed into one or the other car. I hope my imitation crocodile-skin bag is in the Ford, because it isn't in the VW. In my next letter to my mother, I don't want to have to say that we've been conned by a Mexican tout and that my farewell gift from her has been left in an Acapulco villa. She won't like that at all.

When we left the villa, Robert piled everything he could see onto a blanket and bundled it into the Ford. Now I see that he's got one of Senor Garcia's vases and some kind of religious statue. David's certain he's left shirts and underwear on Senor Garcia's clothes line, and Stuart's vegetable stew is percolating away on Senor Garcia's stove. Bill reckons there's no danger that anyone will eat it.

I find my imitation crocodile skin bag and the Yashica camera I got from my mother for my twenty-first birthday in the Ford, so I don't give a bugger about anything else. But most have lost something.

We sit on the sand drowning our sorrows with cerveza. The alcohol has Bill and Malcolm planning a raid on Senor Garcia's villa, but the rest of us make-up stories about how bad Mexican jails are. The raid gets cancelled. We all need a good night's sleep.

We must sleep too soundly because morning has us cursing the thieves who during the night slunk amongst us. They took the VW car keys from the pocket of Stuart's shorts that he'd tucked securely under his sleeping-bag pillow, unlocked the car and stole our valuables. The thieves have good taste because they've stuffed their booty into the imitation-crocodile-skin overnight bag I bought for my mum, and I'm dreading having to write to my mother that it's gone.

The police are surprised to see us, but they listen to our woes. Then they laugh. Laughing in Mexican sounds the same as laughing in English—the bastards.

There's nothing left for us in Acapulco, so David, Stuart and I say to Robert, Malcolm and Bill, 'Hooroo, see you later.' But we know we won't.

~

Two weeks later, outside a cheap hotel in the Mexican east-coast seaport of Veracruz, Stuart and David, companions who know me as well as companions can, go off in their VW Beetle on a three thousand-mile journey to Calgary in western Canada. And all we say is, "Hooroo, see you later.' But we know we won't. There's much more that should be said, but no more is said. That's the way it is.

I rent a room on the bottom floor of the bottom-class hotel, and I feel melancholy and lonely. Every day for a week, I'm on the wharves of

Veracruz searching for work as a seaman—or anything. On the few occasions there's a possibility of a berth I'm asked for my seaman's book. Not only do I not have one, but also I don't know what it is. When I get to talk to a ship's officer looking for crew, I'm asked what ship I came from and when I paid-off. I tell lies about ships that had been in port and left, that I got drunk and was left ashore, that's why I haven't got any documentation apart from my passport. When a sympathetic French ship's officer looked at my passport, he saw that I've been nowhere.

He says, 'You ave not been at zee. Zis passport zes you entered Canada az a pazzenger.'

And he's right.

I don't know why a person having little money seeks solace in alcohol, but that's what I do, and so do many others in Veracruz's cantina bars. Not many Mexicans, and they're the only ones in the cantinas, want to speak to an obviously down-and-out man who doesn't speak Spanish and who sits for hour after hour drowning his sorrows.

I get hardly anything right. I order *huevos* for breakfast because I know that's an egg. When asked how I want the egg, I select natural, and it arrives raw in a glass. I figure my finances, but whatever way I do it, it ends the same way: I'm on the cusp of financial disaster.

The town has a cinema, but all I see advertised are Spanish-speaking films. I hardly believe my eyes when I see that *Summer of the Seventeenth Doll* is showing.

I'm one of only twenty people in the stinking-hot theatre. But I don't care. On the screen is Sydney and Sydney Harbour and Fort Denison, and there's Ernest Borgnine doing his best to speak with an Australian accent. I'm homesick. I'm missing my mother and family and the security of certainty. Also, it's four weeks to Christmas, and I don't have enough money to send gifts. This year all my family will receive is a card. And that's not good enough.

In a bar later, a female entertainer sings *El Gallo Colorado*, and I'm drunk enough to sing it with her.

Someone behind me speaking perfect English says, 'Do you know what you're singing about?'

There's no reason to turn around; I just say, 'No.'

'It's about a red rooster, a fighting cock.'

Now I turn around. '*Yeah?*'

The man who spoke has to be a seaman. He's got a classic seaman's beard and he's carrying a duffle bag. 'Hello, I'm George.'

I'm very pleased to meet George. He and I drink a lot of alcohol. He drinks tequila in shot glasses then puts salt on the back of his hand, sucks it up, then sucks on lemon. I try it, but it tastes terrible and sends my head spinning, so I go back to drinking cerveza.

George says he's been ashore for three weeks. He's got a third-mate's ticket and paid off his last ship on the Mexican West Coast. He hopes to get a berth on the British ship the *Custodian* that's due in port tomorrow. I'm all ears because George might be able to help me get a berth. He reckons that'll be unlikely and that my best option is to get to New Orleans while I have enough money to buy a bus ticket. He reckons that once there I should go to the Scandinavian Seaman's Union and take any job on offer. He also reckons that if I don't get a berth there, I should go to Dutch's Bar.

'Dutch will get you a berth; it might take time, but he'll do it. The trouble is that unless you have the money to pay him, he'll get your first month's pay from the skipper of the ship. You'll work a month for nothing.'

'Yeah?'

'Yeah. The trouble is that without seaman's papers, he'll have to get you on a Liberian ship or some other scrapheap that's sailing under a flag of convenience. The seaman's union is your best bet.'

We drink and talk and sing *El Gallo Colorado* into the early hours.

In the morning I find that I'm lying on a hard bed, sweating and hearing Mexicans arguing. I've got a mighty big headache and wonder if I should open my eyes. When I do, I see a window with steel bars. I close my eyes. My head is spinning. I feel really sick and reckon I'm in a jail. I hear cars and trucks, the clicking of high heels and street noises. I open my eyes. The window with bars is in the bottom room of the bottom-class hotel. The voices are outside on the street. Bloody hell, I'm sick.

I seem not to be in danger. My legs and arms are still joined to my body, and I've got clothes on. I say, 'What happened?'

No answer. I go through the events of last night: drinking with George the English seaman; Tequila; hot Mexican food; Mexican women dancers, and me singing and dancing and …?

Bloody hell I'm sick.

My bag and clothes are here, so I haven't been robbed. *Robbed?* I feel for my wallet and passport. *Oh hell, where are they?*

They've gone. I've been robbed. *Fucking George.*

I throw back the bed sheet and discover I'm lying on my wallet and passport. So I haven't been robbed. I check in my wallet. My money's still there. I lie back on the bed. I'll have to stay here all day.

By the time it grows dark, I'm feeling good. I'm hungry, so I go back to the bar. The barman greets me like I'm his brother. *This can't be good.* Others in the bar smile and give me a wave. Now I'm *certain* it's not good.

Coffee is all I want, but the barman puts a shot glass of tequila in front of me and says, 'Gratis for my Australiano amigo.'

There's no way I can drink alcohol, let alone the potent tequila, so while the barman isn't looking I pour it into the coffee cup. I don't drink that either.

I understand bits of the Spanish and broken English spoken by those around me, and I hear that George and I were the life of the party.

One Mexican says, 'Senor, you dance and sing very well.'

I know that I'm a lousy dancer and singer. I have no idea what he's on about, but I say, '*Muchas gracias.*' I ask the barman, 'Senor George, the man I was with last night, where is he? *Donde estar el senor* George?'

He just shrugs his shoulders and says, '*No comprende.*'

Across Veracruz harbor, a ship flies the British flag. I reckon it must be the *Custodian* because it wasn't tied up there yesterday. Apart from this ship being my last chance of getting a berth out of Veracruz, I want to find out if George got his berth as third mate.

When I get there and look up the gangway of the *Custodian*, a seaman on the ship yells to me, 'Fuck off.'

I yell back, 'Fuck off yourself, you bastard.'

He yells, 'So you're not a Mexican wanting to sell something.'

I yell, 'No, can I come aboard?'

He yells, 'Yes.'

The top of the gangway is as far as I get because the seaman tells me there's no berths; an Englishman named George hasn't got a berth either, and the captain will beach him if he allows anyone that's not crew on board. He concludes with, 'So, mate, fuck off.'

And I do.

10 December 1961.
C/- Hotel Royalty
Veracruz Mexico.
Dear Mum.

I've not got a ship yet, but a British ship comes into port tomorrow. I've tried every ship here, but they all have a full crew.

George, an English bloke I met, is also trying to get a job, although he has a third mate's ticket.

The ship in tomorrow is the 'Custodian'. Here's hoping.

An option could be to go back to New Orleans. When I was there months ago, there were lots of ships. George told me that the Scandinavian Seaman's Union or someone called Dutch Carlson gets jobs for seamen.

It's cheap living in Veracruz, but I could sit here for months and run out of money. I have seventy dollars left—not enough for a bus ticket to Calgary. So if it doesn't work out tomorrow, I may be off to New Orleans.

It looks like I won't get any mail for a while because anything you sent to Mexico City, has been forwarded to London. Write to me in New Orleans c/- American Express.

Love Barry.

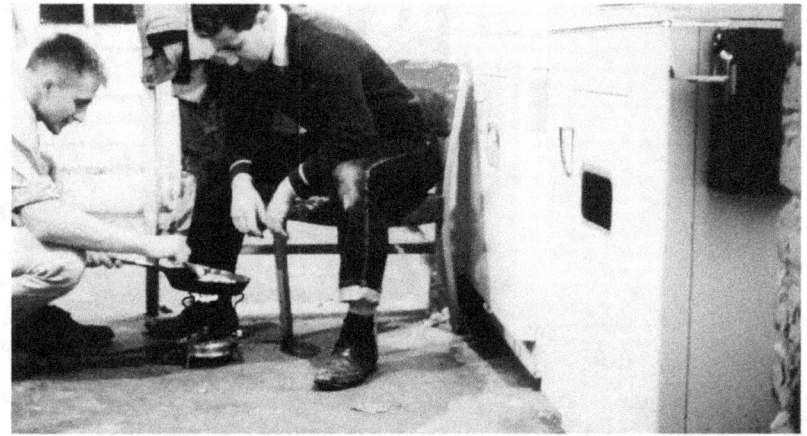
1961, Washington D.C.: Barry and Stewart cook dinner inside a camping ground laundry.

1961, Mexico: Barry on the morning beach.

Mexico Floating Gardens: David Acason, Mike Schonberg & Barry.

1961, Mexico: Veracruz main street. The arch fronted building is where Gerorge the English seaman and I drink Tequila.

Shoe shine in Veracruz.

Chapter Ten

Four buses carry me from Veracruz in Mexico to New Orleans. There's nothing good about the part of town I'm in. I want out. I want to be back in Australia where everything's ordered, normal and clean. Where people are civil; where there's food I can eat and my own bed. I want to be with my mother and family, go to work on the seven o'clock train and get a wage packet at the end of every week. I'm sick and tired of struggling, being broke and not knowing what tomorrow will bring.

But none of that can happen.

I sat on those stinking-hot buses for five days, hearing their high-revving engines go through thousands of gear changes and the drivers announcing the arrival at unmemorable small towns. Buses are supposed to take passengers to where there are friends or relatives or a future, but I reckon I've been taken to nowhere. I don't know anyone, and my immediate future looks bleak. Forty dollars is all I have. I'm near to a financial disaster and the end of my adventures.

The Scandinavian Seaman's Union building doesn't reflect the Scandinavian reputation for good architecture, but their second-floor office is at least near the waterfront. Apart from notices in a Scandinavian language, there's nothing on the walls. My guess is that the notices are union rules, or instructions about filling in forms, or that there's no eating or drinking in here.

A man stands in front of a hole in the wall, talking to another man framed by the hole. He says, 'Zere iz nozing except for a *messegutt*.'

The man on my side of the hole says, 'I vill not vork as a messboy.' Then he goes away.

I'm left staring at what seems like a framed picture of the man behind the wall. He says, 'Yes?'

I don't immediately answer because I think about what a messboy might be required to do, and I reckon high qualifications are not required.

I say to the man behind the wall, 'I'm a *messegutt*.'

He says, 'Ah, goot,' and goes to get some forms.

There's going to be questions, all the things seamen are asked; I'm going to lie.

I have some knowledge of what happens at sea but only because I was in the Australian Sea Cadet Corps, a group funded by the Navy League to get young Australians interested in joining the Navy. My great sailing adventure was being selected to sail on the HMAS *Sydney*, the aircraft carrier the British Government flogged to the Australian Government because it was too old for their navy. It steamed out of Sydney Harbour bound for Jervis Bay then Port Phillip Bay with no aircraft apart from one on the lower deck that didn't fly, seven pretend-to-be naval ratings and a pretend-to-be officer.

My sixteen-year old self found it all very exciting to salute everyone who looked like they should've been saluted, and many I saluted wondered why the hell this pimply-faced pretend-sailor was saluting them. They put our group of pretend-sailors in a parachute-folding cabin and expected us to sleep on the hard steel deck, which we did because no one wanted to look like a sissy. When we got into open waters all we did was paint parts of the ship that had been painted hundreds of times by real sailors who had nothing else to do. I painted a hinged hatch cover that went backwards and forwards with the rocking motion of the ship, and it made me seasick. I spewed over the side. All the real sailors laughed at me.

In the mess queue, the master at arms confronted me because we pretend sailors didn't have regulation uniforms, just bits and pieces of working and dress uniforms. The arrogant bastard said to me, 'Name?'

'White ... sir.'

'Rank?'

'Petty officer ... sir.'

'Petty officer?'

'Sea Cadet Petty Officer, sir.'

'Oh, one of those. Piss off, son, and get back into line.'

'Yes, sir.' And I went to get my roast beef and three veggies.

When the ship arrived in Port Phillip Bay we docked at Williamstown, and we pretend sailors were set loose on Melbourne. We replaced our Sea Cadet Corps hat tally band for stolen HMAS ones and strutted around as if we were real sailors—albeit pimply-faced. As a test of our disguise, two of us older ones went into Young and Jackson's Hotel to be served a beer and perve on the famous Chloe painting and we got away with it. When the seasickness rumbles still percolating in my stomach and bowels met the beer, a chemical reaction ensued, and I quickly had to use the hotel toilet. But there was no toilet paper, so I had to use the tram tickets I was saving as a souvenir of Melbourne.

Then the ship sailed out into Port Phillip Bay and we battened down for a planned, simulated nuclear attack. All the hatches and companionways were closed, and the ship's dinghies put things in the water that oozed pretend radio-active smoke. Then the ship got buzzed by jet aircraft, dummy rounds of pom-pom shells were shot at the planes and the sailor who was responsible for us told us that it was all a big fucking joke, that we'd all be dead if this was real.

The Scandinavian man, who speaks very good English, brings me back to the present by returning to the hole in the wall. He says, 'Seaman's papers?'

'Stolen.'

'Stolen?'

'Yeah.'

He seems unconcerned. 'Ah, it happens.'

'Your last ship?'

'Liberian … I forget the name.'

'It happens.'

He asks questions and I lie away using sea terms I learnt in the Navy cadets: below decks, starboard, bulkhead and first mate, and for good measure I throw in the names of a few sailor knots that mean nothing to him. Mention of a Sheepshank has him shaking his head in wonder.

He says, 'You will need a medical examination. The doctor's report will be sent to the Norwegian Consulate and you will ship out tomorrow. Okay?'

'Okay. Ah, where's the ship bound?'

He looks at a pile of papers, fumbles through them, but doesn't find what he's looking for. 'Europe and India, I think. Does it matter?'

'No.'

The Norwegian flag flutters on the M/T *Varvara*, and the ship does not have, like in Mexico, a crewmember stationed at the top of its gangway to tell people to fuck-off. I'm aboard for five minutes waiting to see someone, anyone, then I hear a voice say, 'Hello to you,' and I say, 'Hello to you too.'

The speaker, a casually dressed man aged in his forties, continues, 'Are you looking for the captain?'

'Yes.'

'Come with me then.'

We go amidships to a cabin. The man ushers me in, then sits behind a small desk. 'I am Captain Nils Kalvenes. What can I do for you?'

'I'm the new messboy.'

'Ah, good, I am expecting a new *messegutt*. You have your papers?'

I give him my brand new *Avregningsbok* that has a *Hyrekontrakt* inside. He reads the *hyrekontrakt*, signs it, takes a copy for himself and says, 'Here is your seaman's book and your copy of our contract.'

My first impression of the Captain is very positive. Two years ago, they did a few voyages from Sydney to Noumea, and he thinks that

Australians are very friendly people. I have difficulty believing that everything's going so well.

After coffee, he says, 'Mister White, on my ship you are to do as ordered by the cook. He will give you your roster, which will be strictly administered by him and his second cook. You will not miss any of your appointed work shifts. Kitchen clothing, the cost of which will be deducted from your pay, will be issued to you, and you will keep this clothing absolutely clean. Understand?'

'Yes sir.'

When I ask where the ship's bound, he says, 'We are a specialist oil tanker. Tomorrow we steam to Baton Rouge where we take on a cargo of oil. We will steam across the Atlantic then through the Suez to Bombay where we will discharge the cargo. Then we steam around the Cape of Good Hope to another American port that's yet to be decided.'

'Oh. And after that?'

'Possibly a few more voyages to the sub-continent.'

'Oh. Not to Europe?'

'No. Unfortunately it will be a long time before my ship is in a European port.'

'As I understand it, my contract states that I can only pay-off in a Northern European port?

''Yes. We will be together for a long time yet.'

I can't argue. There's nothing I can do. I'm broke. I have no power.

~

I finish washing up the breakfast dishes impregnated with egg yoke that sticks like glue and the pots and pans covered in fat and grease marks, then I stand on deck looking at the Mississippi River banks choked with industry, mostly petroleum. I feel secure, but wonder why I'm again doing a job that's done by the lowest of the low.

Apart from one Spanish seaman, the rest of the crew is from Norway, Sweden or Denmark. Some of them are already treating me like

I'm shit. The cook told me in no uncertain terms that he's God as far as I'm concerned, and he'll closely inspect my work. Two seamen do their best to be bloody rude, and I reckon they think they're gods, too.

I figure there's nothing I can do until we put to sea. So for now, I take their abuse.

Surprisingly, in Baton Rouge I'm given shore leave after lunch, and the officer on watch tells me the ship sails at eleven, sharp. He says, '*Messegutt*, ships wait for no one.'

The Spaniard says he's going ashore and I should go with him, which is all right, but when we get our feet on solid ground, he asks me how much money I have.

I've got thirty-one dollars, sixty-five cents but I don't tell him anything. There's no way this Spaniard is getting any of it. As soon as we get away from the dock area, I lose him by telling him I need a toilet when he goes into a shop. That's the end of our shore leave together.

I remember how I spent my last five Canadian dollars buying warm socks before going into the Northwest Territory camp, and I reckon I'll have to do something like that now, but here it'll be a woollen jumper and a waterproof jacket. Beer and scotch and a good time would be better, but it'd be stupid, and I've done enough stupid things for now.

A song plays in a record store I pass: *Seaman, stop your roaming/come home from the sea.* Even though I've only had one night on the ship, I connect to the words. I'm a now seaman.

It's not a lot of fun being the *messegutt*, but the officers' female *messegutt* is a fun surprise. I slave away washing dishes in stainless steel tubs of hot dishwashing water and a young woman does the same two feet behind me, but with officers' better crockery. Most in the crew have good English, but she has little. She knows how to say sorry, hello, no and yes. Occasionally, when I back up and she does too, our bums meet, then both of us say, 'Sorry,' and we laugh. Days later I test her understanding when I ask her if she'll sleep with me; she answers with, 'Hello.' When I see her on deck with the engineering officer, I lose interest, and that's smart because he can easily arrange to push me head first down a companionway.

Some of the crew were on the *Varvara* in Australia, and they tell me how they enjoyed hotel fights. I don't know what they mean or at which hotels they fought, but I've got an image to create so I say that I love that kind of fighting too. They tell some of the other crew, and soon I'm being treated with respect, except by a big Dane.

I'm amazed, surprised and relieved that no one wants to test my fighting, but I reckon it's not going to be long before the big Danish bloke does. He has to.

~

I've been on the ship since the nineteenth of December, and it feels strange to be celebrating Christmas day at sea with Scandinavians. Everyone's saying, '*Godt Nyttår*,' and they're opening mail sent to the ship in New Orleans and only now distributed. The first officer gives each of the crew, and me also, a Christmas post card from a Norwegian school child. I feel special. I ask the cook, 'Why do I get a card? No one knows me.'

He says, 'Every seaman on every Norwegian ship gets a postcard from a Norwegian school child.'

My card is from an Aslaig Nilsson who lives in Tromso in the far North of Norway. The card shows Tromso Bridge, which I now know is one-thousand and thirty-six meters long.

I reckon the Captain of the ship should pay double rates to those working on Christmas day, especially to me because there's loads of washing up. But everyone's in a good mood. Even the sea is calmer and so is the Danish bloke who has it in for me. I risk a few more accidentally on purpose bumps with the officers' *messegutt* thinking that she might, because of Christmas spirit, invite me to her cabin. But she's still saying, 'Sorry.'

I'm pleased when Christmas day has been and gone because my homesick feelings might go now. Late on Christmas night, on the long walkway between amidships and the very front of the ship's bow, I lie on deck in the moonlight with my head through the anchor-cable scuttle. The wind whistles in and around my ears, and I yell and sing and cry, and I see dolphins defying death by dodging under and around the cutting edge of the ship's bow. For an hour, I lean further out, defying death, then at midnight the ship's horn blows, and I'm back to reality. My Christmas melancholia is settled for another year.

Due to the coaching the second cook gives me, I become experienced at laying the tables. He's got me placing cutlery to be used in each part of the meal from the outside in, and making sure that the knife cutting edges are faced inwards. He's even got me trying to serve food using a fork and spoon held in one hand. I reckon I'm doing very well. But the Danish bloke doesn't think so, and he makes wise cracks in Danish that I don't understand, but I get the innuendo.

The dessert tonight is creamed rice. The Dane says he doesn't like creamed rice, so he gets the big stainless-steel bowl and chucks it against the bulkhead. Everyone looks at him, and I do too because the cook will expect me to clean it all up. I'm not going to do that. He sits down, but I'm standing, and I grab a handful of his hair, pull his head back and I say, 'You fucking-well clean that up.'

He struggles so I pull his head further back. I take a tight grip on his shoulder near his neck and feel bone. 'You hear me? Clean that fucking stuff up.'

I reckon he should be shaking with fear, because I am.

No one says anything. But I reckon they're wondering whether they should or shouldn't help him. I pull his hair with all my strength, and I'm uncertain if that's causing him his pain or if it's my grip on his shoulder blades, but whatever it is, he screams blue murder, and the cook rushes from the kitchen holding a kitchen knife. He sees the mess of rice dripping down the bulkhead to the deck and takes its presence there as a personal affront to his cooking. He says, something in Norwegian that has threat in it. I reckon he's said he'll cut the throat of whoever threw his world-famous creamed rice at the bulkhead.

The throat that's most visible and accessible is the Dane's, and the Dane knows that. Panicking, he yells, 'I vill clean it; I *vill clean it*; I vill clean it.'

He tries to sweep it with a broom, but it congeals and refuses to be swept. We all laugh at his efforts. I could never have achieved this result alone, but the crew thinks so, and so does the Dane, so I let them think exactly that.

There's going to be a party to celebrate the New Year. The Captain has released two bottles of beer each, but we must drink it while we're eating our dinner and not at midnight. That's all right with us. The cooks get all competitive, and there's going to be Norwegian and Danish and Swedish pastries to go with our beer. That's also all right with us.

From somewhere, and against regulations, some schnapps, whiskey and vodka is produced and drunk from coffee cups. Everyone's having a good time. Captain Nils Kalvenes comes to wish us happy New Year, and then he goes back to where he won't have to witness any breaking of regulations—probably to the officers' mess where they'll break regulations, too.

My popularity has risen since my successful disagreement with the big Danish bloke, and I'm getting a good variety of what's against regulations poured into my coffee cup, which is not good for my head. I try every pastry, too, which is not good for my stomach. At nine o'clock I don't give a bugger about my *messegutt* duties, and I lie on my cabin bunk. The rocking-chair-like rising and falling of the ship completes the ingredients for sound sleep, and I'm off with the pixies until morning.

But there's something wrong because in the middle of the Atlantic the ship should have no reason to sound its horn. The first blast has me awake, the second has me thinking that we're going to port, the third means we're going astern and that's very unlikely. Then there's the fifth blast, which means get out of my way I can't get out of yours. I reckon there's trouble. But the blasts continue, and I'm on my feet on the deck with my life jacket which I'm struggling to put on, then I'm out of the cabin in the companionway.

Two crew there have just come off watch. They seem not to be too alarmed. In fact they're pointing at me and laughing.

I reckon the ship sinking in the middle of the Atlantic is no laughing matter, but all they do is say, *'Happy New Year,'* and continue laughing at me.

At breakfast time, I'm confronted with the largest cleaning and washing-up job ever, and that's all right. But what is not all right is how the crew all laugh at me.

'Abandon ship! Abandon ship,' they yell, and they fall about laughing.

I don't like being a *messegutt*, and I wish I wasn't here washing dishes. But what's that wish got to do with reality? Nothing. The reality is that I'm stuck with washing dishes for a long time yet, unless I can get transferred to seaman's duties.

I tell the first cook what I'd like to do and he laughs. 'You are a *messegutt*, that's all. You are not a seaman.'

I say, 'But I can be a seaman.'

He says, 'No, you can't.'

There's got to be a way. I reckon that a serious skin disease on my hands is *that* way. So I use abrasive soap to scrub my skin red, soak my hands in dishwashing powder and ask to see Captain Nils.

Captain Nils is a busy man so I have to wait a day to see him. All the while I'm scrubbing away at my hands, and I've got them looking very much like I've got a serious, contagious even, disease that will ravage the ship's crew if I have to continue washing up.

I knock on Captain Nils' door, and while I wait for him to answer, I rub my hands on the steel bulkhead and draw some blood.

I hear Captain Nils' yell to come in, and I'm pleased to see that he's smiling. 'Ah,' he says, *'Our* Australian. What can I do for you?'

It will be good if he suggests having our discussion while drinking a cup of coffee, but I don't reckon he's going to do that.

'Captain Nils, I have a medical problem with my hands ... I think it's a disease, and I don't believe I should be handling dishes that the crew eats off.'

Still smiling, he says, 'And what do you think we should do about your ... disease?'

'I think it would be a good idea to give me seaman's duties and have someone else be the *messegutt*.'

'I see. And which seaman do you think I should appoint as *messegutt*?'

It'd be dumb for me to suggest the Danish bloke because Captain Nils is a good Captain, and he must know about the creamed-rice incident. He must know that the Dane and I are enemies. I say to him, 'Anyone that you think can do the job.'

'So I should tell one of my seamen that they are no longer a seaman. That they are now a *messegutt*. Is that what I should do?'

'Yes.'

'And what do you think that seaman will say to me? Do you believe he will say thank you, Captain Nils? Will he say that?'

'Ah ... perhaps.'

'He will not. He will tell me no. He will discuss it with the crew, and I will have trouble. Now, my Australian, do you think I want to have trouble with my crew?'

'No.'

'Well then, I suggest you stop injuring your own hands, put on rubber gloves and go to do your duties.'

Captain Nils is not the pushover I though him to be. He's as smart as a shithouse rat, but I am, too. I say to him, 'I refuse to work.'

'You refuse to work? Do you know anything about the law at sea? Anything at all?'

'Ah, no.'

'You might be surprised that as captain of this ship I have a great deal of power. I am like the President, or, what do you have in Australia?'

'A Prime Minister.'

'Yes. I'm like the Prime Minister of this ship. Now, did I hear you say that you refuse to work?'

I'd said something that a smart shithouse rat wouldn't have said. I was dumb. Now I'll be smart. I say, 'Captain Nils, because of medical reasons, I refuse to do the *messegutt* job, and I request transfer to seamen's duties.'

He says, 'Forgive me for being blunt, but if I were to say to you that when we reach Augusta you should leave the ship, would you be upset?'

I must contain myself. I must not yell yippee! I must not let him see that's what I want. I say to him, 'If that's what you *must* do.'

I'm wondering why he's still smiling. This is no smiling matter. This is serious. This is the difference between a year's sentence to washing dishes, or freedom.

Captain Nils says, 'You will return to your duties, you will wear gloves, and I will call for you tomorrow to give you my answer.'

The interview is over. He doesn't offer coffee.

The words of the song, *Seaman, stop your roaming/come home from the sea* goes through my mind. I've been a seaman for only three weeks, and already I want to come home from the sea. I sit on my bunk doing financial calculations that a seven-year-old could do, and I speak aloud like a seven-year-old working out his pocket money.

'Money? I've got ah … fifteen dollars American. Money I have in the bank? Ah … none, I don't have a bank. Money needed to get from Augusta to London? Ah … unknown, but a lot more than fifteen dollars. Money I'll get from working on the ship? Ah … little if anything. My seaman's contract states that if I leave the ship at other than a Northern European port, I'll have to pay my replacement's travelling costs, from Norway. Money available … oh shit!' I've forgotten cigarettes and toiletries and the kitchen clothes I've bought on account from the ship's quartermaster.

I seriously think about asking to see Captain Nils so I can tell him I love my job as *messegutt*, that I'm happy and want to stay on his beautiful ship.

My depression takes me back to the very front of the ship's bow. I put my head through the anchor scuttle. It would be so easy to end things.

The first cook says, 'Captain Nils wants to see you.' I drag myself to his cabin prepared to eat crow, crawl, and clean his boots, to do almost anything except bare my bum.

I knock on his door and get happy-sounding, 'Come in!'

Inside the cabin I smell percolating coffee. I see a plate of pastries on his desk. He must be expecting someone else.

'Ah,' he says, 'Sit down, Mister White.'

Mister White is now even more nervous because no one calls anyone Mister here.

'You will take coffee and pastries with me?'

'Ah … yeah. Thank you.'

He pours, and I think about the pastries. I reckon they're better than those available in the crew's mess.

He sits. 'Now, to our little problem.'

I want to interrupt him and ask for forgiveness but I'm busy with a mouthful of pastry.

'Your problem is that you want to leave the ship at Augusta, correct?'

The pastry has a thick custard inside and it clogs my mouth. I say, 'Gruggsgollup.'

'And my problem is that I need a *messegutt*, correct?'

'Gruggsgollup.'

'Good, then that's understood. You are also aware that I must replace you with a *messegutt* from Norway, and that you will have deducted from your pay the cost of his transportation, correct?'

'Gruggsgollup.'

'Good. Mister White, I have told you about my time with this ship in Australia. What I haven't told you is how much I enjoyed your country and your people and that I am now prepared to allow you to pay off my ship at Augusta.'

'Gruggsgollup?'

'Um, you are enjoying the pastry?'

'Gruggs … yes, it's very nice; it's very … ah, custard.'

'What I must say to you is this. Your threat of refusing to work verged on being unlawful. I will not have any of that. Have you mentioned our last conversation to any of the crew?'

'No.'

'Well don't. This is between you and me. Tomorrow we enter the Mediterranean. We take on oil and water at Ceuta, and then we'll be at Augusta next day. You are very fortunate that I have found a Norwegian in Naples who will take your place, the cost to you will be …'

He looks through a pile of papers while I hold my breath.

'… nothing.'

'*Nothing?*'

'Correct. But I must say this to you. I am aware that many young Australians travel the world doing this kind of thing. You've got away with it, but others will not. I will consider my position when I am next offered Australian crew.'

I'm very prepared to polish his shoes but he wants nothing from me.

~

At Augusta the first mate gives me a Statement of Affairs that says I'm to get six-hundred and one kroner. He gives me a document:

M/T Varvara, at sea.

To whom it may concern.

I hereby declare that I sign off the Norwegian M/T Varvara at Augusta, Italy, according to my own wish, and I do emphasis that all pay and rights I have according to my contract have been fulfilled by ship.

I don't even consider pointing out the mistakes in the document, that it should say 'emphasise'. I only ever see CaptainNils again when he's hanging out of the bridge manoeuvring his ship in the tight harbor. He smiles and throws me a wave.

15 January 1962
In Italy.
Dear Mum,
I don't know where I am, somewhere north of Rome.
I caught the wrong train and am now waiting for a connection to Genoa.
Everything is going fine. I will write more details in a few days.
I put a cross on this postcard where the Italian customs in Augusta took two cartons of cigarettes from me. I should be in Switzerland tonight, France tomorrow night and London in three days. I received three letters from you in Augusta.
Love Barry.

January ,1962: Oil Tanker M.T. Varvara somewhere in the Atlantic Ocean.

Four of the M.T. Varvara crew at Augusta, Sicily after 'paying-off' the ship

Chapter Eleven

The journey from Augusta in Sicily, to London went awry. I reckoned I knew enough Italian to keep out of trouble. But I got into trouble anyway—large Italian railway stations have too many options.

Augusta station had one train line going north, to Messina. Only one ferry went from there to the Italian mainland. After that, one train line went north to Naples, so I got to where I should've been. In Naples there was a good chance I'd get on the wrong train, but somehow I got it right. Trains leave from Rome for all over the country, and I couldn't understand the many fast-spoken announcements. I got it wrong and found myself on a train to Milan. I didn't want to go to Milan.

The mistake wasn't entirely my fault. Since I'd arrived in Italy, heaps of officious railway guards had demanded to see my ticket, so surely the guard in Rome knew I was getting on the wrong train.

But it was in Rome that one of the railway men yelled at me, so I'd yelled at him and he'd yelled back at me. I told him he was a cranky old bastard. He replied with long sentences in Italian that included the word *bastardo*, so I reckon he sent me to the wrong train.

I've finally arrived at London's Paddington railway station. I can understand the announcements, but there are still many options. Eight a.m. is not a good time to ask for directions. Everyone's in a great hurry to get somewhere, probably to work. The main concourse is very wide with many platforms. Travelers hurry about like worker ants, except ants are better organized—they follow trails. They don't go every which way. I ask an English gentleman for assistance—his bowler hat, well-cut suit, waistcoat and furled umbrella identify him.

'Mate,' I say, and that's a mistake because how can a gentleman be a mate? 'Where do I get a train—?'

'I haven't got time,' he says.

'Well, get fucked then.' He must have heard me swear. He can't be that deaf.

Two young pommie men standing near me say, 'Hey! What did you say?'

'I wasn't speaking to you. I was speaking to that stuck-up prick there.' It's stupid of me to swear, especially in one of the world's busiest railway stations, but I'm not in the right frame of mind to be smart. I've been travelling in trains for three-and-a-half days. I'm tired. I'm dirty. I'm unshaven, and I don't know where to go.

'Mate,' one of the pommies says, 'the bloody coppers will arrest you for swearing.'

They're not pommies! 'Oh. Thanks.'

'Where've you come from?'

'Sicily.'

'A long way.'

'Yeah. And that's probably why I'm a bit short tempered. I'm rooted.'

'Where are you going?'

'Barons Court.'

So two New Zealanders get me onto the correct train.

~

Barons Court is a nice-sounding name, so I expect a nice suburb, but there's nothing nice about it. Most of the houses are one-room-and-a-hallway wide, three-levels high and have basements that must be freezing cold. I would hate to live below ground in one of those.

It wouldn't be so bad if there were parks and gardens, but Talgarth Road is very busy, and grime and the slush of January weather is everywhere. Barons Court is dull and depressing.

I can understand why the door of 145 Talgarth Road hasn't been opened. Probably the loud, continuous traffic noise is filtering inside the house. So I try harder. I kick the door a few times. Now it's opened. A woman stares at me with a blank I-don't-know-you stare, but I reckon she's about to smile and say hello. She slams the door shut, treating me as if I'm an encyclopaedia or life-insurance salesman.

I don't expect that kind of reception here. This is supposed to be the country of good manners. This is mother England and I'm from Australia. She might be one of the children I helped save during the Second World War. I collected food for Britain in my squeaky-wheeled wheelbarrow, food that probably stopped that woman starving. She probably got the cans of Letona Peaches, Tom Piper Camp Pie, Arnotts Biscuits and Moran and Cato Pure Tea that I collected from my Bauman's Road, Peakhurst neighbours. And her kid probably got the hand-knitted wool socks that I should've got, the socks that were put in the Food and Clothes for Britain box at Peakhurst Primary School.

Is this all the thanks I get?

I sit on the front steps of the narrow-gutted building to consider my next move. A door to the freezing-cold basement opens, and a voice says, 'I'll bet you're David's mate from Australia.'

'Ah, yeah. I am.'

'Well, you'd better come in then.'

I'm at the correct address; it's just that I should've gone to the basement.

The place is scruffy. It's certain that blokes live in this cave-like hole. The Crimean-war vintage linoleum has almost as many holes as there are patterns on the linoleum. The kitchen furniture is decrepit; a Salvation Army shop would be embarrassed to stock the rickety table and four unmatched chairs. Boiled-over-mistakes cake the gas stove, and a single light bulb that's probably only forty watts strength hangs from the close-to-our-head ceiling. The place feels as cold as an ice chest.

The man's friendly enough. He says, 'My name's Albert. I'm the only one home at the moment. Take your jumper off, and we'll have a cup of tea.'

There's no way I'm taking any clothing off, in fact if I had something warmer I'd put it on. Albert tries to get a gas ring going, but it doesn't light.

He says, 'You wouldn't by any chance have a shilling on you?'

'Yeah, I think so. Why?'

'The meter.'

'The meter what?'

'The gas meter. It's out of money.'

I think, *Jesus, what am I doing here?*

While the tea brews, I look to see if Albert uses any of the Moran and Cato tea that was amongst the food for Britain I collected. But he doesn't. He chucks into a crazed teapot something that looks like dust.

He says, 'Strong or weak? Milk or not? Sugar?'

I say, 'Bush tea, thanks,' because I'm itching for him to ask me to explain.

But Albert doesn't ask me what bush tea is. He says, 'Yes, I know; as hot as hell, black as night and as sweet as love. Our Aussie flat mate says exactly the same thing. I'd give you a biscuit, if we had any.'

He's got to give me something. I'm starving. Surely he's got a dry biscuit and cheese.

The cave door opens and two other men enter. Albert tells me their names are Terry and Pat.

Terry asks. 'How's David doing?'

'Good. The last time I saw him and his brother Stuart they were heading for Los Angeles. They'd be back in Calgary now.'

Pat says nothing. He's a long streak of misery who is bloody rude—he's already got his head in a book.

Albert says, 'We ought to celebrate your successful arrival in London. Terry, why don't we go down to the pub for a few ales?'

Terry says, 'I've got no money.'

Pat doesn't even look up from his book to say the same thing, but he does say it with an Irish accent.

'Isn't there a bottle of beer in the refrigerator? We could open that?'

Pat still doesn't look away from his book when he says, 'I drank it this morning.'

In Australia visitors would be offered Iced Vo-Vo biscuits or at least a Sao cracker with a bit of tomato on top. In Canada we always kept grog in the fridge for visitors, and the ship I was on a week ago always had Danish pastries available for the crew. Now, I'm in what's supposed to be one of the great cities of the world and they can't even give me a dog biscuit.

My haversack is sitting on the vintage linoleum and is in the way. I want it to be in the way because one of the cave dwellers will soon have to ask me if I've got a bed tonight. Pat, the Irish bloke, puts down the book he's reading so I can now see the cover; it's about fifteenth-century painters—way outside of my interests.

He gets a saucepan that's still got the remains of a few boiled-over meals stuck to the outside, opens a can of something and tips the contents into the saucepan. Then he tentatively turns a knob on the gas stove. 'Ah,' he says, 'We've got gas.'

Albert says, 'I put a shilling in the meter.'

I reckon he should have said he bludged a shilling from Barry, the poor tired bloke that's looking for a bed tonight so how about we offer him a place to lay his head.

The front door to the cave opens. In comes a short, thickset man with no front teeth and swatches of long hair valiantly trying to cover his mid-skull baldness. He says, 'The bloody bastards haven't got the shit house opened at the railway station.' He rushes through a doorway and I hear his hurried footsteps on a staircase.

Pat says, 'That's Don. He's Australian.'

He has to be Australian, but where's he gone? Obviously he needed a toilet, but it sounds to me like he's gone to the top of the building.

A rush of water goes through a cast iron pipe fixed to the kitchen wall. Don has flushed.

More casual footsteps come down the staircase, and Don comes into the kitchen. 'I just made that,' he says, then looks at my haversack. 'Could this belong to David's mate?'

I say, 'Yeah, it's mine.'

'Ah, at last you made it. We expected you weeks ago. Albert reckoned you were probably lost and doing circuits of the underground.'

Don's a friendly bloke. He shakes my hand, lifts my haversack and says, 'Come, I'll show you your bed.'

Terry says, *'Bed?'*

'Bed? Oh, that's right, we haven't got one spare at the moment; come and I'll show you your stretcher.'

He shows me to a room with two unmade single beds and one window that's caked on the outside with what's probably coal dust. The traffic noise coming from Talgarth Road is continuous. Sleeping here won't be pleasant. Ropes stretch from one wall to the other, and what looks like damp laundry hangs carelessly on one of the ropes—no clothes pegs. The other rope seems to be dedicated to hanging washed and dried clothing: clearly, ironing is done infrequently.

I look at the old, much-used stretcher, but I don't say, 'I'm not sleeping on that.' I can't say that because I've got no other option.

Don's still wearing a black duffel coat, which I reckon is sensible, because the room's as cold as buggery. One of the beds has to be his—the one he empties the contents of his duffel coat pocket onto—packets of tea, jars of jam, tins of herrings and other stuff I don't recognize. I wonder why he doesn't have them all in a bag.

'Been shopping?'

He laughs, 'Yeah. I shop every day.' He takes one of the tins. 'I reckon I'll have the Paté de foie gras tonight.'

I don't say anything because I don't know what he's talking about, but if that small tin has his evening meal inside, he won't be putting on any weight.

'And you? Will you join me having paté?'

'I'll eat anything; I could eat the leg off a horse.'

When I taste the stuff that comes from the small tin I think it to be fish paste. He tells me it's goose's liver, so I decide to never again accept any meal offers from Don. Out-of-place foodstuffs sit on the kitchen table: Queen bee honey, spreads with the Royal Seal and 'By Appointment to her Majesty the Queen' on them. I'm itching to ask how and why? But it turns out I don't have to because Albert asks about Don's boss.

Don says, 'Fortnum and Mason shouldn't have a man like that in charge of their storeroom because he's a dickhead'.

I ask, 'What's Fornum Mason?'

I'm corrected, 'It's Fortnum and Mason; they're the grocers to Her Majesty the Queen.'

I'm surprised. 'The Queen has her own grocery shop? Do you see her in there getting her oatmeal and sugar and sago?'

They laugh. They think I'm kidding, but I'm not. I don't know what the Queen of England does about getting her groceries. It's all right for the blokes that live in this cave at Barons Court because they're used to being in England, so they know about those things. Of course I'm surprised about the Queen having Her own grocer, and I realise that She'd have Her groceries delivered to Her Palace. She can't just arrive at Her shop and expect everyone to swan-about after Her. She can't expect that they'd have everything She'd want.

I expect She'd do what my mum did. My mum had my sister or me take the list of groceries to Mister Jenkins' shop on Forest Road, and next day he's outside our house in his Morris panel van with all her things packed in a fruit carton. I don't expect that Her Charles or Her Anne would take Her list to Fortnum & Mason, I know She'd phone the order through or have Her housekeeper take Her list there.

I don't like people laughing at my expense, especially pommies, so I say, 'I fucking well know that the bloody Queen doesn't actually front up at the shop to get her stuff. I know that she has a lackey do that for her.' But they still laugh.

Don says, 'As a socialist it's my philosophical duty to have the same food that the Queen of England eats. My duffel coat pocket is the transporter of By Appointment foods to the masses.'

'Masses?' Albert says.

'All right, perhaps not the masses ... to us, we that object to elitism and hereditary rule and ownership of assets and royalty.'

'You steal the food,' Terry says.

'Steal? No. Confiscate, or acquire? Yes.'

I'm warming to Don. He's got to know a lot about lurks and perks because only lurk men use the word 'acquire'.

Pat the Irishman starts rambling on about capitalism and socialism and communism and workers' rights and fair distribution of income and assets, but I haven't got a clue what he's on about, so I say nothing. And I say nothing for the next three hours, because it'll be obvious to them that I don't have my school Intermediate Certificate. I reckon they've got theirs, or even the Leaving Certificate; maybe they've been to a University. No one I know has been to a University.

At seven thirty in the morning, I hear the blokes leave the cave to go to their jobs, but it doesn't look right because it's still pitch dark outside. I quickly need to do what they're doing—go to a job—so I mobilize myself for action. Every room in the cave has stacks of day-old, week-old, month-old newspapers the same size as *The Sydney Morning Herald*, so that's where I start looking. But those papers don't have anything much in them apart from news, stories and opinions about stuff I know nothing about. Some newspapers are called *The Manchester Guardian*. I guess that's Albert's favourite paper, because he said he comes from a place called Salford in Manchester, and I suppose he likes to keep up with local things. Others are the London *Times*. I suppose that's Terry's favourite. There are a few *Irish Times* so there's no doubt whose favourite that is, and there's some called *The Observer*, which I guess is Don's favourite. None of those *Sydney Morning Herald* lookalikes, those arm-stretching can't-open-in-a-crowded-train papers, have jobs advertised apart from jobs for doctors, engineers, accountants and historians. None of them are advertising real jobs, no plumbing jobs.

I breakfast on bread that tastes like it's a year old and spread it with the By-Appointment-to-Her-Majesty-the-Queen strawberry jam, then I go look for work.

I see old buildings and houses everywhere, and that's difficult for me to reconcile because I thought Hitler's planes bombed London to smithereens and much of it had to be rebuilt, but I don't see much that's new.

I look at newspapers the same size as the Sydney *Sun*, the kind of newspapers that you can open in a crowded train, then I see one that has the same name as a paper in Sydney, the *Daily Mirror*. This one's just like Sydney's *Mirror*, a rag, so there's got to be job advertisements for plumbers. There are.

~

I find a job and no longer feel inferior to the other inhabitants of the Barons Court cave. Also, at Australia House there's mail for me, and amongst it is a cheque for seventy dollars sent by the Canadian Taxation department. The cheque has to be banked, then I have to wait a week to get the money; life is getting better. Again, I've just made it.

In Canada I got down to having only five dollars, then I got work in the North West Territory. Here in England, I'm down to five shillings when I get my first pay envelope of ten-pounds, five shillings. I'd avoided telling the inhabitants of the Barons Court cave about my plight. I guessed that none of them were very flush, but I reckoned Don would've loaned me a few quid, if he'd had it.

I now have a ritual in my life that I enjoy: going to work where I do what I know best. I put up pipes, weld, screw threads, and beat and shape bits of sheet lead and copper that are used to waterproof roofs. After work I return to a home base where there's security I've not had for six months. The tools of my trade and my other possessions arrive from Canada, so Stuart's front room in Calgary now has space for other travellers' left luggage that's to be sent on to Peru or Japan or somewhere else.

An education process is going on that I'm unaware of, but in which I'm a willing participant. I listen a lot to Albert, Terry, Pat and Don, and although I reckon they sometimes fit a description I learn from them—intellectual snobs—they are bloody smart. I hear that the Prime Minister of Britain, Mister Harold Macmillan, is a bastard, but the Labour Party leader, Hugh Gaitskell, is not a bastard. I hear that the Russian ballet dancer Rudolf Nureyev is a great partner to Margot Fonteyn; a bloke named Francis Bacon has written a load of things called essays; Mahatma Gandhi was the saviour of the Indian people; Dylan Thomas is the voice of the Welsh people, and James Joyce is the voice of the Irish people. It's all so confusing. There's so much to learn.

Working is good because I know what I'm doing and I do it well. The pommie plumbers I work beside are bludgers of the highest order. They don't give a stuff about anything, and they hardly ever do their job correctly. Sometimes I say to them, 'That's not right, mate,' and they reply with, 'You're just a bloomin colonial; how would you know?'

Well, they're wrong, because I do know, and that's proven when the boss asks me if I can lead-burn, and I say, 'I can,' and he pays me overtime rates to work on a roof at a place called Crystal Palace.

I must be good at working on roofs because the boss has me on another one, and the view's great, especially of the office on the other side of the road and particularly of the female Indian receptionist. I do roof-to-office hand signals to arrange a meeting. We go to a pub where I have beer and she has something called Babycham, and in the darkness of a London shop entrance I have with her my first knee trembler. It's hard work.

The blokes in the cave are always arguing about issues. When I try to say something they say, 'It's *not* relevant.' It seems that unless I start reading the newspapers they read, unless I start reading books, unless I start listening to the BBC, I'll never know about issues, and I'll always be *not* relevant.

Don's a big surprise package. He looks no smarter than me. He does low-skilled work; he drinks too much; he's a lousy dresser and he's broke the day after he gets paid. But he knows lots about everything. He's always quoting people that I've never heard of. Lately it's been a Bertrand Russell who he says is a rationalist, and when I say to him, 'I don't know much about religion,' he roars with laughter. And that's a problem for me. I hate it when people laugh at something I say. I'm a learner; I don't know a lot, yet.

Then he's on about the Catholic Archbishop of Melbourne, Cardinal Mannix, who he says is evil, but the novelist Frank Hardy is a saint. I don't know either of them, so I simply nod. And that's the way I'm learning about issues. I know hardly anything about anything, which means I'm doing a lot of nodding while Don and Terry and Albert and Pat are doing lots of talking. I get the courage to ask Don why Archbishop Mannix is evil. He can't be; he's a church leader. He's the Archbishop of Melbourne.

He says, 'He rooted the Australian Labour Party by orchestrating a split that caused the DLP to form. His henchman was Santamaria.'

All I say is, 'Oh.' I ask him why Frank Hardy, whoever he is, is a saint.

He says, 'Because he exposes the ruling class. You read *Power Without Glory* didn't you?

'Ah ... no.'

'What? You haven't read the most important book written by an Australian this century?'

'No.'

Don goes into his bedroom and returns with two books. He tosses one on the table. 'Here, read this.'

I don't read many books. I read two Carter Brown detective yarns, they were good, but this book doesn't look like something I'd invest a month reading.

He doesn't toss the other book; he places it on the table and says, 'When I finish reading Frank's new book—this one, *The Hard Way*—you can read it. It about Hardy's legal battle; the battle he had with the ruling class who didn't like his first book.'

I thank him. I should tell him that I'm never going to read either book, but he looks and speaks with such passion, I don't have the heart.

Pat the Irishman doesn't look up from the book he's reading—titled *Early Irish History and Mythology*—when he says, 'And I thought we Irish were the only ones to fight hopeless causes.'

My first interpretation of his comment is that he reckons Frank Hardy's cause was hopeless, then I think he means I'm the hopeless cause. I say to him, 'You're a smart arse.'

He says, 'Yes, I am rather.'

I now have to read both of Don's books.

Sometimes the issue under discussion is the War and Hitler, and Winston Churchill. That's when I do say something. I say Hitler was a cunt, but they ask me what I know about the economic hardships endured by the German people following World War One. I don't know anything about that. I say that Winston Churchill is a great man, and they say he's a cunt, and then they speak about things Churchill did, and if what they say is true, then he is a cunt.

I wouldn't mind having the radio tuned to pop music, jazz and rock and roll. I'd very much like to hear that new group called The Beatles; they've got a song called *Please Please Me*, but I can't because they've always got the radio tuned to classical music. They listen to music composed by people with names I can't even pronounce—Russians and Germans and French and someone from Finland.

One night they say they're going to have a get-together, which I assume means a party. Loads of people come to the cave, and I have my eye on some girls. I'm ready for my first English party. But all they do is lounge around and eat crisps, dry biscuits and hunks of cheese, and all they drink is sherry and Spanish plonk. Struth. I hate sherry. Then some bloke puts the first of what looks to be hundreds of records on, and something called *The Ring Cycle* plays for hours and hours. Every time I try to make conversation with one of the girls, I'm told to shush.

Next morning they say it was a great get together, which for them it may have been. But it was a lousy party.

~

The boss transferred me to a hotel named the Waldorf, which is in Aldwych. I like it here very much. Rooms and bathrooms are being upgraded while the hotel still operates, so there's not only building workers but also guests and maids. I do an occasional reconnoitre of the still-operating part of the hotel, and I get a lot of attention from the maids. I'm the only building worker wearing work shorts, and although it's far too cold for shorts, I'm wearing them because that's how Australian plumbers dress. I say g'day to them all. I even whistle, *Tie Me Kangaroo Down Sport* so they can tell I'm not a pommie plumber, that I'm an Aussie, and if they play their cards right they can go out with me. Then they can whistle *Is he an Aussie? Is he Lizzie? Is he an Aussie. Is he, eh?*

Juggling going out with the Waldorf's maids is complicated and expensive. Few of them are willing to drink beer—they all want to drink that Babycham stuff—and they all want to munch on crisps.

And not too many of them are totally co-operative, either. I reckon a night out with me buying them Babycham and crisps should end up with me receiving some passionate recompense. But only a few of them understand that, and those who do only agree to a bit of passion in the back row of a cinema, or in a lane-way near their home.

They've got to understand that I've got to keep busy sowing my oats. That my buying them Babycham and crisps entitles me to try for more than a bit of passion; that's the way things are.

I'm not the only one that's doing some reconnoitring of the hotel. Others sneak in, but they have different motivation: theft. The Waldorf's management tells the building company that construction people, the tradesmen, must not be in the hotel proper without approval from the duty manager. This instruction is taken as a slur on our characters, so we're not happy. The building company appoints a carpenter to do security patrols, so we've now got a 'corridor policeman'. We don't like this idea, and we don't like the carpenter, because he's now a boss's stooge, but most of us continue doing our reconnoitring.

A cockney labourer tells me, 'It's our bloomin right to go anywhere on the bloomin job.'

I know that some of the construction workers breakfast on foods stolen from unattended room-service trolleys and some have acquired bedding from vacated rooms. I know that nearly everyone uses no other soap than the Waldorf's soap. I also know that someone, a master of a lurk man, has been outstandingly crafty and acquired a large painting that used to hang in a corridor. We believe this to be the primary reason for the corridor policeman's appointment.

We're all going to a non-authorized stop-work meeting called to deal with what the union office says is 'the restriction by management on the basic rights of the workers'.

I've had a bit of experience with union matters. When I was an apprentice plumber, I did renovations to the Colonial Sugar Refinery building in Bent Street Sydney. My leather jacket was stolen, so I reported the theft to the union delegate. I told him, 'I need my leather jacket to keep me warm when I'm riding my motorbike to work.'

He came to inspect the scene of this great crime and told me there were too many men using the small area. According to regulation something or other, ten square feet of area per man must be provided. He said to me, 'Son, you've got them by the short and curlies; they'll have to get you a new jacket.'

So I told my boss Mister Jack Stephens this, and he exploded, saying, 'There was no need to go to the union; you should have told me, and I would have sorted it out, son.'

But I knew that was bullshit. I knew what he'd have said about my claim. He'd have said, 'Tough luck, son.'

And that's why I'm a member of the union; that's why I pay the apprentices' cost of membership of twenty-five shillings a year.

Mister Jack Stephens signed my apprenticeship indentures, so he could do anything he liked with me. And he did. He sent me to the new Qantas Building site to be under the supervision of the dreaded 'Guts' Byron, the most feared foreman. But that was all right because Mister Jack Stephens gave me ten pounds to replace my leather jacket.

Here in London, I'm one of three that organize a meeting of everyone who opposes the appointment of the corridor policeman, and we're surprised how many construction workers turn up. We've all gathered in the tank room, and we're all angry.

I yell, 'Attention; attention; attention.' But no one pays attention, so I yell, 'Shut up, you bastards.' But even that doesn't stop the angry chatter, so I bang on a water pipe that feeds the hotel system. It's an interesting sound, so I do more organized banging. I tap dot-dot-dot, dash-dash-dash, dot-dot-dot. It's the code for SOS, but I don't realise my Navy Sea Cadet experience of Morse code is still in my brain.

Everyone shuts up, and a pommie plumber stands on a plinth and he yells out all manner of union-inspired stuff about workers' rights and the capitalists and the proletariat.

I'm not much interested in those things. What I'm interested in is being able to wander the corridors seeing my chambermaid friends, so I go to do some wandering.

I hear voices of authority and see the hotel's duty manager and a London policeman. *Shit.*

The duty manager says to me, 'Did you *hear* it? Did you hear the tapping?'

'Tapping? No,' I reply.

'It was ringing through the whole hotel; you must have heard it.'

I shake my head. 'No.'

'It was an SOS call. I ought to know because I was in the signal corps.'

'I heard nothing.'

The London policeman says, 'Let's go to another floor. Perhaps someone heard it there.'

And off they go.

I'm amused by all of this. They're going to discover that hardly anyone's doing any constructing, and, I reckon, they won't think about going to the tank room.

This is my opportunity to duplicate some bastardry done on a Sydney building site that I believe was a beautiful bit of work. I go to the workers' change room carrying a rather nice Ramset explosive cartridge power tool and look for options. The best option is to shoot fixing bolts through the corridor policeman's going-home shoes. To fix them so well to the concrete floor that he'll never move them.

Bang! But the first shot's too strong; it goes right through the sole of the shoe and into the concrete. Bang! The second shot, using a weaker cartridge, is just right. At least he won't be able to move one shoe, but the other one is buggered.

I decide I shouldn't pass up the opportunity of doing the same thing to an enamel mug that's got the corridor policeman's name on its side. Bang! Then I go back to doing some plumbing.

The policeman arrives and asks me, 'Did you hear it? Did you hear the gunshots?'

'No.'

'But you must have. It could be heard throughout the hotel.'

I hold up the Ramset gun and say, 'You don't mean this do you? I was just shooting some pipe brackets to the wall.'

The London policeman says, 'Oh.' And he and the duty manager go away to continue their SOS search.

Because the tank room meeting is interrupted by the sound of a Ramset gun, and because no one but a scab could be using a Ramset gun, the meeting is abandoned. Everyone goes to investigate who's scabbing, who should be at the meeting but isn't.

I say 'copper' to the first worker I see; the word 'copper' goes through the building, and we all go back to doing what we're supposed to be doing. And so does the corridor policeman.

According to Don, the Waldorf Hotel and I are strange bedfellows. I don't know what he means by that. I say to him, 'I have nothing to do with the beds ... except for trying to get acquainted with some of the chambermaids.'

He says, 'The fucking place is elitist. Only the toffs stay. What you're doing by working there is pampering to the toffs.'

I know what a toff is, but how on earth am I pampering them? I'm just a plumber doing his job. I'm not much good at arguing issues, but I am good at defending myself. I don't give a damn who it is or what they are, no one's going to accuse me of toff pampering.

I say to Don, '*What*? I'm born in bloody Redfern. My parents were born in bloody Redfern and so were my grandparents. My great-grandfather drove a horse and cart; he was a tip-carter, and my grandfather was a bloody rat catcher! And you've got the bloody hide to say I'm toff pampering? What you're saying is not relevant.' Don's a lot smaller than I am, so I finish with, 'I ought to knock your bloody block off.'

He may be smaller, but he's no coward, so we're off dancing around the Barons Court cave's kitchen issuing reluctant-to-fight challenges: yeah, come on then; go for it, you start; throw a punch, come on, throw one.

Neither of us does.

Don says to me, 'I bet you use the tradesmen's entrance to go into the Waldorf hotel.'

'Of course I do. I'm a plumber there. I'm a tradesman.'

He says, 'It's elitism; it's their way of separating us, the workers, from them, the capitalists.'

I'm damned if I can fathom why Terry and Albert are laughing their heads off.

Terry says, 'And what about you Don? Do you walk in the front door of Fortnum and fucking Mason, eh?'

I wish I'd thought of that question, but it prompts me to ask a supplementary one. 'And where does the money come from to pay your wages? From the elite! That's where it comes from. The same fucking elite that you accuse me of pampering to.' I reckon I've got him, but Don's a far-too-experienced defender of lost causes to concede.

He says, 'Yeah, I take their money, but I also acquire their food. I'm using *my* duffel coat pockets to take from *their* pockets; I'm reducing the dividends that go to the capitalists. That's the difference. And … why do you think I have so many days off? Why? I'll tell you why. If I get to work on time, I go in through the side door, not the tradesmen's entrance. But if I'm late, that door's closed, so there's only the front door or the tradesmen's entrance to go in. They won't allow me to go in the front door, and I won't use the tradesmen's entrance; so I don't go to work at all … see?'

I'm impressed. He is a man of conviction.

The blokes in the cave conspire to take me with them to the Royal Albert Hall to a concert. I'm not keen to go, but they tell me The Band of the Grenadier Guards is playing. I'd like to hear and see them.

Don, Terry, Albert and Pat are all excited, saying that the Tchaikovsky program will be spectacular. Because I know nothing about it, I say nothing.

It's worth the ten bob just to see inside the Albert Hall: it's huge.

Don's says, 'It's the violin concerto that interests me.'

Bugger the violin; I want the Guard's Band.

Albert says, 'The first piano concerto is my favourite.'

I think that we'll never hear a piano in this large hall, but we'll certainly hear the Guard's Band

Pat's a bit strange because he likes ballet. He says he'll close his eyes and drift through the Swan Lake Suite, and I reckon that's about the best thing to do with ballet.

Terry says, 'The 1812 in the Albert will be spectacular,' but I don't give a bugger because I can't wait until the Grenadier Guards start marching in.

Everything gets going, and not a single person talks. I hope the London Symphony Orchestra isn't embarrassing themselves, that when they finish some in the hall will clap them. I decide to.

After a bloke plays something on the piano that seems to go on and on, there's a half-time break. We go outside for a smoke, and Don raves on about how good it is.

I reckon it's pretty good, too, but I don't say anything because they might ask me a question and I'll say something that's not relevant.

We go inside again, and I notice Don wiggling his hand in time with the music, then a bloke begins playing a violin. Don's got his eyes closed, and I reckon I see some tears near his eyes. Actually, I don't reckon it's all that bad. It's certainly not bad enough to cry about.

Now I'm ready for the band to march in, but they don't. A spotlight comes on, and the band's been sitting at the side all the time. I say to Don, 'Isn't the Grenadier Band going—'

He tells me to shut up and I do.

The music gets going, but the Grenadiers are twiddling their thumbs, and I reckon it's because the conductor doesn't want them marching about spoiling what his orchestra is playing. Then loads of stuff happens: the Grenadiers play, and the London Symphony does too; bells ring and there's explosions and smoke. I reckon the IRA must be attacking. Jesus it's good. Bloody good.

We walk home to the Barons Court cave with the cave dwellers raving about the night, me too. I can't wait to do it again. Next time they won't have to conspire to get me there.

~

The issue constantly being discussed in the cave is something called the Common Market. I definitely don't know anything about that, but the cave dwellers know a lot, and they're all against it. But the British government's all for it.

Not much happens in the world that the cave dwellers aren't against. They're against Mister Harold Macmillan, the Prime Minister. They're against anyone that's a member of the royal family or a lord or a duke or a prince or an earl. They're against anything done by Americans or America, and against anything that's done with the atomic bomb. I'm hardly against anything, but if I make a single comment, no matter what it is, I'm told it's irrelevant. I'm fed up being irrelevant, so I make it my business to at least read the front pages of the newspapers that come into the cave.

I read in one that Australia is sending a few military advisors to Vietnam, that Mister Robert Menzies our Prime Minister says it's a good thing to do, that we must stop the reds in their tracks, because if we don't, something called the domino effect will happen. I don't know what a domino effect is.

Don goes off his brain about all of this. He says, 'That fucking Menzies is going to get us involved in something we shouldn't be in.'

I say to him, 'But Mister Menzies reckons we must stop the reds in their tracks. That we must help a fellow democracy. That just a few advisors are going there.'

But Don starts cursing and spluttering and calling Mister Menzies a bastard.

I say to Don, 'What about the domino effect?'

He says, 'So … what about it?'

'It's a game, isn't it?'

'*Exactly*. That's the first sensible thing you've said since you arrived here. It's all a big political game.'

I'm pleased, because at last I've said something that's not irrelevant.

Now that I've got a regular job and I've got some spare money, I buy a duffel coat. My coat is fawn whereas the other cave dwellers have black coats. I reckon fawn looks best, but the others reckon it's not, and they laugh at my choice. They reckon I'll be the only one wearing a fawn duffel coat when we go to the London ban-the-bomb march. And they're right.

I'm amazed that so many people want to ban the bomb. I wonder if they realise how important it is that we have the bomb, that we must at least be equal to the commos, if not one step ahead. They seem not to realise that, because thousands of them are yelling out, 'Ban the bomb! Ban the bomb!' And the London bobbies just stand about doing nothing. If Mister Menzies were here, he'd do something about it. He'd get the police to straighten them out. He'd have a lot of those black duffel-coated commos arrested. He knows a lot about the commos. He reckons there's a red under every bed. He had his police straighten out the commos that were trying to take Mrs Petrov from Australia and back to Soviet Russia, so he knows how to handle them.

In a packed train, I see on the front page of someone's newspaper that Marilyn Monroe has died. That's very bad news. I can't wait to get back to the cave to discuss this because I do know a lot about Marilyn; I saw her in the film *River of No Return*. But when I bring it up as an issue, they tell me she's irrelevant; it's not an issue; it's not relevant.

Apart from me, none of the cave dwellers have been to America, but they always criticize everything Americans do. I'm beginning to think they're communists, and that's a dangerous thing to be. Our Prime Minister Robert Menzies has told all Australians that the commos want to take over the world, that we must be on guard at all times, but I don't reckon the cave dwellers are very dangerous.

It's an exciting day at the Waldorf Hotel. The boss asks me if I'll transfer to a nuclear-reactor power station being constructed in Wales. He says, 'Barry, this is a very important promotion. We want you to be a supervisor.'

'A *supervisor*?'

'Yes, the company will pay your travelling expenses, your board and lodgings; you'll get plenty of overtime because the job's working every day. And we want you to join the Worshipful Company of Plumbers.'

'The *what?*'

'The Worshipful Company, the elite of plumbers.'

'Jesus!'

'I'll propose you, and I'll get a seconder, and when you're a member, you put the letters R.P. after your name.'

Bloody hell, I'll be Barry White R.P. None in my family has ever had letters following their name; I'll be like a university graduate. I think this is great. The boat fare to Australia is one-hundred-and-sixty pounds. So six months working in Wales will get me back to Australia. I say to the boss, 'Will there be an increase in wages?'

'You'll get sixpence an hour more, six-shillings and seven-pence an hour.'

So that's the end of that. I must go.

When I tell the cave dwellers my news about being a member of the Worshipful Company of Plumbers that was chartered in 1588, they say it's irrelevant.

I'll leave London in two weeks, and there's so much to do. I go to see a man named Oswald Mosley sprout racist opinions and see him get pelted with rotten tomatoes, right under Nelson's Column. Then I go to see where Don works at Fortnum & Mason, and I can't believe that the counter-jumpers are dressed in morning suits. The Queen wasn't shopping there, so I duck down to Buckingham Palace, and she wasn't there either. The cave dwellers take me to a place named Bath. Five of us plus a driver squeeze into an Austin A30, and by the time we get there, we all need a bath, but no one's allowed in the water. And when we arrive back at the Barons Court cave, they moan about each of us having to pay five shillings for petrol. Jesus I'll be glad to get away from these misers.

For the last time, I get out at the Covent Garden underground station to walk to the Waldorf hotel. Every day for months I've passed the Covent Garden Opera House and the nearby markets, and I've not been inside either. A uniformed man stands outside the theatre, so I say to him, 'Mate, what happens in there?'

He says, 'You've never been here?'

'No. I'm a plumber.'

This uniformed man must like plumbers because he says, 'Come in and have a look.'

I do. And I'm astounded. Inside is much, much bigger and better than Sydney's State Theatre. It's like nothing I've seen, even fancier than the Albert Hall.

'What do they do here?'

'Opera.'

At lunch time while all the building workers sit to have their sandwiches and cup of tea, I go back to the Covent Garden Opera house wearing my Australian plumber's shorts and buy a ticket for that night. The woman selling tickets looks down her nose at me and says, 'Gods?'

I don't know what she means so I just nod.

I return to the Waldorf Hotel to do my last afternoon's work, and I debate if I should or shouldn't go in through the front entrance?

I've got only one foot on the entrance steps when the concierge says, 'Stop.' I don't stop. I walk past him. He yells, 'Stop!'

He doesn't hear when I say, 'Get fucked.'

I look forward to telling Don what I did.

The cave dwellers aren't too excited about my going to Wales and that's because my twenty-six shillings rent money will be missed.

Terry says to me, 'How about we arrange a get-together as your farewell?'

I remember the last get-together in the cave and know it means listening to records of that damned *Ring Cycle* and drinking bloody sherry. I say, 'Thanks for offering, but I think not.'

Albert says, 'We can *do it easily*. I'll take five bob down to the phone box and phone everyone.'

'No, but thanks anyway.'

Pat's keen for a get-together because he gets to speak about relevant things like fifteenth-century painters and the incidence of lice on polar bears and why Ireland has more intellectuals, pro rata, than any other country.

Don's got a better suggestion. 'Let's go to the Royal George in Earls Court and get a skin-full of Fosters.'

I don't want to do any of those, although the Royal George is a good idea. I say to them, 'I'm sorry but I've got a ticket to be with the Gods at Covent Garden, so your suggestions are irrelevant.'

Jesus I loved saying that to them.

19 March 1962.
Barons Court London.
Dear Mum,

I was told today that I am to leave for Wales on Monday. I am to get the 10.30 a.m. train and I should arrive at 5.30 p.m. the same day.

I don't know the name of the town but I suppose I'll be told in the next few days.

Thanks for the information about the Irish Whites. I don't know what to think about them being 'nothing to skite about'. What did Aunty Hazel mean by that?

Mum, I think you should keep the house. I know it's a financial burden and it's easy to give you advice from way over here. I believe that Janice will give you the same advice.

No, I have not yet seen the Queen.

I was surprised to get a letter from Stuart Acason today. It was from Australia. I thought he was going to work his passage home on a ship, but it seems he pooled all his money and bought a boat ticket.

Love Barry.

1962. London: The barons of Barons Court - Don, Terry and Albert.

The kitchen at Barons Court.

The entrance gates to the Barons Court cave.

Aldermaston to London 'Ban the Bomb' march arrives in Hyde Park.

Chapter Twelve

Because the plumbing company that's transferred me to Wales is going to reimburse me for money I spend on food, I'm supposed to get dockets. But it's not easy getting dockets, especially from pubs. When I ask a publican in Chester for a docket, he says, 'Why?'

I tell him about the generous payback by the company and he says, 'They're not going to pay for your beer.'

'Why not?'

'Because, companies don't pay people to drink beer.'

'But they told me they'd pay my expenses.'

'Yes, I've heard of things like that, but they won't pay for your beer.'

'But beer is food, isn't it?'

'Food? Umm ... I suppose it is. But it's not what accountants consider as food. Accountants consider food to be eatable, something you chew.'

This revelation by the publican is going to force me to re-appraise my docket collecting: I'm actually going to have to buy food that's chewable

It was a long journey from London to Porthmadog in Northern Wales. My first impressions of everything—the railway station, the temperature, the rain and that no one is here to meet me—is that I hate the place.

I'm lugging a suitcase and my Australian Army ammunition box that holds my tools of trade that weighs a ton, but the bloke who's to take me to wherever the nuclear power station is being built isn't here. But I do see a pub that's open. It's called the Australian Inn.

The pub is obviously the drinking hole for those who live hereabouts, and there's no way I can be taken for a local, so I get severely eyeballed by everyone. The man serving behind the bar reluctantly comes over but says nothing; he just looks at me with a hostile stare. I stare back. I can see he's feeling uncomfortable, so he'll soon have to speak … I think.

Someone away from us says something in a foreign language I've never heard before, possibly a Scandinavian language, 'Glluffgulldydeyde og og?' And I reckon he's saying, 'Who is he?'

The men in the pub stare at me saying, 'Glluffgulldydeyde og og,' so I decide that this is not the time to be standoffish. I say to the barman, 'Gimme a cold beer, mate; and make it a big one.'

At least his hostile stare is now one of curiosity. He says, 'AreyouavisitortoPorthmadog?'

I think he said, 'Are you a visitor to Porthmadog?'

'Yes, I'm from …' I begin to say London, but that's not going to win me any friends here, so I say, 'Australia.'

He says, 'Oh, it'sfromAustraliayouare.'

I think I understand him, and I think I'm supposed to say yes, so I do.

'Oh, soyournotanEnglishman?'

Everything the man says is lyrical and joined, and I reckon it's just as well I'm Australian, because we speak as quickly as anyone does, we speak like he does.

I say, 'I'm Australian; here-to-work-at-the-Trawsfynydd-power-station.'

'Oh, so it's the power station you'd be working on. Well, that's near BlaenauFfestiniog.' Then he says to his regular customers, 'He'sfromAustralia, and hesgoingtoworkatTrawsfynydd.'

Everyone says, 'Oh, Australian.' And now they've all got smiles.

I'll have to be certain to use my Australian nationality everywhere in Wales; they don't seem to like the English.

Someone in the room buys me the second beer, but I don't know whom to thank because they're all looking at me and they're all smiling.

Two men come into the pub. They hesitate at the door as if they're looking for someone, then, even though they still seem hesitant, they go to the bar. Everyone looks at them and I hear said, 'Glluffgulldydeyde og og?' So they must be strangers. Another man comes in, and the three newcomers go to a corner. Lots of strangers visit the Australian Inn today.

The barman gives the three men the same reception I got: he stares at them.

One of the three come to the bar and says, 'Three beers, mate.'

They're bloody Australians!

I nod to the man and say, 'G'day,' but he doesn't speak to me; he simply nods. They're ignorant bloody Australians.

The man takes his three beers, then the barman comes to me saying, 'ThatmanIjustservedisalsoanAustralian.'

'Yeah, I know.'

The three men have their heads close. They whisper and look my way. I look at them, and I know something's going on. These are not average Australians on their adventure tour of Britain.

A third beer comes from someone with a smiling face, and I'm feeling pretty good.

Another of the three mystery men comes to the bar, orders beers and gives me the once over. He says, 'Will you have a beer?'

I slowly turn my head because I'm being cool. I say, 'I've already got one, mate.'

'Let me get you another?'

'No. I'm right.'

He looks back at his two mates and shrugs. Then one of those two comes close and says, 'What are you doing here?'

His blunt question isn't the reasonable curiosity that one traveller might have of another. His question has threat, authority even. I've already sized him up, and I reckon he can handle himself, so I quickly consider my options. I can give him my I'm-a-tough-bloke-too reply, but I'm not a tough bloke and I don't like the odds, or I can be the innocent plumber that's going to his job.

'Mate, I've got a job at the nuclear power station. I'm a plumber there. Someone was supposed to meet me at the station, but they didn't turn up.'

He studies my face, then gives a small smile. 'Ah, so you're travelling on?'

'Yeah. And you?'

'Travelling through. We've got a yacht in the harbour.'

'Travelling to where?'

'Oh, just travelling.'

He's telling me not to ask any more questions, so I don't

I tell the barman I want to telephone the power station's office, and instead of offering me his phone, he sends me to the railway station. He's looking after me.

I'm pleased to be away from the Australian Inn because those three are up to no good, and I reckon that the no good they're up to might be smuggling arms to Northern Ireland. That or worse.

A tall, athletic-looking man ambles into the railway station's waiting room; he looks at me and says, 'Are you the plumber from London?'

There's just a railway attendant and me there, and I'm the only one with baggage and a toolbox. I should be polite; I want to be polite, but this man's got an attitude problem, and because of that I've now got an attitude problem. I say to him, 'Of course I'm the fucking plumber from London.'

He makes no attempt to assist me with my baggage, just says, 'Follow me.'

And I do.

He walks towards a van parked well away from the station, and while we walk I realise I have to do something assertive. He opens the van's doors and stands there, so I place my suitcase on the ground, and in a move that takes all my strength, I fling the heavy tool box at him and say, 'Put this in the back.'

He attempts a grab it, realises it's heavy, does another grab, but it hits him on the thighs. He utters, 'Aha,' then his hands do a mad scramble to catch it before it drops on his feet.

'Oh, sorry, mate. It's a bit heavy, is it?'

'No, it's just that I wasn't ready.'

I've got this bastard, so I need to drive home my advantage. I say, 'Well, it pays to be ready, doesn't it?'

We drive ten miles without anything being said, so I break the silence. 'There's nothing in Australia this green.'

I can see he's thinking. 'Australia! You've been there?'

'Been there! I was born there.'

'Oh. I thought you were English. I thought you were from London.'

'No! Well, yes and no. I worked for the company in London; they transferred me here. I'm following the big money.'

He says, 'Aren't we all. There's no other reason to be in this god-forsaken hole. No one's here for enjoyment.'

Because the man seemed not welcoming to the English, he's not one of them, so I ask him, 'And you, where are you from?'

'Originally Ireland, but I've been over here for a long while now. My parents came to the UK in the nineteen-fifties. My name's Riley.'

'Oh. My name's Barry White. My great grandfather went to Australia from Ireland.'

'Forced to go there?'

'Probably.'

Riley says, 'There's not many of us here that get along with the English, that is, apart from the other English. The majority of us are Welsh, or Scottish, or Irish …'

'And now an Australian.'

'Yes, and now an Australian.'

'You should've said you were Australian in Porthmadog; we could've had a few jugs.'

'We can have a few at the next pub.'

'Not in Blaenau Ffestiniog; there are too many eyes there.'

Now the bloke won't shut up. He asks if I know his relatives in Sydney, that their name's Riley, too. And if he goes to Australia, will he get a job? And what's the cost of living. And why are Australians so tough?

It's not the first time I've been asked this question, but I never answer it truthfully. I'm guilty of perpetuating the myth. I'm not so tough, and neither are the people I know, but some Australians are tough; it's just that I'm not one of them. But I can act tough, and so can most young Australians, especially those on their big adventure. It feels good.

I say to Riley, 'Tough? Yeah, some are. It's the country that makes us tough. It's the bush, the outback and all of that.'

I'm definitely not telling this man that I've only been as far West as Bathurst; that I'm born and bred in Sydney and can't ride a horse; that the few fights I've been in, I've lost by a big margin, because I can take punishment—I can go the distance—but I can't give punishment. I hate hitting people, so that means I can't fight for nuts. I can't tell him that I'm starting to enjoy classical music and ballet. I'm not telling him any of this because I'm an Australian, and as he's just said, all Australians are tough.

We speed along a narrow road with high hedges on both sides, and the tough Australian is nervous, especially at blind corners.

Riley says, 'This is a shortcut. I thought you'd like to see some of the countryside.'

'Yeah, it's great.'

'You must have a lot of experience working on power stations to be given the job of supervisor.'

I can't tell him that I've got no such experience, and I'm mystified why I was asked to come here. I can't tell him I'm not even a licensed plumber in Australia, that I failed my last exam, that I'm just an ordinary tradesman like him. 'Yeah, I've got some experience.'

We arrive at a cluster of caravans that the Canadians would call trailers, and Riley proudly says, 'It's a big camp, isn't it?'

I think about the camp at Pincher Creek in the Canadian Rocky Mountains that was three times this size, but all I say is, 'Yes, it's big.'

'We'll get your bags inside, then I'll take you to the site to meet the boss.'

'The boss; what's he like?'

'You want it straight?'

'Yeah.'

'He's a bastard. No one likes him. He's arrogant; he's unfair; he doesn't like the Scots; he doesn't like the Irish; he doesn't like the Welsh; he hates everyone.'

'The English?'

'Oh, he likes them because he's one.'

I say, 'I'm looking forward to meeting him.'

The site is huge. I have no idea that power generated by nuclear reactors requires such large buildings. Two look the same, each housing a nuclear reactor, and there's a massive turbine hall. These buildings dwarf the workers; they have an ant-like presence. A spread of construction paraphernalia surrounds it all: pipes and ducts, steel structures, trucks, sheds, offices, and a high security fence around the whole site.

Close to the outer edge of this fence is a large lake skirted by very green fields and marshes, the still water reflecting everything surrounding it, mostly exposed craggy rock hillocks that might be the result of ice-age activity.

It's too beautiful here for a power station.

In London, I told the boss of the plumbing company that I'd worked on a power station constructed in Sydney, but I didn't go into much detail, because I don't know any. When he asked me the generation capacity, I had no idea how to answer, but I know there are kilowatt and megawatt things, so I told him about those and got the names wrong. He didn't understand what I said, so I told him that in Australia we use different names. And that's rubbish. Then he asked me about welding procedures for pressure pipes and vessels. I know nothing about that either, so I started talking about cricket, which confused him even more.

I had no intention of telling him that in 1953 at the Casula Power Station, I only worked erecting the rainwater down-pipes. I did that job because I didn't mind sitting in a 'bosun's chair', dangling from long ropes that came from holes in the concrete roof. He didn't need to know that as the bosun's chair worker, I got three-pence an hour more than the other plumbing apprentices or that I enjoyed sitting high in the air where I swung towards the wall and just before smashing into it, I pushed away with my legs and sent myself spinning and swinging around. He didn't need to know that technical stuff.

Now, I'm beginning to wonder *why me?* Why am I here to work as a supervisor? All I know about power-plant plumbing is putting down-pipes up, or down-pipes down, and swinging through the air like a monkey.

The power station's security guard gives me the once over, and I do the same to him. He doesn't like to be given the once over, so he's strict. He says, 'There's been no notification about a security pass, so you can't come in.'

Riley says, 'Well, telephone the plumbing foreman and get the notification.'

The security guard says, 'I'm phoning no one. You've got your pass so you go see the plumbing foreman and get it sorted.'

I sit outside the high-security fence looking at the security man who has a smirk on his face. I say to him, 'Mate, you're a fucking drongo.'

He won't know what a drongo is, but his facial expression tells me he's got a fair idea.

He says, 'This is a high security area, so no one gets in here without a pass.'

'Mate, this is fucking Wales, not fucking Russia. I don't reckon there are too many spies around here, and I'm certainly not a spy who's working for the Australian government.'

'An Australian! I should have guessed, another convict returning home.'

It's certain that this man and I will again clash.

The man wearing overalls and a necktie has to be the plumbing foreman. He goes to the security man, gives him some paper—probably a form designed by a bureaucrat—the security guard only gives it a cursory glance, then wallops a rubber stamp on it. He says, 'Take him in.'

All the plumbing foreman says is, 'Follow me.'

And I do.

Riley is sitting outside a site shed. The plumbing foreman mustn't like him sitting there because he says to him, 'You, get back to work.'

And he does.

I reckon I don't like this plumbing foreman.

The plumbing foreman says, 'My name's Thompson.'

'G'day Thompson, I'm pleased to meet you.'

'Mister Thompson, if you please.'

'Oh, Thompson's your last name?'

'Yes. Mister Thompson.'

I know there's going to be trouble between this bloke and me.

During the passage of my life there were times when I was forced to address people by the title of mister. When aged less than ten years, every older male is addressed as mister. All schoolteachers are a miss or a mister; there's no way around it. When I got my first job interview as a copy boy at *The Sydney Morning Herald*, Mister Jarvis was the man who interviewed me. When I was promoted to head boy, one of my responsibilities was placing the daily newspapers on the desks of the senior executives; they were all misters. The oldest of the Fairfax brothers, Mister Warwick, always said, 'Good morning, boy' to me, so I didn't mind calling him mister. Nor did I mind using the title for his brother, Mister Vincent or the other senior executives: Mister Rupert Albert Geary Henderson and Mister John Douglas Pringle.

During my plumber's apprenticeship, my bosses got the title Mister Stephens and Mister Chatterton when I was in trouble, otherwise it was Jack and Bill. That's the way it's done.

So if this poncy Englishman, this man who's a plumber just like I am, thinks I'm going to give him the title of mister, he's dreaming.

I say to Thompson, 'Mate, I'm not calling you mister. From me you're going to get George; you can call me Barry.'

He fumes—this man spends a lot of time fuming. He says, 'You will give me the title mister; and that's the end of it.'

'Oh no; that's not the end of it. You're going to get your first name or you're going to get, mate. All right, mate?'

The man's face goes very red. If he doesn't start breathing properly, he's going to burst. A strong out-rush of air comes from his mouth with the word, 'Rubbish! You, you, colonial upstart.'

I think: surely he doesn't believe that to be an insult? It's a badge of honour to be a colonial upstart.

Thompson goes to the door, opens it and says, 'You're out of here; you're off my site.'

But I don't move.

'What about we telephone London? What about you tell them you're sending your new supervisor off the site, eh?'

He's thinking and so am I. It's now my considered opinion that this bloke is stuffing things up, that there's loads of problems here that I've not been told about, and that he knows that London knows that he's the problem. We'll soon find out.

I get the phone and dial random numbers. I dial far too many numbers; but he doesn't know that.

He says, 'Put the telephone down.'

And I do.

'What did London tell you?'

'They told me enough.'

'What?'

'That's between London and me. What's between you and me is this; if you don't wake up to yourself, if you don't stop this fucking elitist bullshit; you're finished.'

He doesn't know I've got no right or authority to say he's finished, so he thinks he will be finished.

I believe I'm winning, but I try for one more strike. I say, 'Listen here, Thompson, how about you address me as Mister White, and I'll address you as Mister Thompson?'

He shakes his head. 'Oh no; oh no; oh no.'

'All right, then; so it's George and Barry.'

I go outside and discover about a dozen men standing near the door to Thompson's shed. One of them is Riley. He says nothing, but he mimes hand clapping and so do the others.

That night in the meal queue the men in front of me mostly select long-ago-fried-foods from a steaming bain-marie. Compared to the Canadian camps this food is inferior, but it's very British. Accommodation though is better than that in Canada—perhaps it means that the British care more about good sleeping than good eating.

I get quite a lot of nods and smiles from the men who queue to get their food, and when I've got the food, I get invitations to sit with groups. I sit with Riley and his cronies, who are Irish.

I look around the room. Near a window is a table covered by a tablecloth on which sits plastic flowers in a vase, and all those who sit there are wearing ties. Thompson sits there.

I say to Riley, 'Who are the blokes wearing ties?'

'Bosses.'

'They sit at different tables?'

'Yes. But so do the Welsh, and so do the Scots, and so do the English who are not bosses. This here is the Irish table, but that's all right because there's not a table for Australians.'

Fuck!

I look up, and Thompson looks up and beckons me to him. I say to Riley, 'Thompson wants to speak to me.'

'Take your dinner with you.'

'Why?'

'Because he wants you to sit at their table.'

'Why?'

'Because you're a supervisor.'

I leave my meal where it sits and go to see Thompson.

He says, 'You're supposed to be sitting with us.'

I say, 'No thanks,' and I go back to Ireland.

For my first day of work I plan to dress in my Australian plumber's shorts, but if I do, it'll be the end of me. There are two-thousand three-hundred workers on this site, none wearing shorts; all wear overalls. Also, everyone wears an American safety hat that I know is a bloody nuisance.

Thompson greets me with a muted, 'Good morning … Barry.'

I give him an enthusiastic, 'Good morning … George.'

He says, 'I spoke to London last night.'

'Good.'

'Not so good for you.'

'Oh, why?'

'They told me why you're here. You're here because you—'

'I'm a good plumber?'

'No; because you're Australian.'

'Oh. What's being an Australian got to do with me being here?'

'Because Australia is a neutral country.'

This is not making sense. 'I didn't know Great Britain was at war.'

'We've been at war for hundreds of years.'

'Yeah, but they're all over. Australia helped you win some of those wars.'

'Not those wars; the ones with the Irish and the Scots and the Welsh. Have you not seen the Home Rule for Wales signs around?

'Yeah, but I don't know what it means.'

Thompson tells me that throughout the building site the Irish, the Scots and the Welsh are not doing what the English supervisors tell them.

And the English won't take orders from a Scot, an Irishman or a Welshman. They'll only take orders from their own countrymen.

I'm only here because I'm a bloody colonial! I don't tell Thompson that this is a blow to my ego, that I thought I was here because I'm the best.

Thompson says, 'So you will contain your supervisory activities to passing on orders, *my orders.*'

~

I love stashing money in my post-office bank account. Each week I get thirteen-pound-seventeen shillings, plus three-pound seventeen-shillings subsistence, two-pound ten-shillings bonus, and twenty-seven hours overtime at six shillings an hour: all up it's twenty-three pounds after tax.

Every week I calculate how many more pays it's going to take to get on a ship to Australia, to get away from all the petty nationalistic tension on the construction site. I know that wars and skirmishes between England and the other countries of Britain happened a long time ago. I know that the English stole the Stone of Scone, their Stone of Destiny, from the Scottish, but the Scots stole it back, then the Scots were forced to give it back to the English—a complicated journey for a stone.

I know that the English took from the Welsh their language and took from the Irish their country, but the Irish got nearly all of that back. But that's all history, all in the past.

But there's still bombing by Welsh nationalists and Scottish nationalists and Northern Irish nationalists, some very serious, and some that only involve blowing up one of Her Majesty's Royal Mail post-office boxes. I reckon mailboxes are fair game. On Empire Day I've blown up a few myself using a few double-bunger crackers tied together, but these mailboxes belonged to unfortunates that lived near me, not to Her Majesty, the Queen of Great Britain and Northern Ireland.

Thompson's like the Phantom, the ghost who walks. He turns up all over the place. Everyone knows he sneaks about, peering around corners and looking through pipe ducts, and someone says he uses binoculars to check on what's happening, that he sits in his comfy office chair in his shed looking for workers that are bludging.

The construction site houses an arsenal of weapons that can easily be used to show Thompson that his activities are unwelcome, and I make the mistake of showing Riley one such weapon. Quarter-inch-diameter copper tube and glaziers putty combine to make a terrific blowgun, but there's not much quarter-inch tubing around. I get a three-foot-long length and hide it. When times are quiet—which is often because this is a British construction site—I practise my aim. From high on the reactor building, I lob putty projectiles on many of the site offices, and whoever's inside comes out to investigate what banged on their roofs.

I decide to share what I'm doing with Riley, but that's a mistake.

Riley gets some tubing, and within days all the Irish plumbers and their helpers have a three-foot-long blowgun, and they're pot-shotting at everything—especially Thompson's office shed. Thompson does what everyone does, he goes outside to investigate what bangs on his roof, and that's when it gets out of hand; the Irish go berserk and shoot at Thompson.

The inevitable happens. A general warning is issued: that the dangerous practice of using glazier's putty as projectiles will cease and anyone found doing same will be instantly dismissed.

But does this stop the Irish? No. They're used to arms smuggling and revolution and skulduggery, so the dangerous practice does continue, and it's more fun now because it's illegal.

My relationship with Thompson is always strained, and I reckon he's still looking for a way to do me in. When he comes to me saying, 'I've got a special job for you,' I think, 'Yeah a suicide mission.'

He says, 'We've got to get the Biological Laboratory plumbing done. London tells me that you've had experience installing polythene waste pipes, so you're it. You're the one to do this job.'

There's nothing special about welding polythene pipe, it just seems that there is.

The Trawsfynydd biological laboratory is on the other side of the lake, miles away from the nuclear reactors and outside the security fenced site. I'm here with a Welsh plumber that I'm supposed to be in charge of, but he's in charge of me. The first thing he does is move a table near a window that has excellent viewing of the long and only road here. Then he sits at the table to read a newspaper.

He says to me, 'There-must-at-all-times-be-one-or-the-other-of-us-sitting-here-to seewhenanyonecomes.'

'Why?'

'Becausewecan'tbecaughtsleeping.'

'Sleeping?'

'Yes. Wedon'thavetodoanyworkhere.'

'Oh. Why don't we have to do any work?'

He tells me that no one else can do the polythene welding, so it doesn't matter how long we take to complete the work; Thompson can't send anyone else. 'There-was-two-Scots-here-for-two-weeks-and-all-they-did-was-burn-holes-in-the-pipes.'

'Oh, so how much work should we do?'

'Sixweldsaday, that'sthemaximum.'

Even in Wales it pays not to be smarter than anyone else.

For reasons I don't recollect, I try to learn Spanish. So I bring my book to work and annoy the Welshman with '*Donde esta el correo?*' But he never answers me because he doesn't know what I'm saying. And he doesn't care either, because all he knows about Spain is that Lord Nelson thrashed the Spanish, and all they have in Spain are olives and cheap wine.

Much of the Welshman's time is spent giving me history lessons. He tells me the Romans built hill forts in the area of Trawsfynydd, but the locals didn't like that so they tried to send the Romans packing. And they did, but it took more than a hundred years to do it.

He says, 'There, lookatthatmound, thatwasaRomanfort.'

All I see is a pile of dirt.

He also tells me that his father and his father and his father worked in the Trawsfynydd Slate Quarries, that much of the slate was sent to Porthmadog, and then to Australia.

I tell him that I'm not that old, that I didn't have to use a slate to write on when I was at school.

He says, 'Noboyo, theslatewasusedonroofs.'

Union enforced stoppages are planned, so the builders, Atomic Power Constructors, play at tactics. They announce that the site will be closed while air pressure testing of a reactor vessel is done, that it will be done on two mid-week days, not on a weekend. The workers don't want this because we won't get paid, and it's no fun hanging around camp because there's nothing to do. On another day, there's a lock-out by the bosses, and the security man who originally refused me entry stands defiantly at the gates stopping twenty-five double-deck buses full of angry workers.

I'm with those that yell, 'Ram the gates!' And I make sure the security man sees me doing some good yelling; but he doesn't care because he's getting paid.

Craft Union delegates get gatherings of their members agitated so there's talk about an overtime ban or a general strike, and that's bad for my savings plan. I ask myself, why I should remain here in the donga to earn what I can easily earn in London?

In the television room, while watching the very first episode broadcast on the BBC of the new American program, *Wagon Train*, the wagon master says, 'Move em out.' I see it as a subliminal message for me; it's time to get out of here.

Back in London, I'm like a prodigal son returning home, but Don doesn't give me the enthusiastic welcome to the Barons Court cave that prodigal sons should get. He just says, 'You ought to be hanging your head in shame. It was a nuclear reactor you were working on, wasn't it?'

'Yeah.'

'Well, that's it for you. I won't be marching in the ban-the-bomb parade with you. You're now contaminated by the senseless use of nuclear reactors. They were probably making fucking atomic bombs up there.'

'No they fucking weren't. They're going to generate power: electricity, so you can have a hot bath—if you ever have a bath—so you can boil your kettle; so you can—'

'We've got gas here,' he says.

'All right then, so you can listen to that stupid fucking BBC.' Jesus, I'm not even past the front door of the Barons Court cave and I'm being attacked by a crazy commo.

And once inside, he still goes on.

He throws *The Observer*, his favourite newspaper, at me. Its front page shows Mister Robert Menzies, the Australian Prime Minister. 'There, see, your capitalist mate's here in his double-breasted, pin-stripe suit. He's here kow-towing to the bond holders and the Royals and the Conservative Party and—'

'Is there a bed free?'

'Ah, no. There's only the stretcher.'

'That'll do. Come and I'll buy you a beer.'

'Yair, good idea; spend some of that blood money you've made.'

It's good to be back to stimulating conversation with crazy commos.

Next day I get a plumbing job on the new Hilton Hotel construction, and when I tell Don I can see into Buckingham Palace's back yard, he wants me to start working out how a glider can be launched off the roof to bomb the Palace. He's crazy this commo.

Now he's got the idea of going to the Soviet Union. He shows me details of a bus tour that goes across Europe into East Germany and Poland. He spreads a map on the Barons Court cave kitchen table and says, 'And from Warsaw they go into the Soviet Union to Minsk, then to Smolensk, then to Moscow then to Leningrad. Then it's out through Finland and Scandinavia.' He looks at me and says, 'What about it?'

I tell him, it's good. 'It'll be like going home for you. You'll be able to see all your KGB mates and compare notes about spying and how the cold war's going and help them paint signs saying "Go home Yankee", and tell them that atomic bombs are being made at a power station in Wales.'

'Yair,' he says. 'It's exciting, isn't it? So how about we go?'

'*We go?*'

'Yair, you and me.'

'I don't want to go to fucking Russia. I'm not a commo.'

David and Stuart Acason, my travelling companions in the United States, had both travelled to the Soviet Union, and they reckoned it was terrific. But I can't see what's terrific about travelling around a country that our Prime Minister Mister Robert Menzies says are our enemies. There might even be a war while we're there. The Russians are still smarting about the American U2 plane piloted by Gary Powers that crashed while on a spying flight, and John Fitzgerald Kennedy the new American President isn't getting on with the Soviet chairman Nikita Khrushchev. But on the other hand, the Soviets have had a big success in putting their cosmonaut Yuri Gagarin into space, so they may not be all that keen to start a war at the moment. They'll want to do a bit of boasting first. They'll want to get the Americans jealous about their success.

I say to Don, 'So what's the cost of going there?'

'Seventy-five quid.'

'Um, that's not too much.'

'Plus food costs and expenses. We'd get out of it for a-hundred-and-twenty quid each. It's bloody cheap.'

'All right; I'll go.'

'Beauty. We leave in three weeks on the seventeenth of August.'

Albert and Terry are jealous about Don and me going off, and I reckon the major reason is because they're trapped; they can't be adventurers. But they're cultured, and they reckon I could be too if they get to finish my education. In one week they get me to see the Royal Shakespearean Theatre Company do *The Caucasian Chalk Circle*; the Royal Ballet do *Les Patineurs* and *Giselle*; and finish that week with dancing the twist at the Hammersmith Palais. The following week, I see the Festival Ballet do Improvisations and Act two of *Swan Lake*; the Royal ballet do *Scheherazade*, and finish that week with getting pissed at the Surrey Hotel.

I like the ballet. And that's proven when I ritualistically settle myself in the comfy chair in the Barons Court cave's front room to watch the Royal Ballet School students go to their school that's five doors away from our cave. I know it's time to get settled in the comfy chair when I hear the eight-fifty train arrive at Barons Court Railway Station, then it's only a minute before they pass our basement window hurrying along in their unique duck-like stride that's been caused by years of barre exercises. I look up at their well-developed legs, slim waists and small breasts, hoping their skirts will blow about, that then I'll get a sighting of their panties. But that doesn't happen often because there's not enough wind on Talgarth Road.

I give Don my final payment for the Soviet Union trip, but he goes missing, 'and we don't know where he are'.

Albert may well be right when he says, he's on the piss, and he's blown all your money on that prostitute he's befriended in Soho.

Don does drink too much, and he does go missing for days, and he is very friendly with a Soho prostitute.

I tell Albert, 'I'm not panicking because he's a mate, and mates don't blow their mate's money on prostitutes. I've got faith in Don.'

And that is true: but I get nervous.

Two days later, five days before we're supposed to leave, Don turns up holding our tickets and vouchers.

'Yeah, I did get involved with the woman, and yeah, I did spend half your money, but I knew I was to get a cheque from Melbourne.

'Melbourne?'

'Yeah, the second last payment on a block of land I'd sold.'

'Oh, I didn't know.'

'Jesus, you didn't think I'd done a runner with your dough, did you?'

'No. I had faith in you. I mean, you're a commo, and commos don't do the dirty on their mates, do they?'

Don finances our farewell party that's as well catered for as anything at Buckingham Palace. On his last day working at Fortnum and Mason, he does a major duffel-coat-pocket shopping spree. He's got something called truffles, Pate de Foie Gras, Queen Bee honey, Darjeeling tea and loads of other foods that have a By Appointment to Her Majesty the Queen boast on their labels. He also buys all the beer.

He says to me, 'Mate, that's what us commo's do.'

28 July 1962.
Barons Court London.
Dear Mum,
It's Saturday night and I'm at home watching TV. The program is called 'Twist'. Mum, you should see these women. I think the twist is terrific, it brings out the animal instincts in a bloke.

As I mentioned in Janice's letter, I'm going on a bit of a trip to Russia and Scandinavia. Don and I leave London in a mini bus in August. Don saw the advertisement when he was in Earls Court last week. The cost is seventy-five pound, plus food.

Russian trips have been hard to get this year, especially the overland tour. David Acason had to book a year in advance when he went, and his brother Stuart had to go by ship to Leningrad then by train to Moscow.

Tomorrow night I'm going to the Albert Hall to hear the 1812 Overture. It fits with the Russian trip. During the last few weeks I've been taking out an Indian girl: I'm learning a lot about India.

John, you asked how much electricians are paid here. First-year apprentices get three pounds; tradesmen get between fifteen to eighteen pounds. I gave my notice to my boss yesterday and he told me I could have my job when I get back.

Mum, how did your bowls game go with that single man?
Love Barry.

Chapter Thirteen

I've never explored Soho, but Don knows the area well. His prostitute friend lives here and it's where we are to assemble.

At the end of a narrow lane is a drab-looking building with a drab-looking van parked outside. It's our van, supposed to take us to Moscow and back.

Five men and three women stand, chatting excitedly, beside the van, their luggage lined up. A frustrated-looking man on the van's roof-rack calls to those chatting: 'I say, hey! Throw that big bag up. It'll have to go on next.'

But no one does what he says; they're all interested in getting acquainted. He stomps between the roof-rack frame on the van's metal roof and it depresses with a clunk. When he lifts his foot, the metal springs back with a tinny sound. He seems not to care about the damage. He sees Don and me and says, 'This could be the last two. Hey, you blokes, are you for the Russian trip?'

'Yeah, that's us,' Don says, then he whispers to me, 'There's three bloody sheilas. That's a bit of a bugger.'

I don't reckon that it's a bugger at all. Two of them are good-looking and the third, well, she can be Don's.

Surprisingly, all the gear gets stowed on the roof-rack, but it's so high we'd better not be going under any low bridges.

The driver tells us his name is Noel. Everyone else says their name, and no one remembers anyone's name, except Noel's.

We've nearly reached Dover before the first disagreement is settled. It's taken that long for Don to bleed from one of the women, a nurse—we call her Nurse One—that there may be some elements of communism that could be incorporated into Western philosophy. His persistence gets us all to declare our political alignment. Two women, Nurses One and Two, are slightly conservative; Lisa, the other woman—we call her Moaner-Lisa—and nearly all the rest are sympathetic socialists. But two of the men, Don and the New Zealander—Kiwi we name him—are raging commos. The van's driver, Noel, is smart because he says nothing about his political leanings. So far he's been supporting Nurses One and Two, and I reckon he's doing that because he's got love on his mind.

None of us chunder while we cross the channel, and that's just as well because the van jumps about more than the channel ferry, and chundering here will mean that when we get to the crook roads of Poland, a chunderer will chunder in the van.

Tent erection on the first night has the women complaining that they shouldn't have to help. Noel says, 'Well, don't help.' Then they complain that they're hungry and how long will it be before they eat?

Noel says, 'I can't cook yet because I've got to get the tent erected.'

So they cook the meal, and Noel establishes a cooking regime that applies for the whole tour. A smart man is Noel.

We enter East Germany through Checkpoint Charlie, and all the border guards are rude. They don't give a bugger who they push and shove and insult or about rights or diplomacy. They don't give a bugger about anything.

Everyone in the van is bitching about the border guards' attitude. Don's doing his best to defend their actions. He says, 'But they're not your fair dinkum commo's; they're Germans. Don't forget that they were the enemy during the war.'

Nurse One says, 'But Don, the war's been over for seventeen years, and they're still angry about losing?'

He mumbles something about hardships and imperialism and the bloody Americans. No one knows what he means and he quickly changes the subject.

Much of what we see—buildings, houses, sheds and roads, especially on the sides of the roads—still bear the results of the retreating German Army's determination to leave the Russians nothing of substance to capture. Groups of workers unenthusiastically hoist large stone parts of building facades with a block and tackle so they can reposition them from where they've fallen. Groups of women hammer big stones into little stones to use as road-base, and everywhere there's a sense of sadness and melancholy. This joint is not jumping.

We're all excited about arriving in Warsaw. Don and the Kiwi are talking up what the commos have done there to improve the lot of the people, but there's little to see that we can enthuse about.

There's nothing grand about Warsaw's Grand Orbis Hotel apart from it being on a corner, the corner of Krucza and Hoza streets. It's Saturday night. Warsaw people seem intent on writing themselves off. There are drunks all over the streets, and I decide, we all decide, not to do any serious eyeballing of good-looking women. The three women travelling with us decide to remain in the hotel Grand Orbis, and I reckon that's a good idea. I don't want to have to consider protecting them from randy young Polish drunks that look as though they could eat me before breakfast.

We draw close to the Soviet border, and Don's so excited he might easily wet himself. He's saying, 'It'll be amazing how things will change once we're in the Soviet Union. Jesus it's going to be great. You'll see.'

At the border, the Russians who do the processing of Western capitalist pigs must have gotten out of the wrong side of the bed, because they're more arrogant and much ruder than the East Germans. Nurse One says, 'And so they should be, because these people taught the East German guards their hospitality skills.'

It's a good laugh.

Don and Kiwi don't laugh.

Don's got a mile-wide smile on his face. He's jumping about as if he were going into Disneyland, but it doesn't look like a Disneyland to me. I've been to the real Disneyland. People laugh there.

The Soviet Border Guards and Immigration Officials do blatant perving on the three women in our group and the women lap it up. Nurse Two says, 'Aren't they nice?'

Noel mumbles, 'Yeah, nice like a tiger.'

But Noel has the most difficulty because he's got the van to deal with. We do what we're told, and we empty the contents of our bags and what's in our pockets so an inventory can be done—of everything. Don gets chipped by a border guard for laughing.

'You vill not be laffing,' says the guard.

Don says, 'I'm only laughing because I'm so happy to be in your country; it's great.'

'You vill not be laffing,' the guard repeats.

Don stops laughing, but we laugh when he says, 'The guard's correct. There's no reason for me to be laughing. I mean, look at what's happened to them. The bloody Germans scorched the Russian earth when they retreated. They blew up everything of value; they murdered the peasants; they left the Russians with nothing.'

None of us argue with Don about his history lesson.

Nurse Two says, 'Don, that was seventeen years ago. And we didn't do it to them; we're Australians.'

Don says, 'But now we're their enemies. Don't forget there's a cold war going on, and we're on the West's side, the side of the capitalists and imperialists.'

So here we are arguing politics with the commos staring at us wondering what's going on.

The guards go all over the van, even into the air-cleaner housing.

Nurse One says, 'Look out, there's capitalist air inside that.'

Don tells her to shut up.

Noel says to our women, 'They tell me they've got to do a body search of you three, but there are no Soviet women on duty, so three of the male guards are going to do it.'

The women panic. Nurse One says, 'If any of them come on to me, I'll knee them in the testicles.'

No kneeing gets done.

We want to get going, but our instructions are to wait for our guide, who will be with us for our entire journey. Everyone knows the guide's going to be more than a guide.

Noel says, 'On my last trip, the guide was certainly an employee of State Security. He was with us to make sure we didn't blow up anything, or do any spying.'

Don says, 'That's bullshit.'

The woman approaching us is obviously a member of the USSR Olympic wrestling team. She says, 'Hello, peoples.'

We say, 'Hello'.

'My name is Nellie; I am your guide. You are vaiting for me, yes?'

'Yes.'

'Dat is good. Ve vill go to the briefing room, now.'

Propaganda that's there to impress decorates the briefing room: photos, drawings and paintings of bridges, dams, buildings and schools, none of which has the slightest hint as to their location or capacity or height.

Nellie tells us that there's a whole lot more we can't do than what we can do. At the end of her presentation, she says, 'Dah peoples of zee Union of Soviet Socialist Republic velcome horstralian comrades to our country.'

'And New Zealand comrades too,' the Kiwi says.

Nurse One and two mumble, 'We're not comrades.'

Nellie hears them and says, 'Ve are all comrades in sa var against capitalist domination.'

Don yells, 'Yair.'

Then she insists that we take notes, and an Australian bloke says, 'Notes! Like we did at school?'

'You will take notes,' Nellie says.

So we take notes.

We write: two-hundred and twenty-million people; nine-thousand kilometres from East to West; one-hundred-thousand rivers; one-hundred nationalities ...

Noel says, 'Jesus Christ, we're getting the lot.'

'Zee choice of zee peoples iz zat ve don't has religious practice in zee Soviet Union.'

Don yells, 'Yair.'

'I vill be with you all zee time you are here in our country.'

Don says, 'From go to whoa, eh?'

A space was left in the van for a Russian guide, but Nellie needs two spaces; she reeks of perspiration and garlic, and she'll be with us for two-thousand kilometres. Noel thinks she'll want the front-passenger seat, traditionally the guide's position, and he's panicking.

He whispers to me, 'She's far too big to sit there. I won't be able to change gear without touching her knee, and she won't like that.'

'She'll love it mate. She'll reckon you're doing a line for her. She'll have you in her tent tonight, and she'll kill you. Look at the size of her.'

'No way. I reckon Don's the bloke for her. I'm going to sit her beside him.'

And he does just that, and Don loves it because he's into capitalist bashing straight away. But Nellie's still trying to understand his saying of 'go to whoa' and he's getting her confused because he's talking about horses and how to stop them. He says, 'Whoa. Stop, you know?'

But she doesn't know.

Nellie remembers all our names, but she often adds an 's' to the end, so we have Dons, Barrys and Noels. I'm impressed that she knows us all after one introduction, but Nurse One says she's probably had a week to memorize them. But she must have a good memory because she knows the name of all of the battles that the Soviet's fought against the Germans and all the numbers and dates.

'In that field there,' she says, 'Tventy soviet patriots defeated a zousand German troops zat vas zaported by ten Germans tanks. Zat cairn in zat field ... no, Noel zere iz no need to stop to go zere ... zat cairn iz dedicated to zhe memory of zhe gallant Soviets. Only vun Soviet vas injured, and all zee Germans vas killed.'

It's the same story for nearly every field. But when we arrive at memorials, usually huge, usually having a bronze sculpture of a steely-jawed Soviet soldier, we read the numbers: hundreds of thousands of soviets were killed.

When Nellie speaks about a Soviet victory, Don says, 'Yeah.' When she speaks about lots of Soviets dying, Don says, 'Bloody Germans.'

He's a bit biased.

At Minsk we get to hear about many more battles fought by the gallant Soviet troops. Don says 'Yair,' all the time, and Nurse Two says, 'Don, all this can't be true, can it?'

Don says, 'Can you see any buildings that aren't fairly new?'

'Only a few.'

'Right, and that's because everything was destroyed.'

Between Minsk and Smolensk, it's the same: war, war, war, and battles, battles, battles. I realise my knowledge of history is flawed. Nellie says that four-million soviets died in the four-hundred kilometres between these cities. And that disgusts me.

I reckon the Smolensk camping area is terrific, but it's raining, and there's nowhere terrific when a tent has to be erected in the rain. The three girls remind Noel, that *his* tour company stated in *their* brochure that *their* guide erects the tent. So they go and sit under a shed. Nellie helps though.

Noel takes our food money to the camp shop and returns with stacks of potatoes and two brown-paper-wrapped bottles. I've seen packages like these in the hands of 'down-and-out' men in Sydney's Belmore Park—it's got to be grog.

He says, 'You won't believe what I got.'

'What?'

'One-hundred-proof Russian Vodka.'

'One-hundred-percent Russian?'

'Yair. Not only is it one-hundred-percent Russian; it's one-hundred-percent proof.'

'What's it like? Can it be drunk? Did you taste it first?'

'Yair. Some Russian blokes in a tent near the shop gave me a taste. It's mule-kicking stuff.'

'Right, let's get into it.'

Noel goes all protective. 'Not until the tent gets erected. There's not going to be any erecting done after you've had this stuff.'

Nurse Two hears us speak about erection. She says, 'Why do you men always have sex on your mind.'

Don says, 'Sex? We've got something much better than sex.'

'Much better?' she says.

We all know none of us is going to strike it lucky and get any of our three females travelling companions into having sex. So we all say, 'Much, *much* better.'

None of our food gets cooked because we're all sipping one-hundred-percent Russian Vodka, and most of us are stupid—even the women. Everyone's singing *Waltzing Matilda* and *Tie Me Kangaroo Down Sport*, and the whole camp-site must hear us. Nellie does.

When she arrives at our hard-ground campsite from where she stays in the Special Cabin for Official Guides, the Kiwi is into his rendition of New Zealand's National Anthem up to: 'Hear our voices we entreat,' and we all yell, 'We don't want to hear your voice!'

Nellie's a bit angry. She says, 'Do not drinks zo much of our Vodka; it iz strong.'

We already know that.

Noel takes us to the tent of the Russian drinkers, and they offer us some of their herrings and cucumbers. They must have plenty of Vodka because they don't sip it; they gulp it down. We sip our Vodka, and they all insist that we gulp, so we do. Don goes to get more vodka from the shop, and we're all done for.

The Russian drinkers speak no English. All we know of Russian is '*da*', and that's what we say when they pour more Vodka.

The Russians mimic kicking a soccer ball, and we reckon they look bloody stupid, but they hand gesture and with a bit of German, Don twigs they're trying to speak about the soccer World Cup.

None of us know anything about soccer. But Don's from Melbourne, and he knows about Australian Rules Football, so he mimics kicking a ball and taking a mark. One of the Russians say, 'Ballet.' And one of them prances about doing ballet steps.

The whole thing's gone crazy.

I attempt to find my way back to the tent, but I trip on another tent's guy ropes and I'm on the rain-sodden hard ground for the night.

In the morning, we're all suffering, and Nellie threatens to cancel that day's travelling, but Noel must be used to pretending he's not drunk when he is, and we're off to Moscow. Not much speaking is done.

There's no reason for Noel to go off the main road, but Nellie is having a sleep, so he does. Ahead is a bridge and beside the bridge is a soldier holding a rifle.

Nurse One says, 'He might shoot us!'

Noel stops the van. The soldier peers at us and twists the casually held rifle to a threatening position.

Nurse One says, 'He's going to shoot us!'

Nellie wakes up mystified. She says something in Russian, then, 'Vot is dis?'

The Russian soldier must do a quick calculation on odds. He takes steps backwards and says, '*Sportovo nyet go*,' or something like that. I reckon he's saying, 'Who in the hell are you that's trying to cross my bridge?'

Nellie goes to get out of the van, and the Russian soldier says, '*Nyet*.' Then she goes off into angry-sounding Russian, and the guard bows and scrapes and points the rifle at the sky.

Back on the road to Moscow, Nellie goes off her brain about protocols and diplomacy and manners and security. She tells us that the guard is from a nearby village, we're the first Westerners he'd ever seen, that he would have used his rifle to defend his bridge, and that he's certainly going to report the incident to his village commissar. She says, 'It vas zee most important happening in his life.'

She's really serious while we are, all apart from Nurse One, joking about the episode.

Noel says, 'It was only a wooden bridge that was on a road going to nowhere.'

Nellie says, *'Was it?'*

Don's on her side, criticizing Noel, and it's just as well Nellie knows no Australian swear words. In the end Noel promises Don that he'll not deviate from the main road again. Don says, 'Are you sure?'

Noel says, 'Not on your sweet nellie.'

Now Don's trying to explain to Nellie that Noel's saying 'not on your sweet nellie' doesn't involve her.

'But he zaid my name; he zaid Nellie.'

'Yes; but he was not talking about you.'

'But it iz my name.'

His explanation goes on for twenty kilometres.

We're glad to get to Moscow because, hopefully, that's the end of memorials and cairns to fallen Soviet soldiers. By my count, we're up to seven million dead. And that disgusts me.

Noel had brought another tour group to Moscow, so he knows what to do and where to go, but Nellie gives him very specific directions.

He says, 'This is different to the last time I was here.'

She says, 'Zere iz new protocols for foreign guests.'

We speculate that there's been new construction, something we're not supposed to see, perhaps a military building. But Don sees nothing sinister in anything Nellie says.

We camp near the Lenin Hills that look over Moscow—a huge and not very attractive city of five-million people. We pass row after row of drab-looking apartment buildings that don't allow for any individualism. Where buildings have small balconies, no one stands or sits on them, and there are definitely no pot plants, not even any brightly coloured laundry hanging to dry. Hundreds of tower cranes are busy lifting building materials that will be used to construct more drab-looking apartment buildings. The only attractive aspect of Moscow we see from our camp is the Moskva River that meanders through the centre of the city and disappears to the horizon. We erect our tent in record time then we're off touring.

Don and Kiwi are excited about everything they see; their comments are all complimentary: if it's not fabulous, it's astounding; if it's not remarkable it's outstanding. Nellie is with us all the time, and she rambles on about facts and figures: Moscow has fifteen-hundred factories, and in one year eighty-thousand new apartments are built, and there's forty-million square meters of dwelling space ... On and on she goes. Nurses one and two ask if we can visit a hospital.

Nellie says, 'Hospitals zar not on zhe itinerary for zhe tourists.'

But something's wrong in her brain because she won't stop telling us useless information; she's a walking encyclopaedia about production of tractors and machine tools and wheat and sugar beets. Even Don's bored by it all. She takes us to the Red Square Mausoleum where we see the upper part of Lenin's body; the rest of him is under a covering and we wonder why? Then she has us near the Kremlin wall to see the graves and bronze busts of other Russian politicians, including Joseph Stalin's, whose body used to lie in state next to Lenin and who now doesn't even rate having a bronze bust. Don gives us a history lesson that includes saying that Stalin was a fucking murdering mongrel and a slaughterer of good Soviet people. Nellie smiles and shakes her head in agreement; this is now the official Soviet line, so she's doing what she should do. She likes Don.

She takes us into the Kremlin, and we all wonder if Nikita Khrushchev will come down from his chambers to say G'day and invite us up to drink a Vodka. But he doesn't. We see a bloody huge bell that's fallen from somewhere and is now in need of repair from a specialist welder.

She takes us to gaze in awe at the domes of St Basil's Cathedral, and we, and everyone else on Red Square who's not a Soviet citizen, arrange ourselves so the domes look like they're coming out of our heads and get our photograph taken.

Then we go to the GUM store, where Russians who have nothing enviously inspect inferior Soviet-made products.

Now we're off to the huge Moscow University that's descriptively mentioned on our tourist map as a tall building.

After that we visit the Economic Achievement Exhibition which has permanent displays representing all fifteen of the sovereign republics that comprise the Soviet Union. On display is a full-size Aeroflot T.U 104 jet aircraft, a bloody huge new jet aircraft, that goes nowhere. And we see a copy of Sputnik 1, the first earth-launched satellite to go into space.

She wants to take us to see all manner of sites on her official list of places to show Western capitalist pigs. But I've had enough and so has Noel, so we get lost.

Without Nellie, we're approached by Russians who want to buy the clothes off our bodies; particularly denim jeans with a label on the outside. Noel has experienced all this before, but I'm astounded at the high prices we're offered.

He says to me, 'Don't sell; keep them until we get to Leningrad. They pay higher prices there.'

'Sell! How the fuck can I sell the clothes I'm dressed in?'

'You don't; you make contacts and come back later. You bring all your stuff in a bag and then flog it. Jesus you're naïve; don't you know about this?'

'No.'

He says, 'I've got loads of good clobber from my mates in London. I'm to sell their stuff in Leningrad and use the money to buy a Russian camera and lenses, and binoculars and fountain pens. And any currency

I've got left over, I'll smuggle out and flog in London for more than the official exchange rate.'

'Oh. What are the chances of getting caught? I don't want to spend a few years in a Russian prison.'

Noel's looks at me, shakes his head and smiles, and speaks to me as if I were a schoolboy. He says, 'You can't be so dumb that you don't know all of this goes on. It happens every trip … *everyone* does it.'

I say, 'I wonder if the girls are getting offers for their clothes?'

'Who'd want pink twin sets?'

We take the Moscow underground, and he continues talking about selling stuff. I reckon nearly everyone in the train carriage is a KGB agent, and we're going to be taken into custody and tortured.

I speak softly, and he says, 'Speak up; I can't hear you.'

And now everyone knows we're Western capitalist pigs.

Nellie looks angry when we rejoin the group. I reckon Noel and I are in big trouble. I say to him, 'Mate, she's going to blow her stack.'

He says, 'What can she do, keep us in after school?'

'No but she can—'

'Leave her to me; I'll do one of my I'm-really-sorry lines. Watch this.' He says, 'Oh, Nellie …'

And that's as far as he gets. There's a man with Nellie who's got 'official' written all over him. He says in perfect English, 'Are *these* the missing tourists?'

She says, '*Da*.'

'Good. At least they haven't been murdered.'

'Murdered? What's with this murdered stuff?'

Nellie says, 'Dere iz zis groups of men who …'

The official gives Nellie a dirty look, so she shuts up. He says to us, 'There will be no repetition of this stupidity for the remaining time you are visitors to our country … *understand?*'

'Oh. All right.'

He smiles and says, 'Get with the rest of your party because we leave now for the ballet.'

'Ballet?'

'Yes. I have been able to obtain for your group tickets for the Bolshoi. Tonight they will dance Swan Lake.'

And so they do, and all of us, even the culture-cretin Noel, is impressed.

~

It takes two days to travel to Leningrad. It can be done in one day, but we've got to stop at more memorials to millions more Soviets killed by the Germans while defending villages, bridges, hills and railway lines.

Nellie tells us that soldiers paraded through Red Square and continued marching straight to the German lines less than twenty kilometres away. The sculpture of young Soviet men on a hill is to commemorate their killing by the Germans. The numbers slaughtered disgusts me, and I'm beginning to realise why there are not so many forty-year-old men on the streets. Nellie is aged about forty so I say to her, 'Were you involved in the war?'

She destroys me with her answer. She says, 'Of course. All Soviets vas in zee vare. Nearly as many womens vas killed as vas mens. But no Germans soldier got to Moscow, or Leningrad.'

Our accommodation at a Leningrad camping ground gets mucked up, and Nellie apologizes, saying we have to stay in the Waldorf Hotel. I worked at London's Waldorf Hotel, so I'm all excited, thinking this must be a plush hotel, too. But it's not. It might be plush for Soviets, but in my reckoning any hotel that doesn't supply washbasin and bath plugs, isn't plush.

Commo's Don and Kiwi are itching to see the warship *Aurora*, the cruiser that's supposed to have fired one of its guns to start the storming of the Czar's Winter Palace in 1917. Nurses One and Two and the rest are itching to get to Palace Square then into the Czar's Winter Palace, which is now the State Hermitage Museum, to see paintings by Rembrandt, Raphael and Leonardo. Nellie is itching to have us all see the

Leningrad Metal Works where they manufacture five-thousand-kilowatt power generators, and to see some memorials that commemorate the death of more millions of Soviet soldiers. Although I'm disgusted by these deaths, I'm itching to walk the streets to see everything, and Noel wants to come, too, because he's itching to make contact with Soviets that want to buy clothes.

He says, 'I'm going to make a killing here.'

The fragmentation of her tourist group disturbs Nellie, and we reckon it's because she's just about at the end of her tourist-minding responsibility, and she's hoping to finish the tour with the same number of Western capitalist pigs that she had when she started.

She says, 'I haff a tour organized for you all to zee zhe USSR Academy of Sciences Library and zhe M. E. Saltykov-Shchedrin Public library. Zhey are famous throughout zhe World.'

Noel says to me, 'A tour of bloody libraries? Not bloody likely. Let's tell her we're going to buy some washbasin and bath plugs.'

When we tell her that, she smiles and says, 'Zat vill keep you busy.' She knows getting that kind of thing in Leningrad is impossible.

Leningrad's got loads of water and bridges, good-looking young women, trolley buses and a huge statue of Mister V.I Lenin holding his arm out. We reckon the pigeons sitting and shitting on his arm have no respect for this famous person.

We walk across a big public square that's called the Field of Mars, and I say to Noel, this must be named after the place in Sydney.

'In Sydney?'

'Yeah. I used to hear bands play at a big area in Western Sydney called the Field of Mars. It was run by some religious mob.'

We see an old war trophy, an armoured car that Mister V.I Lenin was supposed to have stood in to make a speech to his commo mates, and I reckon it's nice that they have something like this—but they could paint it or polish it.

Some Russian blokes seem interested in us, and we reckon they like the look of our clothes. Noel is really careful because he's heard that the

Leningrad police are aware of what goes on and have plain-clothed men patrolling the streets looking out for Western capitalist pigs that sell their jeans and shirts with labels on them.

I don't have much I can sell, just my well-worn American jeans, a Canadian western shirt and my in-need-of-a-clean tennis sandshoes.

A Russian bloke looks in my bag at the goods and says to me, 'Ten roubles.'

I say, 'Twenty roubles.'

He says, 'Fifteen roubles.'

So I sell my clothes.

Noel doesn't think much of my dealings. He reckons I should've laughed at the Russian's first offer, that I should've told him the price was thirty roubles. He says, 'They all haggle, and they know you're going to haggle, so they make their first offer ridiculously low.'

I don't know too much about haggling with Russians because I've only haggled with Mexicans. Mexicans haven't had millions of their people killed by German soldiers, and they haven't had to live in a city that was under siege for two years, so I reckon that's why Russians are good at haggling. Noel though, he's been through the Suez Canal, and he's been ashore at Port Said, so he's had experience at haggling with the master hagglers, the Arabs. And he's been to Russia before. So it's not fair of him to criticize my dealings.

Nurses One and Two rave about the Hermitage and, as would be expected of commos, Don and Kiwi rave about the ship Aurora, and Nellie tells us that we missed a very outstanding viewing of Saltykov-Shchedrin Library. I don't care because I've now got fifteen roubles to spend.

I convince Noel and Don that we should at least look inside the Hermitage, that we should at least take a look at the Rembrandt paintings, and then try to find a place that sells beer. We get involved in looking at things that are said to be masterpieces. They have a lot of masterpieces here, and we keep saying, 'One more hall; one more hall.' But we don't realise that the hermitage has two-million exhibits displayed in one-hundred-and-twenty halls. When we get outside, it's time for dinner.

Noel has a big smile on his face, and I reckon he's smiling because he's seen so many masterpieces. But it's not that; it's because he's made contact with an art-loving Russian that's also in the market for big quantities of capitalist pig's clothes. He's very happy.

At the Waldorf Hotel, Nellie is relieved to see us, but she's surprised to hear that Noel must take the van to an electrician who is going to look at its lights. She says, 'But Noel, how vill you know vere to go?'

'A man who works for Intourist told me.'

'But I vork for Intourist. How did you know vhere zee Intourist office iz?'

'Ah … a man came up to me while we were at the Hermitage, while we were looking at the wonderful Rembrandt paintings; he told me.'

'But how doez he knows you are hazing trouble with zee lights?'

'Coincidence.'

She says, 'It iz vone big coincidence, eh?'

In the Waldorf's dining room, we eat borscht, but that's not exciting because we get that everywhere. Then we have a main course option of either a fish stew that looks like spew, or a chicken dish that's loaded with sour cream. Noel and Brian, an Australian who's sat in the rear of the van since London and who says nothing, miss having their dinner. I reckon they don't mind because they're out doing good negotiations with Russian clothes buyers. I'm feeling a bit sorry for the poor Russian hagglers because they're up against a master haggler in Noel, and Brian's a big-muscled bloke, so he'll add an intimidation factor.

In the foyer of the hotel, I spend two of my fifteen roubles on a set of five wooden dolls that come apart and fit into one big doll. I think no one else back home in Penshurst will have these, and when I get back to Australia, I'll give them to my mother as a gift. That is, provided I ever get back to Australia.

I see Noel and Brian coming from the car parking area that's especially for foreign capitalist pigs. They have a huge contrast in attitude. Noel is waving his arms about and saying he's fucking-well going to do this and that, and Brian's laughing his head off.

In the hotel's foyer sits an old man who always seems to be there drinking tea he gets from a nearby Samovar. We reckon he's a retired KGB agent earning his old-age pension by reporting to his commissar any unusual activity by the Western capitalist pigs, and I reckon he's about to have something to report.

I hear Noel say, 'The bastards, the dirty rotten bastards, *the mongrels.*'

Brian gets hold of him and says, 'Shush, shush.'

Brian says to me, 'It was so funny; Jesus you ought to have seen it.' And he laughs and laughs.

The retired KGB agent doesn't quite know what to make of it all, but he's alert; he puts his tea cup down.

In Noel's hotel room, away from the retired KGB agent, Noel says, 'How about coming with Brian and me, and we'll look for the thieving bastards?'

'No. I mean, what happened? Who you want to go looking for?'

Brian says, 'So we're parked outside this food shop, and we wait for the Russians to front and …' He laughs again, tears coming from his eyes. 'And … and the Russians tell us to follow them, and we've got the van in a dead-end street.' He laughs so much that Noel tells him to fucking-well shut up.

Noel says, 'So they get out of their car, and I take them to the back of the van and show them the goods. They like what they see, and we start haggling, and I reckon I'm doing very well, I've got from them an unbelievably high price, right?

'Yeah, go on.'

'So the Russian pulls out a huge roll of money, and in the darkness I'm trying to see. I'm trying to make sure he counts correctly. He's counting out five rouble notes and he's only up to twenty five—'

'Is that all you got?'

'Listen to me; I'm not finished yet. I'm to get a hundred and twenty-five—'

'Hell! That's a great price.'

Brian's laughing again, and he says, 'Wait for it, there's more.'

Noel says, 'And then there's a loud noise, and the Russians panic, and one of them says, "Police." So I panic and the Russian gives me his whole roll of money. I reckon I've got more than I should get, so I'm happy. The Russians grab the clothes, and they're off. I put the roll of money in my pocket, and we're in the van, and we're off.'

Brian says, 'And then?'

Noel, looking sheepish, says, 'Then when I get to a street light, I stop to count the money, and, and …'

Brian says, 'Listen to this; you'll love it.'

Noel gives him a shove and says, 'For Christ's sake, shut up … so when I start to count the money, I realise there's something wrong. The money looks different; what I'm counting are—'

'Fucking old lottery tickets,' Brian says, and he roars with laughter.'

'Yeah. The fucking Russians gave me old lottery tickets; here look …' He takes them from his pocket. 'Tell me if they look like Russian roubles to *you*, will you?'

I give the notes a cursory glance. 'They're old lottery tickets.'

He says, 'Of course they're fucking old lottery tickets; I can see that now. I can see that now when it's light, but I couldn't in that laneway. They looked like fair dinkum roubles then.'

I should be sympathetic. I mustn't do what Brian's doing, but I can't; it's too funny, so I laugh.

Noel says, 'Okay, so it's funny. But what's not funny is how I tell my mates in London. How do I tell a big South African that some bloody Russians ripped me off, and that's why I haven't got his binoculars? How do I tell the bloke in our office, a bloke who's been here with four tour groups and who gave me clothes that were still in their wrapping, that I haven't got the camera he was going to give his girlfriend? I'm rooted. They're going to thump hell out of me.'

I tell Noel his only solution is that he'll have to buy the things. He'll have to pay for everything.

~

When the van is packed ready for heading to the Russian border with Finland, Noel puts me in the back where I have to sit next to Nellie. She stinks of perspiration and garlic.

We're only five kilometres from the border where the Russian customs are located and where Nellie gets rid of her Western capitalist pigs. She seems genuinely sorry to leave us and refuses to take a twenty roubles tip. Nurse Two cries about this, so Nellie reluctantly takes the roubles.

Russian customs officials order us to unload all our baggage from the roof-rack, and then order Noel to drive the van onto a ramp. The officials crawl all over it, looking for anything we're not supposed to take out of Russia. Noel's certain that the camera he's bought for his boss and the binoculars he's bought for the big South African are exportable; there's no duty to pay. And he's right.

Nurse One says, 'We've got a dwarf in the glove box who's defecting.'

A Russian official doesn't understand; but he understands the word 'defecting' and looks alarmed.

No roubles, not even one, are allowed out of the country, but I have one coin in my shoe, and it's causing me to limp, so I put a pained look on my face. Noel knows I put it there. He says to me in a loud voice and in front of a Russian, 'Have you got a problem with your foot? Take your shoe off, and I'll have a look at it.'

I say to him, 'You bastard!'

Our baggage gets hurriedly loaded back onto the roof-rack, and a Russian customs man tells us that they allow fifteen minutes for us to travel five kilometres to the frontier, that if it takes longer, the frontier guards will dispatch a patrol to look for us. It's no worries, because we can easily do it.

We're all very happy and talking about what we'll do in Helsinki. We'll get stuck into their beer, and we'll be able to buy Western cigarettes and not have to smoke the Russian kind with a tube on the end. The road is bumpy so Noel takes it slowly. Nurse Two starts singing and Noel joins in, rocking the van from side to side, and that's when the roof-rack brackets let go. The rack, bags, tent and everything hit the ground then much of it rolls down an embankment onto a railway line.

Oh.

There's lots of swearing and concern, and Kiwi says, 'What if a train comes?'

We scramble down the embankment and get a human chain going to get everything back. There's not time to pack it all, so Noel gets the roof-rack back on top and wires it there, and we shove all the stuff inside. The inside of the van is crowded.

The border guards see what's happened, and they reckon it's very funny that the Western capitalist pigs can't even fix their roof-rack to the top of their Western capitalist pig of-a-van.

Just a kilometre inside Finland, everything's different. There's a shop plastered with Coca-Cola, ice cream and cigarette advertising signs— normality.

Noel orders a re-packing of stuff that's to go on the roof-rack, and while he's packing his things, he looks inside. The Russian camera and binoculars are smashed beyond repair.

22 September 1962.
London.
Dear Mum,
We're in London at last and I'm pleased to be back.
During the last stages of the trip I was tired of roughing it, of sleeping in wet tents and not being able to wash properly.
When I was in North America I thought it was the centre of the world and that Europe would be old and drab. To my surprise it's not.
London is the drabbest city, but the Scandinavian and Benelux countries are quite modern.

Stockholm was fantastic. I guess one of the reasons were the beautiful girls. All the cities we visited in Holland were impressive. I could quite easily live in that country. The people were only too willing to help and go out of their way to make us comfortable.

I have left Leningrad to last because it deserves more than a few lines.

We were supposed to camp there, but the camping area was closed for the winter. Instead, we were housed at the Waldorf Hotel, which was very nice indeed.

I was told that quite a few Australians go to Leningrad, but neither of our guides had met an Aussie. They were very amused by our antics and even spent their own time with us

The Hermitage Museum was unbelievable. The best in the world (even to some non-communists).

I'm broke again.
Love Barry.

1962, Russia: We lose the roof rack near the Finland border.

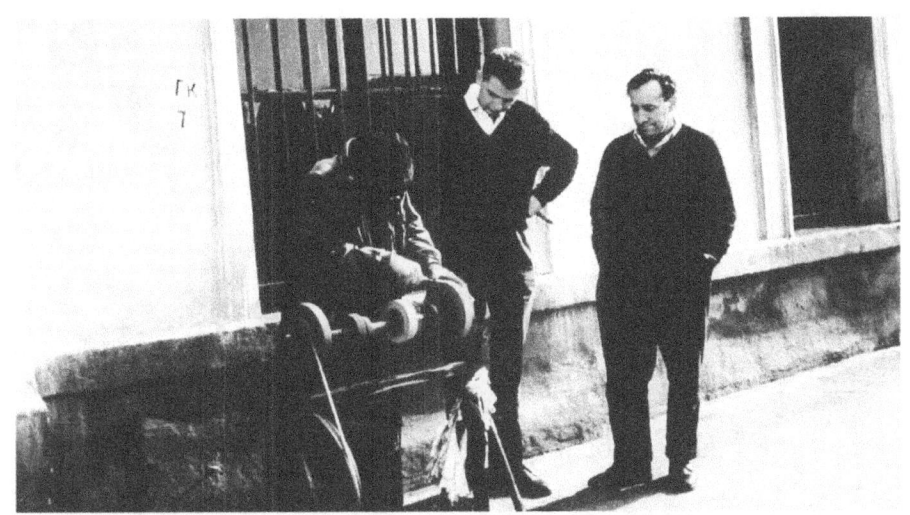
Don Harper and our Aussie driver have their knives sharpened.

The door-mobile outside our Warsaw hotel.

Chapter Fourteen

Months of the year are not important, unless there's a direct connection to the weather. September in London means rain, a precursor to a long miserable winter. The Barons Court cave is just bearable in summer—we all wear jumpers while inside—but in winter it's horrible.

I want to return to Australia. I want to see my mum. I want to go to Cronulla beach. I want to live in comfortable surroundings. I want out. But I've got very little money, and everything I want requires money.

Getting a job is easy. The boss of the plumbing company I used to work for said he'd start me tomorrow. But how can I fit into the humdrum of going to work when it's dark, and coming home when it's dark and working with people whose minds are in the dark? People that only want to talk about Tottenham Hotspur and Chelsea and Manchester United football teams. People who still believe that Britannia rules the waves. People that think good food is fish and bloody chips.

I do the money calculations. My income as a plumber will be thirteen pounds a week, less living costs of nine pounds, so I can save four pounds. It's going to take at least forty weeks to buy a boat ticket to Australia! That's one lousy English winter and one lousy English summer. It's a death sentence.

Albert's got his head in his favourite newspaper, *The Manchester Guardian,* and I know he can't be reading the comic section, because it has none. I reckon it can't be a good newspaper if it has no comics. '

I say to Albert, 'Where's Qatar?'

He says, 'What's Qatar?'

'It's a country.'

'Never heard of it.'

'What? How come you've never heard of it? It's a British protectorate.

He says, 'I don't know the names of all the countries that Britain is supposed to protect.

I reckon he's very narrow-minded. I reckon every English person should know the names and locations of countries they're protecting. Englishmen of Albert's age are supposed to be prepared to put on their country's uniform and go wherever their Prime Minister says there are people that need some protecting.

Albert says, 'Why don't you go to the Hammersmith Library? They'll have a book with it in; probably an atlas.

But I don't want to waste my valuable unemployment time traipsing to the Hammersmith Library to look at an atlas, so I wait until Terry arrives home from work.

Terry only has his foot in the door when I say, 'Do you know where Qatar is?

He says, 'I never had it. I've never used it … look in the cupboard.

The Hammersmith librarian is amused that she has an Australian in her library asking about British protectorates. She says to me, 'Why do you want to know about British protectorates?'

I say, 'Because it says that in the advertisement.'

'What advertisement?'

'This one. I got it from the London *Observer*.' I show the librarian the section of paper I stole from Don's favourite newspaper.

She looks at the advertisement. 'You read a very good newspaper.'

I could tell her it's Don's paper and that he bought it yesterday just prior to him leaving the Barons Court cave to go to Rotterdam in Holland. I could tell her that Don's a mug to have gone there because he's got no sea experience, no seaman's papers and no hope of getting a berth on a ship going to Australia—or anywhere. None of this I tell her. Instead, I say, 'I like to read a good newspaper, don't you?'

'Yes, I do. Now what's written here? It says it's a Scottish-American Company that wants experienced oil-drilling workers.' She looks at me. 'Oh, so you're an experienced oil worker?'

'Ah … kind of.' There's no need to tell her that while I was in the Canadian Northwest Territory working with a seismic exploration crew, I learned some of the key words that oil drilling people use, and that I'm planning to use that knowledge to bluff my way into getting a job. 'But where's Qatar?'

She reads from the advertisement: *Keir & Cawder Arrow Drilling will interview applicants in our London office. Those who are successful must be prepared for immediate relocation to Qatar.*

She looks at me and says, 'Qatar?'

'Yes, Qatar. Where is it?'

We look in an atlas, and discover that Qatar is a small peninsula of land that protrudes into the Persian Gulf.

The librarian says, 'Oh; so that's where Qatar is.'

'Yes, it's a place that Britain is supposed to protect.'

She says, 'From whom?'

I have no idea.

Back in the Barons Court cave, I give Albert and Terry a geography lesson by drawing on page three of *The Manchester Guardian* my interpretation of where Qatar is. Geography was my best subject at school, so I draw the outlines of continents pretty well, but Albert keeps saying, 'Compared to Malta, where's Qatar?'

I'm buggered if I know where Malta is, so I don't include it on my drawn map, and so neither of them learn where Qatar is. In the end I say, 'It's in the bloody Persian Gulf.'

Next day I leave the Barons Court cave in the darkness of early morning and work with people who only know about football, page 3 *Mirror* girls and how much they hate the Irish. It's dreadful.

During my lunch break I telephone the Keir & Cawder Arrow Drilling Company where I speak to an American who asks me questions that I seem to answer well. He wants to meet with me tomorrow. I'm amazed.

Albert and Terry advised me to wear a suit and tie, but I go to the meeting dressed as a plumber does, and the American doesn't appear surprised. I say to him, 'My suit is at the dry cleaners.'

He says, 'We're not looking at suits. We're looking for good people.'

I tell the American that I'm a plumber with experience in the oil fields of Canada, and to add emphasis, I include an oil term in every sentence of lies. I speak quickly, hoping it will baffle him. I say, 'I was a derrick-man on a rig drilling for Richfield Oil. All the roughnecks were Canadian; the tool-pusher was American; we drilled to eight thousand feet, cased and cemented the hole.'

He's unimpressed. He says, 'We'll let you know.'

A telegram arrives addressed to me. Albert treats it as though it's news from the War Office saying that a soldier has died.

It reads:

REFERENCE INTERVIEW STOP NOW OFFER POSITION AS DERRICKMAN IN QATAR STOP PLEASE ATTEND WITH PASSPORT AND VACCINATION CERTIFICATES FOR MEDICAL DOCTOR PHELIN FIFTY THREE GREAT CUMBERLAND PLACE WEST ONE AT TWO THIRTY FRIDAY TWELVE OCTOBER STOP CONFIRM BY TELEPHONE AT NINE THIRTY FRIDAY TO FINCHAM GROSVENOR FOUR EIGHT FIVE ONE STOP

The Hammersmith librarian is surprised that I've now returned to search for information about the British protectorate of Qatar. She says, 'Do you really need to know more?'

'Yes. I'm going there. I'll be there before this week ends.'

She's amazed. She tells me she's never met anyone that's been to a British protectorate, so she wants to help me. She finds a book. We read that Qatar is a country of eleven-thousand five-hundred square kilometres, has a population of one-hundred and eighty-thousand, and an average rainfall of ten centimetres. The ruler is Sheik Suhaim, and the country's only income is from oil which is eight-hundred-thousand pounds Sterling a month.

The librarian says, 'You must be a very experienced person to have got such an important job?'

'Yes, I'm very experienced.'

When she leaves me, I go to the children's section of the library where I find a picture book with an illustration of an oil derrick. I'm prepared with a piece of grease-proof paper that I lay over the illustration while I carefully copy the oil derrick and write the names of the various components. Now I'm experienced.

~

I'm in a line with others preparing to board a Middle East Airways comet four jet aircraft, and I feel important.

I've only ever been in two aircraft: a joy flight over Terrigal in 1957 when I was a passenger in an old and strange-looking, twin-wing twin-engine Avro that seemed to be glued together, and in Canada I flew in a single-engine plane that had skis and landed on snow.

But I've seen lots of big aircraft.

My father sometimes used to drive my mother, my sister and my brothers in his Dodge utility truck to Mascot Airport on Sundays to see the planes. We'd wait at the fence of the airport to experience the Qantas or B.O.A.C or Pan American Super Constellations roar over us, then us kids would jump onto the back of the truck and dad would race around to the terminal. There, we'd stand on the open balcony to watch important people walk down the gangway and across the tarmac to the terminal. Just about all the important men wore well-cut, double-breasted suits, and nearly everyone had a hat. The ladies always wore nice clothes and a hat, and they wore one glove and carried the other. Mum reckoned that was what ladies did.

At other times my father took us to see spectacular landings of flying boats at Rose Bay. Those were my favourites. We strained our eyes to get a first glimpse, and whoever did would yell, 'There it is,' and they'd point. Then came the good part when the flying boat got close to the water, skimming a few feet above it prior to touching in a wash of spray. We never saw anyone get off because the plane slowly taxied to a wharf and we weren't allowed in there.

I'd say to my father, 'Will I fly in a big plane one day?'

He'd say, 'Yes, son ... one day.'

Well, this is the day, and I'm feeling important, and I'm not paying anything. Keir & Cawder Arrow Drilling are paying for my ticket, and I'm going to be the first in my whole family to fly in a big plane.

But I do have some concerns.

Albert and Terry told me that the British Aircraft Industry's pride and joy, the Comet jet passenger aircraft, has had a lot of crashes. They reckon that one went down in the Alps, another into the Mediterranean and others down somewhere else. I told them that was bullshit, that they're just trying to scare me and don't want me to leave the Barons Court cave because they'll have to pay more rent.

I sit next to a cockney named Bill who's also going to Qatar to work on the oilrig. He says, 'I hope this is one of their good planes.'

I say to him, 'Do they have good and bad?"

'What do you think?'

I don't know what to think. I say, 'If I was selling British planes and I was British, I'd make sure my best planes went to a British airline.'

'Exactly. Here we are in a plane that's owned by Middle East Airlines ... the Arabs.'

He's right; we're probably going to die. But all the cabin crew is English, so that's something.

An announcement from the cockpit says, 'G'day ladies and gentlemen. My name's Bruce, and I'm your captain ...'

You beauty, the pilot's Australian; we're probably not going to die.

I stare at the Swiss Alps a few thousand feet below. I'm almost mesmerized, but a hinged thing on the wing is flapping up and down and breaks my concentration. It's going like the clappers. Whatever it is, should it be doing what it's doing? Hinges wear out; the pin eventually goes, and if this happens, will air roar into the opening and upset the plane's stability? Was this the cause of the Comet crashes?

I say to Cockney Bill, 'Look at that; see that flap that's going like the clappers. See it there?'

'What about it?'

'Well, do you reckon we should tell Bruce about it?'

'Bruce? Bruce who?'

'Bruce the pilot.'

'Why?'

'Because it might be important. It might mean there's a problem.'

'You can tell the hostess if you want to, but she's going to laugh at you.'

'Laugh? Why would she laugh?'

'She'll laugh because it means nothing. It's just a flap going up and down.'

So I say nothing to Bruce or the hostess, but if the plane crashes I'm going to beat the living Christ out of Cockney Bill.

The plane successfully lands at Rome Airport, and while the Comet's parked, the flight engineer walks around looking at things and tapping things and kicking tyres. Surely he'll get on the wing and look at that flap? He doesn't.

We fly to Damascus with the flap still going like the clappers, so perhaps Cockney Bill's right; perhaps it's supposed to do what it's doing.

Damascus is hot.

I feel relief when the Comet lands at Abadan and even more relief when we're told we can't leave the air-conditioned aircraft. Bruce, the Australian captain, says, 'Ladies and gentlemen, we won't be here long. We're only taking a few passengers on board.'

But at the entrance to the plane there's lots of yelling and screaming in Arabic that means nothing to me, but it sounds like trouble.

Cockney Bill and I watch Bruce come from the cockpit; he ambles along the aisle-way smiling and saying G'day to everyone. He doesn't appear worried.

More yelling comes from the rear of the cabin, and I hear Bruce's Australian accent. His voice is calm, but he's saying lots of 'bloodys'. Bruce sorts out the problem and ambles back to his cockpit, then he's got the Comet going slowly to the end of the tarmac to the take-off location. But there's a rotten smell permeating the cabin air. It's terrible.

The plane stops and again Bruce comes from the cockpit, but this time he's not smiling, he's angry, and he doesn't say G'day to anyone. Everyone hears Bruce's voice saying a lot more 'bloodys', then we hear the Comet's high-revving engines, so the door must be open, but someone shuts it quickly. Bruce hurries back to his cockpit and revs the jet engines; the flap on the wing goes like the clappers and then the plane's in the air.

Bruce's voice says, 'Middle East Airways apologises for the short delay at Abadan. The aroma in the aircraft was from foodstuffs carried onto the aircraft; they've now been ditched.'

Bruce's use of 'ditched' is slightly alarming because we're now over the Persian Gulf, and I didn't closely watch the hostess's demonstration of how to tie a lifejacket. I was watching her beautifully shaped lips mouth words that started with 'p'. When her lips formed to pronounce every 'p', I was imagining how nice it would be to kiss her lips.

The hostess goes past our seats, and Cockney Bill says to her, 'Love'—He's got a hide addressing the woman I want to kiss as 'love', but cockneys can do things like that and get away with it—'What was going on at the back of the plane?'

Now that she's near us, I can smell her perfume—a mixture of enticing aromas that has my penis twitching. I wouldn't be surprised if the perfume was named 'Orgasm'; it should be.

She says, 'A passenger'—it's a 'p' word. Her lips are near me, and I'd like to be brave enough to get up right now and give her a big kiss. A cockney would get away with that—'carried on board a hooded hunting Falcon that he wanted to take to Doha. Bruce had it taken off, but the passenger'—Another 'p'; her lips are fabulous—'also had some dead animals for his Falcon to feed on, a kind of in-flight meal. They were rotten and the smell was going throughout the cabin, so Bruce ditched them.'

'Oh. So everything's all right now?'

'Yes, sir.'

Her 'Orgasm' perfume has gone right up my nostrils, and I want more, so I say to her, 'That flap on the wing that's going like the clappers, what is it?'

Cockney Bill gives me a dirty look, but I don't care because she's leaning across to look out of the window. Her breasts touch me, and I could orgasm at any moment.

She says, 'I've not noticed it before, but I'm certain it's quite normal.'

I say, 'Are you sure? Do you want to have another look?'

She gives me a wonderful smile. 'If it concerns you, I'll mention it to Captain Bruce.'

Cockney Bill says, 'Love, forget about it; say nothing to the Captain. This bloke's an Australian. They know nothing about flying.'

She says, 'The Captain is Australian.' And she goes away.

Bruce announces that the plane is about to land at Doha Airport and everyone should fasten his or her seatbelt. Mine has never been unfastened.

Doha doesn't much look like a capital city of a country. It's mostly single-level, white-painted buildings with a few having two levels, some with a minaret on the roof. The few trees are all date palms. A very large building that could be a supermarket sits to the west of the city, but Bruce announces that the building on the right of the aircraft is the Sheik's Palace.

I reckon Doha might be just right for commos to come and balance the economic ledger.

Buildings appear to move about in the haze of heat rising from the bitumen tarmac, and while the Comet taxies towards a jumble of buildings that must be the terminal, I contemplate my future.

It's certain that the American who interviewed me has told the drilling manager here that he's sending him a very experienced Australian oil worker, and that's what they'll expect. So will there be trouble for me?

Cockney Bill is a roughneck who'll work on the platform of the derrick where some oil drilling knowledge is required, but much more needs to be known by a derrick-man. He needs to know about rigging and ropes and splicing wire ropes and not be afraid of heights. Although I'm not afraid of heights, I've never done anything as dangerous as this.

If everything goes wrong and I'm fired, what will happen to me then? I've got no money, and even if I had some money, just enough to get me out of Qatar, where would I go? Bahrain or Kuwait or Iraq? And what would I do there? Only work on oil derricks, exactly what I'm to do here. So I've got to make this a success; there is no alternative.

It must be one-hundred-and-thirty degrees on the tarmac and at least one-hundred in the terminal. Qatar Customs don't pay much attention to anyone coming to their country to work on oil derricks, and that's because they believe that anyone who comes here is quite mad, or an escaped murderer or bigamist, certainly a person who places no value on quality of life.

A tall Arab, who drives a taxi on permanent hire to the oil company, meets me and Cockney Bill and takes us one-hundred miles south on an atrocious road to Umm Said and the Dukhan oil fields. There's no conversation. Not even between Cockney Bill and me. It's too hot, dusty and sticky. It's bloody awful.

The camp comprises ten Alberta Company trailers that must have been shipped from Calgary in Canada surrounded by a high wire fence topped with barbed wire. Two uniformed soldiers holding some kind of machine gun wait at the entrance-gate. The Arab taxi driver, who isn't allowed behind the fence, says, 'The soldiers are for your protection.'

Oil drilling is a twenty-four hour operation, so it's usual to have one crew on the rig drilling, one crew sleeping and one crew relaxing. The crew that's relaxing give us a muted welcome. A few bother to shake hands; a few nod and crack a small smile, and a few do nothing. All of them have a questioning look, wondering why we're here in this hot hole.

The manager says to the clerk, 'Hoppy, take these guys to their bunkhouse, and then bring them back to meet the tool-pusher.'

We follow the limping Hoppy to the trailers, and I'm surprised to get a single room with an air-conditioner fixed to its outside wall. When I go into the room, my eyes weep from the heat. I say to Hoppy, 'They could've turned the air-conditioner on.'

He says, 'Yes, I could've done that. But I didn't.'

It seems that everyone's tough here.

The boss, the tool-pusher and Hoppy are Yanks; the three drillers are Canadian, and the rest—the mechanic, the roughnecks and derrickmen—are Scottish and English. Hoppy tells me that apart from the Sheik's doctor, I'm the only other Australian in the country.

This is the first time I've ever gone to work at four in the afternoon. The driller on my shift, a Saskatchewan Canadian who has the unlikely name of Mans Sherwood, spends half a year cutting railway sleepers from the Canadian bush and the other half in hell holes like Qatar. He's a muscly mountain of a man—well over six-feet tall—and not talkative. He drives a Ford pick-up with his crew of seven Arabs sitting in the back. They laugh and chatter away as though they're going to a picnic.

Mans eventually speaks. In a voice that rasps like scraping metal, he says, 'What rigs have you worked on?'

I can't come straight out and say none, so I say, 'A few.'

'What fucking few?'

This is the moment I've been dreading. I hoped I'd be working with someone with empathy for what I'm doing, someone who'd understand that young Australians go travelling the world doing something here and something there, anything to earn some money to travel to the next place. But this bloke won't understand that.

I say, 'I wintered with a seismic crew in the Northwest Territory.'

'I didn't ask about that. I asked you what rigs you worked on.'

'Well … ah. None actually.'

He says nothing. The pick-up hits a few bumps on the road, and the Arabs in the back bounce about, laughing and chattering. He's got to say something, soon.

In the distance is the oilrig, located on a rise adjacent to the access road. It's the first oilrig I've been close to, and I'm surprised at the amount of equipment surrounding it—mostly water-storage tanks, drilling and mud-filtering devices, and hundreds of lengths of large-diameter pipe.

The chattering Arab crew gets out of the pick-up truck and walks unenthusiastically to the derrick. Then Mans explodes. He says, 'You goddamned sonofabitch. Are you telling me that you've *never* worked on a rig?'

'Ah … yes.'

'Shit. I've been landed with a greenhorn.' He thumps his hands repeatedly against the steering wheel, and with every thump he says, '*Goddamn.*'

I sit there wondering what happens next. Do I get fired immediately? Do I get sent back to camp and then get fired? Should I get out of the pickup before he starts thumping me? I decide to stay put.

One of the Arab workers comes back to the pickup and says, 'Mister Mans; some trouble?'

Mans says to him, 'Get your goddamned arse onto the rig ready to change shift.'

The Arab scurries away.

'Have you ever done any hard work?' Mans asks.

'Yeah, of course I have. I'm a plumber.'

He laughs. 'A plumber! You think that's hard work? This job's going to kill you. You ain't done hard work if you ain't worked on a rig. You cocksucking limeys come out here with your union rules and rights and cups of tea … ah, shit.'

There's absolutely no chance that I'm going to take on this bloke that towers head and shoulders over me and whose body looks like it's been wrought from ironbark. I have no oil-drilling experience, but I have a strong sense of self-preservation. What I must immediately do is try to calm him and allay his fears about my capacity to do hard work.

I say to him, 'Mate, firstly I'm not a limey; I'm Australian. Secondly, I've worked in Canada, and I know how hard you Canadians work … and you're quite correct about the English, they wouldn't work in an iron lung. But I'm here now, and I'm prepared to learn quickly, and you need someone, so how about giving me a go?'

He narrows his eyes, thinking.

I look at the oil derrick. A platform sits more than halfway up the structure, presumably, where I'm to work. A man up there hangs out over a pipe that goes from the drilling platform up the inside of the structure. He unhooks something; the pipe wobbles; the man wobbles, then he pushes the pipe into a rack with the sound of metal smashing against metal. I'm thinking that getting fired here and now might be for the best.

Mans says, 'This is what's going to happen. You'll work the goddamned shift, you'll do everything I goddamn tell you to do, and you'll say nothing to any of the goddamned crew. *Right?*'

'Right.'

'I'm going to send Joseph up top with you, and you'll do everything he says, *right?*'

'Right.'

'Now get out of this goddamned pickup and up to the goddamned rig and keep your goddamned mouth shut. *Right?*'

'Right.'

I hope God doesn't connect me to all the goddamns he's said. If I die today I don't want His wrath; I don't want His vengeance taken out on me.

The tower of the drilling rig shakes and shudders, and I wonder how Joseph climbed the vertical, steel-rung ladder with such ease and confidence. My first thought is that Australian unions wouldn't let this ladder be used without having a circular safety shell behind it, and the grease cleaned from the rungs, and sharp bits of metal ground off, and dodgy welds re-welded. But I'm not going to say anything to Mans. I climb and concentrate: left foot, right foot; right hand, left hand, and I never not have one hand on the sides.

Goddamn.

Joseph is talking to a man on the platform, and that man says to me in a Scottish accent, 'Come on, hurry up; it's end of shift.'

I say to him, 'Give us a break, Jock. It's my first day.'

But he doesn't even answer. He just gets onto the ladder and literally slides down to the drilling platform.

Joseph smiles and says, 'Him, Mister Angus, he funny.'

I hear Mans voice yelling from below. 'Hey, *up there*. We've got the drill bit on. We're going to be sending pipe down. *Now.*'

Joseph says to me, 'You stay. You watch, okay?'

I watch him while the sun sets, then in the evening light, then in floodlit darkness as he walks like a trapeze artist ninety feet in the air on greasy steel to grab seventy-foot long, six-inch diameter steel drill stem from the rack and attach it to a threaded socket. He whistles, and a steel-wire rope lifts the drill stem up, then it's deftly lowered onto drill stem that's already in the hole on its journey four-thousand feet below. Feverish activity goes on, more whistles come from below, the steel-wire rope races up to where Joseph is, and the whole procedure is done over and over. It's bloody hard and dangerous work. All I see below are figures rushing about under floodlights, and I hear Mans' voice yelling orders.

Now, there's a change in the mechanical noises. The drill stem is revolving. Joseph has a satisfied look. He says, 'It go very good, Mister Barry. We rest now.'

I think, *wow*.

Around us, as near as a kilometre away, flares burn off the gas that could power a town, and past those wild flames, scores more reach to the horizon.

An hour later Mans yells, 'One of you come down and eat.' I go down the vertical ladder slowly, meticulously, making certain I always have one hand tightly gripping the steel side rail. Ah, safety.

Mans is in a small enclosure, pushing and pulling levers and yelling goddamns to the Arab roughneck platform crew. They seem to not care that they're being goddamned, and they chatter away in Arabic.

He says to me, 'Australian, eh?'

'Yeah. Australian.'

'Not a limey, eh?'

'No.'

'Okay, then. We'll try to make it work. I'll keep Joseph up there for two more shifts, after that, you're on your own. Okay?'

'Yeah.'

The Arab crew rides in the back of the pickup, laughing and chattering away as though they're coming home from a picnic.

I say as little as I can, but something that happened during the shift intrigues me. I have to ask. 'Mans,' I say, 'Where did the crew disappear to during the shift?'

'Prayers. They're Muslims.'

'Oh, I see.'

But I don't see. I have no idea what he means. I know Arabs have their very strict religion, but I know nothing about it. All I know is it's something to do with Islam and Mecca and Mohammed, and that the Arabs and the Jews don't get on; that's all I know. But I'm not going to ask Mans any more. I'll learn.

Before arriving at the wire fence with barbwire on top that surrounds our trailers, the Arabs jump from the rear of the pickup and, still laughing and chattering, walk to what looks like a hovel.

I have a hot shower and change my clothing, and then go to the dining trailer to eat dinner. It's nearly one in the morning. Apart from the cook, Mans and I are alone.

He says to me, 'Well, at least you didn't kill yourself.'

'I tried hard not to, but I can see how it can happen.'

'Yes, it's different over here. We try to have reasonable housekeeping on the rig, but the Arabs don't see life as we do. Many of them seem keen to meet Allah. My tip to you is to be careful, but not so careful that you slow things up. You got to know that I've got a drilling program, and if I don't get footage, the tool-pusher gets up my arse.'

'All right.'

The cook brings Mans a huge steak which smells delicious. He looks at the steak, loads vegetables onto his plate, then he's into it. I've not seen steak this size since being in Australia and Canada.

The cook says to me, 'Same for you?'

'Yeah. *Great.*'

Mans grunts a lot. He's like an animal eating a kill, and he holds his knife with the same grip I've seen other American and Canadians use, a grip one would use when holding a dagger. Etiquette is not going to be important here.

The cook brings my steak. It's too rare for me, but I say nothing. The cook joins us holding a small shot-glass that's probably got rye whiskey in it. I hesitate to ask how he can have alcohol in this Muslim country. He says to Mans, 'You want a drink?'

'Got any Scotch?'

'Yes. You want a couple of fingers?'

'Make it three fingers, then I'll hit the sack.'

The cook goes to the kitchen, stops at the doorway, and says to me, 'And you?'

'No thanks. I reckon I'll hit my bunk.'

It's been a long day. Sleeping will come easily.

~

I soon get used to what happens here, but I can't get used to the oilrig's dangers. I'm traumatized when Mans tells me to take the grease gun to the very top of the rig, one-hundred and fifty-feet from the ground, to grease the top bearings. The rig shakes, and I feel vibrations from the spinning drill travel along my hands and arms. I wonder if it's customary to be up here while the rig's drilling. I hear him abusing me for my slowness, but it's difficult carrying the grease gun and keeping at least one hand on the ladder. I'm not going to allow him to get at me. I want to stay alive. Unlike the Arabs, I'm in no hurry to meet their Allah, or anyone else's God.

I'm only a few meters down the ladder and I hear him yell, 'Goddamn it, hurry up. We're going to replace the drill. I'm going to pull it all out.'

I wonder why he wants to pull five-thousand feet of drill stem up? How does he know the diamond-tipped drill needs replacing? I'd like to yell to him that we should wait for two hours so the next shift can do all of that.

The drill stems are wet and caked with mud; the steel cable has needle-sharp slivers of wire; the steel clip that lifts the stems from five-thousand feet below is difficult to loosen, and I have to lean out over a ninety foot drop to twist a gathering rope around the stems. Then when the threaded joint is uncoupled from below and the drill stems are positioned under me, I uncouple the steel clip and fling the fifty-foot long length into a finger rack. It's dangerous and tiring work.

But when all that's done, and the drill bit is replaced, it all happens in reverse; everything gets screwed together and five-thousand feet of stem goes back into the hole.

When Mans believes I'm slowing down, he sends Joseph up to help me, but that happens on no other shift, and it's a reflection of my reluctance to risk my life and limbs.

Joseph says to me, 'Mister Barry, you no like this work, eh?'

'I don't like it at all, Joseph; I hate it. It's too dangerous.'

He says, 'Dangerous?'

'Yes. Dangerous. One slip up here and we're dead.'

'But Mister Barry, we no slip. Why we want to slip?'

He and I have different values. He comes from Somalia where the people scratch out a mere existence, and if they die old, it's at the age of forty. In Somalia a lost life isn't important.

I look at Joseph's patched and torn clothes ingrained with grease, oil and drilling mud. His shoes are totally inadequate, and he wears no work gloves to protect his skin from cuts and abrasion. He's black, but his hands are red with dried blood.

He says to me, 'Mister Barry, we can rest now; the drill go slowly. We not having to put more stem on this shift.'

I feel ridiculous being addressed as Mister Barry. I've always hated using the title for others, and I definitely hate it used for me. I say to Joseph, 'I wish you'd stop calling me Mister Barry.'

'Why? What you say that to me for?'

'Because I don't want to be a mister. I don't call you Mister Joseph, do I?'

He gives a big laugh and says, 'You are a mister; I not a mister. I am Somalian.'

I say, 'Well, from now on you are a mister; I'm calling you Mister Joseph, Mister Joseph.'

Now he's really laughing. 'Hah, hah, hah. You can't do this.'

'Oh, yes, I can. Mister Joseph; Mister Joseph; Mister Joseph.'

'But, Mister Barry, I must say Mister Barry. All workers must say mister to white people.'

'There's no reason to. It's elitist. White people are no better than you are. I tell you what, at least stop calling me mister when we're up here on the derrick; I'm Barry and you're Joseph, all right?'

Joseph reluctantly agrees. But he doesn't stop. I'm always going to be a mister to him.

A shift rotation has Mans and his crew working in daylight, and I learn why no one likes days. By eight in the morning the temperature is eighty degrees, and by noon it's just under a hundred. My body is constantly wet from perspiration; it stings my eyes and makes it easy to mistake getting proper footing and secure handgrips. On one occasion, we withdraw five-thousand six-hundred feet of drill stem, seventy-four lengths of heavy pipe, and then, when the drill's replaced, down it all goes again. Then the drill comes off and Mans goes off his brain and tells us we're all useless sons of bitches because he's now got to fish for the lost drill. So seventy-four lengths are withdrawn again, and Mans does delicate searching, fishing for the lost drill bit.

At the end of the shift, I shower and sleep. I'm too tired to eat. It's the hardest day's work I'll ever do.

No, it's not.

Mans says to me next morning, 'We're going to have a big one today.'

'Oh,' I say, 'I thought we had a big one yesterday.'

'Hell, no, that was nothing. That's the stuff that goes on. It's the luck of the draw what happens on a shift. The tool-pusher got up me for losing that bit and having to fish for it. But I'll tell you what, those goddamned Arabs won't screw me again. I'll kick their arsehole so hard it'll come out of their mouths.'

I reckon he could do that. He's big and mean enough to.

We lug lots of large-diameter steel pipe up to the platform, and it all goes down the drill hole. It takes a whole shift to accomplish this, and I'm buggered.

It's time for the shift change and Mans says to me, 'The other crew will bring us something to eat.'

'*Bring*? Why?'

'We're going to work a double shift. We're going to help them cement the hole.'

I'm alarmed. A double shift? I'm barely able to move after this shift casing the hole. I say to him, 'This is no fucking good. We shouldn't have to work another fucking shift. Mate, I'm buggered.'

He laughs. 'You'll goddamned do what I tell you to do. We're going to be here until morning.'

When the Arabs open bags of cement, the dust flies all over and completely covers them and everything else. It's in our eyes and up our noses and in our mouths, and our own juices mix with the dust, so we're all chewing wet cement.

I want to … I *have* to stop soon. But Mans will thump the Christ out of me if I complain. There's a need for an electric-welding job to join some steel casing, and the rig mechanic that does this has gone to camp for spare parts. Mans and the tool-pusher are really pissed-off, and they're goddamning everyone and everything.

I say to the tool-pusher, 'I can do it.'

'You?'

'Yeah. I'm a plumber, and it's just a bit of pipe.'

He almost gives me a smile, and that's the first from him. This Yank's a bastard of the highest calibre. A smile from him must almost break the unused-to-smiling skin on his face.

He says, 'Goddamn, that's good. You do this weld, and I'll take you back to camp and we'll get drunk.'

I have loads of experience at welding, but only with acetylene and oxygen, but as a plumbing apprentice my teacher at the St George Technical College did give us one lesson doing electric welding. So I reckon I can do this job.

The tool-pusher points to a vertical weld. I can only electric weld when the metal's on a bench and when there's no gap; and even then it's risky.

I say to him, 'There'll be no stress on the weld, will there?'

'Hell, yes. When the weld's done we'll drop the top of the casing. There's going to be five-thousand feet of casing attached.'

I get the welding mask on and guess at power settings. I strike an arc, but none of the welding rod sticks to the pipe. I guess at another setting, I strike the arc, and this time it sticks—kind of. Over half an hour I weld and weld, and grind off mistakes, and weld again. It's a terrible job. It can't possibly hold.

Mans orders the Arab roughnecks to connect the steel-wire rope. He gingerly lifts the casing pipe; the holding tongs are removed, then he slowly lowers the casing pipe. It holds.

Back at camp I feign sickness by rushing to the toilet, then coming out, then rushing in again. The tool-pusher says, 'Let's get some whiskey.'

I say to him, 'Ah, I've got some trouble in my stomach. Can I cancel out? Can I have a drink with you tomorrow?'

'Hell, yes. Tomorrow's fine. We'll go to the Dukhan Beach and Sailing Club.'

'Sailing Club?'

'Yeah; some limey ex-pats have got a club down on the Gulf.'

'For sailing?'

'Hell no. All that happens there is drinking.'

I sleep for eight hours.

When I ask Hoppy, the clerk, about the Beach and Sailing club, he tells me the limeys started it, that it's five miles from camp on the Gulf, and that it and the oil camp compounds are the only places where alcohol is allowed. He says it's the only place you'll see any Western women, and they're the wives of the limey oil crews. 'But a warning, don't get involved. Their husbands will kill you.'

'Yeah?'

'Yeah, an Irishman had an accident a month ago. He fell from a drilling platform.'

'An accident?'

'Yeah. That's what the husband of the woman the Irishman screwed said. He slipped and fell.'

'Oh.'

~

Being at the Dukhan Beach and Sailing Club is like being at an after-game Rugby party. Mostly I hear British accents yelling, telling jokes and singing, but there's an occasional American and Canadian accent. I've not seen a European woman for a month, and it's difficult keeping my eyes where they sensibly should be. Everyone knows there's a new stranger in the club, and everyone knows it's me, and that I'm Australian. I get a warm welcome, and I've got drinks lined up that someone has bought, and I'm doing what I can to act like a stereotypical Australian. But it's tough.

I feel good, and when songs are sung that I know, I sing along, and that's uncommon. After a while I lung about and quip back to smart remarks about colonials and convicts and Australians sleeping with and fucking sheep. I stand on a barstool to sing a slurred-voiced version of *Waltzing Matilda*, but I'm yelled at to get down and shut up. I don't.

The Beach and Sailing Club is closing, and four-wheel-drive Land Rovers are driven away by those that shouldn't be driving. I look about to get my bearings then go towards where my camp should be.

My alarm clock goes off at six-thirty, but it's change of shift and there's no work for me today. And that's just as well. I lie stupefied on my bunk. With my eyes closed, I analyse last night's movements. I was drunk, but I was scrupulously careful not to say anything out of line to any expatriate's wife, so I shouldn't get murdered. But the Beach and Sailing Club's five miles distant, so how did I get back to camp?

Of the compass directions, northwest is where I needed to walk. East is the Gulf and south is the desert and death. How did I know in which direction to walk? Am I Christ? I hold my arms out like I'm welcoming the masses. I'm Christ. I really believe I'm Jesus Christ.

A Land Rover comes to our camp and goes straight past the armed soldier on guard at the gate. Europeans don't get challenged.

An Englishman says to me, 'Are you ready?'

'*Ready?*'

'Yes, ready for cricket practice.'

'*Cricket practice?*'

He smiles. You don't remember, do you?'

'No.'

'All right then. Last night we told you about the test match that's coming up: England versus India. Do you remember that?'

'No.'

'Oh. You don't remember saying that you played district cricket in Australia, that Australia's opener Arthur Morris is a friend of yours, and that you played cricket with him?'

'No.'

'That's unfortunate. Because we had a selection meeting at the Beach club, and we've put you in the team; you'll go in third drop for England.'

'Oh, mate, to tell you the truth I'm feeling quite sick, hungover I suppose. Can I give it a miss? Drop me from the team, eh?'

'Drop you? Oh, no. We won't do that. The game's next Saturday. You told us you're on shift then, but we'll do something about it. It'll be fine.'

And off he goes shaking his head repeating, 'Arthur Morris, Arthur Morris …'

I played cricket for the Peakhurst Waratahs Club under-sixteen's in 1951. I wasn't an outstanding cricketer. Mister Morris, the father of the famous Australian cricketer Arthur Morris, was my sixth-class schoolteacher at Beverly Hills Public School. I've never met Arthur. But my now dead father did buy a second-hand refrigerator from Sid Barnes, and I did see the famous Don Bradman at the Sydney Cricket Ground in one of his last games.

Hell; what did I say to them last night?

The Darwish General Store is near our camp. I'm uncertain if it's run by a man named Darwish, or Darwish is where it's located, but I go there to get shaving cream, cigarettes and chocolate. Everything I buy there must be remarkably good because the busy little Arab that runs the store always says it has a lifetime guarantee. There's a notice board there that's mostly used by English-speaking people to sell unwanted things, probably when they're being repatriated to Britain, and it's where social events are advertised. A printed notice has details of the upcoming England-versus-India test match and there's a handwritten appeal at the bottom asking for catering help. Lisa needs willing workers.

I've been giving this cricket match more thought. It could be interesting and a good way to meet others for a social game, but the advertisement suggests that it's more than a social game, and if Lisa needs willing workers, there'll be plenty of spectators. If I were a good cricketer, I'd love to have people yell out, 'Good shot, Barry,' or to clap and cheer me when I hit a four, but I'm not capable of either. I must at all costs not play in this cricket game.

I was becoming friendly with Derek, the 'Jack-of-all-trades' drilling-rig mechanic—a demanding job. He's got my sympathy because he's always getting radio messages about problems at the rig. I admire how he can fix the huge Autocar trucks, and rig machinery and electricity, and do the welding. He deserves to get well paid, and he's told me that this tour of work will give him and his wife enough money to put a deposit on their dream cottage in outer London. But I won't get any friendlier with him now because while he was driving to Doha airport to pick up spare parts for the rig, an old ex-Army Blitz wagon ahead of him dropped one of its load of large rocks. The odds of it bouncing from the road, then through the front window of his pickup truck were small, but it did, and he was killed.

There's a collection in camp to buy a wreath that will be at his funeral in England. Derek is repatriated in a metal casket, and now everyone's talking about him as if he were a saint.

It's a week of disasters on the drilling rig. An Arab roughneck gets his hand mangled in the draw-works machinery; another Arab roughneck gets all his front teeth knocked out by a steel sling and another Arab roughneck gets his jaw broken by a revolving chain. Then five Arabs get hurt when a bus rolls over, and on another drilling rig ten miles away, a derrick-man falls ninety feet to his death. Safety harnesses are to be used by us derrick-men while we're on the monkey-board, but they're a damn nuisance—too restricting.

The derrick-man I replaced fell with his harness attached, his stomach muscles were torn, and his head was bashed in as he swung in mid-air.

A prerequisite to coming to Qatar was that a last will and testaments be prepared in London by Keir & Cawder Arrow Drilling's solicitors. I'd never had a will because I have nothing to leave anyone, so the forced preparation of one should've made me aware that there are big dangers in this job. I mailed the will to my sister in Australia and wrote that she mustn't tell mum about it. She wrote back demanding to know why a will, and was it dangerous working on an oil derrick? I wrote back saying, 'No, it's perfectly safe.'

Some western newspapers are mailed to camp, but by the time they arrive, the news is old. A few men have radios with a short-wave band and tune into the BBC, but there's static, and raising and lowering of volume, and squeaking and squawking.

Hoppy says to me, 'There might be war.'

'War? Against who?'

'Us against *them* ... the Russians.'

I'm aware there's a cold war between the western powers and the Russians, but a cold war's not a war. I say to Hoppy, 'Don't be stupid. I've been to Russia, and I know the Russian people don't want a war. It'll take them fifty years to recover from the last one.'

He says, 'Believe me, Kennedy's not going to take any crap from that arsehole Khrushchev. Last night on BBC it was said that the Ruskies have missiles in Cuba. Goddamned Cuba ... on *America's* back door.'

I say to him, 'I reckon it's all crap. The Russians wouldn't want a war with America. They'd lose. But I tell you what, when I was in Russia I never saw an overweight soldier, they looked fit.'

'So are our boys.'

'Oh yeah, nearly every American soldier I saw looked fat, far too much ice cream and the easy life. '

'Are you a commie?'

'No. I'm not a fucking commie. I went there to, ah... sell some clothes.'

'Eh?'

'I'll tell you about it one day.'

Next day Hoppy's telling me that BBC radio reported that President Kennedy and Khrushchev are threatening each other with atomic annihilation unless the Cuban missiles are removed, and I'm glad my last will and testament is made.

All the Americans in our dining trailer are saying, 'Let's nuke the Russian sons-of-bitches.'

I hope that their President Kennedy doesn't want to do that.

An American driller says to me, 'I hear you're a commie.'

'No. I'm not.'

'Hoppy told me that you are; that you've been to Russia for training, and you're spying for them, reporting to them about oil production.'

'That's fucking bullshit.'

'According to him it's not. He says we've got to keep our eyes on you.'

I'm not surprised that the Americans think communist sympathizers are everywhere. They're like that, fanatical about commos, but *me* a Communist?

I say to him, 'You've got me. I've got a radio in my trailer, and I report every night to Moscow about how deep we've drilled the hole, and what we have to eat, and I'm convincing the Arabs to have an uprising and murder all you Americans in your beds, you fucking drongo.'

Now the American's going around telling everyone I'm a radical and I might just be crazy.

Mans Sherwood corners me, and he looks as though he's going to punch my head in. I'm not looking forward to that. He says, 'You goddamned cock-sucking son-of-a-bitch, what are you doing to me?'

Anyone that does anything to Mans is dead; we all know that, so I'm concerned. I say to him, 'Ah … tell me?'

He says, 'You've got the shifts changed over a day early so you can play goddamned cricket with the goddamned limeys.'

'No, I didn't. I don't even want to play cricket. The blokes at the Beach club want me to, but I'm not going to play.'

'The tool-pusher told me that a limey tool-pusher on another rig asked him to take you off shift. You're needed to play a game, because you're an Australian champion.'

Christ!

I say to Mans, 'I'm not a champion at anything, and I don't want … no, I won't play in the fucking game. Tell the tool-pusher to tell them to go to buggery.'

I cringe and take a slow step backwards while Mans digests what I say. But I reckon I'm the right distance away from him to be hit with a haymaker punch, so I go forward to where I was. I can wrestle him from here, then quickly bugger off.

He says, 'It was nothing to do with you?'

'*No.*'

'Okay; well it's done now, so I'll be coming to watch you beat the crap out of the limeys. You *have to.*'

~

I wear daggy sandshoes that have travelled with me from Australia and white shorts and shirt that someone told me to wear, and everyone's saying hello. A pommie bloke says to me, 'I'm the skipper. Douglas is my name; great to have you on our side.'

'Thanks. But, mate, about the Arthur Morris business, I—'

'Oh, yes! I'm told you played with him.'

'No, I ah—'

'Just a moment,' he says as he takes an Indian man by the shoulders, 'Naresh, meet our Australian player. Meet Barry.'

Naresh says, 'Oh, very-verygladtomeetyou. I hope you're not going to be too hard on us today? So it's Arthur Morris you played with, eh?'

'No. I don't know how …'

He grabs a tall Indian by his waist and says, 'Meet Barry, he's played with the great Arthur Morris.'

'Very- verygladtomeetyou,' he says.

Now there's nothing I can do about the great Arthur Morris and me. Somehow, I've got to go through with the charade.

Some of us are on the field, which is not a field because it's all sand, then the coin is tossed and we hear that India's batting. Great.

The Indian openers are good and hit balls all over the place. I pray that none are hit near me at second slip. A ball goes well above my head, so I do a ballet-like jump into the air with my arms extended, and I'm relieved that it's way too high.

The captain says to me, 'Good try; well done.'

The India team's all out for nearly one-hundred-and-fifty runs when we go to lunch, and as we casually walk from the field congratulating each other for getting them all out, I see Mans Sherwood sitting under the shade of a tree. He smiles, and that's unusual for him.

Douglas, England's captain comes to me and says, 'I have to put our regular openers in. You'll go in third drop. I hope you don't mind?' He laughs. 'I suppose you and Arthur used to open the innings, eh?'

I say nothing. I'm hoping that the players before me break all world records and get enough to win without a wicket falling. But they don't.

The tall Indian bowler seems to go much further back for his run-up to bowl to me. I stand at the crease, hit the ground a few times with the cricket bat, ask the umpire to give me middle stump, scratch a mark on the crease and hold the bat in the air while I look around the field. My hands, arms, head and body run with sweat, and it's stinging my eyes. I sense movement behind me; the wicketkeeper is going back a few paces.

Shit!

The tall Indian bowler starts his run, and I hear Mans' Canadian voice yell, 'Come on Aussie!'

Shit!

This tall Indian bowler ought to run the one-hundred metres for India in the Olympics, because he's coming at me like an express train.

Shit!

I know I can't skilfully block the ball like the great Arthur Morris. I don't know how to do that. My only hope of saving face is to wallop the ball for six.

The ball's in the air somewhere between the bowler's hands and me, so I close my eyes and swing. There's the sound of stumps breaking behind me. The all-Indian team jump into the air and say, *'How's that?'*

It's a lonely walk from the wicket to where Lisa has her willing workers employed pouring cups of tea and buttering scones, but I do the walk with dignity. I hold aloft my cricket bat and nod thanks while everyone says things like, 'Bad luck.'

Mans Sherwood says nothing. He's got a scowl on his face.

India beats England, and, regretfully, the end-of-game drinks at the Beach Club don't include the Indian players. They're not allowed in.

I don't get selected for the second test match.

~

Mans Sherwood is yelling at everyone on his shift, pushing them to go faster to get more footage drilled. I desperately want to tell him to get fucked. And I often do tell him that, but only when my back's to him or when he can't possibly hear what I say. The Arab crew is treated far worse than I am, and I marvel at their ability to take it, but I know they have no option.

I see danger in almost every aspect of my work, and it's having a psychological effect. I'm hesitant climbing and descending the derrick ladder. I'm moving slowly on the monkey-board, and I fear greasing the derrick's top bearing. I spend much time thinking about my situation, considering the possibilities for getting out. The contract I've signed states that I must stay with the company twelve months, and should I leave before that, I have to pay to have a replacement come from London. I haven't yet earned enough to do that.

One English worker has been repatriated to London at the company's cost. The tool-pusher got rid of him because he was doing irrational things that endangered his and others' lives. I'm told that the Englishman was a good actor, that he contrived his dismissal. Somehow, I'm going to find a way to get myself fired. Feigning madness is not an option, it takes too long to establish madness, besides, it's already been done once by that bloody Englishman.

Everyone knows Mans is a bastard, even the boss. But Mans is a key person. I'm not.

At the end of a graveyard shift, I stand on the derrick platform looking at the long licks of flames coming from gas flares. The first is close—about a mile away—and then they're randomly spaced, circling us all the way to the horizon. It reminds me of the flame that burns on the gas flare at Sydney's Kurnell oil refinery, and I think of home in Australia and everything I miss, then I think about what seems like my prison sentence here. I count how much longer I have to serve—nine months minimum, the same time it takes for life to gestate in the womb. Mans Sherwood is my prison warder.

How does one defeat a prison warder? I can't think of an example, not even a movie where Humphrey Bogart, the toughest of the tough, does it. So how can I?

From below me, I hear my prison warder yell, 'Hey! Don't bother to come down.'

I look at my watch. It's the end of the shift. What did Mans mean about not going down?

I yell to him, 'Why not?'

He yells, 'We've got to do more cementing.'

I yell, 'That's for the day shift to do.'

He yells, 'Stay up there.' He runs to the bottom of the ladder and clambers up, taking two rungs at a time. Mans is not the least afraid of heights. He says, 'The tool pusher wants two crews to do the cementing. It'll be quicker.'

'But … that's not fair. We did the last cementing. It's a bastard of a job.'

He goes down the ladder hardly touching any rungs with his feet and yells, 'You fucking stay up there.'

It's over eighty degrees and everyone's sweating. Two-hundred bags of cement are torn open in a frenzy to keep up with Mans' taunts of hurry-hurry-hurry. About one-hundred bags go in the hole, and about one-hundred waft as a dust that eventually falls on everything. It leaves its most dramatic impression on sweaty bodies: we're like moving Norman Lindsay sculptures.

Anyone who stops moving feels the beginnings of the cement setting on their body. When they move, it cracks like glaze crazing.

It's nearly three in the afternoon; we've worked for fifteen hours. Mans goes around telling everyone they've done a good job, but we're so tired we don't think about anything apart from rest.

Mans says to me, 'Don't tell the crew yet, but we've got to work part of the next shift.'

I don't immediately absorb what he's saying. I don't believe him. He's yards away from me when I do absorb it. I yell, *'What?'* But he continues going. I yell at him, 'Hey, you bastard, *stop right there!*'

He stops and I realise what I've just said. Now he stands there with his back to me, not moving. I hope he thought he heard something, but he's not certain what it was. That he'll turn and ask what I said and I'll say, 'Oh, nothing.'

He turns and I can tell from his face that he did hear me.

He says, 'You goddamnedcocksuckingsonofabitch. No one talks to me like that. I'm going to kill you.'

I know he can do that easily. We're standing on a slippery steel platform twenty feet above ground. Near us is a spinning drill, the draw-works machinery, the heavy pipe pliers and eight Arab roughnecks that know something exciting is going to happen.

My mind races. If he decides to hit me, I'm done for, because once he starts punching, he'll not stop, and I'll not get a chance to hit him. And even if I do get to land some blows, it'll be like hitting steel. I'm uncertain what to do.

He stands right in front of me. I stare at his top shirt button and think about kicking him in the testicles—it's about the only way I can win. But he shapes up like a prize-fighter, dances away from me, then to me, then away again. He says, 'I'll throw you off the goddamned rig.'

I realise that he means *physically* throw me off—he's capable of flinging me fifty yards. 'So … you're firing me?'

He stares at me. He doesn't mean that at all.

I goad him. 'You can't fire me. Only the tool-pusher can fire me.' And I laugh.

He says, 'Oh, can't I? Okay, buddy, you're *goddamned fired.*'

So I scurry down the ladder to the ground and I'm off.

He yells, 'Get back here you sonofabitch.'

'No way,' I yell. 'You've fired me.'

He's not going to come after me because he's far too professional; he'll never leave his rig while it's drilling.

The pickup truck waits nearby with the key in the ignition, so I'm off to camp. and I'm happy. *I'm fired; I'm fired; I'm fired.*

The tool-pusher attempts to mediate, but I tell him over and over that I've been sacked, and I can't possibly work with someone that's sacked me. Apparently Mans also says he's not going to work with someone he's sacked.

Cockney Bill sees me and says, 'You lucky bastard; how did you do it?'

'Do what?'

'Get Mans to fire you?'

But I'm not telling Cockney Bill anything because he's got a big mouth.

Amazingly, a rumour gets around that I stood my ground against Mans, that I was going to fight him, and that I'm tough. Mans hears this, too, and he corners me in the ablution trailer and asks me if I want to sort things out, *now*. I tell him he'd be stupid to punch Christ out of me, that he'd get sacked, so we should leave things as they are. He agrees.

The tool-pusher tells me that due to a clash of personalities, I'm to pack my bag and fly to London tomorrow.

Joseph hears I'm leaving and waits outside the wire fence. He calls out, 'Mister Barry!'

I shake hands with him, and he passes me something. I don't immediately look at it, but it feels solid. I'm walking with my back turned to him when I do look. It's a flick-blade knife! Its plastic handle is decorated with a gold bull and a silver bullfighter that's holding a red cape.

Joseph calls out, 'Barry, it will be good for you in fights.'

~

A Canadian pilots the Comet aircraft I'm sitting in, and I hope he's not related to Mans. Qatar is behind us and we're landing at Bahrain. Why? I don't know.

In the stinking hot terminal, I buy a souvenir. An Arab curved-blade knife in a brass scabbard.

In London a British Customs officer asks if I've anything to declare. As he concludes his question, the Arab knife drops from its wrapping onto the terminal floor.

I say to him, 'Ah … yes, a knife.'

He's a good-humoured British customs man. He says, 'That's just a toy.'

I say, 'Yes, it's for my little brother in Australia.'

So he doesn't search the rest of my baggage, and the serious flick-blade knife from Joseph goes into Britain.

I visit the Keir & Cawder Arrow Drilling office to get an unknown amount of money. I may get three months' pay that's been banked for me in London, or I may get that amount less the cost of my airfare, or I may get very little.

The American behind the desk is sickeningly apologetic. But why? There's no reason for him to be. Perhaps he's feeling embarrassed about the awfully bright tie he's wearing. He tells me to sit down, and when I do my bum movement causes the soft-leather seat covering to squeak. I apologise.

He says, 'We're very sorry to have you back in London.'

'I'm very sorry to be back in London … I loved working in Qatar.'

He raises his eyebrows. 'Loved it, eh?'

'Yes.'

He taps his finger on his desk, thinking, then he says, 'The best we can do for you is pay all your banked wages, right?'

'Right.'

'And we'll pay the cost of the airfare to get you back, right?'

'Right.'

'And all we can give you as severance pay is one month's wages, right.'

'*Right*!'

I want to kiss this American and tell him his tie is terrific and that I'll celebrate American Independence Day forever and that I love his President Kennedy, hate Nikita Khrushchev, and I'm glad the commos were kicked out of Cuba. I restrain myself until I'm outside and near the American Embassy. Then I yell out *'You little beauty!'*

I'm going to be able to return to Australia.

15 December 1962.
Dukhan Qatar.
Dear Mum,

For the past week I've been scheming to get away from this place and I think it has worked. I had an argument with the driller and he more or less fired me.

I asked the tool-pusher, the second in charge, if he thought I was fired.

He told me that if I have quit, I would lose a lot of money. As far as I'm concerned, I'm fired.

Yesterday the manager tried to talk me into staying, but I gave him a line of 'bull' and I told him I would not work with the driller. I told him that if I weren't fired, I'd quit.

Later, Hoppy the accountant came to my trailer and asked if tomorrow's plane would be all right. It was very confusing.

I had planned that if I had to quit, I would get a plane to Aden and get a ship from there, but I won't have enough money.

If I'm sacked my fare gets paid back to London, and then I'll have enough money to come home. I might try the Trans-Siberian railway.

Many of the blokes here want me to stay, but I'm acting all hurt by the events. For my liking, things are getting too dangerous on the rig. There have been lots of accidents: one death.

I've had a few slips but managed to save myself. Now I know why we're insured for 10,000 pounds.

Christmas in London won't be all that bad. Write to me at Barons Court.

Love Barry.

1962, Qatar, Doha

Barry in front of the oil rig.

An Arab riding a camel rode out through the desert to the oil rig.

Mohomad and the derrick prepared to move.

Joseph the Somali derrickman and another Somali oil-worker.

Chapter Fifteen

A big farewell party would be nice, but instead of that I'm haggling about money. The Barons Court barons, Albert and Terry, reckon I've put European coins in the gas meter. They have three lots of coins from various countries that are the same size as British coins; the country most represented is Belgium.

Albert says, 'It must be you. Terry and I haven't been to Belgium.'

I know I'm not the present culprit. I have been guilty of putting into the meter's slot the occasional non-British coin; but that was months ago. I say to him, 'Not fucking guilty.'

'Well who else would've done it, a ghost?'

'*Not* fucking guilty.'

Albert is over six-feet tall and he's fat. He stands over me and says, 'So it was a ghost, eh?'

I'm fed up with disagreements about rent money and gas meter money and who stole whose food from the crappy refrigerator, and arguments about whose turn it is to mop the cave floor. Tomorrow I leave for Paris, then to Marseilles to board a ship that's sailing for Japan. The last thing I expected to be accused of was placing delinquent Belgian coins in the gas meter.

~

In Marseilles I argue with a French railway-station attendant. I asked him how to get to the wharves and reckon he's understood my question, but he's determined not to say anything in English to this English pig. He's rambling on. I say to him, 'Mate, I don't speak French, so will you tell me your answer in English?

He answers in French and the only word I understand is *'bateau'*.

I'm surprised at the size of the Messageries Maritimes ship *Cambodge*. It's said to be 15,200 tones, but it looks smaller. Travelling on it will be three classes of passengers; one hundred and seventeen in first class, one hundred and ten in tourist, and fifty-two in Troisiemès. First and tourist class passengers look to have good size cabins, but in Troisiemès, us less-affluent travellers are four to a small cabin.

Another surprise is the large amount of cargo being loaded: machinery, cars, cartons, a small boat with a deck-mounted gun, and sling loads of hessian bags containing something powdery.

The ship's officer says to me in French, 'Welcome aboard, sir.'

I give him my ticket, he looks at it and then says in English, 'Other gangway. All third class passengers use other gangway.'

He doesn't give me a 'sir'.

The food served on the first day at sea is exactly the same as that served on the second day, and I'm already tired of it. I say to the cook, 'Is there anything else but rice?'

He says, 'Wee, monsieur, we ave Riz au Cari.'

I say to him, 'No, no, no. I asked you for something else. You've given us boiled riz for breakfast and fried riz for lunch and dinner. Have you got anything else?'

'No, monsieur. Every passenger like having the riz.'

And he's quite right. Everyone else travelling in third class is Asian or Indian, and that's what they like to eat.

I share a cabin with three Mandarin-speaking Asians, so we have nodding and hand-gesturing communication. They think I'm British, and nothing I do can convince them otherwise; I even try whistling *Waltzing*

Matilda and hopping around like a kangaroo. They probably believe I'm mad.

Third class is located in the front of the ship. I can hear the sound of the bow breaking through every wave, especially in the toilets at the very front. Third class has little outside deck space and no deck chairs. I see mostly European passengers having a good time on the second class area. They're lolling in the sun on nice deck chairs with waiters bringing them fancy drinks. Between the 'them' and the 'us' is a companionway guarded by a bored French seaman who takes pleasure in stopping any Asian that tries to go out of Troisièmes to above their station.

I go past him, and he says nothing but 'Bonjour.'

I 'Bonjour' him back.

When I sit in a deck chair a man says, 'Hello, I haven't seen you before.'

'No, that's because I've just sneaked up from third class.'

'Third class? What's it like down there?'

'Basic. Yeah, basic; that's about the best word to describe it.'

'But I thought there are only Asians travelling there?'

'There are—Asians and me, an Australian.'

'Ah; Australian?'

'Yeah …' I think about what I said to him. It might sound like I was slighting Asians, being racist. 'But there's nothing wrong with being Asian.'

He nods. 'No; of course not. But they are different.'

'Different? Of course they're different. They're bloody Asians. They come from Asia.'

The man goes away mumbling and moments later a crewman comes and says to me, 'Monsieur, what ize your cabin number?' He escorts me back to riz class.

Again we've got only riz for dinner, so I say to the chef, 'Mate, please give me something else. The curry in your riz is killing me. My stomach's aching, and I'm spending half my day in the toilet.'

I reckon he pretends not to know more English than he speaks. He says, 'Nozing else, ve only aze riz, riz au curi.'

I pass the current companionway guard and sniff real food. I reckon it's meat, probably beef stew, and I'm salivating.

A tall, gangling man says to me in a very public-school British accent, 'Hello, old chap, who are you?'

'Barry's my name. Barry White.'

'And where is Barry White from?'

'Do you mean five minutes ago, or what country?'

'Both, old chap.'

'Five minutes ago I was in curry-class, but I'm from Australia.'

'Curry class?'

'Yeah, the crowd in the front of the ship.'

'A rather amusing description … curry-class. Well, I'm Clifford; pleased to meet you Barry White.'

I don't know what to make of this Clifford. He's the epitome of everything I hate: upper-class elitism and speech wrought by an English Public School education.

Clifford says, 'I'm an ornithologist; what do you do?' I look at him with a blank stare, and he says, 'Birds, it's to do with birds.'

'I'm a plumber, and I know it's to do with birds. I'm not a fucking idiot.'

'How interesting.'

Perhaps I should say to him that his job as an ornithologist is interesting, but I don't; it must be awfully boring.

Clifford says, 'Oh look, there's John. John, I'm over here!'

John is also English. He doesn't speak like a Public School educated Englishman, but he probably should because he's a solicitor.

I strike up a friendship, have no trouble passing the companionway guard and engage in pleasant meetings in second class. They even have waiters bring them cups of tea and biscuits.

John says, 'We're in Port Said tomorrow; what are you planning to do?'

I'm planning nothing because everything in the ship's newsletter—that's not available in third class—costs money. I say, 'I'm just going to walk around.'

'So am I,' says Clifford.

Clifford and I visit a marketplace, but I'm not comfortable with him because he's dressed like a Russian Cossack. His red-silk shirt buttons across his chest and has floppy sleeves, and his riding britches tuck into high-topped riding boots. He's weird.

He says, 'Have you heard of the Aswan Dam?'

'No.'

'The Russians are building it. It's going to stop the flow of the Nile River.'

'Never heard of it.'

'You don't know much, do you?'

'I mightn't know much about Russian dams, but I know you look stupid. Why are you dressed like that? Where did you get that fucking stupid shirt?'

'This, fucking stupid shirt, as you put it, is going to keep us out of trouble.'

'How?'

'Because the Egyptians are afraid of the Russians and …'

Three small boys, a small Egyptian gang, run to us offering anything and everything: their sister or mothers or brothers for fucking, and their valuable family antiques that came from under the pyramids, and anything else the Effendis want.

Clifford says to them in a gruff tone, like how a Russian KGB agent would speak, 'Nyet!'

And they run away.

We travel by taxi to the centre of Port Said, a short two-mile journey. The driver wants to be paid two pounds. I say, '*What?*'

Clifford tells me to pay the man. But I'm not going to pay him because he's exploiting us. I argue with Clifford, and he says, 'Then I'll pay him.'

I say, 'No; neither of us is paying two pounds when the journey's only worth a maximum of five shillings.'

'Pay the man,' Clifford says.

The taxi driver knows I'm reluctant to pay, so he focuses on Clifford. He says, 'Mister, two pounds is very fair; you must pay two pounds.'

I try to remember some Arabic words used in Qatar. I want to tell this man what I think, but I only remember the word for hurry and get the hammer—both inappropriate.

A crowd gathers around the taxi, so it would be foolish for either of us to get out. But I do get out, and I stand at the driver's window telling him he's a robbing bastard.

Clifford's still in the taxi and he says in a loud voice, *'Pay the man his money. Pay him two pounds.'*

The crowd gets bigger. Arabs scream at me, and I regret getting out of the taxi. I hear someone yell orders in Arabic at the rear of the crowd. The crowd parts, and a uniformed man wearing Sam Browne webbing and a pistol comes through the gap. He gives more orders and pushes people away. He's not friendly.

Clifford says to me, 'I'll handle this.' He yells a jumble of words that might be Russian or gibberish.

The policeman looks at him: he's curious.

Clifford yells some more Russian or gibberish, and the policeman changes his attitude; he even looks afraid.

Clifford changes to speaking broken English. 'Comrade policeman; we have a little misunderstanding, we ask you to give the driver his money.' He gives the policeman two pounds, says, '*Spasibo*,' then tows me away from the crowd saying, 'Ruski; Ruski; Ruski.' He says to me, 'Old boy, you very nearly had us in a spot of bother.'

I realise I acted stupidly. I'm an experienced traveller, but what I did was worthy of a new chum, a greenhorn, a wet-behind-the-ears adventurer. I can understand that a first-time adventurer from Australia, someone on their way to England, might do what I did, but not me. But

I'm not going to admit it to this weirdly dressed pommy ornithologist that's going to spend his life doing something useless like looking at birds.

He's a strange bird himself—the way he dresses, speaks and acts. I wouldn't be surprised if he were a poofter or went looking for those young Arabs. Come to think of it, why did he befriend me? Did he believe that because I'm travelling third class I might like to be his 'bum-boy'? I've been travelling for nearly three years, and this is the first time I think I've been targeted by a poofter. I need to be careful.

~

I'm standing in blazing heat at the ship's handrail watching the activity on the banks of the Suez Canal. Behind me, second class passengers are doing the same, but they're in comfortable deck chairs, and above us, first class passengers are doing it in style under a canvas canopy.

Few others in third class bother to be here. They know it's not smart to be in the sun. A French seaman says to me, '*Ca va.*'

'Sorry but I speak no French.'

'Ah, English.'

'No, Australian.'

'Australian, so you ave to speak English, eh?'

'Of course.'

'What port you leave zee ship?'

'Yokohama.'

'Ah, so you are with uz all zee way? Very good.' Then he leaves.

I see Clifford with a group of people and they're all laughing. He sees me and gestures to me to join them. I gesture to him a very positive, no. I'm going to keep away from Clifford.

We dock at Aden, another hot Arab City full of struggling people who, legitimately, want to exploit affluent Europeans.

The same French seaman says, 'You are not going ashore monsieur?'

'No.'

'Good, zhere is little to zee here. Iz it zat you ave no monies to spend?'

He's quite right. But he doesn't have to be brilliant to know that. I'm the only non-Asian in riz class. I say to him, 'From Japan I get a ship to Australia. I'm going home. I think I'll have enough money to do that, but I've got nothing to spare.'

'Zo, a lettle extra monies vould be nice?'

'A lettle extra monies vould be *very* nice.' If I say anything more to him I'm definitely not going to mimic his English pronunciation.

'Ah, perhapz I can be of azzistance with zat.'

I've got a fair idea what he's going to suggest. I reckon I've struck another poofter, one thinking I'm desperate enough to take a turn in the barrel—or whatever name French sailors have for that English sailor's term. I say to him, 'Fuck off, mate.'

'All it vould mean iz taking zee small package ashore in Bombay.'

I regret saying fuck off. 'Oh, and what would be in the small package?'

'Ah, it iz not important. Perhapz you vill zhink about it. Ve vill speak again. Zo for now, au revoir, monsieur.'

'Yeah; arev warr.'

I'm desperate to have a few cold beers, but I can only do that in second class, so I must risk seeing Clifford. I sit alone at the small bar. I've had four drinks when John joins me. We have many beers and are soon telling our life stories.

He's going back to his Chinese wife in Hong Kong after a failed attempt at extracting money from his reasonably-well-to-do English family. When we're both nearly drunk he tells me that his law practice in Hong Kong needs an injection of funds, otherwise he's going to embarrass the family and be declared bankrupt. 'But they don't care. They've never approved of me having a Chinese wife.'

The French seaman actively seeks me out and is very persuasive. He's got the actions of a spiv—always looking over his shoulder before he speaks, then whispers with his eyes darting about. I hate it when he whispers because he comes close, and he has the vilest breath.

'Zo, monsieur, ave you conzidered my propozal?'

'Yes, but I need to know more. I need to know what's in your little package.'

'Er … ze truth iz zat ze Indian Customs menz do a full body search of ze crews, but zhey don't do it to zee English; understand?'

'Yes.'

'Zo, I aze a body belt zat you vill vear ashore, understand?'

'Yes; but what's in the body belt?'

'I vill tell youze, but I must ave your assurance. I must know your attitude, understand?'

'What's in the fucking body belt? Drugs?'

He acts, or really is, very offended. 'Ohhhh, monsieur, nozing liks zat. I propose zat you zhinks about my proposal.'

'Okay. But what kind of money are you talking about?'

'Ve will discuss zis, but it vill be good.'

I do need money. I believe I have enough to buy a boat ticket from Japan to Australia—maybe. 'So I can decide, you must tell me now what's going to be in the body belt; okay?'

He looks around; his eyes dart about and his stinking breath is next to my face. 'Et iz just a little gold.'

'Gold!'

'Shush, shush *shush*; not zo loud.'

'Gold; what do you mean by *a little*? If it were only a little it'll fit easily into a pocket, there'd be no need for a body belt.'

'Ahhh, vell, it iz actually, ah, four bars.'

'Four bars!'

'Shush; please monsieur; *speak softly*.' He goes away saying, 'Ve vill speak tomorrow, eh?'

I want the money the French seaman is offering, but are the risks worth taking?

I think about the heat of Bombay and how I'll be dressed—a short sleeve shirt and long trousers. How on earth can a body belt containing four bars of gold be concealed under those clothes? How much will it weigh? And how do I disguise carrying this weight? I suspect that Indian customs are practised at detecting smugglers, so an Australian that's got an unusually thick waistline would surely be searched. My mental picture of a Bombay gaol isn't nice. I see disease and squalor and beatings and bastardization, and possible death.

I decide I don't want a bar of the French seaman's gold bars, but how do I tell him?

I know about his smuggling plans. If he decides he can't take the risk of me telling others, he'll dump me over the side of the ship: it'd be easy. All he has to do is get me to meet him at night, then he and a fellow smuggler each take one side of me, and plonk; I'm in the Arabian Sea.

The French seaman is much more comfortable speaking to me in darkness. He says, 'Vell monsieur; you will do it?'

'No, I can't risk it.'

'Monsier, az I zaid, zear iz little risk.'

'Ah, but there is. I didn't tell you I have a criminal record in Australia. The Australian police know I'm out of Australia, and they've, probably, advised the Indian police that if I enter through an Indian port, I'm worth looking at, that I may be smuggling, say, ah, gold bars.'

'*Merde!*'

I know about ten French words; *'merde'* is not one of them, but if I had to guess it's meaning, I'd say he's swearing. I say to him, 'So you can understand why I won't do your smuggling?'

'Of course, of course. I am grateful. You must not do it.'

It gets around the ship's crew that I'm an Australian master criminal and remarkable things happen. The crew greets me with a friendly, '*Ca va?*' And I say, '*Ca va?*' to them, and the third-class chef asks if he can cook me some meat. Crime does pay.

The night prior to reaching Bombay, the French seaman gives me a friendly '*Ca va?*' and shakes my hand. I feel something passed into my hand, and when I look, I see ten pounds. He says, 'Please enjoy Bombay.'

But no one can possibly enjoy Bombay. The Indian Customs and Immigration inspection is easy: a look at the face, a look at the passport and a stamp on a blank page. Outside the wharf, on the streets of Bombay, is the reality of India—abject poverty.

Not staring is difficult. How can an Australian whose major disappointment as a child was not getting the filling he wanted on his school lunch sandwiches, not be affected. How can I not stare at six-year old children that have ulcers on their eyes and mouth where flies cluster? How can I not stare at a man without arms and legs that gets about on a bit of wood with pram wheels on it? How can I not be repelled by a policeman wielding a long flexible stick onto the backs of begging children?

As the ship sails from port I'm pleased to see the gateway to India get smaller and smaller. I see the French crewman and he looks happy. The gold bars must have got ashore, somehow.

A man I thought to be Indian speaks to me with a perfect English accent. He says, 'I saw the chef give you a meat stew.'

I'm careful because I don't know who he is. 'Did you?'

'Yes, it appeared to be a good stew.'

'It was.'

'My name is Harry; I'm travelling to Colombo.'

'Good.'

'It's uncommon to have a European with us.'

'With us?'

'Us from the sub-continent ... *us* travelling in third class.'

I like him, so I think I trust him. 'Barry is my name; I'm Australian.'

'Yes, I know. We all know about you in third class. We know you don't like curried rice and that you take excursions into second class; we can't do that.'

We lean on the ship's handrail for more than an hour. He delicately, diplomatically, probes me for answers, and I tell him as much as I want to. He does exactly the same with my probes about him.

He tells me that he's in the Ceylonese Army, has been studying at Sandhurst Military College and has been recalled to Ceylon by his commanding officer.

I tell him about my travels, that I'm on my way home to Australia.

He asks my profession.

'Profession? I'm a plumber.'

He can't, or doesn't want to mask his surprise. 'A plumber! And you can afford to travel?'

I can't say to someone from Ceylon who has probably never met a plumber and would treat a person that worked with their hands as inferior that I'm as good as any professional. That I'm a professional plumber. I'm proud to be one. I say to him, 'Our countries are different.'

'Yes, very different.'

I decide not to be delicate or diplomatic. 'Harry, what does being recalled mean?'

'It is not a good thing to have happen. There are some problems in my country ... it will be difficult for you to understand.'

'So you don't want to say too much?'

'I can't say too much. What I can tell you is that my father is a retired High Court Judge with a high profile and we have many political problems in Ceylon.'

'I thought Mrs Bandaranayaka was a good Prime Minister.'

'You know of her?'

'Yes. I read *The Observer* newspaper. I've read that there's a bit of trouble with the Sinhalese and the Burghers and other ethnic groups.'

'You are very well informed. They are the reason for my recall. My superior officers are having some, ah, difficulties. That's why I'm travelling, ah, third class. They fly me to Britain, and I return third class in a ship.'

'That's how it goes.'

We stare at the moon's reflection on the sea and at some lights on the horizon, probably the lights of Goa. The vibration of the ship's propeller shaft is transferred to the handrail, but we only hear the breaking of water from the ship's bow.

Harry says, 'Would you like to meet my parents?'

'Yes.'

'Would you consider staying with us and having dinner?'

'Yes. The ship's at Colombo for two days. That'd be good.'

So a plumber is about to meet a High Court Judge. I doubt if anyone from Chatterton and Stephen, the company I did my plumbing apprenticeship with, has ever stayed with a High Court judge.

I'm anxious to make a good impression with the retired High Court Judge, so I ask a second-class passenger to sneak past the companionway guard to first class to get me a library book. In the book I read that ethnic Tamils have lived in Ceylon for two-thousand five-hundred years and they now want their independence from the rest of Ceylon. It's a land of tea, coffee and gems—mostly rubies, sapphires and moonstone.

I'm ready for the Judge.

Official-looking people meet and escort Harry from the ship. It appears my free meal is gone, but when I walk from the wharf, a car containing Harry and his family stops. The meal's on again.

At their house, his mother gives me a sarong to wear and asks what food I enjoy. I say, 'Nothing too hot.'

But we *do* get hot. I perspire through the meal, and during the night I do an embarrassing search in darkness for their toilet.

All night and in the morning there are people outside Harry's house that appear to be 'official'. When I ask about them, Harry says, 'It's best you ask me little.'

At Singapore, two Canadians join me in rice class and life gets better. Brian and Joe are adventurers that are going to Tokyo, but they've only paid their fare to Kobe. Joe says he should have a cheque waiting for him in Tokyo. I trust them, so I bankroll them their drinking money.

The *Cambodge's* Captain tells passengers they should not go on deck during the ship's passage up the Saigon River. We reckon it's a ridiculous instruction because there's so much to see—dense tropical jungle, small villages and outrigger canoes.

I say to Brian, 'What's that strange-looking boat following us?'

He looks. 'That's a … why that's an Army landing barge.'

'Are they guns on its front?'

'Yes.'

'And those boats coming towards us?'

'Ah, more landing barges; they've got soldiers in them. Hell, and there's two gunboats.'

We go below deck and stay there.

Saigon streets, especially around the wharf area, are interesting but uncomfortable. Sandbagged defence posts on the street corners have armed soldiers behind them, and madmen and women ride very-overloaded under-powered small motorbikes. Sinewy-bodied men pull rickshaws with well-fed Americans dressed in civilian clothes sitting in them—they're obviously soldiers.

Tanks wait outside Ngo Dinh Diem, the President of South Vietnam's, palace. We learn that his own air-force strafed his palace a week earlier.

Brian, Joe and I decide that the safest things to do in Saigon are to drink grog and perve on women.

'Let's get back to the wharf area,' Joe says. 'The prices will be lower there; there's too many Americans in the city centre.'

And they are. We drink in a bar directly opposite the ship's berth with some of our ship's crewmen; they shout us beer. Brian goes away and returns thirty minutes later. He says to a crewman, 'The customs didn't even ask to look at it.'

'Look at it! Look at what?' I ask.

'The package I took on board ship.' He tells us that the reason we're being bought beer is that he's told the Frenchmen we'll take some packages onto the ship.

'What's in them?' I ask.

'They told me its bottles of rice wine.'

'Why the fuck can't they take their own rice wine onto the ship?'

'It's customs and duty and regulations … something like that.'

But they wouldn't drink rice wine; they'd drink French wine. The French are very particular about their wines. We don't understand why they'd want rice wine, but what we do understand is that they'll continue buying us beer while we continue taking wine onto the ship, so we probably smuggle something that could get us put in a Saigon gaol for a long time.

I consult with my image-maker, the French seaman that labelled me as an Australian criminal, about the location in Saigon of young women that may be sympathetic to young travellers sowing some of their wild oats. He says to me, 'Monsieur, I aze made many trips to Saigon, so I can tells you zat near ze wharf is dangerous womens. Zhey vill give you the, ah … disease. You must go elzewhere.'

The taxi driver who takes us to the Caravel Hotel must believe we're well off, because we pass the President's Palace twice. Joe reckons he must be used to carrying stupid Americans that have plenty of money so he says he's going to sort him out. I don't know how he's going to do that, but he speaks in French to him, and I understand only one word: *regrette*. The driver does a u-turn, and he and Joe chatter away in French. I'm very impressed with Joe's French and reckon he's going to be useful on the ship.

Joe says to us, 'It's all arranged.'

'What's arranged?'

'Meeting the women. Later tonight he's going to take us to meet some nice girls.'

'Nice girls?'

'Ones that won't give us any diseases.'

Wild oats are going to be sown.

We go to an upstairs bar in the Caravel Hotel because we've learnt there's bombings of easily accessible bars. Vietcong sympathizers speed past on motor scooters and chuck bombs at Americans mainly, but we look as though we could be Americans, so we're not taking any chances. American servicemen dressed in civilian clothes are all over the place, but they're not difficult to spot, what with their short haircuts and superior strutting walk.

My budget for buying beer gets spent in the first hour, so I have to cash another traveller's cheque, my second last. I'm hoping the Canadians are cheap drunks, but they're not because they're drinking Seagram's Canadian Club. I drink the cheap local Export 33 beer.

Three hours pass and the Canadians are very near to being drunk. I'm feeling pretty good, too, but I'm nervous about being taken by a taxi driver I don't trust to see his 'nice girls'. I say to Joe and Brian, 'We could buy some bottles and take them to the ship to drink.'

They're not excited about my idea.

Brian says, 'But we've got to meet the taxi driver in half an hour; he's taking us to the girls.'

'Mate, we should've given this more thought. We don't know where he's taking us, what it's going to cost and what the girls are like … they might be old hags.'

He says, 'Have you seen an old hag in Saigon yet?'

He's right. The Vietnamese women are beautiful. They mostly wear silk-like trousers and a long, white pinafore-style dress that's split to above their knees. They have beautiful long black hair, and they're always smiling. I'd like to sow some wild oats with one of them. But I'm nervous.

I say, 'What about we give it a miss; what about we do some serious drinking instead, eh?'

Joe says, 'What! Is there something wrong with you? Don't you like women? Are you a homo?'

I can't allow Joe to say that I'm a homo. 'Of course I like women, but I'm not getting myself a load of the clap just for a fuck.'

'But the taxi driver said they're nice girls, *nice girls*, right?'

Joe and Brian fall asleep on the back seat of the speeding taxi, but there's no chance I'll do the same because I reckon this driver is conning us. We pass Hong Thap and Phan Thanh Gian and other streets, and I try to remember their names, but it's hopeless.

I turn around and push Joe, 'Wake up.' They should know what all good adventurers know; that one should never ever go to sleep in a taxi in a strange city.

Joe says, 'Where are we?'

'Dunno; we passed the Independence Palace five minutes ago, and with the speed this driver's going we'll soon be in Cambodia.'

Brian wakes up. 'Cambodia? We're not allowed to go there.'

Sometimes I look behind and see the results of collision-avoiding manoeuvres—bicycle riders waving their arms about in anger at our driver. But he seems not to care. He weaves between lots of bikes, some of them coming towards us.

We drive onto streets without lights, and I reckon we're being abducted, that the taxi driver is probably a Vietcong, and he's taking us to his cadre, or he's a kidnapper that's going to hold us for ransom. We see lights in the distance. Joe says something in French to the driver, and he says something in French to Joe.

Joe says, 'We're there.'

'There? Where?'

'That village.'

'Where?'

'Those lights.' He points to a dozen small ramshackled huts.

Brian says, 'What? *There*?'

The village has few lights, mostly just low-wattage bulbs hung over doorways. Figures in shadows watch the taxi arrive. The driver gets out, and I lean across to take the licence held to his sun visor by rubber bands. The taxi's headlights shine as though illuminating a stage. He speaks in Vietnamese to an older woman. She waves her arms about and shakes her head. It's a *no* and I'm pleased.

He remonstrates with her and passes her money. Now she's smiling—a toothless smile.

The taxi driver says in broken English, 'This woman say okay.'

Brian says, 'Okay to what?'

He tries to laugh, but it's a nervous stutter. 'Okay for you to see nice girls.'

Joe and Brian are out of the taxi and they both preen: Joe lifts his trousers higher; Brian strokes his hair. Joe chatters away in French to the taxi driver, who nods yes. Joe says to me, 'Come on. It's all arranged.'

I'd rather stay where I am, but the taxi driver comes back and opens the car door. 'Okay, okay.' He drags me to a woman that's aged about a thousand years. He speaks to her; she nods, then he says to me, 'Ten American dollars.'

I say, *'No way … no way. No.'*

A young girl, about ten-years old, comes from a dimly lit doorway and stands there nervous and afraid.

I understand what's going on. This is one of the nice girls. This little thing who's got her life ahead of her is being offered as a prostitute. *Bloody hell!* I'm revolted. I say to the taxi driver, 'You bastard.' But he doesn't understand. He's still smiling. I say, 'You mongrel bastard … if you think I'm going to abuse this kid … why, you fucking *mongrel bastard.*'

Just then, almost as if it were scripted, we hear truck engines. Searchlights shine around and at least twenty armed soldiers run about.

Fuck!

A soldier, an officer, approaches us, yelling in Vietnamese.

Fuck!

Brian and Joe come from a hut, looking confused.

The intense searchlight beam makes me blink. I shade my eyes and see at least three Army trucks. The officer has a pistol in his hand, and I reckon he won't be reluctant to use it. I try to appear calm but I'm panicking. I say to him, *'Australian, Australian.'* But that doesn't meaning anything to him. He's yelling away in Vietnamese and, although I don't know what he's saying, it's abusive. Joe and Brian join me. They ask questions and yell things I really don't hear.

I say to Joe, 'Explain in French to the officer. Tell him we're not—'

'What? Tell him what?'

The officer says, 'Here, here; you all come here.'

But I stand behind him. I'm staying close to him. I reckon his men won't shoot at me if there's a danger of hitting their officer. He moves a bit, and I move a bit.

The taxi driver explains in Vietnamese why he's there; Joe speaks over him in French, and the Army officer looks confused. He snaps something to the taxi driver, and the driver looks afraid. Joe tells the officer that we're photographers in the village looking for subjects to shoot photographs of tomorrow. His mention of *shoot* unnerves me.

The driver is asked for his licence. He goes to get it, sees it's not where it should be and panics. I take his licence from my pocket and give it to him. He's relieved, and the officer looks more confused. He must say to the driver, 'Why has that nasty European got your license?' The driver shrugs. We show our passports; the officer takes details, and then he dismisses us. 'You go now,' he says.

Little is said while we are driven back to the wharf. We're contemplating what could have happened. We didn't know there was a curfew and that the V.C. are active outside of Saigon at night. The taxi driver takes a direct route to the ship.

At the wharf I tell Joe and Brian to go, that I'll pay the driver. They go. I give the driver two American dollars and say, 'That's all you're getting.' He looks miffed.

We don't leave the ship again while in Saigon.

~

A cyclone in the South China Sea makes nearly all of us, including the crew, seasick. Because I'm now a very experienced adventurer, I'm trying to maintain a degree of sophistication about my seasickness, but I'm in the toilets with everyone else. All the cubicles that have doors have someone behind them, and there's someone at all the washbasin positions. I'm dry-reaching, and so is John, who's beside me.

He says, 'Arhh. What are you arhhh doing in Hong arhhh Kong?'

'Arhh, nothing in partic arhh ular. '

He says, 'You'd better arhh spend the night with Tossi and arhh me.'

John, his wife Tossi and I drink in Hong Kong's Condor's bar, where lots of John's friends are welcoming him home. The owner, Condor, is Australian, and he introduces me around.

An Englishman says to me, 'What do you do?'

'I'm a traveller. What do you do?'

'I'm a journalist.'

'Oh. I worked for *The Sydney Morning Herald.*'

'Really?'

I should tell him that I was a copy boy at the *Herald,* but I don't.

'He says, are you looking for a job?'

'Doing what?'

'Sports: writing sports.'

The Sydney Morning Herald used to send two copy boys with a photographer to Warwick Farm racecourse. Our job was to wait outside in a staff car while the photographer took photos of the race finishes. He'd stand in line with the finishing post and photograph the winners, then after race three, he'd bring the photographic plates outside the gate, give them to one of us boys and say, 'Run.' And one of us would go like the wind to Warwick Farm Railway Station to get a train to Sydney. Then at the end of the fifth race, the photographer would come out with more plates, and off the other boy would run. At the Herald's photography department, we were welcomed as though we were messengers from God.

But the Royal Easter Show was the best. A chauffeur-driven car took a photographer and a copy boy to the Sydney Showground where, with special entry passes, we'd drive in the main gate, then slowly wind between the show-goers to the *Herald's* show office. The car was impressive. The *Herald* had American made cars that had long two-way whip-radio aerials on their roofs, an uncommon car in Sydney.

I reckon I'd like to be a sports writer.

I say to the journalist, 'I used to be in the sports department at the *Herald*.'

'So you could do it, then?'

'Yes. I could do it.'

Condor's beer has me taking the job, but afterwards, in the sober light of a new day, I speculate on my chances of a successful career in journalism. I can't use a typewriter; I can't spell that well; I'm not good at writing. I'd last as long as my first story. Then I'd be marooned in Hong Kong; I'd never get back to Australia.

Prior to the *Cambodge* leaving Hong Kong, Joe, Brian and I shop for the lowest priced Johnnie Walker Black Label Scotch Whiskey, which when sold in Japan, should be worth double what it cost. We take a solemn pledge not to open any of the three bottles.

~

I'm excited about arriving in Kobe, but Joe and Brian are nervous because the money they're expecting from their parents will be in Tokyo. Their boat ticket takes them only to Kobe, and they've no money to go any further.

I offer to allow them to stow-away in my cabin. It's only one night steaming to Yokohama; there shouldn't be any difficulties.

Somehow, they get through immigration. Joe tells me it involved phone calls to the Canadian Embassy, then a phone call to their parents' bank. They take their luggage ashore to Kobe railway station where it's left to be freighted to Tokyo, then they return to the *Cambodge* to pretend to farewell us.

The chef in riz class can hardly believe that I've taken a liking to his 'riz au cari'. He's pleased when I take a loaded plate away. I say to him, 'It's for the stowaways hiding in my cabin.'

He laughs.

Joe and Brian reluctantly eat it.

A knock on my cabin door has us panicking. There's nowhere for the Canadians to hide.

I say, 'Yes; who is it?'

'Purser. It's zhe purser's mate, monsieur.'

'What do you want?'

'Documents must be signed.'

'Now?'

'Wee, monsieur; Japanese immigration vill board zhe ship early tomowow.'

I slightly open the cabin door and take the papers, but I drop them and the purser's mate sees my mates.

He says, 'Oh!'

Brian invites the purser's mate in. But he doesn't want to come in—he knows something's not quite right. Brian takes him by his shoulder and pulls him inside. 'Sit on that *fucking* bunk,' he orders.

Joe rattles away to the purser's mate in French. His expression goes from fear, to anguish, then acceptance.

Joe says, 'He doesn't care what we're doing.'

I go close to the purser's mate and say, 'If you tell anyone about this, I'll … I'll throw you overboard.'

Anguish returns to his face. 'Wee, monsieur. I know who you are. You are the Australian criminal.'

Joe and Brian say, 'Australian *criminal?*'

I tell them to shut up, then I say to the purser's mate, 'Monsieur; you keep your mouth shut, all right?'

'All right.'

Joe says, something to him in French, then he hurries away.

Brian says, 'What's all this about being *a criminal?*'

I tell them how I got the title, and they laugh. We celebrate by consuming one bottle of our Johnnie Walker Scotch. We reckon we've been tough, scary even, but later we realise that the purser's mate was smart; he had nothing to gain and everything to lose by disclosing the stowaways. There were no medals in it for him.

An American travelling in second class is nervous. He knows Japanese immigration officers will demand to see evidence that he and his absolutely stunning girlfriend have the financial resources to buy tickets out of Japan. They only have funds enough for one of them.

I can help. I have enough funds in traveller's cheques to pay for my boat ticket to Australia, and all the immigration want to see is evidence. I say to him, 'Why doesn't your girlfriend go through immigration with me? We'll pretend to be lovers.'

The American says, 'You wouldn't do that, *would you?*'

'Yeah.'

His girlfriend cries with gratitude and hugs me, and I feel my penis rising. I say to them, 'We'll have to look convincing. We'll have to look like we're lovers.'

In the immigration queue, the American woman's all over me. We kiss and rub against each other, and I wish it would go on forever. Behind us Joe and Brian are rehearsing their explanation of evidence of funds, and why they have no baggage. But I don't care about them; I'm more interested in evidencing my passion for the American girl.

The immigration officer smiles at us, stamps our passports, then says, 'Next,' and Joe and Brian start their convincing.

On Yokohama railway station, I'm dumped by the American girl and picked-up by Joe and Brian. It's Saturday, and they need somewhere to sleep. On Monday, when the banks are open, they'll get their money; hopefully.

I take a basic room at the Tokyo Station Hotel. The hotel has a back staircase that the Canadians use to get to my room. They're amazed how easy it is to get past the reception desk.

Brian says, 'These Japanese are so trusting.'

I'm not comfortable being in Japan, nor am I interested in trusting the Japanese. I've watched Sydney's Anzac Day march every year since the end of World War Two, and I have uncles that fought Japanese soldiers.

One uncle was in Changi prison and slaved on the construction of the Burma Railway. He returned a shattered and spirit-broken man; the only employment he could get was as a railway station attendant. He did that for three years, then when he was too slow completing a crossing of the railway tracks, he got run over; both his legs were amputated.

Few Australians like the Japanese. Nearly everyone has a relation or friend that experienced some manner of abuse, degradation or torture from Japanese soldiers. 'Those bastards', is the description generally used.

Joe and Brian offer to steal food. They reckon it'll be easy. So off they sneak down the hotel's back staircase, and off I go to the Ginza to sell my Johnnie Walker Black Label Scotch. I have no trouble getting interest in it, but I want a fair price. I want double what I paid in Hong Kong.

The short Japanese barman is aged about forty, old enough to have been a soldier—perhaps he was at Changi. He's trying to get my price down, but I won't bring it down. He says something in Japanese that sounds insulting, and I go off my brain. I'm yelling insults at him that he has no chance of understanding. Then I push two glasses off the bar-top and they smash onto the floor. I yell at him, 'You bastard; the whole lot of you are cruel bastards.' And I take my Johnnie Walker back to the hotel.

Joe and Brian are waiting near the back staircase. They're not pleased, either. Brian says, 'All we could steal was chocolates.' So we eat chocolates for two days. But they do go to the Ginza to sell my scotch.

When they return Joe says, 'Johnnie Walker's gone to a good home.'

I go to the Peninsula and Orient line office where I get a passage on the S.S. *Arcadia* sailing for Sydney. Brian and Joe go to their bank where it's proved that their parents do love them—their money is there. So they finance a long night drinking in the Ginza. We're careful not to buy back any of our Johnny Walker.

Two days later they leave the Tokyo Station Hotel by the back staircase, and I leave by the front door; we are simply ships passing in the night.

~

The Peninsula and Orient ship *Arcadia* arrives in Sydney on 25th March 1963 on a dull day. Nothing like I dreamed it would be. For two weeks I've watched happy passengers frolicking in the ship's bars and dancing in the cabaret room, meeting and romancing, and going ashore in Manila to do exciting tours. I have no money; I do none of that.

The ship eases close to the Pyrmont wharf, and I see my family waving their arms. My mother appears to be crying. After three years of adventuring, all I have to give her are a few souvenir teaspoons and a Russian doll that pulls apart. In my pocket is one-shilling and nine pence. That's all I've got left. I give the coins to my mother.

~

Ceylon, Colombo: Harry and his family - the Judge on the right.

Saigon streets, 1963.

It's 2018

I suspect that many characters mentioned in this memoir are now dead, including my mother who died age ninety-eight on the 25th February 2014.

I'm now aged 81 and live on the NSW South Coast at Jamberoo. Ray Bartlett lives on the NSW North Coast at Nambucca Heads. Stuart Acason lives at Allora in Queensland. David Acason was killed in a vehicle accident near Allora. Mike 'Son of a Moose' Schonberg is possibly living in Mexico and still gambling at cards.

The reader of this memoir might be interested in what wise counsel this old man can give. My answer is: nothing, absolutely nothing.

Our life's journey is simply that, OUR JOURNEY.

I have been married twice, both times to wonderful women.

No children resulted from the marriages but in 1978 I deposited some semen in a vial which was tested by a pathologist in Sydney's Hurstville. I was very pleased when my doctor in Lugarno said to me: 'All's well: you're fertile.' In the unlikely event that anyone resulting from that incident reads this memoir, they may be interested to know that the pathologist was located in a building that replaced the Savoy Picture Theatre, the same theatre where in 1955 my widowed mother served ice creams and milk shakes to earn a quid.

Barry and Ray thirty-three years later at Nambucca Heads, NSW.

Forty-five years later: Stuart Acason, David Acason and Barry White.

A Note from the Author

Did you enjoy my book?

If so, I would be very grateful if you could write a review and publish it at your point of purchase. Your review, even a brief one, will help other readers to decide whether or not they'll enjoy my work.

Do you want to be notified of new releases?

If so, please [sign up to the AIA Publishing email list.](#) You'll find the sign-up button on the right-hand side under the photo at www.aiapublishing.com. Of course, your information will never be shared, and the publisher won't inundate you with emails, just let you know of new releases.

About the Author

Barry White, a third-generation Australian, was born in 1937 in Redfern, Sydney. He served an apprenticeship as a plumber, then following his return to Australia in 1963, he worked as a sales manager in hardware, refractories, and then as a teacher with TAFE.

His life now involves writing, metal sculpture, painting, drawing, and living influenced by Zen Buddhism and contemporary philosophy. He resides on the NSW South Coast at 'Stone Cottage', Jamberoo.

www.ingramcontent.com/pod-product-compliance
Lightning Source LLC
Chambersburg PA
CBHW081352290426

44110CB00018B/2355